Case Studies on Modern European Economy

The last two centuries have been the scene of dramatic change throughout Europe. And one of the main causes of these tremendous and spectacular changes was the economy. These transformations were achieved by people—scientists and political thinkers, inventors and entrepreneurs, educators, skilled and educated workers—who not only invented machines and computers, but were able to renew economic and political systems. This volume, therefore, presents a new approach to the period by looking at case studies to understand how these changes came about and the impact they had on modern Europe.

Ivan T. Berend presents the spectacular history of modern European economy as a chain of "small" events, actions, and the ideas of individuals, as the influence of institutions and bold entrepreneurs. The essays are grouped into six chapters and discuss the power of entrepreneurship; the power of institutions; economic regimes and the permanent renewal of capitalism; the power of ideas and inventions; pioneering companies; from the rise of industrial cities to post-industrial suburbanization; and bubbles, great depressions, and economic cycles. All of the single episodes and personal stories offer a cross-section of the complex and interrelated history of modern Europe.

Case Studies on Modern European Economy will be essential reading for students of economic and modern European history.

Ivan T. Berend is a professor in the history department at the University of California, Los Angeles. His publications include *An Economic History of Nineteenth-Century Europe: Diversity and Industrialization* (2013), *Europe Since 1980* (2010), *From the Soviet Bloc to the European Union* (2009), *An Economic History of Twentieth-Century Europe* (2006) and *History Derailed* (2003).

Case Studies on Modern European Economy

Entrepreneurs, Inventions, Institutions

Ivan T. Berend

Routledge
Taylor & Francis Group

LONDON AND NEW YORK

First published 2013
by Routledge
2 Park Square, Milton Park, Abingdon, Oxon OX14 4RN

Simultaneously published in the USA and Canada by Routledge
711 Third Avenue, New York, NY 10017

Routledge is an imprint of the Taylor & Francis Group, an informa business

British Library Cataloguing in Publication Data
A catalogue record for this book is available from the British Library

Library of Congress Cataloging in Publication Data
Berend, T. Iván (Tibor Iván), 1930-
Case studies on modern European economy : entrepreneurs, inventions, institutions / Ivan T. Berend.
p. cm.
Europe – Economic conditions. 2. Entrepreneurship – Europe – Case studies. 3. Capitalism – Europe – Case studies. 4. Economic development – Europe – Case studies. I. Title.
HC240.B3946 2013
330.94 – dc23
2012039802

ISBN: 978-0-415-63994-1 (hbk)
ISBN: 978-0-415-63995-8 (pbk)
ISBN: 978-0-203-55040-3 (ebk)

Typeset in Times
by Taylor & Francis Books

Printed and bound in Great Britain by
TJ International Ltd, Padstow, Cornwall

To Kati as always

Contents

5   From the rise of industrial cities to post-industrial suburbanization   **176**

6   Bubbles, great depressions: economic cycles   **214**

Preface

The idea to write this book emerged while I was working on my comprehensive European economic histories of the nineteenth and twentieth centuries.[1] To break up their several hundred pages of macro-economic discussion, analyses, and statistical documentation, I added micro-economic illustrations in the form of short, easily readable, colorful case studies. Within three books I attached about three dozen case studies on topics such as the invention of the steam engine, the birth of department stores, pre-modern cultural-behavioral patterns and the lack of education in some peripheral countries. All were very well received by readers and reviewers alike.

Here I present a whole volume of case studies—a micro-historical illustration of macro-historical processes. The process of selecting roughly 70 examples from among thousands of possibilities is an unavoidably risky enterprise, not least because the choices may appear to be arbitrary. What criteria can be applied to structure choices? Which of the entrepreneurs, inventions, ideas, or companies are "the most important" in a more than 200-year-long history? The list might easily be almost endless. I have had to develop a rational framework to guide both the selection of cases and their presentation within this volume. What I offer here, although only a small sample, consists of cases typical, significant, and highly interesting, selected for their ability to illustrate six different topics and organized one chapter for each topic. My firm belief is that together my choices represent the factors most important in stimulating the development of the modern European economy.

The development of the modern economy occurred in conjunction with the emergence of the individual—the entrepreneur—as a significant economic actor. So important was this change that Joseph Schumpeter, one of the greatest economists of the twentieth century, could imagine the entrepreneur as the hero of the capitalist market economy and the prime-mover of innovation.[2] In Chapter 1 I introduce a group of exceptionally innovative entrepreneurs who left their fingerprints all over the modern European economy.

Entrepreneurs, however, always have had to work within institutional frameworks, and therefore Chapter 2 offers case studies on the legal, political, and social institutions that have hammered out the structures and rules of modern economic activity. As Douglass North and Barry Weingast maintained in their famous and often quoted study, institutions and legal structures are the "rules of the game." They create the possibilities and constraints of human actions.[3] Institutional systems, however, are not always working well. They are not always good to all of the players. Dissatisfaction and disappointment often led to changes, reforms, or even revolutions. When nineteenth-century free market capitalism failed to produce the imagined and desired outcome for the peripheral countries of Europe, revolutions after World War I introduced alternative economic regimes. Both right- and left-wing alternatives failed. Systemic competition, however, especially during the Cold War half-century, generated reforms and capitalism renewed itself.

The case studies in Chapter 3 dig deeper into the causes of institutional and systemic change by discussing certain revolutionary ideas and inventions—cultural and scientific factors—that played central roles in both societal and economic development. Broad cultural movements such as the Enlightenment and Romanticism, as well as the works of individuals such as Newton and Darwin shaped the modern way of thinking, institution creation, and economic transformation. Scientific and technological inventions provided a foundation for economic innovation and company formation during the great economic revolutions: the late-eighteenth-century first and turn-of-the-twentieth-century second industrial revolutions, and the turn-of-the-twenty-first-century communications revolution. Case studies on these topics reflect their central role in transforming human life.

Chapter 4 presents a bunch of companies at the forefront of the technological and managerial transformations in modern times. Some of the companies have centuries-long histories and pioneering roles in the creation of modern economy. They introduced managerial innovations and new technologies and some started operating as multinational companies a century ago.

Chapter 5 discusses the impact of economic development on the settlement structure. Industrialization gave a significant impetus for urbanization, the rise of industrial cities. Early urban settlements, however, were overcrowded and unhealthy places. At a later stage that generated major attempts to humanize the urban environment. This led to the idea of building garden cities, and then suburbanization around the big cities to combine urban and healthy countryside lifestyle.

Finally, Chapter 6 offers an important counterpoint to the story of human ingenuity, entrepreneurial power, and company formation as the engine of economic progress outlined in the first four chapters. Regular entrepreneurial miscalculations, over-optimistic investment during boom years, and the passion to gain more and more that led to speculative business transactions, can undermine prosperity and halt development. Modern economic development has never been a linear process. Recessions, depressions, especially the so-called Great Depressions have caused cyclical turns, and speculative bubbles have accompanied the market economy from early modern times to the present. All these still may cause a lot of human suffering: Indeed, as this book was being written, Europe was descending into its most severe economic crisis since the twentieth-century interwar era.

The six chapters described above, with their nearly 70 case studies may move readers towards a much better understanding of the most important features of modern economy. I very much hope that the audience for this volume will include not only educators and students at high school and university levels, but also the interested general reading public. Those who like to search for and understand the causes of events, who are interested in human creativity and innovativeness, who want to enhance their understanding of the age, the institutions, and the economy in which they live might find here important and interesting stories to read and think about.

Notes

1 Ivan T. Berend, *An Economic History of Nineteenth Century Europe: Diversity and Industrialization*, Cambridge: Cambridge University Press, 2013; Ivan T. Berend, *An Economic History of Twentieth Century Europe: Economic Regimes from Laissez-Faire to Globalization*, Cambridge: Cambridge University Press, 2006; Ivan T. Berend, *From the Soviet Bloc to the European Union: The Economic and Social Transformation of Central and Eastern Europe*, Cambridge: Cambridge University Press, 2009.
2 Joseph A. Schumpeter, *History of Economic Analysis*, New York: Oxford University Press, 1954.
3 Douglass C. North and Barry R. Weingast, "Constitutions and Commitment: The Evolution of Institutions Governing Public Choice in Seventeenth-Century Britain," *The Journal of Economic History*, Vol. 49, No. 4, 1989, 803–32.

Introduction

This brief introduction offers a general framework for the case studies in the volume. It is a macro-economic skeleton for the blood-and-flesh micro-economic cases. In summarizing the process of modern transformation—what happened and why—in the modern European economy, this description may help to signpost the various case studies, thus helping the reader to set them properly into the bigger framework.

The saga of the modern European economy can be dated back to the seventeenth century when the socio-economic and cultural structures and practices in certain northwestern European countries—England and the Low Countries, the Dutch Republic in particular—began to diverge from the norms that had prevailed over the European continent for hundreds of years. In these countries, the absence of feudal structures in some parts and their very early disappearance in others combined with special cultural trends such as the Reformation and a capitalist mentality, the value of hard work and thriftiness, to give a green light to scientific progress, new forms of education, secularization, and urbanization, much earlier than in any other parts of the world. These developments prepared the soil for modern transformation that, at the end of the eighteenth century, began to manifest itself in the British Industrial Revolution, truly the opening of a new chapter in European and human history. From Britain, industrial transformation spread first to Western Europe and then to Scandinavia in the nineteenth century, reaching the peripheral regions—the Mediterranean and Central and Eastern Europe—in the twentieth century. In other words, during the nineteenth and twentieth centuries, all of Europe experienced enormously dramatic change. Statistics readily demonstrate all of these general observations.

Over two centuries, Europeans have become notably richer, with the goods and services readily available to the average inhabitant increasing by nearly 40 times. This abundance has meant not only much more and better food to eat, and much more and better clothing to wear, but also healthier, incomparably more comfortable housing, more education, along with several more years on average in school, much better healthcare and more effective medications, all of which together have led to a dramatic increase in life expectancy. Greater wealth also has meant longer vacations, more entertainment during vastly increased free time, and more traveling at speeds so much faster than before that other countries and continents have become much easier to reach.

At the beginning of these two transformational centuries, Europeans generally spent 80–90% of their income on food and basic necessities, but at the end of that period they spent only 10–15%. At the beginning of the period, people worked 12–16 hours per day and 70–90 hours per week; at the end of the period, they worked 36–40 hours per week, with two-day weekends and about 5–6 weeks paid vacation per year. At the beginning, 60–90% of the people were illiterate; at the end, virtually everyone completed elementary and some kind of secondary education, while nearly half of 18- to 24-year-olds enrolled in university. Two hundred years ago, the average life expectancy at birth was 25 years; today it has increased to 80 years, due in part to the dramatic decline of infant mortality and to the near-elimination of diseases such as plague, cholera, smallpox, tuberculosis, polio, and syphilis, which used to decimate the adult population. Vaccinations, modern hospitals, the invention of antibiotics, and a sophisticated pharmaceutical industry have led to the disappearance of those medieval scourges and to the cure of several others. Of course, modern times have also generated or increased the incidence of new mass diseases, among them diabetes, heart conditions, and AIDS, but continuing medical research and discovery have helped to counter and cope with many of them.

At the beginning of the nineteenth century, the huge majority of people died in the village of their birth. Mobility was extremely limited, and traveling, at the average speed of about 20 kilometers per hour, was enormously difficult, slow, and often risky. By the end of the twentieth century, millions of people were in permanent movement. Cars now run at 120–30 kilometers per hour, trains at 200–400 kilometers per hour, airplanes at 600–900, or about 80% of the speed of sound. Meanwhile Europe, which sent about 60 million people to settle in the Americas, Australia, New Zealand, and Africa in the nineteenth century, today is a destination for migration, with immigrants from other continents comprising about 8–10% of its population.

Living conditions, even for most migrants, have improved enormously. At the beginning of the nineteenth century, three generations of a single family, often 30–40 people, lived together under one roof in most parts of agricultural Europe. In the industrial cities, people lived in overcrowded rooms, attics, and cellars, sleeping several to a single bed and sharing one "toilet"—actually a big hole at the edge of the yard—with the other residents of a whole apartment block. By the end of the twentieth century, in contrast, a huge part of the population was living in comfortable single-family homes or in apartments shared by 2–4 people, in a strongly suburbanized environment.

What was the principle cause of these tremendous and spectacular changes? In a word: *the economy.* More specifically, radical transformations to the economy. These began with the key changes in the husbanding of the land for purposes of food production that collectively comprise the agricultural revolution: In the place of practices that required leaving half or one-third of land fallow, modern crop rotation allowed all fields to be planted each year, while animal fertilizers and the hybridization of new crops increased yields per acre. These innovations are represented in this volume with the case study "Inventing and reinventing agriculture." Their consequences cannot be overstated. First of all, as these practices spread, the supply of food became more dependable and abundant. Crop shortages and famine had once been regular visitors to European lands. In the medieval centuries, famine hit Britain 95 times and France 75 times. A late sixteenth-century famine killed one-third of Finland's population, and in the second half of the eighteenth century, nine famines hit Scandinavia. The last major famine in Ireland, which killed one million people in 1845–49, pushed two million people to emigrate. And in Finland again, persistent famine between 1866 and 1868 killed 8% of the population. By the end of the nineteenth century, however, agricultural productivity had increased so dramatically that peacetime famine had all but disappeared from the European lands. The only real exceptions occurred in economically backward peripheral countries such as Russia, where, in the second half of the nineteenth century and up until 1922, crop failures and food shortages caused terrible starvation 11 times, revisiting again in the early 1930s during Stalin's forced collectivization drive. Second, along with increased dependability and abundance came greater agricultural productivity. As a consequence, fewer people produced the food needed to sustain Europe. Today only 3–5% of Europeans cultivate the land, whereas at the beginning of the nineteenth century, 60–80% had been so engaged; what is more, today that 3–5% produces several times more food than before. Europe has even become a food exporter. The liberation of the majority of people from toil in the fields supplied the labor necessary for the growth of emerging industries. The last two centuries thus became the period of industrialization and of the mechanization of nearly all forms of production and work. Case studies in this volume, in particular "James Nasmyth, the pioneer of standardized mass production of tools and machines" and "Killing the killers: from vaccinations to antibiotics," illustrate these developments.

As the European economy modernized, it became increasingly science- and knowledge-based, with industrialized research and invention driving economic transformation and development. At roughly 100-year intervals—at the turn of the nineteenth, twentieth, and twenty-first centuries—major industrial-technological revolutions unfolded, each new one building on the one that had preceded. The first industrial revolution in England, at the turn of the nineteenth century, produced the steam engine, the modern textile and iron industries, and mechanized factories. A new mineral energy source, coal, transformed the economy by eliminating the constraints associated with reliance on organic sources such as wood.[1] With these developments, even though Britain's economy remained largely pre-industrial until the mid-nineteenth century, the gates had been opened to allow for sustained economic growth.

The industrialization of continental European countries followed in the footsteps of Britain and, as the nineteenth century progressed, contributed new revolutionary changes to the economy. The process of industrializing was hugely strengthened around the middle of the century by the construction of railroads. Case studies such as "Revolutionizing transportation with the steam engine" and "From the macadam road to the autobahn" help in understanding the revolutionary impact of these changes. In the last third of the century, a strongly science-based industrial revolution, with Germany in the leading role, created the organic chemical industry, as well as the electricity and automobile industries. This second industrial revolution caused an even greater discontinuity in history than did its predecessor a century before. Several case studies address these topics. Among them: "The creation of synthetic dyes," "Werner and Wilhelm Siemens and the second industrial revolution," "William R. Morris and the British car industry," "Louis Renault and the French car industry," "Emil and Walther Rathenau: the birth of the German electric and electro-chemical industries."

The third revolution, the one in electronics that began in the second half of the twentieth century, is still unfolding today, especially in the form of the so-called communications revolution, with its twin inventions, the personal computer and the internet. These innovations, discussed in "The computer, the internet, and the world wide web," seem to be creating an economy engaged in the relentless transformation of technology and of the conditions in which human beings in Europe and throughout the world are living.

But endless technological revolution actually can be said to have begun a century ago, during and after the second industrial revolution when offices and households began to be mechanized. Today, refrigerators, washing machines, dishwashers, vacuum cleaners, and air conditioning join with computers, printers, scanners, and Xerox machines, to name only a few examples, to make life incomparably more efficient and comfortable. These have been joined by novelties such as the movie, and by military advances such as the guided missile. Case studies present these last two examples in "The birth of the movie" and "Wernher von Braun: the visionary pioneer of missile technology—and an 'apolitical' war criminal."

Technology-driven revolution fundamentally altered transportation. On the water, sail boats lost out in competition with steamships, and canals shortened shipping routes while also reducing costs. The case of "The Universal Suez Ship Canal Company" represents these developments. On land, horse-driven coaches were replaced by railroads, which would eventually crisscross all of Europe, connecting all European countries together and making possible the rapid movement of goods and people. These exciting developments are documented in this volume by "The Orientalische Eisenbahnen company and German colonization plans" and by "The port of Rotterdam—'port of Europe.'" In line with the pattern of relentless technological movement, nineteenth-century steam technology would be replaced by electric and diesel technology in the twentieth century, eventually making possible today's bullet trains running at 400 kilometers per hour. From the 1930s, and especially after World War II, new highway networks would be built and slowly transportation by automobile would become dominant, such that today, on average, one of every two people in Europe has a car, and nearly every family has access to this private and flexible form of transportation. Urban public transportation, including tram, bus, and subway networks, would further enhance mobility. Finally, also in the early twentieth century, transportation by air would emerge on its spectacular path, as illustrated here by the case study "The first airlines: Air France, KLM, and Lufthansa."

The effects of these technological revolutions restructured the traditional European economy and transformed what had been, for centuries, a primarily agricultural region. Britain, in 1841, became the first country in the world where industrial employment surpassed agricultural employment. This process continued steadily so that by the end of the twentieth century, agriculture, which had once employed about 80% of the European working population, now provided work for only 4–6%. Industrial employment also had shown sharp declines, with industry contributing only 27% of aggregate European income as the twentieth century closed. In effect, most of the active, working-age population had been liberated from hard physical work: only 25–30% worked in the combined agriculture and blue-collar industrial sectors with the rest, 70–75%, working in service industries.

The age of industrialization ignited historic migrations—from Europe to other continents and from the countryside to emerging cities. Approximately 60 million people left Europe before World War I, but the region's population nevertheless nearly trebled in the same period, bringing pressure for changes to settlement patterns. In the early nineteenth century a new type of settlement, the industrial city, emerged and attracted millions of uprooted peasants from the countryside. The scale of internal migration was enormous: at the end of the twentieth century, more than 90 percent of the population in some West European countries lived already in urban settlements. Case studies such as "The world's first industrial city: Manchester" (England), "Lyon: the silk center of Europe" (France), "Turin: the industrial capital of Italy," "The rise of Brno (Brünn), Central Europe's foremost industrial city" (the Czech lands), "Łødź—the Polish Manchester," and "Budapest: an old capital city becomes a new industrial center" (Hungary) represent the phenomenon of rapid urbanization.

Overcrowded, unhealthy cities would themselves change in response to the influx of people. In the second half of the nineteenth century major cities would be modernized gradually, as illustrated here by the case study "Rebuilding of Paris and Prague in the second half of the nineteenth century." From the early twentieth century, moreover, the centripetal motion towards cities would be met with an opposing centrifugal pattern, suburbanization. This latter pattern would accelerate into a real de-urbanization trend in the late twentieth century, as significant numbers of people moved out from crowded towns into rapidly growing suburbs extending for 10 to 50 kilometers around big cities. Seaboards, too, would change dramatically, becoming the site of low-density settlements stretching out for many kilometers. Today, in advanced countries, 60–80% of the population lives in family-owned homes. The settlement structure of Europe was, obviously, dramatically altered during the two centuries of modernization. "Humanizing the cities: the garden city and pedestrianization," "The emergence of post-industrial cities: suburbanization," and "The two major types of urban sprawl" illustrate the spectacular transformation of urban settlements, while reflecting in particular on the advantages that have been reaped by integrating aspects of rural lifestyle into the urban experience.

What forces enabled these spectacular economic changes? Principally *accumulated knowledge and a transformed culture.* For more than 200 years, the scientific revolution and its intellectual siblings and offspring together have gradually marginalized superstition, fear of an "unknowable" natural world, and religious intolerance, and have enabled the flowering of social and scientific innovation and invention. Case studies such as "Enlightenment and Romanticism: the ideas of modern society and the nation-state," "Liberal and secular values that formed the modern capitalistic attitude," and "The two books that contributed the most to creating the modern world: Newton and Darwin" present the power of the ideas that changed the economy and the world. People learned not to accept uncritically what they had inherited from previous ages. From the eighteenth century, an "industrial Enlightenment," as Joel Mokyr has called it, translated experimentation and applied science into commonplaces.[2] Books, encyclopedias, and popular lecture series spread mathematical and physical knowledge, as well as practical know-how. Social organizations, from amateur art- and science-promoting private institutions to the various Royal Societies, sponsored research, initiated competitions, and awarded inventions. Thousands of skilled technicians and instrument-makers started working on machines and new industrial production procedures. And with inventions and innovations came improved technology.

The accumulation of scientific knowledge depended in part on the provision of institutional support for scientific investigation. Research universities such as the pioneering Göttingen and Humboldt Universities in Germany and the famous École Polytechnique in France, and laboratories provided the first of such homes for professional research and experimentation. Somewhat later, large factories established laboratories and employed scholars to work towards developing new products and technologies. The field of organic chemistry, for example, spawned the modern chemical industry, and basic research on electricity generated a new energy system along with its infrastructure and related applications. In the twentieth century, especially in its second half, research itself became industrialized, with state-sponsored institutions and huge, mostly multinational companies monopolizing "research and development" (R&D) projects, thereby opening new fields of knowledge and initiating new areas of industrial production. Knowledge-based industries and services also emerged, eventually to become the dominant sectors in advanced economies in the late twentieth century.

Together, scientific discoveries, knowledge of the natural world and of human society, and new attitudes towards both strengthened the consciousness that institutions and systems were not given for all time but rather subject to change. And indeed they were already changing, even before the revolutionary decades at the end of the eighteenth century. In particular, a secular way of thinking and a gradually secularizing society were making it possible for the ideal of tolerance to replace religious bigotry. Enlightened ideas about state governance, societal organization, and state administration, and about the institutional forms most able to optimize human performance would provide the conceptual materials for thoroughly restructured social and political institutions. But even before that, in the sixteenth and seventeenth centuries, autocratic and authoritarian regimes were being questioned, attacked, and destroyed. The Dutch fight for independence against Spain, begun in the last half of the sixteenth century, was the first bourgeois revolution in a society that was strongly urbanized and free from feudal institutions. The British "Glorious Revolution" in 1688 introduced constitutional monarchy and a powerful parliamentarian system. The French Revolution, begun in 1789, made "liberté, égalité, fraternité" fundamental socio-political principles.

While kingdoms were secularizing and slowly taking on the characteristics of modern nation-states, a new kind of society, the bourgeois society, was also being born. So too were the legal frameworks—modern property rights, copyright law, and basic human and citizenship rights—that would regulate this new form of society and its economy. For example, the Code Napoleon, with its principle of universal law applying to every citizen of a given nation, introduced modern civil, business, and criminal laws that were copied throughout Europe. Mass education spread and, in the mid- to late nineteenth century, the introduction of compulsory and free elementary education in the advanced Western countries, gradually eliminated illiteracy. The peripheries were unable to follow suit with these developments because major historical and cultural road-blocks did not allow it, as the case studies on "Pre-modern culture that blocked the road to the modern capitalist transformation" and the "The birth of the Vizcaya iron industry in Spain," or "The Ganz Works: a cutting edge engineering company in a less developed country" illustrate. The peripheries finally began traveling the road of the West in the first half of the twentieth century. In these nations, in the interwar decades, but most of all in the second half of the century, free secondary education became a mass phenomenon. Then, in the second half of the twentieth century, even university education became free, and over time one-third to one-half of college-age young people would matriculate.

All of these improvements were achieved by people who revolted against autocracy and who provided a rock-solid base for a new, free society. Scientists and political thinkers, inventors and entrepreneurs, educators, and skilled or educated workers, all helped the dream of freedom to become reality. Case studies introduce some of these figures: "Mayer Amschel Bauer and the foundation of the House of Rothschild," "The Morozov dynasty: from illiterate serfs to Russia's richest industrialists," and "Jewish entrepreneurship in Hungary." Other studies describe companies that pioneered the transition from the early modern to modern economic forms: "The empires' companies and the companies' empires," "The Thyssen empire: from local to global," or "Vickers-Armstrong: the multi-arms military giant," and "Rolex—one of the most successful Swiss watch-makers."

Throughout the two centuries of principle concern here, revolutionary ideas would spur creative change. Scholars and political thinkers would play central roles in modern economic transformation, while innovators would not only create modern banking, machines, and computers, but also help to renew economic and political systems. Autocratic power would be replaced by representative democracy, serfdom would disappear from the continent, and personal freedom and human rights would gradually gain ground. And most recently, a still incomplete revolution in gender relations would begin opening the gates for women to become decisive participants in the modern economy. Two case studies offer illustrations of the role of women outside the home: "Women in business and management," and "Women in work and on the labor market."

The complexion of the last two centuries cannot be understood without taking into account the variety of socio-political and economic systems that arose in response to the demands and experiences of mass dislocation, industrialization, and urbanization. Case studies on the fascist and communist economic regimes illustrate approaches that attempted to address problems by instituting major socio-institutional change, sometimes involving desperate experiments. Other studies discuss the rise and fall of the laissez-faire regime, the renewal of capitalism by means of major institutional changes, and the rise and fall of alternative economic regimes. These historical dramas are reflected in "The cycle of protectionism and laissez-faire in the market economy," "German wartime *Planwirtschaft*: the cradle of new economic regimes," "The economic regime of fascist modernization dictatorship," "The non-market, centrally planned economic regime," and "The Nazi *Grossraumwirtschaft* and the Soviet-led Comecon—regional autarchy."

After two devastating total wars, Europe has elected to replace brutal conflict between nation-states with continental integration and to turn away from exploitative capitalism. The European welfare states have elevated the people and reinterpreted civil rights to include the right to social security. Case studies on this topic—"Trade unions and *Sozialpartnerschaft*," "Renewal of capitalism: the welfare state," "Renewal of capitalism: the regulated market system," and "The European Union's redistributive system: towards a homogenous Europe"—present these historical changes.

With the integrated European Union, the process of trying systematically to eliminate the traditionally huge economic divisions between Western and Eastern Europe, between the center and the peripheries, has begun. The catching-up process started with the common market of Europe, although the core–periphery relation, which had characterized the world economic system since its emergence in the early modern centuries, did not disappear. But even though some of the European peripheries had nearly reached the advanced

West European level in 2008, when the present economic crisis took hold, their economies were still more vulnerable than those of their Western brethren. These stories are presented in the case studies "How to make a state bankrupt: Greece, 1981–2010" and "The European peripheries and the 2008–12 economic crisis."

All the transformations associated with the modern economy not only required centuries to come to fruition but also were uneven in their development, with cycles of great progress and severe backsliding. Medium- and long-term economic waves created a regular pulsation in the economy. Speculative business led to ballooning bubbles that would burst and cause tremendous loss and suffering. Great depressions and recessions regularly visited Europe, and other parts of the world. Many of these setbacks, from the seventeenth century to the present, as well as the theories that discovered the causes, are represented by case studies in this volume: "The pharaoh's dream and modern economic cycles," "A shocking new recognition: Nikolai Kondratiev and the long economic cycles," "From the Dutch tulip bubble (1637) to the Irish housing-market bubble (2008)," "The greatest economic crash ever: the Great Depression of the 1930s," "The anatomy of bank crashes in the 1930s," and, as an extremely interesting personal case, "Ivar Kreuger's suicide in 1932: the sensation and symbol of the Great Depression."

Sometimes great progress in the economy and social relations was halted by great depressions, stagnations, and the return of dictatorships and wars: what had been reached before was taken away after. Economic, social, and political development is not linear and does not move toward any predetermined end. Nevertheless, the two centuries of modernization in Europe, despite their troubled periods and failure to distribute development equally across geographical regions, have definitely transformed the normal everyday life of Europeans for the better.

Throughout its history, European capitalism has exhibited great flexibility. Colonies, which played an important role in the birth of capitalism and capitalist states, but which became a liability after World War II, provide a clear example of the ability to respond and evolve. Colonial capitalist regimes, flexible like any others organized on the capitalist model, evolved such that eventually the imperial powers—Britain, the Netherlands, and France—withdrew, either by choice or in response to political, military, and economic pressure. The case study entitled "The birth and renewal of capitalism: colonization and decolonization" discusses this issue. The inhumane working conditions of early capitalism provide yet another example of flexibility and evolution. In the earliest capitalist states, work days of 12–16 hours were the norm, as were child labor, penurious wages, and deplorable housing conditions. Over time, the capitalist regimes responded to poor conditions and demands by introducing labor and finance legislation and welfare institutions. The eventual result was the modern European welfare state.

As this brief excursion has made clear, this volume offers a history of innovative people—obsessed amateurs, lone scholars, geniuses, and ordinary researchers—working sometimes independently but more often with the support of university or company laboratories. It offers, too, the amazing story of pioneering companies, influential thoughts and ideas, important events, and dramatic historical episodes; and it tells of new institutions—the modern agricultural rotation system, the factory system, and the first modern banks, for example—which nowadays seem pedestrian, commonplace, but which, at the time of their birth, opened doors that would redefine the future. Finally, this volume provides a glimpse through its case studies and essays of the spectacular history of modern European economy, represented as a chain of "small" events, actions, individual ideas, institutional influence, and bold entrepreneurship. Taken as a whole, these stories offer dozens of interesting and even exciting episodes, which together present a cross-section of a complex history of interrelated phenomena; that is, they allow us to re-experience modern Europe coming into being.[3]

Notes

1 Edward Anthony Wrigley, *Continuity, Chance and Change: The Character of the Industrial Revolution in England*, Cambridge: Cambridge University Press, 1988; Paulo Malanima, "The Path Towards the Modern Economy: The Role of Energy," at www.paolomalanima.it/ DEFAULT … / ENERGY_ AND_ GROWTH.pdf.
2 Joel Mokyr, *The Gift of Athena: Historical Origins of the Knowledge Economy*, Princeton: Princeton University Press, 2002.
3 Several major comprehensive histories of the European economy have covered this long, amazing, and exciting saga. Others have explored specific parts of the story, or have tried to integrate the experience of Europe in these two centuries into a wider and longer historical framework. Mentioning only a few very important works: Alan Milward and S.B. Saul, *The Economic Development of Continental Europe, 1780–1870*, London: Allen and Unwin, 1973, and *The Development of the Economies of Continental Europe, 1850–1914*, London: Allen and Unwin, 1977; Clive Trebilcock, *The Industrialization of the Continental Powers 1780–1914*, London: Longman, 1981; Carlo Cipolla (ed.), *The Fontana Economic History of Europe: The Emergence of Industrial Societies*, Vol. 4, Pt. 2, London: Fontana Books, 1973; Richard Sylla and Gianni Toniolo (eds), *Patterns of European Industrialization: The Nineteenth Century*, London: Routledge, 1991; Stephen Broadberry and Kevin H. O'Rourke (eds), *The Cambridge Economic History of Modern Europe: 1700 to the Present*, Vols. 1&2, Cambridge: Cambridge University Press, 2010; Nicholas Craft and Gianni Toniolo (eds), *Economic Growth in Europe Since 1945*, Cambridge: Cambridge University Press, 1996; Barry Echengreen, *The European Economy Since 1945: Co-ordinated Capitalism and Beyond*, Princeton: Princeton University Press, 2008. As mentioned before, I published two volumes on nineteenth- and twentieth-century economic history of Europe in 2006 and 2013.

1 The power of entrepreneurship

Introduction

The modern market system has its own rules and mechanism. If fully introduced, it has a decisive impact on economic development. The geopolitical situation of a continent or a country, the possibility of water transportation, nearby seas and navigable rivers, its natural endowments, e.g., its possession or lack of crucial raw materials of the age such as water, coal, iron ore, or oil, also have decisive influence on economic growth.

Nevertheless, the most important factor in modern economic development is people. The majority of people in a society collectively share certain values and principles that may assist or block the road of economic development. Equally important, however, was the role of the armies of workers who learned the skill and developed their proud identities with their work and companies. Invented or imported technology, the prime mover of economic development, would not work without the *social capability* of the given society, as the Stanford University economist, Moses Abramovitz, called it. Social capability includes a certain educational level, but it also includes social habits, attitudes, and behavioral patterns, or, to put it in a different way, the culture of the society.

Within the army of actors in a modern economy, the special, talented, and courageous individuals, the captains of industry, the pioneering bankers, entrepreneurs, and managers whose innovative talent put them into the driver's seat, deserve special attention. Their work and initiative may make tremendous difference. As already noted in the Preface, economist Joseph Schumpeter maintained that entrepreneurs are the central figures of the modern market economy. Schumpeter stressed the role of entrepreneurs as innovators who introduce new products and new production methods, discover new markets, and realize new forms of organization of work. Actually he calls only those to be an entrepreneur who carry out innovation: "The entrepreneur may, but need not, be the inventor ... may, but need not, be the person who furnishes the capital ... It is leadership rather than ownership that matters."[1] The entrepreneurial spirit is the engine of innovation and technological change. Entrepreneurs are often called the "spark in the engine of economy." Two main characteristics made them successful: creativity and risk-taking. Calculated risk-taking, however, had to be cautious and not hazardous. Good entrepreneurs, often obsessed by certain ideas, are never gamblers. "Casino-type" entrepreneurship may ruin the entire business. Entrepreneurs establish firms to compete in the market, and they have to introduce something new to be successful. They have to put ideas into effect. These ideas are sometimes their own invention, sometimes just a superb realization of others' technological invention. Good entrepreneurial instinct helps to find, and often to create, a need of the people and satisfies it. To gain profit and maximize it required a highly competitive spirit. Entrepreneurs of big companies, with huge financial resources, might play an especially crucial role in investing in research and development projects and create positive economic change.

This chapter presents a few portraits of an endless number of entrepreneurs, among them the first bankers of modern Europe, the Rothschilds, who emerged from antique business and money exchange; and the inventor and producer of the steam-hammer, James Nasmyth, who became a leading entrepreneur from his craft and small business. Some of them established entire dynasties and sons continued their fathers' business. Amazing stories help us to understand the role of entrepreneurs, such as the story in this chapter of the illiterate peasant-serf Morozov family that emerged to be one of the richest textile dynasties of Russia. A quite different type of entrepreneur is illustrated by the British William R. Morris and the French Louis Renault, skilled and obsessed entrepreneurs who established a whole industrial branch from experimenting in their garages. A very different type again is the university-educated scholar-entrepreneurs such as the pioneers of the German electro-chemical industry, the Rathenaus, or the Siemens brothers, central heroes of the second industrial revolution. A case study presents the problem of females in business and management. Half of the society, the women, were excluded from holding an equal role in business for a long time, but they always had an important role that, at last, was recognized and was even assisted by social programs. The essays in this chapter illustrate the role of the human, entrepreneurial factor in the development of the modern European economy.

Mayer Amschel Bauer and the foundation of the House of Rothschild[2]

The Rothschild family opened a separate chapter in European banking. Mayer Amschel Bauer, who started using the name of Rothschild permanently, emerged as the most prominent banker of the age. He kept his oldest son in Frankfurt, but sent his other four sons to London, Paris, Vienna, and Naples, and, after his death in 1812, the five collaborating brothers ran major Rothschild banks throughout Europe. The banking dynasty played a central role in nineteenth-century investment banking, railroad construction, and industrial investment all over Europe, significantly contributing to the industrialization of the continent.

Only scattered information is available on the family during the previous centuries. What is known is that, in the 1560s, Isak, son of Elchanan, built a house called "zum Roten Schild." From that time on, the Bauer family also often used the name of Rothschield. Sixteenth- and seventeenth-century Bauer-Rothschilds were relatively successful small business people. Their taxable income doubled from the late sixteenth to the late seventeenth century. However, Mayer Amschel's father, Amschel Moses, lived in the same small house where the family moved in the seventeenth century. He was a goldsmith and also dealt with money-changing.

Here, in the Judenstrasse, in the walled ghetto of Frankfurt am Main, Mayer Amschel was born in 1744. Jews had to wear a special sign on their clothes, were not allowed to enter inns or coffee houses, parks or promenades. On Sundays, they were banned from leaving the ghetto. To leave Frankfurt, they had to apply for a special pass. In the early eighteenth century, about 3,000 people lived in this ghetto. The young Mayer Amschel, after having completed his primary education, was sent to Fürth to a rabbinical school. At the age of 12, however, both of his parents died in an epidemic, and his three older siblings sent him to Hanover as an apprentice to learn business at the Wolf Jacob Oppenheim merchant firm. The Oppenheims were court agents, a continued practice of the medieval "court Jews." This experience certainly influenced Mayer Amschel during his entire life.

His first independent business activity after 1764, when he returned to Frankfurt, was selling rare coins and medals, and soon other kinds of antiques. The buyers of these goods were mostly recruited from the aristocracy and via this business he came into contact with William, Hereditary Prince, later Elector (or Kurfürst) of Hesse-Kassel and one of the biggest capitalists of the age. This connection determined Mayer Amschel's later success, since he established permanent business contact with the Prince as his financial agent. In 1769, he gained the rank of court agent. Next year, the 26-year-old merchant married the 16-year-old Gutle Schnapper, the daughter of the court agent of the Prince of Saxe-Meiningen. Between 1871 and 1892, Gutle Rothschild delivered 19 children, virtually one per year. Ten of them, five girls and five boys, survived. These boys, Amschel Mayer, Salomon Mayer, Nathan Mayer, Kalman (Carl) Mayer, and Jacob (James) Mayer became employees, and later partners, in their father's business. After the birth of his last child, Jacob, Mayer Amschel started his banking activities. This was a general custom for merchants and goldsmiths at that time, since their business was connected with crediting and money exchange.

As one of the best Rothschild historians, Niall Ferguson, stated, "At the beginning of the 1790s, Mayer Amschel Rothschild was no more than a prosperous antique-dealer."[3] Within the space of a decade, however, he emerged as one of the richest men in the country and the founder of Europe's most famous banking house. What really happened? One of the main secrets behind the spectacular rise, beside the genuine aptitude and superb manner and talent for contact-building, was Mayer Amschel's fruitful court connection. In the medieval and early modern centuries, the institution of "court Jew" played a central role in money-lending and primitive banking. This institution was rooted in the Church's banning of usury, i.e. medieval money-lending, and also in the strict bans that excluded Jews from activities other than trade or the money business. Jews filled the "lücken Positionen," as Karl Marx called the gap positions in societies.

Mayer Amschel joined this group of court Jews, many of whom, in the nineteenth century, became court bankers. Rothschild built and maintained personal contacts with the court and started lending money, investing and handling Kurfürst William's huge wealth, including the Prince's English investments. Managing this portfolio was a great business. In a few years, for example, Rothschild purchased securities for the Prince nine times with a total amount of £664,850. He got one-eighth of 1% as the brokerage fee, but gained 2% from the difference between the agreed and real purchasing price, and some other amount from the difference between the agreed and real exchange rate. Furthermore, most of the transactions were conducted by using Rothschild's money as a loan to the Prince who only later paid back the amount, with interest. Until the securities were fully paid, they remained in Rothschild's ownership. Altogether the banking profit was high. The same was true with the discounting business. Mayer Amschel also discounted hundreds of thousands of gulden bonds for various courts that needed the money promptly, and he later sold the bonds at a higher price. Just one transaction of 290,000 gulden made a profit of several tens of thousand guldens. As a consequence, the Rothschilds' wealth jumped from 108,504 gulden (£10,000) in 1797 to 800,000 gulden (£80,000) by 1810.

He also started lending to foreign governments, first to Denmark. His business activities had a huge geographical range, including Hamburg, Berlin, and all other parts of Germany, but also Vienna, London, and Paris. During the French occupation, he established the same banking business with the French authorities in Germany. Via his son, Nathan, and the established London branch, the Rothschilds financed the war against France. The British government entrusted the Rothschilds to manage its payments to its continental allies. In this way, Rothschild established contacts with almost all of the European ruling houses. In the early 1800s, Mayer Amschel Rothschild was appointed court agent to the Order of St. John, the Prince of Thurn und Taxis, the Count of Büdingen, the Landgrave of Hesse-Darmstadt, and most of all, the Emperor of Austria. The court banker's role became especially lucrative during the years of the Napoleonic wars, when the House of Rothschild established its huge wealth.

Banking was a multinational business from the beginning and the House of Rothschild was a genuine multinational company. Mobile, cosmopolitan minority people had a genuine advantage in that early stage of banking. Daniel Chirot suggests that it was their own identities and cultures that were the basis of success in the transnational networks: "Their 'Greekness,' 'Jewishness,' 'Armenianness' … meant an entry ticket to an international business network, because the diaspora entrepreneurs were always more loyal to international capital than to the nation in which they lived."[4]

The Rothschilds also entered the English textile business during the British industrial revolution. Nathan, one of the most successful sons of Mayer Amschel, moved to Manchester in 1799 and began to be involved in textile export to the continent. During the war years and the banning of trade by continental blockade, he conducted the business by smuggling. Nathan then moved to London, and entered into banking operations. The London branch of the Rothschild house became one of the pillars of the British banking system, similarly to the family's private banks in Paris, run by Jacob, Vienna, headed by Salomon, and Naples, established by Karl. The century's most influential European banking network was created. Mayer Amschel, as the surviving correspondence proves, commanded the business. Except for official business letters, his letters to his sons were written in German, but using Hebrew letters to be strictly confidential, and guided them closely. He kept the entire organization in family hands. He excluded his daughters from the business. And while his sons-in-law were often employed by the family business, they never belonged to the top leadership. In 1810, at the age of 66 and seriously ill, Mayer Amschel signed an agreement with his sons to establish "Mayer Amschel Rothschild & Sons," a family company. His daughters, sons-in-law, and their heirs had no share in the capital of the firm. In a will written hours before his death in September 1812, he reiterated the guiding principles of the company, including the rule that the oldest son is always the head of the House, unless the majority of the family decides otherwise.

After the death of the founder, the family council elected as head of the family the talented and successful Nathan Mayer, who was the fourth child and third son of Mayer Amschel, and also head of the London branch. As the second son, Salomon stated, "My brother in London is the commanding general, I am his field marshal." Nevertheless, as the Brockhause Encyclopaedia's 1827 article on the Rothschilds stated, the number one guiding principle "obliged the five brothers to conduct their combined business in an uninterrupted community ... Since his [Mayer Amschel's] death, any proposal ... is the object of collective discussion; each operation ... is carried out according to an agreed plan."

The Rothschild dynasty emerged from Frankfurt's Judengasse and dominated nineteenth- and twentieth-century European banking. All five brothers got hereditary nobility and established a life of aristocracy. Unlike most of the enriched German Jews, the Rothschilds did not convert, and continued helping their community. Mayer Amschel not only paid out 10% of his income, according to the Jewish rule for the community, but worked on the emancipation of Jews both in Frankfurt and in many other countries where he had business. His sons became major donors in various areas.

During the ensuing two centuries, eight generations followed each other and nearly 100 German, English, French, and Austrian Rothschilds were born and lived in their home countries. The sons were involved in family business, while other members turned to various occupations. There were black sheep such as Nathan Mayer's daughter, Hannah Mayer, who—against the will of the family elders—married the Gentile Henry FitzRoy in 1839 and converted to Christianity. It shocked the family, which then shunned her. A few male members of the fifth generation rejected banking. Walter studied natural science, and his brother Charles became an amateur entomologist who published 150 papers, but he later committed suicide. From the French branch of the same generation, Jimmy became a liberal MP, and his brother Maurice an art collector. In the life of the seventh generation, it was natural that Emma Rothschild would become an excellent British historian; she married Amartya Sen, the Nobel laureate economist of Indian origin. The history of the Rothschilds has significantly broadened and not ended.

James Nasmyth, the pioneer of standardized mass production of tools and machines[5]

Early engineering during the industrial revolution was a bottleneck for industrialization because it remained behind in the age of handicraft work. The production of tools and the first newly invented machines, including steam engines, was thus expensive and lacked precision. "Engineers" were handicraft workers, used manual tools and worked without precise standardization. James Nasmyth stated in 1841: "Up to within the last thirty years nearly every part of a machine had to be made and finished ... by mere manual labour ... consequently the enormous expense [as well as inaccuracy] ... proved a formidable barrier."[6]

Around the turn of the nineteenth century, however, some brilliant London pioneers, among them Joseph Bramah and most of all Henry Maudslay, who invented machine-making tools and machines, started changing the practice. Maudslay is considered to be the founder of machine tool technology because he revolutionized the production of component parts with his slide-rest lathe and the first screw-cutting lathe that allowed the standardization of screw thread sizes. Some of his pupils, the second generation of "London and Manchester engineers gradually solved the problem of mechanizing machine making, inventing machines to make machines – self-acting tools, such as lathes, planing machines, drilling machines, grooving, slotting, and paring machines ... [that made possible] 'almost mathematical accuracy and precision' in the manufacture of machinery."[7] In the first half of the nineteenth century, the engineering industry gradually stopped general engineering production and started specialized work. Various companies specialized in producing machines for the huge market of the textile industry. Producing textile machines was one of the very first fields of specialized machine production. The machine-tool industry also became an independent branch. Richard Roberts, a pupil of Maudslay, invented the self-acting spinning mule and produced cutting engines for gear wheels. The Sharp brothers specialized to produce standardized cotton-spinning machinery and later also locomotives. William

Fairbairn, a self-educated Scotsman who emerged from a farming family, also belonged to the prominent British pioneers of standardized mass production, producing automatic tools, iron ships, and other machines, and he employed 2,000 workers in his Manchester and Millwall factories by 1835.

Contemporary authors wrote about the changes with great admiration in 1835: "admirable automatic instruments, which have so greatly facilitated the construction and repair of factory machines [by producing] many counterparts or similar pieces … are all made so perfectly identical in form and size, by the self-acting tools … that any one of them will at once fit into the position of any [other machine]."[8] The path towards standardized mass production of machines, produced in a modern organizational and management system, was paved by, among others, a Scottish Renaissance man, James Nasmyth. He was born in 1808, son of Alexander Nasmyth, a famous Edinburgh architect, painter, builder, and amateur mechanic who made experiments in his workroom at his house. James' mother was from a landed aristocratic family. In this environment, young James received a good education, including evening classes for five years at the Edinburgh School of Arts, one of the very first technical colleges, and he worked as private assistant to the genius mechanic Henry Maudslay for two years in London. Those years with Maudslay certainly changed the life of the young Nasmyth. The 17-year-old James, in his father's workroom, built a model steam engine for Professor Leslie to use during his lectures at the University of Edinburgh. At the age of 20, Nasmyth produced a steam carriage. As assistant to Maudslay, he invented his first machine tool with a revolving cutter to cut square or hexagonal nuts or bolt-heads. His interests in science, his friendship with Michael Faraday and John Herschel, and the several lectures he later presented at the Manchester Literary and Philosophical Society, at the British Association, and even at the Royal Society, clearly reflects that he was, at least, as Musson called him, a "scientific engineer."

In 1831, Nasmyth established his first, temporary workshop in Edinburgh and in 1834 he moved to Manchester and founded his Bridgewater Foundry, or Nasmyth, Gaskell & Co., next to the Bridgewater Canal, the Manchester Ship Canal, and the junction of the Manchester–Liverpool Railway. Because he had only £69 saved, Holbrook Gaskell and some others gave him the money he need to open the business and to build several workshops, including an impressive five-story factory and cottages for workers initially on four acres, but later on 14. He planned the construction of his factory buildings according to a new assembly-line principle that he pioneered.

A booklet of 1836 described his "straight line" factory system. The main floor of the workshop, 400 feet long, 70 feet wide and 21 feet high, was organized according to the production process. Thus at the one end stood the drawing office, the pattern-makers, the foundry, the iron and brass molders, and all the other departments in a line, ending with the departments where "erectors" put together the machines and applied the final touches. The molten iron was delivered by railcar in huge, 6–7-ton-pots and lifted by cranes. In this system, carrying material and goods forwards and backwards and lifting them up and down were avoided. Each procedure was the responsibility of a specialized department, led by a foreman or manager who also coordinated the work with the connected departments. Nasmyth invented the first factory assembly-line system.

His other major managerial invention was the introduction of standardized mass-production of tools and machines without advance orders. Before him, tools were produced for individual clients based on special orders. Mass production in the cotton industry already existed, but in machine-building the old handicraft practice dominated. Mass production of machines became a real breakthrough in the industrialization process. Nasmyth realized that the need for various machines and tools was immense. As he wrote to his partner during construction of their factory, "It is now as foolish to wait for orders for such machines as to wait for orders for a ton of iron bars and tell the parties when they apply to you that you must have four months as the ore has to be got out of the ground before you can supply."[9] Accordingly, he introduced the standardized mass production of various machines and tools and advertised them in catalogues.

Among the main mass-produced products were small steam engines and locomotives, and various "self-acting" machine-tools. He built his first locomotive in 1838–39, but by 1853 the factory had produced 109, partly for continental railroads. His small mass-produced high-pressure steam engines were used mostly to directly drive various machines. The factory also built hydraulic presses and iron ships. Several of his products were based on his own, often patented inventions. Among them the various sizes of planing machines that replaced the previous unsatisfactory process of chipping and filing, and produced the plane surfaces that are most often required in machine-building. He invented and produced a nut-cutting and facing machine, a bolt-screwing machine, teeth cutters for iron or wooden wheels, a boiler-making machine, a spiral-wire drive for small drills, a paring or shaping machine called the Nasmyth Steam Arm, and, his most famous invention, the steam-hammer.

The mass production of 13 sizes of self-acting steam-hammers up to 5 tons that were able to make 220 blows per minute made it possible to shape large pieces of wrought iron and reduced the price of the products by more than 50%. The handler of the hammer was able to control the force and frequency of the blows, especially because the force of the blow was power-assisted. By 1850, the company had sold nearly 500 steam-hammers. The following year, the steam-hammer was exhibited at the famous Crystal Palace Exhibition. Nasmyth used the same principle in 1843 to create his steam-powered pile-driver that was able to drive a pile in 4.5 minutes; this had taken 12 hours using traditional technology. Small wonder that his machine was broadly used by construction workers. Within three years of the establishment of the firm, 300 workers were employed, but their number increased to 1,500 by 1868, although the introduced self-acting machines reduced the labor force by half.

Nasmyth, a ruthless employer, got tired of making deals with trade unions, and he retired in 1856 to live 34 more quiet years preoccupied with his hobbies. His machines were still used in various factories in the early 1920s.

The door was thus opened to 200 years of unstoppable automation and standardization, and to ever-newer forms of modern mass production.

The Morozov dynasty: from illiterate serfs to Russia's richest industrialists[10]

Savva Morozov was born in 1770 in a serf peasant family in autocratic, backward Russia. His father, Vassili, belonged to the Old Believers, the Orthodox Raskolnik minority who rejected the reform of the Orthodox Church by Patriarch Nikon, and preserved the old customs. They had a strict and close community, did not drink alcohol, and led an ascetic life with hard work as a value. They were persecuted and escaped to small, far-away villages. The Morozovs lived in a small village, Zuyevo, 50 miles east of Moscow on the bank of River Kliazma. Due to their small parcels of land and the need to pay feudal fees, most of serfs were unable to make a living and had to have additional income. A strong peasant cottage industry emerged in the Ivanovo region, where every third peasant household produced linen products. The properties of the serfs belonged to their noble owners, but the so-called peasant *kustar* industry flourished.

Young Savva was sent to work as a weaver in Kononov's silk factory. He was then selected by the community to serve for life in the army. He asked for a loan from his employer to send a substitute, and he paid back the loan in two years. The Old Believer community offered an excellent financial infrastructure and provided credits from the communal holdings. When Savva saved enough money, he asked the permission of Count Riumin, to whom he belonged as a serf, and established a silk ribbon shop in 1797 where he worked with his wife, Uliana. During the Napoleonic wars, he added a wool cloth factory on the other side of the river that became Nikolsk. When their sons Elissei and Zakhar became 14 and 10 respectively, they also joined and worked with their parents. By 1820, the Morozovs had four sons; the elder two were now 22 and 18, Abram was 13, and Ivan was 8 years old.

The strong, heavily built Savva walked the 50 miles to Moscow from time to time with a huge bundle strapped to his back to sell his silk ribbons and delicate linens by knocking on the doors of rich houses. In 1820, when he had saved enough money, he bought freedom for his family for 17,000 rubles, but when their youngest son, Timofei, was born in 1823, he had to pay an additional amount to liberate him.

Savva permanently reinvested their income and expanded the business. By 1837, the cloth mill filled 11 buildings. During the 1830s, he recognized the importance of cotton, and converted his factory to cotton weaving. Cotton was already produced in Russia from the early eighteenth century. Savva imported power looms from England, and he added a cotton spinning factory to his Nikolsk branch and, when it was allowed, he imported spinning jennies and water frames. By 1850, he employed 1,000 workers.

By that time he was already in his 80s, and he passed management of the company to his youngest and ablest son, Timofei, who, in 1851, opened the fourth unit of the family factories in Tver. The other sons, Elissei, Zakhar, and Abram, also independently ran certain branches of the family business, but all of them died early in the 1850s and 1860s, as did their brother Ivan. Savva died at the age of 92 in 1862.

Timofei was a very shrewd businessman, and he enlarged the family empire significantly. In 1872, he charged his two nephews, Abram's two sons, with managing the Tver factory, and he himself focused on his parents' Zuyevo-Nikolsk enterprise. He also reorganized the firm into a limited liability company, but kept the largest part of the shares. He also invited British engineers, employed expert staff, and established a factory for mechanical tools. By 1880, Timofei was the leading industrialist in Russia, the Zuyevo-Nikolsk factory complex occupied 2.5 square miles, employed 8,000 workers, and earned 2 million rubles profit yearly. In 1885, a major strike against Timofei's cruel factory rules and inhuman manner regarding his workers shut down the factories. This strike became a milestone in the history of Russian socialism.

Timofei's first son, Savva, was born after the serfs were liberated in Russia, in 1862. He and his brother attended a gymnasium, and then he continued his studies at the Moscow State University studying chemistry. The grandson of the illiterate founder of the dynasty was sent to Cambridge, England, to continue his studies in chemistry. He patented some of his own innovations. After his father fell ill, Savva took over the directorship of the family business in 1887 at the age of 25. This continued after his father's death, with Savva as director while his widowed mother remained the owner.

The third-generation Morozovs, however, exhibited the typical third-generation complexes, e.g., the lack of brutal strength that characterized their parents and especially their grandparents. This syndrome is brilliantly described and analyzed by Thomas Mann in his Buddenbrooks saga. The third generation became interested in arts and lost interest in business. Savva was a talented businessman whose direction further strengthened the Morozov estate. He increased the company's profit by one-third, and made the company competitive with Britain on the Iranian and Chinese markets. However, he also became an art lover and spent an unheard of 500,000 rubles assisting the Moscow art theaters of Konstantin Stanislavski and Vladimir Nemirovich-Danchenko. He donated a huge amount to the Red Cross. Most of all, since he took over the management two years after the shocking strike that influenced him strongly, he started humanizing the factory regime in the family complex, built modern living quarters, and introduced medical service for his workers. Because of his love affair with a left-leaning actress, he also assisted the Bolsheviks by financing their illegal newspaper, *Iskra*. He hid Bolsheviks in his own house, and sent fur jackets to Siberia for exiled students. When Savva wanted to introduce profit-sharing in the Morozov factories, his mother—the owner of the estate—dismissed him as director. A few weeks later, he travelled to Cannes and, at the age of 43, committed suicide in 1905.

His attitude also characterized Mikhail, Ivan, and Arseny, the grandsons of Abram, second cousins of Savva and fourth-generation Morozovs. Mikhail and Arseny built extreme palaces, including a Moorish-style castle. Ivan, an art lover, often traveled to Paris, and he had a permanent agent there to buy impressionist paintings from Monet, Sisley, Renoir and Pissarro, who were not recognized at the time. He became one of the leading early collectors of Picasso and Matisse. When the Bolsheviks nationalized the Morozov estate after the 1917 revolution, his collection became the core of the modern part of the State Hermitage Museum.

By the First World War, the Morozov textile empire was one of the biggest industrial enterprises in Russia with nearly 40,000 workers. It was nationalized by the Bolsheviks and remained in operation for decades. The company finally closed during the dramatic decline of Russian industry after the collapse of the Soviet Union.

Werner and Wilhelm Siemens and the second industrial revolution[11]

The name of Siemens is inseparable from German industrialization and the second industrial revolution that started with the steel, electricity, and chemical industries. The Siemens brothers left their fingerprints all over the electric and steel revolution. No one could foresee that future in 1816 and 1823, respectively, when Ernst Werner and Carl Wilhelm (known as Werner and Wilhelm) were born into the relatively poor farmer family of Christian Ferdinand Siemens. Christian, like his father, rented land from big landowners, first near Hanover and then from the Duke of Mecklenburg, and cultivated it. The family had 14 children, 10 of whom survived. They did not have enough money to send the boys to school, and Werner, the eldest, was home taught until the age of 11. Technology attracted the young boy, but university training was out of the question. At the age of 19, Werner joined the Prussian army, and, as he planned, he was enrolled in the army's Artillery and Engineering Academy in Berlin. He served 15 years as an officer. Wilhelm, seven years his junior, was educated at the Magdeburg Gewerbe Schule, and his brother taught him mathematics. He studied only a few semesters at the university, and, at the age of 19, he started his training as a machine technician.

The ten children lost both their parents within six months in 1839–40. The 23-year-old Werner became the head of the family, and he took care of the education of 16-year-old Wilhelm, as well as that of Friedrich (aged 13), Carl (10), and Walter (6). When they reached adulthood, all of them worked with their eldest brother.

Werner was a genuine talent who, as he later stated in his memoir, "belonged by natural endowment and inclination in a far higher degree to science than to practice. Scientific research was my first, my early love ... "[12] Indeed, he was attracted and intrigued by the rising age of electricity. The theory of electricity, a brand new field of physics, was not much older than Werner Siemens. It was born at the end of the eighteenth century when Luigi Galvani discovered contact electricity; Georg Simon Ohm discovered the law of relation between electric current, voltage, and resistance; André-Marie Ampère discovered the interaction between two parallel conductors carrying electric currents; and Hans Christian Ørsted established the science of electromagnetism. Two towering geniuses, Michael Faraday and James Maxwell, contemporaries of Siemens, created the theories for using electricity as a practical form of energy.

The theory was at hand, but its practical uses were extremely limited. "The first product of low-current technology 'industry,' which ... was still based on a centralized workshop type of production, was the electrical telegraph, the overhead lines and the cable for long distance telecommunication ... Siemens was among the leading personalities who created the conditions for the development of electrical technology from the initial experimental stage into the modern electric industry."[13]

Werner's first major invention was the pointer telegraph, actually a major improvement of the British Wheatstone's machine, that, unlike Morse's code system, produced a readable text because a needle, moved by the electric signals, pointed to the right letters. This invention created the base for the first business enterprise of the Siemens. The hunger for communication in the rising age of modern shipping, railroads, and international trade was tremendous, and the brothers recognized it. Wilhelm, who settled in England in 1844 to sell his brother's findings, learned about the gutta-percha, natural latex from the evergreen palaquium gutta tree in Asia. He got the idea to use it for insulating telegraph cables. Werner constructed an insulating machine, and in 1847, with the master mechanic Johann Georg Halske, founded the Siemans & Halske Telegraph Construction Company, with the financial contribution of Werner's cousin, Johann Georg Siemens.

The company, in 1848, began laying down telegraph cable systems, first between Berlin and Frankfurt. They continued this work in the Prussian Rhineland. During the 1850s, a booming business in Russia followed, and the company founded its St. Petersburg branch, run by brother Carl. The company built a large network of telegraph systems in Russia. The British branch, headed by Wilhelm, who became a British citizen in 1859 and changed his name to William, specialized in maritime cable-building. He even planned and developed a deep-sea cable-laying ship, named *Faraday*. The Siemens brothers built telegraph connections between Europe and India, Europe and the United States, connected Spain to North Africa, and laid cables in Brazil. The German mother company and the British and Russian branches all established cable factories. Werner's invention of a galvanometer helped discover faults in the cables. The Siemens Company established itself as a pioneering firm of the new, emerging electric industry.

After the period of the telegraph business, the Siemens turned to various other applications of electricity. The marriage of science and technology in the persons of the Siemens brothers led to new areas. The invention of the hand-powered generator to replace batteries was the first step in the new direction. Werner's inductor, based on Faraday's theory of electromagnetic power, created the so-called Siemens armature. A decade later, 50-year-old Werner developed the inductor into the first self-excited dynamo, which he demonstrated before a group of scientists at the Berlin Academy in 1866. The principle of the dynamo was almost simultaneously invented by other scholars as well, but Siemens worked for 14 years to produce reliable dynamos. The discovery of the dynamo electric principle and its practical working out opened new roads for the application of electric energy in various practical uses. It founded the emergence of electric engineering. The Siemens Company started the mass production of the dynamo in 1878.

A series of crucial inventions and applications followed. Werner was interested in electric propulsion, and the groundbreaking result of this was the building of an electric railway locomotive. The Siemens demonstrated it at the Berlin trade fair in 1879. In two years, they built the first electric tram in the Spandau suburb of Berlin and an electric railway line in Austria. Werner also became the father of the trolley bus and built the first line in Berlin in 1882. Two years before that he had built the first electric elevator in Mannheim. He also worked out a plan for a two-level Berlin transportation system, one on ground level and one at an elevated level. Construction was started in 1896, four years after his death, by Werner's sons and cousin Georg. Before the war, four main lines were opened that created the nucleus of the famous S-bahn system that later grew to 15 lines.

The Siemens company, using arc-lamp techniques—before Edison's light bulb invention and the new age that started around 1880—pioneered electric lighting for public places and streets in Berlin, and created the lighting of St. Petersburg's famous Nevsky Prospect and the Winter Palace. In 1882, however, Siemens produced its own incandescent lamp, which became the most important area of the London branch's activity. The company, including its Vienna branch, built electric power stations as well.

As an entrepreneur, Werner Siemens was also innovative and established widespread welfare institutions in his company. In 1872, on the 25th anniversary of the foundation of the company, he introduced a pension system that offered two-thirds of the wages after 30 years of service, and a support system for orphans and widows. He stated in his memoirs: "It had very early become clear to me that ... the growing firm must depend on securing ... the co-operation of all the workers ... It seemed to be essential that all who belonged to the firm should share in the profits according to their performances ... This principle came to be adopted in all our establishments ... These arrangements have worked remarkably well during the nearly twenty years of their existence."[14] As a politician—Werner was elected and served in Parliament in 1862—he added: "Every large factory ought to form such a pension fund, to which the workmen contribute nothing."[15]

Besides the widespread and permanently broadening activities in the electric industry, another epoch-making invention, this time by Friedrich and

William Siemens in London, revolutionized the glass and steel industries. The first industrial revolution, beside the textile revolution, introduced the modern iron industry. The opening of the second industrial revolution or, one should say, the meeting point of the first and second industrial revolutions, was the invention of modern and cheap steel production. The first step towards this new wave of revolution was made by the British Henry Bessemer with his 1856 invention. The Bessemer procedure, however, was not faultless. The real breakthrough came through a combined German and French invention, the Siemens-Martin procedure. The Siemens brothers patented their new, regenerative furnace that created a much higher temperature in the furnaces using pre-heated gas and air. This became immediately successful in the glass industry, but it did not work at first in iron and steel production. Based on this patent, however, the Frenchman Pierre-Émile Martin added scrap iron to the molt. Eventually, the Siemens-Martin procedure revolutionized steel-making from the 1860s and was used for an entire century.

Siemens' minor inventions—such as the fire alarm system, water meter, and their contribution to radio and lighting technology, later producing electric motors, heating appliances, various components for electric installations, and several others—led to the permanent expansion of the company.

When Georg Halske retired from the business in 1867, Werner's two sons, Wilhelm and Carl, also joined as partners with a certain share of the capital, alongside the three brothers, Werner, William, and Carl. The Siemens preserved the close family character of the business for a long time.[16] However, the Siemens Company not only accomplished foreign orders, but established subsidiaries in three countries besides Germany—Britain, Russia, and Austria—and attempted to do so in France. The family company thus became one of the very first pioneering multinationals in the mid-nineteenth century.

Werner Siemens, the founder, actually reached his goal as he expressed it: "My guiding idea was to establish a lasting firm which might one day, in the hands of our sons, become a world-wide concern like that of the Rothschilds, bringing fame to the name of Siemens all over the world."[17] Werner and William were elected members of the Berlin Royal Prussian Academy and the Royal Society, respectively, and both were awarded hereditary nobility in their countries.

In 1892, when Werner died, the Siemens Company employed 6,500 people, 4,800 of them in Germany. Around the turn of the century several mergers, including the foundation of the Siemens-Schuckertwerke in 1902, led to a strong concentration in the new industry: before the war, Siemens and AEG controlled 75% of the German electric markets.

The spectacular rise of the Siemens Company was based from the beginning on the unique combination of research and development. Werner, as he stated, loved science, but was also challenged by its practical use and became one of the first superb electrical engineers. Quoting from his memoir: "I have certainly always felt the impulse to make scientific attainments useful for practical life ... Science does not exist for its own sake ... but to raise mankind to a higher level of civilization."[18] Besides, he also sought to realize the inventions by himself as an entrepreneur and manager of his own factory.

The combination of research, development, and good entrepreneurship as well as transnational operations remained a permanent legacy of the Siemens Company. In 2010, 163 years after its foundation with ten workers at 19 Schöneberger Strasse in Berlin, Siemens had more than 200,000 employees and only one-fifth of its revenue came from Germany. Almost another fifth comes from Asia, one-quarter from the United States, and the remainder from Europe.

Siemens preserved its technology leadership for more than 150 years, nowadays in automation and water treatment technology, offshore wind farms, air pollution control technology, and imaging technology for hospitals. The company is among the best at utilizing energy-efficient technology in power plant construction, making transformers and gas turbines. In one single year in 2006, continuing in the footsteps of the founder brothers, Siemens registered more than 10,000 inventions and 6,000 of them were patented. The company was the world leader in patent application.

William R. Morris and the British car industry[19]

William Morris' life story is astounding. From a farming family, via an apprenticeship in a bicycle repair shop, he became the biggest car producer in Britain and was ennobled as Lord Nuffield. Although his own education ended at the age of 14, he received honorary doctorates from six leading universities and became the founder of Nuffield College, Oxford.

His father, Frederick Morris, was not a fortunate man. He tried his luck in America and Canada, but could only deliver mail. He returned to England, married, and the first of his seven children, William, was born in 1877. In 1879, the family moved to Oxford to cultivate the farm of his wife's family. William studied only until the age of 14 and then became an apprentice in a bicycle repair shop. "When I was but 16," he later stated, "I realized that the security I needed for my parents and myself would depend solely on my own personal efforts."[20] And efforts he made.

The ambitious young man realized that he could earn more alone, and after nine months, having learned the skill, he left the apprenticeship and, at the age of 15, in a shed behind his parents' house, established his own bicycle repair shop. It was 1892, and the bicycle business flourished, especially in Oxford where cycling remains one of the main forms of transportation even in the twenty-first century. Morris soon realized that producing bicycles was more profitable than repairing them. He rented a stable near New College, hired three men and one boy, and started producing two types of bicycles, a solid one and a lightweight one for racing. His business boomed, and he soon opened a shop in the center of the city on the elegant High Street. To "advertise" his product, Morris started cycling training in the early mornings and evenings, and he became champion of popular bicycle races in three counties: Oxfordshire, Berkshire, and Buckinghamshire. Within two years, he had seven employees.

The restless William's interest turned to motors, the most fascinating new phenomenon of the turn of the century. He watched motor mechanics and motorcycle owners taking the motors apart and then put them back together, read manuals, and learned fast how to do it. Morris decided to produce motorcycles. With two partners, he established the Oxford Automobile & Cycle Agency, but it went bankrupt, and Morris split with his partners and started repairing and producing bicycles again. The skillful and hardworking Morris soon re-established his business, and by 1906, he already employed 15–20 people. He looked ahead and what really excited him was the car. In 1905, he bought one for himself. In 1907, the entrepreneurial William founded the Morris Garage, a car rental and dealership.

In the early twentieth century, the car was only a toy for rich people who dressed like fighter pilots. They had to stop and fix tires or the engine several times in a short trip and had to buy the gasoline in containers from grocery shops. There were only 30,000 cars on the British roads. However, the car was the future and America already heralded it.

Morris bought parts and started to build a car in a corner of his shop in 1910. In two years, the first Morris Oxford, a two-seat, four-cylinder, water-cooled, 10-horsepower car was exhibited at the Motor Show. Production started at Temple Cowley in a former military training college. Morris bought almost all the parts from various producers. Engines, carburetors, and gear boxes were delivered by White and Poppe in Coventry, the body from Raworth, axles and other parts from Wrigley of Birmingham. Morris' factory was an assembly line. The only part that was his design was the "face" of the car, the so-called bull-nosed radiator. In a year, he sold more than 1,000 cars.

The First World War stopped the car boom, but Morris started working for the army and enlarged the factory during the war years. After the war, the car continued its triumphant conquest, and by 1921, 226,000 cars were in operation in Britain. Morris produced 7% of the country's car output. Morris Motor Ltd., as it was called from 1919, rapidly gained ground. One of the main secrets of his success was the low price of his cars. He cut the cost of production all the time and became a price leader. Morris still bought the parts and assembled them, but as the business enlarged, he established an iron foundry to cast cylinder blocks, and started buying out the companies that supplied him. After 1923, and until the 1950s, he started purchasing his suppliers— the Birmingham engineering work of Wrigley, one of his main competitors, the Wolseley Motor, the S.U. Carburetter Co., and the Coventry firm—and at last, Morris Industries Ltd, a holding company, became self-sufficient, controlling ten separate businesses and two subsidiaries with 10,000 workers in all. By 1925, Morris produced 67,000 cars, more than one-third of the country's car output, and his income surpassed £1 million. In those years, 1,750 dealerships sold Morris cars. The company became the largest car producer in Britain, marketing more than half of the cars that the biggest six car factories produced.

William Morris was and remained an autocratic entrepreneur. The giant enterprise, although already a joint stock company with a board of directors, was still firmly in his hands. The everyday operation was part of his role, but he had the last word in technical and production issues as well as marketing. Everybody was directly responsible to him, and the managers of the branch factories, as one of them stated, "lay plans in the light of what we thought he was thinking."[21] Morris could not stop the management style he developed as a small-scale bicycle producer. He still had excellent ideas such as the pioneering establishment of the Technical Service Department and the introduction of service manuals and the after-sale service with standardized prices. He cultivated the high wage policy and a kind of profit-sharing. "My experience is that if you look after your men, they will look after you. A low wage is the most expensive method of producing."[22] The Nuffield Benefaction for Employees distributed bonuses from the profit of the company among the employees every year.

The competitors, however, learned from the success of Morris, whose company was not managed according to the requirements of the age, was not flexible enough, and did not produce a great variety of types. As one of his leading managers stated, "By nature, Morris was an adapter rather than a creator, and it was terribly hard to persuade him to let the drawing office start from the clean sheet of paper stage."[23] Until the late 1920s, he still sold only two basic types, the Oxford and the Cowley, and in 1933 there were still only nine basic types. The other big car-makers, including Ford and other Americans in Britain, offered 64 types of cars in 1933–34, and Morris lagged behind. By 1933, it produced only 21% of the country's car production.

William was still only aged around 50, and ready to learn the hard lesson. After 1933, a major reorganization began. He employed good managers and engineers, and reorganized the company along the American production and management line. He introduced a single management, with independent profiles for each of his firms, and the moving assembly line. William Morris, at last, gave up his autocratic management style, started playing golf, and took long vacations in Australia and South Africa. Meanwhile he continued purchasing connected companies, and Morris gradually regained its position. His excellent business instinct, especially as a seller, still worked very well, and he introduced the cheap people's car years before Porsche got the idea and realized it with the help of Hitler to produce the popular Volkswagen. The Morris Minor, a small, fuel-efficient, 8-horsepower car, became an instant success. In the mid-1930s, Morris sold 1,000 units per week of the £135 car. Instead of the 82,000 cars he produced in 1929, he sold 305,000 cars in 1939. Between 1933 and 1938 the company sold 108,000 cars overseas, representing 28% of British car exports. His status was well represented by the fact that in 1934, Morris became a Baron, and in 1938, Viscount Nuffield of Nuffield in the County of Oxford.

In the 1930s, unlike many, he foresaw what was coming. The great entrepreneur began preparing for war production. He had an idea already at the end of the 1920s to enter the aircraft business. In 1935 and after, Morris made several offers to the Air Ministry to produce cheaper high quality aircraft engines, but he was rejected. The four monopolist companies blocked his road. As compensation, he received an order for producing tanks. Morris hired one of the best American expert engineers, Walter Christie, and by the outbreak of the war, several prototypes were ready for production.

During World War II, the Morris Company played a key position in war production. They produced the "Crusader" tank for the African war, and the "Cromwell" that played its role in liberating the continent. Lord Nuffield was appointed unpaid civilian Director General of Maintenance in the Air Ministry and repaired damaged RAF aircrafts: between 1940 and 1945, 75,000 fighting machines were sent back into the air from the Morris factory. He also bought the Bofors patent from Sweden and produced anti-aircraft guns for the defense of Britain, and the Centaur bulldozer that was used in liberated Germany for the reconstruction of cities. The company significantly enlarged and employed 30,000 workers.

After the war, the giant company that had assembly works abroad, including in Australia, continued reorganization. Morris withdrew from managing the company, giving it over to talented managing directors who continued the reorganization that had begun in the 1930s. Major capital injections were granted by issuing shares. Morris merged with its most important competitor, Austin, in 1952, and the new British Motor Corporation, with William Morris as its President, dominated the British market. In his mid- to late 70s, Lord Nuffield virtually retired from management, and in 1954, retired entirely to his estate in Nuffield. He could not establish a dynasty, however, and he died in 1963 at the age of 85 without children.

Louis Renault and the French car industry[24]

The combustion engine-driven car was a German invention, but France became the first and leading car producer in Europe around the turn of the century. Three towering personalities played a central role in this development: Armand Peugeot, André Citroën, and Louis Renault.

The Peugeot family entered modern business in the eighteenth century, producing coffee and pepper grinders, crinoline dresses with steel rods, umbrella frames, and then bicycles. In 1890, after buying a Daimler license, the company started building its first cars and was the first to use rubber tires in 1895. The real Peugeot story, however, started in 1896 when Armand established his independent company and produced his first engine.

André Citroën's name is closely connected with an improved gear mechanism, and most of all, with Europe's first mass-produced cars after World War I. He produced the largest numbers of cars by far, but he went bankrupt in 1935, and died in the same year. The Citroën factory merged with Peugeot in 1975.

Louis Renault emerged as a leading car producer because of his special interest in and talent for mechanics. He was born into a well-to-do family in 1877. His father, Alfred, was a fabric merchant and button manufacturer, and after his death in 1891, his two elder brothers entered the family business. Louis rejected joining. He was not a good student, and his only interest was machines. He rejected studying at the famous Ecole Centrale, and instead started working in a boiler factory before being recruited into the army. When he returned to civilian life, he bought a 0.75-horsepower tricycle for himself. He did not like it and started rebuilding it into a light, two-seat, four-wheel car in the workshop he arranged in a garden shed of the family house in Billancourt (which later became a suburb of Paris). Louis constructed all the parts of his car, from the axles to the chassis. He was dissatisfied with the transmissions the car industry used at that time and began experimenting to change it. In the end, his first major invention was born: the direct drive. He replaced the chain drive system in which each gear had to be connected by belt or chain to the engine by separate gear wheels. His system was simple. He used a universal joint in the drive shaft that allowed the axle to rise and fall and did not apply belt or chain. The modern transmission, his first patent, established his success.

In two and half months, in December 1898, his first car, constructed partly from bicycle parts, was ready. The car became an instant success and some friends and bystanders ordered similar cars from him. His two brothers, Fernand and Marcel, recognizing the potential of the new car business, joined and invested capital in 1899 in the newly established firm, the Renault Frères. The light, 0.75-horsepower "Voiturette" Renault car targeted a wider circle of potential owners, was exhibited in the Salon l'Automobile in the same year, and generated 60 orders.

The garden shed was not enough any longer, and the brothers bought an old boathouse on the other side of the river, opposite Billancourt, and reconstructed it into a workshop. Louis himself did most of the carpentry, engineering, and roofing. He employed assistants and, by 1900, had sold 200 cars.

The decade around the turn of the century was the period of regular car races between cities and capitals. These extremely popular auto races attracted mass interest and made the best advertisement for the winners' products. Louis and Marcel Renault regularly drove their cars at the races, first in 1899 at the Paris–Trouville race, and the next year they became the winner of the Paris–Toulouse race, which instantly generated 500 orders. In 1901, Renault won first place in the light car category in the Paris–Berlin race. Next year, the chief designer of the Dion factory, Viet, offered his new four-cylinder engine to Renault and the new car, driven by Marcel Renault, won the Paris–Vienna race in 1902, putting the company on the map. The success was tremendous since the average speed Marcel achieved was 39 miles per hour, including the crossing of Arlberg Pass. He reached a higher speed than that of the Arlberg express. After that success, Marcel was killed in an accident during the Paris–Madrid race in 1903, and the inter-capital car races ended.

Louis Renault's life was his factory, the car, and newer and newer inventions. After the early death of his oldest brother, Fernand, in 1909, he tactfully bought back his brothers' shares and became the sole owner of the firm. Louis kept all the financial transactions in his own hands and did not turn to banks. When it became unavoidable to transform the enterprise into a joint stock company, he kept 98% of the shares. He worked in his overalls with his workers, avoided any form of social life that was boring for him and, although he had a mistress for ten years, he did not marry until he was 40. He had a rude, unsophisticated manner, and made enemies easily. He was not interested in money and reinvested the profit into the factory to enlarge and develop it. He was not educated, made severe mistakes in spelling and speech, and remained suspicious of educated people, even preferring to employ mechanics who lacked a higher degree.

Working day and night, Louis produced a huge number of inventions and patents. To quote one of his biographers, "Renault was now inventing prolifically, and every month a fat letter went off to the Government patent office. One was a device for increasing the gas pressure in the cylinders; another for ignition without a magneto, working with a single distributor. He invented a method for advancing and retarding ignition; a separable multi-piece sparking-plug ... He patented a starter worked by compressed air from the engine. He had several different patents for carburetors, air intakes and petrol mixtures."[25] Besides his first transmission patent, the most important of his inventions, however, were the drum brake and the hydraulic shock absorber that remained in use for a century.

The business flourished. Renault produced taxi cabs for Paris and London, and in 1906 his first buses appeared on the streets of Paris. Commercial vehicles established his major business success, and he preserved his lead in that area in France: besides buses, he produced sanitary vehicles, and two-, three-, and five-ton delivery vans. In 1907, the factory produced its first eight-cylinder airplane engine. By the start of World War I, the 36-year-old Louis employed 5,200 workers and had sold more than 10,000 vehicles, one-fifth of the total French production. He had selling agencies in New York and Madrid and sold vehicles in Japan, India, and Russia. King Edward VII of Britain used a Renault car.

The Renault factory's success was crowned during World War I. The company had produced 80-horsepower airplane engines for the army since 1910, but because of German technical competition, it constructed 200-, and then 300-horsepower engines that gave aerial supremacy to France. Renault introduced the production of shells, machine-gun carriers, tens of thousands of trucks, and carriers for the eight-ton cannons. With these vehicles, the French army was able to concentrate more than 1,300 heavy guns at Verdun. His light tank design was produced by several companies and played an important role in the last phase of the war. The famous and often-cited episode of the war at the River Marne put Renault's name into the history books since his taxies transported the troops that defended Paris from the deadly German offensive. For his contribution towards winning the war, Louis Renault was the first industrialist in France to become one of the highly prestigious Officier de la Légion d'Honneur.

The interwar decades brought both success and difficulties. Renault, who had visited the Ford factory in the United States before the war, was impressed by Ford's "vertical integration" system and introduced the Fordist system to his own factories. He bought all of the factories that supplied Renault, and established his own steel foundry, smelting plant, glass factory, and even a hydro-electric power station. He owned his own tool factory, saw-mills, and a cotton and wool factory. He produced bricks for constructing new buildings. Consequently, Renault, via a whole set of satellite companies, became self-sufficient and produced everything the company needed for production.

He also studied American Taylorism, the most modern management system that introduced norms for piece work and rationalized the workers' time, including banning the smoking of cigarettes during work time. The implementation of these systems in the Renault factory met with a severe resistance from the workers. During the second half of the 1930s, violent strikes and factory occupations disturbed the Renault empire. Louis was dissatisfied with the entire political atmosphere of the Popular Front government, and he sympathized with those regimes in the neighborhood that created order. In 1938, he met Hitler at the Berlin auto show.

In 1939, the Renault empire employed 82,000 people and produced 18,000 cars, but about one-fifth of the production was not cars. Renault produced giant diesel engines for battleships and airplane engines for, among others, the first planes that started the regular Paris–London commercial air traffic, and served the Air Union (later Air France). He produced light camionnettes and heavy trucks and served the government with an elegant chauffeured limousine service.

However, World War II, unlike the first, led to disaster and the fall of Louis Renault. He had serious conflicts with the war authorities and did not satisfy government orders. Was it connected with the decline of his health, a mysterious difficulty to speak? To handle the factory more easily, the government asked him to go to the United States, and even to meet with President Roosevelt before the war erupted. By that time he was already a married man with a son, so he needed to go with his entire family. After the French defeat, however, he returned to the occupied country to direct his company personally. Together with most French industrialists, his motto was "business as usual." Quoting again his biographer about those industrialists, including Renault: "Before the Second World War, daily contact with their German colleagues and admiration for German output and efficiency persuaded them to regard a Europe unified under German economic leadership favourably ... "[26]

All in all, under permanent German control, Renault worked for Nazi Germany and strengthened its war efforts. When his main factory was bombed and heavily damaged three times, he rushed to rebuild and even modernize his works and continued production. Unlike several of his industrialist colleagues who also served Hitler's Germany, he flatly refused to support the resistance movement financially. When the war ended and the political forces of liberated France turned against the collaborators with vicious anger, Renault was arrested in September 1944. He claimed to have been physically abused at this time. He died the following month.

Although he died before his trial, the Renault empire was nationalized by a decree of January 16, 1945, signed by General Charles de Gaulle, head of the Provisional Government of France. "For reasons which are psychological as well as economic and moral," stated De Gaulle later, "there was a need after the liberation of France to pursue a nationalization policy ... This is what I have done."[27]

Postwar nationalization was widespread in Western Europe, including Britain, France, and Austria. Vast parts of the economies of Germany, Italy, and Spain were also state-owned. Western Europe built up a mixed, private and state-owned economic system. Until the 1980s, 94% of the energy sector, 83% of telecommunications, 46% of transportation, 44% of banking and 6% of other industries were in the hands of the French state. The nationalized Renault factory became a part of the mixed economic system in France.

Emil and Walther Rathenau: the birth of the German electric and electrochemical industries[28]

The Rathenaus, father and son, contributed significantly to the birth of the two most important new industries around the turn of the twentieth century, and to Germany's rise to the top as an industrial powerhouse of Europe. The birth of the second industrial revolution during the second half of the nineteenth century emerged from university laboratories and new striking scientific discoveries, most of all in electricity and chemistry. Germany had the best technical education system in the world and outstanding research universities with modern laboratories. If the first industrial revolution happened in Britain, the second was an American and German affair.

The road from the laboratories to industrial mass production is long and bumpy, however. Capital investment and entrepreneurial talent paved the way. One of the most important entrepreneurs of the new era was Emil Rathenau. He was born in 1838 to Moritz Rathenau and Therese Lieberman in a well-to-do Jewish merchant family. Their predecessors in the eighteenth century were *Schutzjuden* or "protected Jews."[29] Emil, the middle child of three, studied in a Berlin gymnasium and then in one of the famous German Engineering Hochschulen in Hannover, and then in Zürich. His "baptism in industry" happened in his grandfather's machine factory in Silesia where he spent four and half years. As an engineer he practiced at the Berlin Borsig company, and he inhaled the atmosphere of industrialization in England as a machine constructor.

In 1865, at the age of 27, Emil Rathenau established his own company with a partner: a small factory with 50 workers in Berlin to produce small steam engines and other engineering products. Chancellor Bismarck's wars for German unification offered a great opportunity to produce for the Prussian army and navy. Those became the years of *Gründerfieber,* a feverish boom of industrial establishments. Rathenau built a bigger factory in Moabit, near Berlin. His ambition and eagerness inspired him to travel to the Philadelphia World Exhibition in 1876.

This trip became a turning point in his life, and also in German economic development. Emil Rathenau was fascinated by American technology and mass production techniques, and he was attracted most of all by the new inventions in electrical technology, such as the electric motor and lighting. Those were the pioneering years of electricity. Newer and newer inventions, newer and newer wonders followed one after the other. At the Paris Electricity Exhibition in 1881, Edison presented his advanced lighting system and new bulbs. Emil immediately wanted to buy the patent and contacted Edison and his Continental Edison Company in Paris. He started the electrification of the Berlin Stock Exchange palace in 1882. With a consortium of interested Berlin bankers, he initiated other electrification works and published a popular study on the "Edison-Light."

In March 1883, he established the *Deutsche Edison Gesellschaft*, and began producing incandescent bulbs, and installing lighting systems. The Munich and Stuttgart theaters were first, followed by the Berlin Grand Hotel, restaurants, several sugar, textile, paper, and machine factories, and even ships. Germany's first electrical municipal railway was constructed by the company. The 45-year-old Rathenau entered the electric industry business in parallel with Siemens & Halske, another pioneering company. They competed with each other, but they soon also found the way of "division of labor" and worked in neighboring and connected, but independent areas. Later, in 1903, the two giant companies' radio departments together established the Gesellschaft für drahtlose Telegrafen mbH, or Telefunken AG as a joint subsidiary.

During his trip in the United States in 1903, Emil Rathenau also made an agreement with General Electric, the world leader in the new industry, to exchange patents and divide markets. The secrets of his immediate success were his deep interest in everything that was new in technology, skillful cooperation with banks, finding and employing talented engineers, and working 12–13 hours a day.

A year after establishing the German Edison Company, in 1884, Emil Rathenau founded the *Allgemeine Elektrizitäts Gesellschaft (AEG)*, producing electrical equipment, light bulbs, motors, generators, and electricity transmission systems, and later cables as well. Soon, 3,000 workers were employed in his Berlin factory. AEG conquered newer and newer fields of the rapidly advancing electrical technology. In another decade, it entered into a brand new area: the combination of the two new industrial branches, electrical and chemical industries.

In the further development of the company, the son of Emil, Walther, born in 1867, also played a central role. The young Rathenau studied physics, chemistry, and philosophy, then turned to electrochemistry as a post-graduate in Munich, worked as an engineer, and then joined the board of AEG in 1899. His special talent, partly inherited from his father, was the "immediate utilization of every technical innovation for mass consumption, and the immediate absorption of every new source of capital for the increase of production."[30] He also assisted his father in establishing horizontal trust organizations that incorporated the most important electrical companies on the continent and made agreements on division of labor, market sharing, and prices.

Walther played the central role in AEG's entering the electrochemical business. In 1893, he became the manager of the newly founded *Electro-Chemische Werke GmbH* in Bitterfeld that employed 3,400 workers, and then another one in 1894, the *Gesellschaft Kraftübertragungswereke Rheinfelden*. The combination of the electrical and chemical industries opened up an enormous new area of industrial activities. In a presentation at the Berlin Postmuseum in 1900, with Kaiser Wilhelm II in the audience, Rathenau spoke about "Electric Alchemy" and about aluminum, one of the most important novelties among the innumerable new products they were producing. The Kaiser, preparing for war, was highly interested in AEG, and he visited the Berlin factory in the same year with his wife. AEG got military orders, including the electrification of railroads and building turbines for the navy. Between 1910 and 1918, the company produced aircraft for the army. AEG played an important role in the foundation of the new aluminum industry that gained military importance during the war. *Aluminium-Industrie Actien-Gesellschaft, Neuheusan,* "the center of European aluminum production,"[31] with several companies from France to Poland (AEG Elektrizität Warschau), became a significant part of the AEG consortium. The huge conglomerate already employed 14,000 workers. Besides that superb organization, and alongside several banks, including the Deutsche Bank and the Schweizerische Kreditanstalt, AEG established the *Elektrobank* in 1895 as "its own financial center,"[32] a "bank for electric companies."

AEG was already one of the most important early multinational companies by World War I. The founder, Emil Rathenau, died in 1915, and Walther took over leadership of the company. His interests, however, went far beyond the company's business that time. In 1914, as a German nationalist, he felt he had to help his country win the war. He worked out a plan for the controlled management and distribution of war materials, a central issue for the German war economy because of the naval blockade. He knocked on the door of the War Ministry, and one week after the outbreak of the war, he was appointed head of the Ministry's *Kriegsrohstoffabteilung,* the department with the responsibility for realizing the Ministry's war plan. That was the beginning of the build-up of the world famous German wartime economic system that influenced the entire world economy after the war.

Although Rathenau resigned from that post when his father died in order to take over the leadership of AEG, his political interest pushed him further. At the end of the war in 1918, understanding the tensions and dangers of the postwar situation, he advocated workers' participation in management. Most importantly, he founded the German Democratic Party, and was appointed Minister of Reconstruction in 1921, and Minister of Foreign Affairs the following year. Rathenau, although an ardent anti-communist, masterminded the Treaty of Rapallo with Bolshevik Russia in April 1922 that normalized diplomatic relations and established trade connections between the two isolated countries. Although Rathenau denounced the Versailles Treaty, he argued that obligations under it should be fulfilled. The far right accused him of treason, and spoke about a Jewish-Bolshevik conspiracy. Two months after signing the Treaty of Rapallo, Rathenau was assassinated by two ultra-nationalist officers near his home on Königsalle at Berlin-Grünewald.

AEG had a troubled history during the interwar period and World War II; several of its factories, located in the Russian occupation zone, were confiscated after the war. Nevertheless, by 1948, AEG had already recovered and employed 20,000 people. During the 1960s and 1970s, the company became an actor in the German economic miracle: by 1970, it employed 178,000 workers worldwide. After 1967, the company's name became AEG-Telefunken, but Daimler-Benz bought it in the 1980s, and in 1997 the company ceased to exist as an independent firm. From 2005, Electrolux bought the prestigious brand name and became AEG-Electrolux.

Jewish entrepreneurship in Hungary[33]

In most of the peripheral countries of Europe, the nobility preserved its monopoly on political power in the surviving authoritarian regimes. The society remained traditionally immobile. The noble elite, including the lower layers of the nobility, the gentry, looked down on business. They considered it an ungentlemanly activity, and they instead monopolized military and bureaucratic-administrative positions in the state and county apparatus. On the other hand, the peasantry was excluded from society, and their upward mobility was extremely limited. However, modern urban, business, and professional areas, inspired by Western business connections, emerged and led to the birth of a politically mostly powerless and subordinated small bourgeoisie. The gap positions between the noble elite and the peasant masses in the peripheral societies were mostly filled by ethnic minorities. A greater part of this small-business elite and modern professional layer was considered non-indigenous foreigners, initially Greeks, and later Germans or Jews. Hungary was one of the countries, together with Russia, Poland, Lithuania, and Romania, where entrepreneurship and professional positions were strongly connected with the Jewry.

Before World War I, the Jewish population of Hungary increased by roughly three times through immigration from the eastern provinces of the Habsburg Empire, such as Galicia, and neared one million people, representing 5% of the country's population. This percentage was much higher than anywhere else in Western Europe, including Germany, and was equal with the situation in Romania, but behind Lithuania (7%) and Poland (10%). Excluded from feudal society, land ownership, and public jobs, and long suffering discrimination through strict legal restrictions on occupation and residence, Jews lived outside the city walls and urban settlements, which opened a window of opportunity for the Jews in trade and small business. A 1768 census showed that two-thirds of the Jewish population in Hungary were occupied in small itinerant trading, going from village to village and selling goods, or leasing noble monopolies such as inns, mills, and distilleries. One-third of them were beggars, impoverished peddlers, rug collectors, and workers.

When the modern transformation slowly began in the nineteenth century, and feudal structures were eliminated in 1848, and especially after 1867 when Jewish emancipation was enacted, the opportunities for Jews were broadened. Actually, they "enjoyed the specific advantage of exclusion, and were thus able with relative ease to become the pioneers of capitalist economy."[34] Many of them migrated to the rapidly growing capital city, Budapest, which emerged as by far the largest business and industrial center of the country. As a consequence, Jews came to make up nearly one-quarter of Budapest's population.

From the 1860s on, several Jewish entrepreneurs rose from small business into the business elite. One important route was the grain trade, the most important and lucrative business activity between agricultural Hungary and the industrializing Western provinces of the Habsburg Empire. Several leading traders recognized the opportunity, and started founding flour mills in Budapest from the 1860s. One of them was Adolf Weiss, a village pipe-maker, who moved to the capital, entered the grain trade, and was among the first of a couple of Jewish grain traders to invest in the flour mill industry. Others, such as the Deutsch family, established sugar refineries, and still others set up distilleries. In agricultural Hungary, the bread basket of Austria-Bohemia, food processing became the capstone of industrialization. Until the early twentieth century, this single sector produced 40% of total industrial output.

Leading merchants who became well-to-do via the Austro-Hungarian trade, and who built successful connections with Austrian and other foreign banking interests, also entered banking. Ferenc Chorin, Adolf Ullmann, Fülöp Weisz, and Leó Lánczy emerged as the leading bankers of the country. The sons of Adolf Weiss, Berthold and Manfred, established a canned food factory, and then Manfred became a leading industrialist and owner of engineering and munitions factories that employed 30,000 workers during World War I. The Weiss family and several other leading Jewish bankers and industrialists in the liberal regime of the late nineteenth century bought noble ranks, becoming for example Baron Manfred Weiss of Csepel and Baron Hatvany-Deutsch.

In the backward eastern part of Hungary, in Carpatho-Ukraine, a huge Jewish working class represented the majority of Jewry, and in the Transylvanian Szatmár, Hassidic communities remained in isolation. Altogether, nearly one-third of Hungarian Jews were lumberjacks and workers, and they had a huge presence in the printing industry in 1910, but business, trade, industry, and banking sectors were overwhelmingly Jewish. More than 20% of Hungarian Jews worked in banking and industry, and their share among clerical employees of the banking sectors reached 53%, in industry 43%, and 80% of the industrial managers were Jewish. Among shopkeepers, Jews made up the majority, 57%.

In the overwhelmingly peasant society (roughly two-thirds of the population were peasants) the Jewish minority had a dramatically different occupational structure: more than 73% of them worked in industry, handicrafts, banking, and commerce, and another 11% worked in various free professions and communication. The percentage of Jews among the self-employed was 53%, and 36% of the Jews were self-employed. In the latter part of the nineteenth century, Jews flooded the professional fields: nearly half of the medical doctors, 42% of the journalists, 38% of private engineers, and 23% of actors were Jewish in 1910. In the legal profession, their share was 45%, but in a typical way, almost none of the judges and prosecutors, and thus none of the state- or publicly employed legal experts were Jews, while they dominated in the private sector. A portion of Jewish business people went to Vienna, and Jewish participation in banking, the stock exchange, and the Chamber of Commerce in the capital of the Habsburg Empire was 60% before the war.

The Hungarian political regime after the 1867 Austro-Hungarian Compromise was liberal, and even at the highest political levels representatives often praised the Jewish contribution to the Hungarian economy and culture. A couple of Jews, Mór Wahrman and Ignác Einhorn (Ede Horn), were even elected to Parliament, and in 1917 the first Jew (Vilmos Vázsonyi) was named to a cabinet post. The liberal regime, however, ended after World War I. The troubled postwar years, with their two revolutions, in the end opened the way for the authoritarian Horthy regime, the first one in Europe to introduce anti-Jewish legislation by limiting the number of Jews at the universities in 1920. That regime, in alliance with Hitler in the 1930s, introduced two pieces of anti-Jewish legislation in 1938 and 1939. The latter took the Nazi Nuremberg Law as a model and virtually eliminated the possibilities for Jews to make a living. Hundreds of thousands lost their livelihoods. The men had to serve in labor battalions and were decimated. In the summer of 1944, the deportation of the countryside-dwelling Jews to Auschwitz took place, and, in the end, half of the country's Jewish population was killed. In 1946, two dramatic pogroms reflected the deeply rooted anti-Semitism in the country. More than half of the survivors emigrated to Israel or the West. In the second half of the twentieth century, about 80,000–100,000 Jews remained in Hungary, most of them in Budapest.

The period after World War II under the Soviet-installed communist regime, especially during the devastating Stalinist era between 1948 and 1953, became the period when Jewish communists dominated the leadership of the Communist Party and the country. In the most paradoxical way, all the Jewish and other businesses were nationalized at that time. As in many other countries of the region, including Poland, Romania, and Lithuania, Jewish entrepreneurship virtually disappeared, along with a significant Jewish minority.

Women in business and management[35]

Women in business, especially big business and management, were a rarity in the earlier years of the development of the modern European economy, and still are even today. In the nineteenth century, as countries industrialized, discrimination against women excluded them from the critical areas of political participation and education that might have given them access to the highest positions. Except in Finland and Norway, women did not even possess voting rights before World War I. Educational opportunities were also limited, due in part to a deeply rooted cultural tradition that tended to pair femaleness with an innate deficit in rationality. Even Jean-Jacques Rousseau, the early prophet of education, distinguished between the kinds of education proper to males and females. Women, he stated in *Émile* (1762), his famous work on the subject, should be educated in "relation to man ... to be pleasing in his sight, to win his respect ... to train him in childhood, to tend him in manhood, to counsel and console, these are the duties of women for all time, and this is what she should be taught while she is young."[36] Nearly 60 years later, in 1820, Poland's first recognized women writer, Klementyna Tanska-Hoffmanova, despite demanding equal recognition for women, maintained that "women certainly have less need to possess knowledge ... study should not be an aim. ... To know how to make her husband happy, to make his life pleasurable, to bring up their children properly, to find new ways of pleasing everyone: that is the system of education for women."[37]

In the later nineteenth century, a new set of middle-class social standards, emphasizing the responsibility of the female for household hygiene, nutrition, and children's health added another set of barriers to the participation of women in the workplace. It became fashionable for a woman to trade her job, upon marrying, for the position of housewife. The husband as the sole breadwinner became a norm and a source of male pride as well; a working wife brought social shame. This new attitude gradually came to predominate in Britain, the Netherlands, and other rich societies. In the 1900s, four out of five employed middle-class women in the Netherlands left their jobs before getting married. Their counterparts in the lower layers of society could not afford to do the same; thus between one-third and one-half of women whose husbands were unskilled workers continued working, even after marriage. Nevertheless, "social classes competitively emulate the social strata above them ... being a housewife became over time the dominant choice among the lower classes as well."[38]

This cultural pattern ruled in Europe until World War I. At the end of the nineteenth century, a feminist Slovak woman writer who demanded proper education for women articulated a bitter complaint about the middle-class male culture: "The majority only wants their wife to be beautiful, charming ... and devoted to them body and soul ... They require her to have only social skills ... Any sort of education ... is a disadvantage, not a benefit ... a husband is the ready-made enemy of his wife's education through his conviction that it leads her away from her duty."[39]

Access to secondary and university education opened for women only in the very late nineteenth century. In Austria, to take the final examination at high school was allowed for girls only in 1872, in Germany in 1895, and in Galicia in 1907. Campaigns to open universities to women were launched in several European countries between the 1860s and 1890s. The very first woman to get a medical degree, Nadezhda Suslova, would receive her diploma from the University of Zürich in 1867; at last medical schools were opened to females. During the 1870s, access improved as the universities of Paris, Edinburgh, London, Ireland, and Denmark all began accepting female students. In Britain, however, Oxford and Cambridge did not follow suit until the 1920s.

Although political, cultural, and educational barriers virtually excluded women from positions as "captains of industry" or as top managers at major companies, they did not entirely prevent nineteenth-century women from playing significant roles behind the scenes. In a few notable cases, widows of leading entrepreneurs took over the responsibilities left vacant by their husbands' deaths. This happened twice in the Krupp family business in Germany. At the turn of the nineteenth century, when the Krupp Company was still very young, the widow of Friedrich Jodocus Krupp, Helene Amalie, bought four coal mines along with the ironworks of Gutehoffnungshütte. She, therefore, was the real founder of the company. Nevertheless, although she retained decision-making power, she appointed her 19-year-old grandson, Friedrich, as manager of the firm. The pattern was repeated after Friedrich Krupp's death in 1826, when the firm became bankrupt. Friedrich's widow took over the company, but, due to the culture of the age, she appointed her 14-year-old son, Alfred Krupp, who dropped out from school, to act as her company manager. A similar story unfolded around the turn of the twentieth century at the Kassel firm Henschel & Son, Germany's largest locomotive factory. Before his death in 1894, the company's owner, Oskar Henschel, conferred sole ownership and control on his wife, Sophie Henschel. She ran the company but arranged a formal partnership with Oskar's son in 1900: Sophie Henschel, "instead of openly acknowledging her power ... assumed a less public role— one that kept her out of the limelight—and promoted the perception of her son's leadership."[40]

More often women were silent business partners, especially in the realm of finance. In the early decades of the nineteenth century, before modern banking was invented, the financial and credit markets depended on private crediting. In Sweden, for example, even in the 1870–80s, in cities such as Kalmar, Falun, and Sala, informal crediting represented two-thirds to three-quarters of total crediting. In several instances, rich women, mostly widows—Helena Renström of Falun is an example—acted as private bankers. Women also became major investors. In 1840, 47.2% of British government securities were held by women. Half of them were widows, the other half spinsters. Of English investments in government securities, women owned about one-third.[41] In Stockholm between 1862 and 1875, 59% of the depositors at large savings banks were women. Moreover, in the last decades of the nineteenth century, 30–40% of the shares of the eight leading Swedish commercial banks were owned by women. As Tom Petersson concluded, the activities of the "publicly active, profit maximizing male entrepreneur represent just one kind of economic agency, while the 'silent' investment activities of middle-class women represent another."[42]

In the twentieth century, gender discrimination started to decrease in Europe. Women gained voting rights in every nation and barriers to post-secondary education disappeared. After World War II, gradually, a female majority emerged at universities. In several countries, women became political leaders, cabinet members, even prime ministers. In the late twentieth century, women filled a majority of cabinet posts in Norway and Spain. Nevertheless, significant remnants of old cultural patterns persisted. The primary responsibilities for looking after children and elderly family members lay with women who, although working in jobs outside the home, also spent twice as much time as men doing household work. In Italy today, an average man spends 1.3 hours per day on domestic work; the average women spends 5.2 hours. In Sweden this difference is much smaller, 2.3 versus 3.4 hours. Given these extra demands on their time, a great many working women prefer working on a part-time basis.

In the business world, women in top positions are still a rarity. Recognizing this situation, the organization of business and professional women established in 1930 in Geneva by Lena Madesin Phillips, today known as BPW International, launched a new campaign in 2011 on "women in economy and leadership," noting that "BPW International was founded on the vision of achieving work place equality ... and equal pay. Eighty years on and the issues are still the same."[43] *The Economist*, meanwhile, recorded in July 2011 that the number of female managers remained still very small. Among the group of leading companies listed either in France's CAC 40 share index or Germany's DAX index, not a single one was run by a woman.[44] Even Scandinavia, certainly the most gender egalitarian region in the world, has room to improve: out of 269 managing directors in Sweden in 2010, only 8 were women. Counting all managerial positions, just one-quarter to one-third are filled by women.[45]

The twenty-first century promises to be a historic turning point. Norway has pioneered a new state campaign. Its Parliament passed a law in 2003, when the number of women named to company boards was only 9%, that required publicly listed firms to fill 40% of board seats with women by 2008. This move motivated the European Union to take over the cause and on October 30, 2009, to initiate a campaign to promote change throughout Europe: "Women are still held back from launching their own companies by a range of barriers including education, stereotypes. ... The EU is working with member states to overcome these obstacles."[46] On July 6, 2011, the European Parliament passed a resolution stating that 40% of companies' board seats must be reserved for women by 2020.[47] The EU appointed "ambassadors for women entrepreneurs," successful business women such as Svana Helen Björnsdóttir of Iceland, an electrical engineer who established an information technology company in

1992, and Zlatica Maria Stubbs of Slovakia, a successful entrepreneur for 20 years in consumer electronics and the automotive industry. These "ambassadors" will travel around encouraging and assisting female entrepreneurs in Europe. Spain enacted a law similar to Norway's in 2007, France in early 2011, and the Netherlands is preparing one. Even major companies followed suit: the multinational Deutsche Telecom announced that by 2015, 30% of its upper and middle managerial positions will be filled by women.

Now, in 2012, the number of female board members at companies has indeed increased significantly and totals 34% in Norway, and 27%, 15%, and 13% in Sweden, France, and Germany, respectively, but progress is uneven. The figures for Spain and Russia are still only 10% and 8%, respectively. In the business world, quota systems often bring mere superficial change, or "face-lifting" initially. Thus, at the top levels of company leadership, in the executive committees, the percentage of women is still very low: 8%, 7%, and 3% in France, Spain and Germany; even in ambitious Norway, a mere 13%. Nevertheless, gender equality in business is most certainly slowly breaking through.

The birth of the Vizcaya iron industry in Spain[48]

Until around the turn of the twentieth century, the dramatic economic transformation of the nineteenth century hardly touched Spain. The former world power, which had been one of the richest countries in the world, declined into peripheral backwardness. The huge belt of latifundio in south and central Spain was frozen in a medieval state. The minifundio in the north, with its extremely small plots, was not market-oriented and was dominated by subsistence farming. Industry, except Catalonian textiles, was virtually non-existent. Spain was also the only country in Europe to remain outside the century's demographic revolution. While some countries increased their population by three to four times, Spain less than doubled its population. Although five revolutions attempted to destroy the *ancien regime*, they were defeated, and until the 1860s the pre-capitalist socio-political environment was conserved. The restoration government, led by the landed aristocracy, was incompetent. There was a lack of entrepreneurial skill and motivation, and an aristocratic "hidalgo" prejudice against hard work and in favor of spending more than earning, and that looked down on frugal social values, still dominated. That was the reason the hundreds of tons of gold and silver that flowed in from the Americas in the previous centuries all disappeared, and in the end enriched the Dutch and the British.

In this ocean of backwardness, however, small advanced islands emerged: textile factories in Catalonia, orange orchards in Valencia, and vineyards in coastal regions. At the northwestern edge of the country, in the Basque region, one of Europe's most important iron and steel industries started working in the last decades of the nineteenth century. How did this happen?

While path-dependence was debilitating, outside effects from a radically transforming Europe had an impact on Spain. The British industrial revolution that revolutionized the cotton, iron, and coal industries also created a hunger for raw materials. Non-phosphorus-laden iron ore was one of the most important raw materials that Britain looked for outside the island. The rich hematite endowment of the Bilbao Bay, located near to the ocean by navigable waterway and then railroad, had attracted British interest. Between 1851—when the Linares Lead Mining Co. was founded—and 1913, 174 British mining companies exploited the rich iron ore, lead, and copper resources of Spain, 56 of them in iron ore mining.[49] From 1870 on, British companies invested in the region's iron ore mining. According to certain calculations, 47% of the profits from iron mining went to Britain. This development was assisted by the replacement of the medieval mining law that gave a monopoly on subterranean resources to the Crown and blocked the road to private enterprises. This was, at last, replaced by the modern Mining Act of 1868. Foreign, mostly British, mining companies rushed to exploit the rich iron resources. Between the late 1870s and 1900, 58 million tons of iron ore, nearly two-thirds of total output, were exported. This quantity represented 86% of all the iron ore sold in Europe.

However, the foreign companies mostly worked in collaboration with established local elites, and some joint enterprises offered huge incomes from the exports for local families. Basque entrepreneurs owned and often leased out mines, entering into joint ventures with the Brits. Consequently, leading Basque entrepreneurs such as the Ibarras and Chávarris families accumulated huge amounts of capital, and, from the 1870s on, they began investing in the local iron and steel industry. Instead of exporting the ore, they started processing it domestically. During the last decades of the nineteenth century, nearly 600 million pesetas in profits accumulated from iron ore exports, half of it in the hands of a few Basque families. Basques, like other minority populations in peripheral countries, e.g., Armenians, Greeks, Germans, and Jews, embodied different values and represented different attitudes towards the economy than the dominant nations. They were highly entrepreneurial and could profit lavishly from the noble negligence of the dominant ethnic groups. Basque entrepreneurs invested more than one billion pesetas in new industrial companies at the Bilbao Stock Exchange.

Basque entrepreneurs could also use the British connection to buy cheap coal from Britain (delivered by the same carriers that transported the ore from Spain to England). British coal was cheaper than Spanish coal, mined in Asturia, because it was transported by water. While one-quarter of investments was channeled into the mining industry, iron and steel, shipbuilding, and other industries were also established. Giant companies emerged such as the Altos Hornos de Vizcaya.

The unique success of the Basque iron and steel industry was also connected to strong state interventionism. Against the dominant post-feudal interest groups, the Bilbao Chamber of Commerce (1886) and then the Liga Vizcaína de Productores (1894), in cooperation with Catalonian industrialists, successfully fought for the defense of the domestic market. The 1891 Tariff Act was followed by an even more extremely protective tariff of 1906, which made Spain one of the most protectionist countries in Europe. In 1896, they succeeded in getting the government to ban imports for the railways, a giant market for the iron industry. The governments also gave special privileges for the Vizcaya shipbuilding industry, including big orders from the navy.

Important modern industrial pockets emerged in two ethnic minority regions, the Basque and Catalonian areas of Spain, but the country still remained in its backward state until World War II. The second half of the twentieth century, with its Spanish economic miracle, led to a process of catching up with Western Europe. That was mostly accomplished during the last decades of the twentieth century, when Spain became an integral part of Europe and a member of the European Union. Nevertheless, the 2008–12 economic crisis still exhibited the impact of the former peripheral weaknesses of the country.

Notes

1 Joseph Schumpeter, *Business Cycles: A Theoretical, Historical, and Statistical Analysis of the Capitalist Process*, New York: McGraw-Hill, 1939, Vol. I, 103.
2 This essay is based on the monumental, 1,309-page book by Niall Ferguson, *The World's Banker: The History of the House of Rothschild*, London: Weidenfeld & Nicolson, 1998; and on Frederic Morton, *The Rothschilds: A Family Portrait*, New York: Atheneum, 1962.
3 Ferguson, 1998, 48.
4 Daniel Chirot, "Conflicting Identities and the Danger of Communalism," in Daniel Chirot and Anthony Reid (eds), *Essential Outsider: Chinese and Jews in the Modern Transformation of Southeast Asia and Central Europe*, Seattle: University of Washington Press, 1997, 13.
5 This essay is based on A.E. Musson and Eric Robinson, *Science and Technology in the Industrial Revolution*, Manchester: Manchester University Press, 1969; www.biographybase.com/biography/Nasmyth_James.html
6 In R. Buchanan, *Practical Essays on Mill Work*, 3rd edition, revised by G. Rennie, 1841, 393–418, quoted by Musson and Robinson, 1969, 474.
7 Musson and Robinson, 1969, 475.
8 Andrew Ure, *The Philosophy of Manufactures*, 1835, 37, quoted by Musson and Robinson, 1969, 478–79.
9 Nasmyth's letter from the collection of the Gaskell family is quoted by Musson and Robinson, 1969, 494.
10 This essay was built on Valentine Tschebotarieff Bill, "The Morozovs," *Russian Review*, Vol. 14, No. 2, 1955, 109–16; Petr Ivanovich Liashchenko, *Istoria narodnogo khoziaistva SSSR*, 4th edition, Moscow, 1956.
11 This essay is based on Werner von Siemens, *Personal Recollections*, New York: D. Appleton, 1898; Wilfried Feldenkirchen, *Werner von Siemens: Inventor and International Entrepreneur*, Columbus: Ohio State University Press, 1994; Kurt Busse, *Werner von Siemens*, Bad Godesberg: Internationes, 1966; Herbert Goetzeler and Lothar Schoen, *Wilhelm und Carl Friedrich von Siemens: Die zweite Unternehmergeneration*, Stuttgart: Franz Steiner Verlag, 1986.
12 Siemens, 1898, 352.
13 Feldenkirchen, 1994, 5–6.
14 Siemens, 1898, 355.
15 Ibid, 357.

16 The London branch became public in 1881, and the Russian branch in 1886. The mother company in Germany became a joint stock company only after the death of Werner in 1892.
17 Quoted by Busse, 1966, 14.
18 Siemens, 1898, 352–53.
19 This essay is based on R.J. Overy, *William Morris, Viscount Nuffield*, London: Europa Publication, 1976; Robert Jackson, *The Nuffield Story*, London: Frederick Muller, 1964; Philip W.S. Andrews and Elizabeth Brunner, *The Life of Lord Nuffield: A Study in Enterprise and Benevolence*, Oxford: Basil Blackwell, 1955.
20 Jackson, 1964, 28.
21 Overy, 1976, 40.
22 Quoted by Overy, 1976, 113.
23 Ibid, 51.
24 This essay is based on Anthony Rhodes, *Louis Renault: A Biography*, London: Cassel, 1969; Laurent Dingli, *Louis Renault*, Paris: Flammarion, 2000; Patrick Boniface, *Automotive History: Louis Renault*, 2008, www.helium.com/items/1192567-biography-louis-renault.
25 Rhodes, 1969, 52.
26 Ibid, 166.
27 Quoted by Bertrand Jacquillat, *Nationalization and Privatization in Contemporary France*, Stanford: Hoover Institution, 1988, 16.
28 This essay is based on Ursula Mader, *Emil und Walther Rathenau in der electro-chemischen Industrie (1888–1907): Eine historische Studie*, Berlin: Trafo Verlag, 2001; Felix Pinner, *Emil Rathenau und das elektrische Zeitalter*, Leipzig: Akademische Verlagsgesellschaft, 1918; Manfred Pohl, *Emil Rathenau und die AEG*, Mainz: Hase & Koehler, 1988.
29 In the Holy Roman Empire, from 1236 on, Jews were considered to be *servi camerae regis*, servants of the royal chamber, a special class protected and taxed by the emperor, and later by free cities and landowner princes, who guaranteed protection for taxes.
30 Harry Kessler, *Walter Rathenau: His Life and Work*, London: Harcourt, Brace & Co., 1928, 16.
31 Mader, 2001, 180.
32 Ibid, 98.
33 This essay is based on Michael K. Silber (ed.), *Jews in the Hungarian Economy 1760–1945*, Jerusalem: Magnes Press, 1992; Ivan T. Berend, *History Derailed: Central and Eastern Europe in the Long Nineteenth Century*, Berkeley: University of California Press, 2003.
34 Peter Hanák, "Jews and the Modernization of Commerce in Hungary, 1760–1848," in Silber, 1992, 26.
35 This study is based on Robert Beachy, Béatrice Craig, and Alastair Owens (eds), *Women, Business and Finance in Nineteenth-Century Europe*, Oxford: Berg, 2006; "Women in Business: Still Lonely at the Top," *The Economist*, July 21, 2011.
36 Jean-Jacques Rousseau, *Émile*, trans. Barbara Foxley, London: J.M. Dent, 1993, 393, quoted by Rachel G. Fuchs and Victoria E. Thomson, *Women in Nineteenth-Century Europe*, Houndmills: Palgrave Macmillan, 2005, 87.
37 Ursula Phillips, "The Upbringing and Education of Women as Represented in Novels by Nineteenth-Century Polish Women Writers," *Slavonic and East European Review*, Vol. 77, No. 2, April 1999.
38 Frans W.A. van Poppel, Hendrick P. van Dalen, and Evelien Walhout, "Diffusion of a Social Norm: Tracing the Emergence of the Housewife in the Netherlands, 1812–1922," *The Economic History Review*, Vol. 62, No. 1, 2009, (99–127), here 100–101, 118.
39 Elena Maróthy Soltésova, "The Need for Women's Education" (1898) in Norma Rudinsky (ed.), *Incipient Feminists: Women Writers in the Slovak National Revival*, Columbus: Slavica Publisher, 1991, 134–36.

40 Robert Beachy, "Profit and Property: Sophie Henschel and Gender Management in the German Locomotive Industry," in Beachy et al., 2006, 69.
41 Alastair Owens, "Making Some Provision for the Contingencies to which their Sex is Particularly Liable: Women and Investment in Early Nineteenth-Century England," in Beachy et al., 2006, 29.
42 Tom Petersson, "The 'Silent Partners': Women, Capital and the Development of the Financial System in Nineteenth-Century Sweden," in Beachy et al., 2006, 50.
43 www.bpw-europe.org.
44 "Women in Business: Still Lonely at the Top," *The Economist*, July 21, 2011.
45 BBC News Europe, "Is Sweden the Best Place to be a Woman?" October 16, 2010, www.bbc.co.uk/news/world-europe-11525804; World Business Culture, "Women in Business in Sweden," www.worldbusinessculture.com/Women-in-Business-in-Sweden. html.
46 European Commission, "Europe Needs More Businesswomen," *Enterprise and Industry Online Magazine*, ec.europa.eu/enterprise/magazine/ articles/smes-entrepreneurship/ article_9724_eu.htm.
47 *The Economist*, 2011.
48 This essay is based on Joseph Harrison, "Heavy Industry, the State, and Economic Development in the Basque Region, 1876–1936," in Pablo Martín-Aceña and James Simpson (eds), *The Economic Development of Spain Since 1870*, Aldershot: Edward Elgar, 1995; Nicolás Sánchez-Albornoz (ed.), *The Economic Modernization of Spain, 1830–1930*, New York: New York University Press, 1987.
49 Charles Harvey and Peter Taylor, "Mineral Wealth and Economic Development: Foreign Investment in Spain, 1851–1913," in Martín-Aceña and Simpson, 1995, 188, 189.

2 The power of institutions

Economic regimes and the permanent renewal of capitalism

Introduction

The modern nineteenth- and twentieth-century industrial economy was born from flourishing merchant capitalism, rapidly growing colonial empires, and developing international trade that led to sufficient accumulation of capital. On the basis of a gradual social and political transformation, and two economic revolutions in the seventeenth and eighteenth centuries, the agricultural and industrial revolutions in northwestern Europe turned a page in history. Although it was nurtured by mercantilist protectionism and state intervention, when industrial capitalism became strong enough, it emerged hand in hand with the rise of the laissez-faire market system in the most advanced core of Europe. This system, initiated by Britain, rapidly spread throughout the continent by trade agreements and the Gold Standard. Laissez-faire, however, did not well serve the latecomers and less developed southern, central, and eastern regions of Europe. Protectionism gained ground from the 1870s, and state interventionism and a creeping economic nationalism, especially after World War I, started transforming free market capitalism.

World War I and the tremendous economic effort to supply history's first industrialized war, led the main belligerent countries, and especially Germany, to introduce a strongly centralized, state-run, and even planned war economic system. Its economic outcome was surprisingly satisfactory. Countries that adopted this system achieved far better results than during peace time. The lessons of the war economy were learned, and elements of that regime started to be used during peace time. John Maynard Keynes, the most influential economist of that age, prophesized the end of laissez-faire in the 1920s.[1] Indeed, three different economic regimes emerged from that experience. The regulated market system took root in Western Europe and gained new impetus during and after the Great Depression of the 1930s. The European peripheries, which joined the laissez-faire regime in the mid–late-nineteenth century, were sorely disappointed in its results. They remained agricultural and backward. Disappointed and frustrated, countries and regions turned inward and invented alternative economic systems, based on the experience of the war economy. The fascist revolution in Italy institutionalized a dirigist economic regime with a huge role for the state, including state ownership of important sectors, "nationalization" of trade unions and introducing a corporative system, and strict, centralized economic regulations. The Bolshevik revolution in Russia invented and developed the world's first non-market economy with total state ownership and central planning. Besides its ideological origins, the wartime economic system also played a major role in its construction. The dirigist regime and the communist non-market system spread and became dominant in several countries of the Mediterranean, and in the Central and Eastern European peripheries, respectively, for a long period of the twentieth century. The regimes of both Hitler and Stalin initiated regional systems of autarchy, mostly based on bilateral agreements and trade in kind.

Economic development in the West, together with the socialist (trade unionist), fascist, and communist challenges to liberal capitalism, generated major institutional reforms and the renewal of the market system. While self-regulating laissez-faire regimes subordinated the society to the economy, reforms were introduced to safeguard the society. Brutal, early industrial capitalism was regulated by social legislations that offered some defense against the negative effects of the market. Thanks to resistance from labor organizations, child labor gradually disappeared, 12–16-hour workdays were cut, and factory inspections moderated the often inhuman circumstances in workplaces. Later in the nineteenth century, pension schemes, health insurance, and other legislation improved the workers' situation in Germany and some of the Scandinavian countries.

Although these reforms began to gain ground in the mid- to late nineteenth century, the welfare state appeared only in the 1930s in Sweden, and became dominant in Europe only after World War II. In the regulated market regime, the role of the redistributing state increased significantly. A mixed private and also partly state-owned economy was institutionalized. Social compromise, the system of the so-called Social Partnership, helped post-World War II reconstruction and the rise of prosperity.

In the late twentieth century, as a consequence of globalization and the collapse of communism—and thus the end of competition between capitalist and communist regimes—the self-regulated laissez-faire market system returned in the 1970–80s. It challenged the welfare state. Although welfare institutions were curbed, the welfare state was not eliminated. A quarter-century later, the financial crises of 2008 in several countries further weakened the welfare state. Meanwhile, they strengthened again the trend of regulation, as in the 1930s, and they in fact probably may end the turn-of-the-century resurgence of the self-regulated market system.

The lessons of two devastating world wars, together with the rising Cold War immediately after World War II, generated a strong integration effort that led to the foundation of the European Economic Community in 1957, later renamed the European Union. The integration process, although far from being a permanent linear trend, led to an integrated common market, the introduction of a common currency, the elimination of borders among the member countries, and the introduction of the so-called cohesion policy to help backward regions catch up with the most advanced parts of the EU. This policy gained special importance when the original six member countries began accepting new applicants and the EU had 27 member states by the early twenty-first century. During the last two centuries, tremendous institutional changes have characterized and influenced the European economy.

In this chapter, various essays offer interesting examples of the role of different institutions. Essays discuss the rise, decline, and rise again of the laissez-faire system, the regulated market economy, and the German war economy as it influenced the rise of fascist and communist economic regimes in the interwar decades. These regimes, which were characterized by a strongly isolationist economic nationalism, also invented autarchic regional trade systems. Other essays illustrate the strong flexibility of capitalism through building and abolishing colonial systems, by introducing *Sozial-partnerschaft*, the welfare state, and the integrated European economic regime with its brand new redistributive system, the cohesion policy, to assist backward regions and countries to catch up.

Globalization is also presented in this chapter. From the 1970s on, globalized capitalism surpassed the framework of the nation-states. A tremendous increase in trade and capital flow, and the determinant role of multinational companies with huge networks of subsidiaries abroad, opened a new chapter of modern capitalism. While globalization was based on revolutionary technological changes, especially the communication and transportation revolutions, it was also the outcome of deliberate policy. The interests of the industrial powers in the second half of the nineteenth century initiated the "first globalization" or, better put, a globalizing, but not yet fully globalized world economy. This generated strong resistance during and after World War I, when a strong back-lash of economic nationalism destroyed globalization. The trend, nevertheless, reemerged after World War II, and especially after the 1970s. The Pax Americana, the Bretton Woods agreement, including the foundation of the International Monetary Fund and the World Bank after the war, the establish-ment of the General Agreement on Tariffs and Trade (GATT) and later the World Trade Organization (WTO), all assisted globalization. The new tech-nological revolution strengthened its objective base significantly. However, globalization was also a policy to replace the collapsed colonial system. It has its winners and its discontented losers, but several countries and regions profited from it, including both advanced and backward regions.

Political, social, and economic institutions have thus played an important role in generating economic performance. In recent decades, economists and economic historians have embraced an institutional interpretation of economic history. Institutions are "the rules of the game in a society ... the humanly devised constraints that shape human action."[2] According to Douglas North and Barry Weingast, the British Glorious Revolution of 1688 and the institutional system that was crafted afterwards, especially that of property rights, created Britain's economic success.[3] "Institutions shed light on why some countries are rich and others poor."[4] In the 2010 *Cambridge Economic History of Modern Europe*, the first sentence of the chapter on "State and Private Institutions" boldly declares: "Economic growth depends upon institutions (rules that constrain human behavior and their enforcement mechanism)."[5]

However, the institutional interpretation of economic history as the single most important factor is one-sided and unavoidably simplistic. The strong entrepreneurial state, which was the product of centuries-long historical development and was influenced by a host of cultural and ideological factors, underwent a gradual social-economic transformation that led to the creation of new "rules of the game." The most legitimate question to ask thus is: "what caused institutions?"[6]

Path-dependent and culturally inspired institutions, or the lack of them, certainly play an important role in economic performance (both success and failure), but one cannot point to them alone, especially not as *the* determinants of economic development. Institutions often serve the interest of a certain layer of society and not society as such. The same institution may have different impacts in different social-cultural environments, since it and other factors are interdependent. The institutions that work best in a given social-cultural environment often do not work in a clientalist and corrupt society.

The cycle of protectionism and laissez-faire in the market economy[7]

The several-hundred-years-long history of capitalism and the market economy exhibits a dramatically changing cycle consisting of periods of protectionism, followed by decades of free trade and laissez-faire, and then back to protectionism, to be replaced again by free trade. While the eighteenth century and the first half of the nineteenth century were characterized by strict protectionism and regulations, laissez-faire gradually gained ground in Europe from 1860–70. Its rule never governed the entire European continent, and a part of Europe (and the United States) soon turned back to protectionism. From the 1870s until World War I, Germany, Italy, and virtually all of the peripheral countries of Europe such as Spain and Russia built up high tariff walls around their borders.

This trend of protectionism became predominant in the interwar years as a reaction to the previous free trade regime and the economic challenges of the war, the tragic Great Depression, and the soon re-emerging war preparations of the 1930s. Some peripheral countries, such as Italy, Spain, and Russia, introduced state-dominated, strictly regulated "modernization dictatorships."

After the 1950s and 1960s, the new wave in the Pax Americana gradually reinstalled the laissez-faire regime, but it became characteristic only in Western Europe, and only in a limited way even there, restricted by welfare measures and state ownership in a mixed economy. Laissez-faire gained a freer hand from the 1970s to the 1980s, when globalization had broken through. The market economy thus exhibited a marked cycle of radical policy changes.

Based on far-reaching anthropological research, Karl Polanyi described pre-capitalist centuries' economic systems in his *Great Transformation: The Political and Economic Origins of Our Time* as guided by social and communal interests, "Man's economy … is submerged in social relationships," and the economic system was run on non-economic motives. "Primitive man" did not have a capitalist psychology as economists later assumed, but a collectivist one, and the main economic motives were social reciprocity and redistribution. During the seventeenth and eighteenth centuries, a flourishing merchant capitalism emerged and was assisted by courageous ocean shipping, aggressive colonization, and developing foreign trade. The economy was still not guided by market rules. State regulations and protective tariffs strictly served the defense of domestic markets against competition. The dominant *mercantilist* economic idea maintained that the wealth of a nation depends on a trade surplus and the accumulation of precious metals. The leading economic policy thus defended the domestic market against foreign imports by high protective tariffs and various kinds of import restrictions and banning the import of certain goods entirely. Meanwhile, the government provided export subsidies and state monopolies to promote industrial output and increase exports.

In seventeenth-century France, Jean-Baptiste Colbert, minister to Louis XIV, embodied this policy. His famous regulations encouraged French exports and discouraged importing from abroad. The ban on the import of woolen products, and the foundation of "manufacture royale" in various industries such as glass, cloth, and the famous royal tapestry works aimed to replace imports and assist exports.

The British government also followed the same ideas and policy. The trademark legislations that symbolized this policy were the Navigation Act (1660), the Calico Law (1720), and the Corn Law (1815). All defended domestic markets. The country banned the export of raw materials, and the colonies were forbidden to sell their product to other countries except Britain. The Prussian state under Frederick the Great, and the Habsburg Empire under Maria Theresa and Joseph II, also followed the same path (they called it Kameralist policy) during the second half of the eighteenth century.

In the first long policy cycle from the seventeenth- to the mid-nineteenth centuries, the economy was strictly regulated and all countries defended their domestic markets against imports, and the state stimulated and subsidized industrial production and exports. However, the self-regulated, free market system gradually gained ground in the nineteenth century. Was that the consequence of a wise recognition of the advantages of free trade and a non-regulated market economy? True, a few genuine talents started seeing economic affairs in a different way in the eighteenth century. Influenced by the Newtonian worldview and the idea of the genuine harmony of the universe, political thinkers discovered the same type of genuine harmony in human relations and the economy. English political thinkers such as John Locke and David Hume spoke about a divine harmony between private advantage and the public good. All of a sudden, outside intervention was condemned as harmful. As Jeremy Bentham maintained, to govern better, one must govern less, and nothing ought to be done by governments.

The first school of economics, the French physiocrats, led by François Quesnay in the last third of the eighteenth century, questioned the mercantilist principle and realized that wealth is not created by a trade surplus and the accumulation of gold, but by human work (although they limited it to agricultural work). Anne-Robert-Jacques Turgot went further by recognizing the advantages of free trade. The real breakthrough, however, arrived with the British school of economics, around the turn of the century. The great trio of Adam Smith, David Ricardo, and John Stuart Mill established the modern free market economic theory in which the "invisible hand" of the market regulates the economy. They maintained that the free market system and competition offer advantages for both advanced (industrial) and backward (agricultural) trading partner nations. Moreover, as Mill stated, a free market is the prerequisite of democratic society. Herbert Spencer, the British sociologist-philosopher, went even further by adapting the concept of biological evolution to the society, creating "social Darwinism" before Darwin with his concept of the "survival of the fittest." Free competition, these schools of thought maintained, builds society and humankind as well.

Nevertheless, the free market system was not born from the realization of great ideas, from books and studies. In fact, it happened the other way around: modern economic theory was born from the developing interests and slowly spreading practices of the most advanced parts of northwestern Europe, most of all Britain. Britain was already the "workshop of the world" in the eighteenth century, when widespread so-called "proto-industry," i.e., the merchants-organized putting-out system based on peasant cottage industry, was for the first time combined with the newly invented factory system. British exports flourished: they doubled in the first half of the eighteenth century, and then more than tripled during the second half of it. Britain became the cradle of the first industrial revolution between 1760 and 1830, with its landmark mechanization of certain branches of industry by the steam engine, the introduction of coal as the main energy source, and the invention and further development of an array of textile machinery. Already by 1820, Britain exported more goods by value than France, Switzerland, Austria, the Low Countries, and Italy combined. During the long nineteenth century, British exports increased thirty-fold.

Britain definitely became interested in the elimination of tariff barriers, and the institutionalization of free trade. Tariffs, however, also represented one of the most important income sources of the state. To eliminate them, substitute state incomes were needed. The first budget that was balanced without tariff income was achieved in Britain only in 1842. From the 1840s on, Britain steadily progressed in the direction of laissez-faire. Radical tariff reductions and the abolition of export duties followed. The Corn Law and the Navigation Act were both repealed in that decade. By the 1860s, tariffs were lifted and free trade policy became triumphant. Britain started internationalizing the free trade system, and, unilaterally introduced the Gold Standard—basing the value of the English pound on gold and making it exchangeable with gold—and advocated its international realization. Both efforts succeeded.

The breakthrough occurred in the 1860s and 1870s. In 1860, the first modern free trade agreement was signed by Britain and France. The Cobden-Chevalier Treaty was the first free trade agreement in the nineteenth century between two leading countries. This also contained the famous "most favored nation clause" that became the engine of the spread of the free trade system through its automatic tariff reduction mechanism. Due to this clause, every tariff reduction made to one trading partner became automatically compulsory in any future trade agreement with other partners. After the milestone British-French agreement, almost 50 bilateral trade agreements soon followed and all of the European countries accepted similar principles.

Free trade was significantly assisted by the introduction of the Gold Standard. An international agreement was signed in 1870 and all the countries that joined—by the 1890s, virtually all of Europe—based their currency on gold. This system gradually replaced the previously existing bimetallic (silver and gold), silver, or paper money regimes in Europe. The unified Gold Standard made the exchange of currencies easy, since their values were indexed to gold. It also helped the progress of multilateral payment networks. All of these gave further impetus for international trade. The half-century before World War I is often called the "first globalization."

The less developed, latecomer, and peripheral countries, however, soon became dissatisfied with free competition with more advanced countries, and, especially after the 1873 depression and deep agricultural crisis, more and more countries questioned the free trade system and returned to protectionism. That happened in Germany, Russia, Spain, and several other countries. Using Karl Polanyi's expression, they turned to self-defense against the uncontrolled rule of the market.

World War I, and then the Great Depression of the 1930s, sounded the death knell of the laissez-faire system, and the era of economic nationalism was opened in most of Europe. During and after the war, a new phase began and virtually all of Europe returned to protectionism. National independence was equated with economic self-sufficiency, an idea that characterized some of the peripheral countries of Europe in an extreme form. Economic isolationism ruled fascist Italy, Franco's Spain, and Stalin's Soviet Union. Nazi Germany established an autarchic regional agreement system with some of her neighboring Central and Eastern European countries. Germany, Poland, and Hungary introduced some kind of state planning as well. Free trade and the gold standard disappeared, and its reintroduction soon failed in Britain.

The post-World War II era of *Pax Americana* urged the reintroduction of the free trade regime. The General Agreement on Tariffs and Trade (GATT) in 1947 aimed at the gradual reduction of tariff and the return to the free trade era. Several subsequent agreements, the so-called Tokyo Round and the Punta del Este Round, pushed the laissez-faire system ahead. In 1995, GATT was replaced by the World Trade Organization (WTO) to further liberalize and supervise international trade. Around the turn of the millennium, 153 countries, representing 97% of the world's population, belonged to this organization, while 30 more so-called observers sought membership.

After 18 years of delay, at the end of 2011, Russia also joined the WTO, so now nearly all of Europe belongs to the WTO. More importantly, European economic integration, the formation of the European Common Market—and later the European Union in 1957—led to the elimination of tariffs and trade restrictions among the member countries, and to the introduction of a Single European Market of 27 countries around the turn of the twenty-first century.

However, the laissez-faire market system was restricted in Europe. After the war, a mixed economic system was formed with a significant state-owned sector of the economy, strict wartime and postwar regulations remained intact for a long time, and the welfare state became dominant with a strong redistributing role and huge social expenditures by the state. Free trade with regulations, a mixed economy, and the welfare state dominated the postwar decades until the mid- to late 1970s.

The crises and stagflation that followed and characterized the period between the mid-1970s and mid-1980s, however, opened a new chapter of globalization and a partly globalized neo-liberal economic theory. This started with strong privatization in the state sector and deregulation of the financial sector, together with the challenge of the welfare state and the need to curb social expenditures. The ideologues of the self-regulating market, the emerging school of neo-liberal economics—Friedrich Hayek, Milton Friedman, and others—maintained that unregulated markets may also solve economic troubles and social problems. They reintroduced the idea that a free market economy is the only system that guarantees freedom and democracy. This one-sided trend was nevertheless partly stopped by the 2008 financial crisis that revitalized the era of regulations and state interventionism, although not at all in its interwar form, and never really challenging international free trade. A regulated market economy tries to combine the advantages of free trade and a role for market mechanisms with social controls to curb speculation and to defend society from the negative side effects of the market.

During the last half-century, the policy cycle manifests a rising laissez-faire trend, but, as several times earlier, it is somewhat limited and not entirely world- or Europe-wide. Is a backlash of late twentieth century globalization possible? Might Europe face a new change, a new phase of policy? Although the future is mostly unpredictable, a more balanced and combined policy of free trade and state-interventionism is seemingly more probable.

The birth and renewal of capitalism: colonization and decolonization[8]

Europe started to build global empires beginning in the early modern centuries. First the Iberian countries, and then, from the seventeenth century, the northwest

European countries established the foundations of their empires. The process began with the migration of European settlers. Between the sixteenth and twentieth centuries, about 60 million emigrants established the European "colonies" in the Americas, Africa, Australia, New Zealand, and Asia. Modern colonialism was inseparable from the birth and rise of modern merchant and then industrial capitalism. It was launched by conquest, or forced agreements and external control and rule. In 1800, European powers already controlled more than one-third of the world's land. Nevertheless, the nineteenth century became the real offstage for the "age of empire," as Eric Hobsbawm called the culmination of that process between 1875 and 1914.[9]

After the Napoleonic Wars, Britain emerged as an unchallenged superpower and began conquering or at least controlling the greatest part of the world. The British Empire was already large, incorporating North America and Australia, and major trading positions in India. The nineteenth century, however, became Britain's imperial century. The new conquests started in 1808 with Sierra Leone, followed by Java, Singapore, Malacca, and Burma. In 1877, Queen Victoria was proclaimed Empress of India. By the 1880s, Beludjistan, Upper-Burma, Malaysia, North-Borneo, and New Guinea were incorporated into the colonial empire. The African enlargement of the Empire began with Zambezi, and Nyassa-land, and the colonization of Africa was crowned by the conquering of Sierra Leone, the Gold Coast (Ghana), Gambia, Bechuanaland, Zanzibar, Nigeria, and the occupation of Egypt and Rhodesia.

After the 1880s, when one single generation enlarged the colonial empire by one-third, income from British foreign investments doubled. The British Empire ruled a nearly 26-million-square-kilometer area with about 400–420 million people before World War I. An "informal empire" enlarged the sphere of interest, controlled and institutionalized by forced agreements such as the Treaty of Nanjing, imposed on China in the early 1840s. The former white colonies, however, became already either independent or lost—like the United States—or turned into self-governed dominions such as Canada, Australia, New Zealand, and South Africa between 1867 and 1910.

France emerged as the second largest colonial empire, colonized Indochina, and built an African empire that was itself bigger than Europe. The world's second-largest colonial empire ruled a territory stretching over more than 12 million square kilometers.

Other Western European countries joined. The Netherlands was one of the earliest colonizers with huge possessions in the East Indies, and in the islands of the West Indies. In Java and the surrounding islands alone, the colonies of the Netherlands had 35 million inhabitants. Belgium owned Congo as the private property of King Leopold II, an area that was 80 times larger than Belgium itself. The latecomer powers, such as post-unification Germany, sought to join the club of colonial empires, a trademark of national greatness at that time. In the 1880s, Germany occupied Togo and Cameroon, an area five times bigger than Germany. Post-unification Italy also made efforts to emerge as a colonial power by occupying Somalia and Libya, but was defeated in Ethiopia.

Modern colonialism and industrial capitalism seemed to be twin brothers. John A. Hobson, a British economist, called attention to the phenomenon and its motivations in 1902 in his influential, 400-page book, *Imperialism: A Study*. Imperialism, in his interpretation, was the natural product of the economic pressures created by a sudden advance in capitalism that cannot find occupation at home and needs foreign markets for goods and for investments.[10] Various goals motivated colonial expansion or imperialism. British policy sought to establish political control and the power to build a guaranteed market for her goods and profitable investments to fully exploit British economic potential. Foreign trade with colonies indeed played an important role in Britain. Between 1892 and 1896, 33.2% of British exports went to the colonies and 22.5% of the nation's required food and materials were imported from the Empire. Of course, the products of plantation economies in sub-tropical and tropical regions, including sugar, coffee, and tea, and the extraction of raw materials such as silver, diamond, copper, oil, and other resources, all inspired colonization.

For several other colonial powers, however, trade did not play such an important role. Colonial expenditures, in the meantime, had risen and sometimes surpassed gains. In the case of France, expenditures surpassed gains by 108 million francs in 1898. The German and Italian latecomer colonizers did not realize gains since they launched risky adventures, bloody and expensive wars to *build* a colonial empire. "Although the new Imperialism has been bad business for the nation," explained Hobson, "it has been good business for certain classes and certain trades within the nation. The vast expenditure on armaments, the costly wars ... though fraught with great injury to the nation, have served well the present business interest of certain industries and professions."[11]

A complex of interests besides economic ones motivated expansionism and empire-building. Colonization (imperialism) was closely connected to nationalism. French colonialism mostly originated from nationalism, an effort to redeem France and reestablish the "gloir," especially after the Napoleonic Wars, severe losses of her possessions to Britain, and the humiliation of the defeat by Germany in 1870–71. It was even more so in the cases of Italy and Germany. They felt themselves inferior and second-rate powers without colonial possessions. No one expressed that better than Heinrich von Treitschke, a leading historian, ideologue, and member of Parliament in late nineteenth-century Germany: "Every virile people have established colonial power ... All great nations in the fullness of their strength have desired to set their mark upon barbarian lands and those who fail to participate in this great rivalry will play a pitiable role in time to come. The colonizing impulse has become a vital question for every great nation."[12]

Social motivations also contributed. In the late nineteenth century, rising social tensions and polarization, and the strong socialist mass movements in some countries, inspired politicians to forge national unity by channeling outrage and passion against outside rival-enemies. They were stressing the need for internal social unity, and by fighting for colonies to elevate the nation.

Enrico Corradini, the leader of the Italian Nationalist Party maintained that "nationalism and imperialism represent the rebirth of the valour of collective existence ... [and spoke about the] sacred mission of imperialism."[13]

A combination of economic, political, and social motivations led to the apex of colonization around the turn of the century. In the end, half of the land area of the globe and one-third of its entire population was under colonial rule by World War I. Marxist theoreticians established the theory that imperialism was a new and highest stage of the development of capitalism. According to Rosa Luxemburg, capitalism needs a "third person" beside the bourgeoisie and proletariat, the non-capitalist sector, including the Third World, as it was dubbed by Alfred Sauvy, the French demographer in 1952.[14] Vladimir I. Lenin, in his 1917 pamphlet, popularized the concept of "imperialism as the last stage of capitalist development" when the globe is divided by the leading imperialist powers who turn against each other for redistributing the possessions. "These wars will generate revolutionary upheavals and dig the grave of capitalism."[15]

In opposition to the idea that capitalism is unable to exist without colonialism and imperialist conquest, and also to the "last stage" theory, Karl Kautsky, the leading theorist of the German Social Democratic Party, stated in his 1914 work, *Der Imperialismus*, that imperialism is only a policy (as child labor and long work days had been in the early stages of capitalism), and might be replaced by other policies. Capitalism, thus, may exist without colonies, and colonial conflicts might be replaced by international cooperation in a future stage of capitalism, what he called *ultra-imperialism.*[16]

It needed another half-century before Kautsky's vision became reality. During the twentieth century, colonial rule weakened and, especially during and after World War II, the entire system was undermined. This was a long process, especially if one includes the liberation of the Spanish colonial empire in Latin America in the nineteenth century, and the formation of independent states from countries that belonged to the so-called mandated territories, founded by the League of Nations to take over the colonies of the Ottoman Empire and Germany, mostly by Britain after World War I.

Liberation movements, peaceful or violent, spread like wildfire. There were several bloody episodes such as the Sétif massacre in Algeria in 1945, the Madagascar massacre in 1947, and the bloody Indochina and Algerian wars. Many heroes of these struggles such as Mohandas Gandhi, Kwame Nkrumah, Sukarno, Gamal Abdel Nasser, and others pushed the movements ahead. In the polarized, Cold War-ridden world system, it was easy to find arms and support. The European powers, weakened by war exhaustion, lost momentum, and many of them, beginning with Britain and the Netherlands, gave up their colonies without resistance. India became independent in 1947, Indonesia in 1949. The African colonies became independent mostly in the 1950s and 1960s. After long wars and humiliating defeats, the French gave up Laos, Cambodia, and Vietnam in the 1950s, and Algeria in 1962. Portugal lost its African colonies in 1974. Virtually the entire colonial system collapsed by the 1960s, as the United Nation's Declaration on the Granting of Independence to Colonial Countries and Peoples marked in 1960.

Decolonization was a major, and in many ways heroic historical event, but the truth is that colonies had lost their importance for the former colonial states. The emerging modern postwar economic structures, and the new technological and service revolutions, made the former raw material resources much less important, and the Third World countries also lost their role as markets for mass consumer goods. Advanced countries turned to each other with high-tech trade and investments. Colonial empires also became more and more expensive and, in the end, a real burden. As John Kenneth Galbraith explained, the engine of economic well-being was shifted within and between the advanced industrial countries, the colonial trade and market lost importance, and the liberation of the colonies was soon compensated by alternative ways to maintain most of the benefits without the burdens of colonial empires.[17]

What Karl Kautsky called "ultra-imperialism" is nowadays called the globalization that followed the collapse of colonialism from the 1970s on. This is not just another term replacing the discredited imperialism as some Third World theorists maintain. Globalization has several losers, but it is a new phenomenon, not a one-way road, and it provided opportunities for prepared peripheral countries to gain capital, new technology, management, and expertise to catch up with the advanced world. While the world became more polarized, huge parts of the former colonies and subordinated countries— first all of the former "white colonies," then South Korea, Singapore, Hong Kong, India, and China—started rising to the core.

German wartime *Planwirtschaft:* the cradle of new economic regimes[18]

World War I ended the prewar liberal free market economic system in Europe. One of the main reasons for that was the invention of a new economic regime, which was required by the economic demands of the first mechanized war. This war was unique in scale and length, but most of all in its new technological requirements. It was the first war between highly industrialized countries, and the two industrial revolutions created an unlimited industrial background for the war. Transportation of troops and armaments was based on railroads and trucks. New long-range artillery with high explosive shells was used for the first time. Mass production of machine guns and automatic rifles, sophisticated hand grenades, flame throwers, and the mass production of weaponry dramatically modernized traditional warfare. More importantly, new weapons appeared, such as tanks, airplanes, giant battleships, as did a brand new naval weapon, the submarine or U-boat.

From 1890 on, a deadly naval arms race began between Germany and Britain, and the Royal Navy delivered the so-called Dreadnoughts, a new battleship with a top speed of 39 kilometers per hour, ten 12-inch (30 centimeter) guns, and 22 12-pounder guns. Later the first super-Dreadnoughts appeared with their 135-inch (342 centimeter) giant guns. Against the British advantage in naval power, Germany introduced the submarine, with powerful diesel engines that changed warfare. Meanwhile, the first anti-aircraft guns and anti-submarine weapons also appeared. Poisonous gas, although banned by the Hague Convention in 1899 and 1907, was also used, first by the Germans in April 1915 at the battle of Ypres, and then phosgene and mustard gas was used by both sides, causing about one million casualties.

The production of war planes advanced tremendously in the war years, and it transformed the vulnerable toy-plane into a deadly weapon—equipped with machine guns—that could be used to gather intelligence as well as bombing enemy lines. The German AEG factory produced hundreds of C.IV and G.IV fighter planes with machine guns and 160- and 260-horsepower engines. Caterpillar tanks with Maxim or Lewis machine guns and heavy armor became a dominant weapon. The British Mark I tank in 1915, and then the more efficient French tanks in 1917—although they traveled at a walking pace—became the most important new weapon that changed the character of war, as the major tank battle at Cambrai proved in 1917.

Mechanized warfare, however, required a different economic system to guarantee raw material and labor supply, and to produce new weapons on time in huge quantities. This requirement became a question of life or death in Germany, which launched parallel wars on two fronts, in the east and the west, and which was surrounded by powerful enemies, including the world's great industrial powers of Britain, France, and later the United States. The German military tactic of running two separate wars, first against France, and then against Russia, almost immediately collapsed. Long and standing trench warfare followed parallel in two fronts.

The tremendous economic burden of the long war pushed ambitious Germany to a new road to establish a highly centralized war economy. The market was unable to regulate such a system. What was needed was an organization, a mechanism that worked like a clock, with cogwheels moving each other forward in a harmonized way. The task was gigantic because the Allied naval blockade limited the raw material resources of the country, and the huge army had to recruit all of the able-bodied male population.

In the summer of 1914, Walther Rathenau, a congenial entrepreneur and manager of the Allgemeine Elektricitäts-Gesellschaft (AEG), one of the giant electric companies of the country, knocked on the door of the War Ministry and offered a plan for the organized distribution and production of strategic materials. He was appointed to run the organization, called the *Kriegsroh-stoffabteilung* (KRA), or department of war raw materials, within the Ministry of War. In October, KRA abolished free market prices and introduced the fixed price system. It also started allocating materials to companies working for the army. Rathenau also initiated the production of *Ersatz*, or substitute, artificial materials. The world's best chemical industry started producing cru-cial substitute materials such as synthetic rubber, synthetic rayon, artificial fat, and coffee. KRA gradually directed two-dozen corporations that produced substitute materials. To be able to supply the army, food rationing was introduced in January 1915, and in May 1916, a special office, the *Kriegsernährungsamt*, was established to regulate and ration the food supply for the population. To be able to recruit a sufficient labor force, a law was enacted in December 1916, the *Gesetz über den vaterländischen Hilfsdienst,* that mobilized the male population between the age of 17 and 64 for mandatory labor service.

Abolishing the free market for materials and food products was not enough. The army needed more and more cannons, airplanes, tanks, and innumerable kinds of weaponry and munitions. A market economy was unable to guarantee a steady supply to the army. The entire war production had to be planned and directed by central offices on a mandatory basis In August 1916, an armament production plan, the Hindenburg Plan, was also introduced. The word *Planwirtschaft*, or planned economy, appeared for the first time in history. To run the planned economy, and in effect to militarize the entire German economy, the *Oberstes Kriegsamt*, Supreme War Office, was established in November 1916 under the direction of the Supreme Army Command. A network of government offices directed the various sectors of the economy. The *Kriegsersatz- und Arbeitsamt* was established with the authority to direct the output of substitute products and to distribute labor. The newly founded *Waffen- und Munitionsbeschaffungsamt* became the authority responsible for the production of weapons and munitions. The Supreme War Office had the right to close down factories if needed, and it did so for factories that produced for the civil population.

State direction naturally incorporated war financing. Taxes were increased, treasury bills were issued for short term credits, and war loans were taken. In these ways, state authorities covered war expenditures to the amount of 150,000,000 marks. The final source of financing, however, was the printing of paper money. Consequently, the amount of money in circulation quintupled and generated inflation during and after the war years.

The German war economy became an extremely efficient, centralized, state-run economic machine that produced all the required results, accelerating war production and supplying the huge army that fought in the west, south, and east of Europe, and competing with the combined economic power of Britain, France, the United States, and Russia. Foreign troops were unable to enter German territory until the very end of the long war. A new economic system was created.

John Maynard Keynes, the British economist who soon became one of the most influential persons in economics and government economic policy, delivered a lecture at Oxford University in 1924, in which he stated: "War experience in the organization of socialized production, has left some near observers optimistically anxious to repeat it in peace conditions. War socialism unquestionably achieved a production of wealth on a scale far greater than we ever know in Peace."[19] The characteristic title of the lecture was "The End of Laissez-Faire."

Keynes himself was inspired to work out the substitute market system that became dominant in Europe between the wars and thereafter for nearly four decades. A strictly regulated market economy was introduced that rejected the idea of perfectly working market automatism in which supply—as formulated by the French economist, Jean-Baptiste Say—creates sufficient demand. Keynes argued—and several governments followed this concept during and after the Great Depression—that state interventions have to create additional demand.

The German war economy served as model for Benito Mussolini in establishing his dirigist, state-run economic system, and for Vladimir Lenin, who, in 1918, suggested taking over the German system as the economic basis for the Soviet Union.

The economic regime of fascist modernization dictatorship[20]

Fascism, a preventive counter-revolution, emerged in Italy's chaotic and revolutionary years after World War I. The Risorgimento that unified the Italian peninsula was unable to create a unified economy. While the advanced north was near the West European economic standard, the backward south remained nearer the Russian economic level. This latecomer country nurtured colonial ambitions that it thought would elevate it among the advanced colonial powers of the West. From this soil grew Italian nationalist proto-fascism around the turn of the century, which maintained that Italy was a "proletarian nation" that had to fight against the "bourgeois countries" to find its place in the sun. The "translation" of the Marxian concept of class struggle into the idea of international conflict and the struggle of nations, put the notion of the supremacy of the state and the unity of the nation into the center of the rising ideology. The experience of the war, especially the lessons learned from the German war economic system, strengthened the notion of an almighty state that would dominate national economy.

Benito Mussolini, a former socialist turned founder of Italian fascism based his ideas on prewar proto-fascist-nationalist concepts. He denied the existence of classes and class struggle, and subordinated individual rights to the state's interest. "The Fascist conception of life stresses the importance of the state and accepts the individual only in so far as his interests coincide with those of the State ... Fascism stands for liberty, and for the only liberty worth having, the liberty of the State ... Outside of it no human values can exist ... " Mussolini was very explicit regarding statism, state dirigisme in the economy, and permanent warfare. The state and the economy "must be militarized ... [because] I consider the Italian nation in a permanent state of war." As he stated, "war alone keys up all human energies to their maximum tension ... Life [is] elevation [and] conquest. [The Fascist state is the] keystone of the fascist doctrine ... [The twentieth century] is the collective century and therefore the century of the State. [The totalitarian state is also] an economic organization of the nation ... The Fascist State lays claim to rule in the economic field ... "[21]

The first realization of this program was the initiation of major public works: the electrification of railroads, the development of hydroelectric power generation, land reclamation and road construction, including the initiation of the world's first *autostrada*, or freeway project. Two major campaigns, the "Battle of Birth" to increase the population from 40 to 60 million inhabitants, and the "Battle of Grain" to reach self-sufficiency in agriculture, were launched in the 1920s. The 1923 Act of Land Reclamation aimed at achieving self-sufficiency by increasing the arable land and productivity, partly by tractorization and by using more artificial fertilizer. The major electro-irrigation and land reclamation plans were realized by huge state investments, four times more than between 1870 and 1922 altogether.

State interventionism significantly increased during the 1930s when state control over foreign trade was introduced, including a permit and then licensing system for imports, price-fixing schemes, and price controls. In 1932, the law of *consorzi obbligatori* established the compulsory cartel organizations that distributed raw materials by fixed quotas, regulated the quantity of production for each company, and worked as government institutions.

From the late 1920s and during the 1930s, a large state-owned sector of the economy was created. In 1926, *Azienda Generale Italiana Petroli* (AGIP), a state company for the exploration and production of oil, was established. In the same year, the Banking Act and then the foundation of the *Istituto Mobiliare Italiano* started the reorganization of the banking system under state tutelage.

The most important step was the foundation of the *Istituto per la Ricostruzione Industriale* (IRI), a dominant state holding company that soon owned the three major banks of the country and 42% of the total joint-stock capital in Italy. In some sectors, such as steel and arms production, it controlled 100% of industry, in shipyards 90%, in shipping and locomotive building 80%, and in electricity output 30%. During that decade, several specialized state companies were also formed. In 1936, the entire banking sector was nationalized or state-controlled. In 1943, after the coup of Marshal Badoglio, and the arrest of Mussolini, "Il Duce" was rescued by a German commando and re-established his power in the Fascist Republic in North Italy. His party announced a new program of "abolishing the capitalist system," and of nationalizing all companies "with a share capital exceeding one million lire or employing one hundred workers."[22]

Creating a mixed, combined state and private economy went hand in hand with the nationalization of the trade unions, banning strikes, the formation of the Fascist Confederation of Workers as the only legal representation of workers, and establishing a consistent corporative system. The corporations, joint institutions of workers, employees, and the representatives of the state, formed the political institutional structure of Italy, replacing the parliamentary system. The state was formally a mediator, but in practice it occupied the key, decisive position. A pyramid of corporative bureaucracy was built up, with a Ministry of Corporation, provincial and federal organizations, and the

National Council of Corporation at the top of it, headed by Mussolini from 1930. Labor Courts were founded to decide labor disputes that were not solvable in the corporative framework. "The Fascist corporate state," wrote a contemporary observer, "has been limited almost exclusively to putting a stamp of approval upon whatever measures the Fascist government has chosen to propose."[23]

The dirigist regime, due to its populist features, also established some basic social security institutions such as maternity and child welfare organization that provided healthcare for about one million mothers and children. Later a national health organization was established. Family allowances, old age and invalidity insurance, and a 40-hour work week were complemented by free two-week vacations for members of the fascist youth organization. The *Opera Nazionale Dopolavoro*, or leisure time organization, maintained libraries and sport facilities and distributed cheap tickets to more than three million members. Public expenditures increased from 20% to 33% of GDP between 1929 and 1936.

The modernization dictatorship had impressive economic success until the Ethiopian adventure in the mid-1930s. The Great Depression had only very limited impact and, by 1939, Italian GDP surpassed its pre-World War I level by 62%. The length of electrified railroads doubled and reached 56% of the network, the number of tractors used in agriculture also doubled, electricity output increased by 50%, and the country became self-sufficient in food production, ending the huge deficit in agricultural trade.

The Italian fascist economic regime became a model that spread in backward Mediterranean Europe, first in Spain and then in Portugal and Greece, and important elements were adapted by Austria and several Central and East European countries, and then by Nazi Germany as well. The fascist dirigist regime collapsed with the war and fascism. In Spain and Portugal, however, the regime survived the war and remained more or less characteristic until the 1970s.

The non-market, centrally planned economic regime[24]

The non-market economic system was born from a theory. In the mid-nineteenth century, Karl Marx and Friedrich Engels, analyzing ascendant British capitalism, reached the conclusion that the "basic contradiction of capitalism" is the contrast between collective production and private expropriation. In the *Communist Manifesto* of 1848, they prophesized the revolution of the exploited proletariat that will "expropriate the expropriators," and "centralize all instruments of production in the hands of the state."[25]

Marx anticipated the "disappearance" of the peasantry, based on England's experience, and thus he did not offer any solution for the landowning peasantry. However, in the late nineteenth century, the then elderly Friedrich Engels had to return to the peasant question, which represented a major challenge for the Marxist socialist movement in Germany. Engels, while recommending the nationalization of the big estates, excluded this solution for peasant lands. He suggested the gradual and deliberate collectivization of independent peasant farms.[26]

Besides the creation of collective—part state and part cooperative—ownership, Marx's analysis of capitalism led him to the idea of a planned economy: "United, cooperative societies are to regulate national production upon a common plan … putting an end to the constant anarchy … of capitalist production."[27]

Last but not least, Marx also offered a program for distribution. In his *Critique of the Gotha Program* of the German Social Democratic Party, Marx provided a two-stage path towards an egalitarian society. At the first stage (socialism), proper equality is not yet possible, and thus everybody has to work according to his ability and "the same amount of labour which he gives to society in one form he receives back in another." At the higher stage of development (communism), the society will be able to realize the principle: "from each according to his ability, to each according to his needs."[28] The theory for an economic system based on state and cooperative ownership, central planning of production, and egalitarian distribution was ready in the mid–late nineteenth century.

The 1917 Bolshevik Revolution in Russia, under the leadership of Vladimir Lenin, turned to the Marxist idea to build up a communist society. But how to start in a backward peasant country that had just survived a long devastating war and a destructive civil war that followed the revolution? In their unfinished work, *The German Ideology* (1847), Marx and Engels clearly expressed that the communist revolution had to happen in the most advanced countries acting together. In one especially backward country, "local communism," as they called it, cannot survive.[29] Lenin and Leon Trotsky, the other leader of the Bolshevik Revolution, were convinced that socialism could not be realized in peasant Russia, and so they developed the theory of the permanent revolution. Russia's role was to start the revolution and ignite proletarian revolutions in the advanced Western countries. If the revolution failed to spread, as Trotsky rephrased Marx's view, the Russian revolution would either be destroyed by a conservative Europe, or eroded by its primitive economic, social, and cultural conditions.[30]

Lenin turned to the German war economy as the solution. In the spring of 1918, he stated: "Take the most concrete example of state capitalism … It is Germany. Here we have 'the last word' in modern large-scale capitalist engineering and planned organization, *subordinated to Junker-bourgeois imperialism.* Cross out the words in italics, and in place of the … imperialist state put *also a state* … a *Soviet* state … and you will have the sum total of the conditions necessary for socialism."[31]

Instead of state capitalism, Lenin suggested building a state socialist system. In 1918, universal nationalization abolished private ownership of the economy. The new Soviet state first turned to so-called war communism, a harsh dictatorship and command economy without using money, but soon they had to retreat and, at least temporarily, introduce the New Economic

Policy (NEP), a return to market economy. Between 1923 and 1926, harsh debates erupted about the required economic system and the fate of the revolution in Russia. Lenin died in January 1924, and the debate was closely connected with the fight for his place. Trotsky and his Left Opposition circle vehemently attacked the NEP and argued for the introduction of a centrally planned "dictatorship of industry." An exact "road map" was worked out by Yevgeni Preobrazhensky in his lecture series in 1924, later published as a book, *Novaya Ekonomika*, in 1926. His point of departure was that in a poor backward country, the central question is capital accumulation and investment so as to generate rapid industrialization and economic growth. The only way to achieve it, he argued, is a forced preliminary (or primitive) capital accumulation at the hands of the state by exploiting the peasantry, the bulk of the population. Preobrazhensky suggested the creation of a "price scissor" by keeping agricultural prices artificially low and industrial prices high. He also recommended reducing the income of the population by inflationary policy. His plan was the destruction of market prices and the market system in general, and the introduction of a state-dictated economic regime that would channel the state accumulation into industrial investments. What Trotsky and Preobrazhensky argued for was a new model of modernization dictatorship in a poor peasant country to force rapid industrialization and growth.

Although the majority of the Bolshevik Party rejected Trotsky and Preobrazhensky's concept, after the eradication of the various oppositions, Joseph Stalin, who emerged as the unquestionable new leader by 1927–28, "borrowed" the program of the eliminated Left Opposition and started its realization, including the brutal collectivization of agriculture, combined with so-called "de-kulakization," the destruction of the well-to-do layer of the peasantry during his first Five-Year Plan. Nikolai Bukharin, the talented Bolshevik economist, denounced this policy as "the feudal-military exploitation of the peasantry." By 1936, 90% of peasant households were already collectivized. Resistance was cruelly crushed and about 10 million peasants died, mostly from the famine caused by forced collectivization. Any kind of private trade and employment were banned and became "criminal activity."

The industrialization drive began with the gigantic construction work of the Dnieper hydraulic power station in 1928. According to the plan, industrial output had to increase by two-and-half times by 1932. New industrial centers were created. A triumphant Stalin announced at the 17th Party Congress in 1934 that the Soviet Union had eliminated "backwardness and medievalism. From an agrarian country it has become an industrial country."[32] During the 1930s, the planned and forced industrialization led to an unprecedented 61% increase in the per capita GDP of the Soviet Union. The isolated country was not hit by the Great Depression that limited the economic growth of Western Europe to 8% during that decade. The per capita GDP of the Soviet Union, compared to Western Europe, increased from 37% in 1913 to 49% by 1950. A catching-up process had begun.

After World War II, the Soviet type of centrally planned economic system spread over to sovietized Central Europe and the Balkans. The so-called Soviet Bloc introduced the same economic regime, and they formed a trade community, the Council of Mutual Economic Aid, or Comecon, that used fixed prices and tried to establish a self-sufficient economic area. Forced accumulation and industrialization, as well as a huge labor input to the economy, led to rapid growth, and the previously agrarian countries became industrialized. The regime, however, resisted required reforms, blocked the path of market incentives, and remained mostly in economic isolation. In the end, remaining outside of the integrating world economy during the period of a new scientific-technological revolution led to the reproduction of backwardness. After the 1973 oil crisis and the structural crisis that followed, the Soviet Bloc countries declined into a deep and permanent crisis that eliminated the regime's advantages of full employment, rapid growth, and increasing living standard. Stagnation and decline undermined the regime, which collapsed in 1989–91.

China, the largest communist country after its 1949 revolution, followed a different path. After the tragic period of the so-called Cultural Revolution, the country preserved its communist political regime, bloodily crushed the revolt against it in 1989, but turned to radical reforms. The political regime, using communist rhetoric, became a classic Asian modernization dictatorship by turning to market reform and creating a state-private, export-oriented economic system after the 1980s. China reached a unique 8–10% annual economic growth, elevated hundreds of millions of people from poverty, and rose as one of the leading economic powers of the world.

The state-owned, centrally planned, egalitarian state socialist economic regime, a major player in twentieth century history, virtually disappeared. Its most important impacts on European history were its social modernization, the ruthless destruction of the old, highly hierarchical, almost caste-like societies in less developed Eastern Europe, and the introduction of educational revolutions. These social consequences are helping the former socialist countries to integrate into the modern European economic system within the European Union.

The Nazi *Grossraumwirtschaft* and the Soviet-led Comecon—regional autarchy[33]

Nazi Germany and communist Soviet Union were arch-enemies. Hitler killed communists in the 1930s, and Stalin's Red Army stayed around Hitler's bunker in Berlin in 1945, forcing him to commit suicide. The two regimes were based on entirely different ideological premises. Internationalist, class-conscious, egalitarian proletarian communism confronted extreme nationalist, racist, and lower-middle-class-based expansionist Nazism. The two countries launched the bloodiest war ever against each other, causing 30–40 million deaths between 1941 and 1945. Not accidentally, the Soviet Union was in alliance with the United States, France, and Britain, the core democratic countries of the world, while Germany led a fascist alliance, called the "Anti-Comintern (anti-Communist) Pact" with Italy, Japan, and some of its Central and East European satellites. Both regimes were dictatorial, one-party, non-parliamentary systems, and both regimes' legitimacy was based on what Max Weber called the charismatic legitimization of an "infallible" leader who delivered on his promises.

The resemblances, however, did not stop there. There were also similarities in their central state interventionist policy and state planning, and both regimes established an agreement system with neighboring countries to run a regional autarchic economic system. It was invented by Hitler's Germany as early as 1934, a year after he took power. Under the direction of Hjalmar Schacht, the *Neuer Plan* targeted economic war preparation by building a self-sufficient parallel international market with neighboring agricultural countries without the usual market rules. As Hans Ernst Posse, a member of Hitler's cabinet stated in 1934, "the time has come for attainment of *Grossraumwirtschaft* [large area economy] to become our most important economic policy goal."[34] Preparing for war, Germany sought to establish an economic backyard nearby to avoid the negative consequences of a potential naval blockade and bombing, and to be able to buy food and raw materials from neighboring Central and Eastern Europe. At the same time, Hitler wanted to hit two birds with one stone by paving the way for the country's economic and political expansion, or as Hannah Arendt called it, continental imperialism,[35] following the ancient *Drang nach Osten* policy. In February 1934, the first bilateral trade agreement was signed with Hungary, followed by similar accords with Yugoslavia, Romania, and Bulgaria. All of the bilateral agreements followed the same pattern. Germany offered import quotas for exact quantities of agricultural products and raw materials, with attached subsidies that increased the export prices for the Central European countries above world market price levels. Germany paid 90% of the price of the imported goods by delivering her industrial products. In other words, trade among the countries in the zone of the *Grossraumwirtschaft* was barter trade or trade in kind without using currency payments. Only the remaining 10% of the German payments were products available only for hard currency. Trade between the eastern neighbors doubled and trebled in a few years, and trade with Germany jumped from 20–25% to 40–50% of the foreign trade of the agricultural countries, and the region's share of German wheat, meat, and bauxite imports totaled 35–60%.

One may not forget that the trade connection with Germany, which offered a fixed market and higher than world market prices in the years of the Great Depression and the especially tragic agricultural crisis, was very lucrative for the poor agricultural countries. They had, however, to pay a high political price for it. As a secret German memo clearly stated at the time of the trade agreement with Hungary, "Germany's intent with the agreement is to link the Hungarian economy strongly and inseparably to the German one by increased trade."[36] Indeed, "the German-led regional economic system prepared the road for Nazi political and military penetration and domination in Central and Eastern Europe."[37] Except for Yugoslavia, which was attacked and occupied by Hitler after a radical takeover by an anti-German government in 1941, the other countries of the region became incorporated into the Anti-Comintern Pact, the Nazi-fascist alliance system, and joined Hitler's war.

At the end of World War II, the Soviet Army liberated Central and Eastern Europe from Nazi occupation and local fascist rule between the summer of 1944 and the spring of 1945. In the emerging Cold War, Stalin followed the old Russian military doctrine to build up a buffer zone between Russia and the West. The Soviet army remained in the region and the countries east of the River Elbe became sovietized as satellite communist regimes. The Soviet Bloc introduced the same type of non-market economic system, a fully nationalized planned economy, and the characteristic Soviet industrialization policy of the 1930s. The more or less uniform regimes established the Soviet-led Council of Mutual Economic Aid, or Comecon, in 1949. Although the process was the other way around compared to Hitler's *Grossraumwirtschaft*, in that it started with political subordination followed by the creation of an autarchic economic bloc, Comecon followed the Nazi trade agreement system. It was based on bilateral agreements and introduced barter trade without using hard currency and world market prices. Actually, due to the five-year-plan mechanism, prices were fixed at the 1950 world market level, and did not change at all until 1957. Deliveries were being paid by counter deliveries at the planned "parallel socialist world market." The only significant difference was the structure of trade. In the *Grossraumwirtschaft*, Germany imported agricultural products and raw material and paid with industrial goods, while the Soviet Union, beside food, mostly imported processed industrial products, machinery, buses, pharmaceutical goods, and a vast amount of industrial consumer goods, and it paid mostly with raw materials such as coal, oil, iron ore, and also with industrial equipment.

After the first decade of its existence, however, Comecon was radically reformed in the post-Stalinist period. Prices were fixed for five years, then adjusted for the world market prices, and then fixed again for another five years. After the 1973 oil crisis, since Soviet oil deliveries dramatically increased to the Soviet Bloc countries, prices were fixed only for a year, based on the previous five-year average price, and changed accordingly every year. Even more importantly, beyond the trade connection, Comecon introduced some division of labor, and member countries started producing for the entire bloc. Hungary, for example got the task of producing buses for the bloc countries, and a monopoly to produce 48 types of machinery for the bloc, while Czechoslovakia produced heavy trucks, Bulgaria manufactured computers, and Romania made diesel locomotives and other industrial products for all the member countries. In other words it was a division of labor by industrial products and not by parts of products. Nevertheless, since deliveries were always uncertain from other member countries, all of the countries gradually returned to supplying themselves as much as possible. Nikita Khrushchev in the early 1960s tried to go further and establish a joint planning office that would make, or dictate, the entire economic plan for the member countries. That would have meant the total economic subordination of the satellite countries, and they rejected this plan. However, economic dependence on the Soviet Union was very strong within the autarchic economic regime.

The artificial, fixed price system contributed to the isolation of the Soviet Bloc countries from the world market. In the 1950s, it led to a huge advantage and gain for the Soviet Union, but from the 1960s to the 1970s, and especially after the oil price explosion, the Soviet Union subsidized Comecon members by cheap oil deliveries. The economic system was a part of Soviet ideological and political control over the region. From the later 1970s and during the 1980s, however, the deep crisis of the entire Soviet Bloc, including the Soviet Union, led to a loosening of the ties. Countries had to turn to the world market to buy goods that were not available in the bloc. Some countries tried deliberately to loosen the economic connections, and in the end Poland, Hungary, and Romania developed a much more balanced trade connection with the West and the Comecon countries.

The gap was even deepened by asking for Western credits after the oil crisis and walking into an indebtedness trap. These changes, however, became part of the steep decline of the regime that led to its collapse in 1989.

Trade unions and *Sozialpartnerschaft*[38]

"Virtually all known forms of wage struggles and their repertoire of actions are as old as the existence of labourers."[39] More than a century ago, one of the earliest works on trade unions gave the following definition of them: "a continuous association of wage earners for the purpose of maintaining or improving the conditions of their employment."[40] The word "continuous" is of major importance here. The history of labor from medieval times has exhibited various forms of labor dissatisfaction and revolt that often generated ad hoc organizations of boycotts, strikes, and other forms of labor self-defense. Long before the industrial revolution and the mass proletarization of the workforce, agricultural workers, craftsmen, and cottage industry workers, as well as those in mining, canal-digging, shipping, and road-building, have from time to time organized themselves to defend their interests. Collective actions "such as embezzlement, go-slows, charivari, mob violence and similar crowd actions"[41] exhibit early labor's attempts at self-defense. Various types of permanent and formal sailors' organizations existed in Europe already as early as 1300. In the fourteenth and fifteenth centuries, sailors' organizations were established in Bruges, Antwerp, Bergen, and the towns of the Hanseatic League. "Organizations of seamen existed continuously in Europe from the late Middle Ages ... "[42] Seasonal workers building Dutch dikes often used the strike as a weapon in the sixteenth century, though their organization was spontaneous. "There are records of strikes by navies in the Low Countries from 1410–13 onwards." British canal-builders had labor disputes in 1768.[43] Boycotts occurred several times between 1718 and 1720 in the pre-industrial-revolution Swedish iron industry, for example in the Leufsta Ironworks, which was boycotted by the charcoal-burning peasants.[44]

Nevertheless, emerging industrial capitalism and the nation-state made a major difference by causing tremendous social upheaval and also furthering the integration of different layers of the society on a national level. That became the prerequisite of the essentially permanent union organizations in Europe. Hundreds of thousands of peasants, former cottage industry workers, and artisans started working in the newly invented factories, and they had to adjust to the never-before experienced factory discipline and endless workdays. The single worker was defenseless and lost. The factory's skilled workers and unskilled laborers—men, women, and children alike—were closed into three- to four-story buildings as members of the new army of industrial laborers, subordinated to the owner, manager, and foremen, in a strict hierarchy. Violations of order were severely punished, wages were miserable, and in cases of economic downturns, depressions, or just lack of sufficient orders, wages were decreased and workers dismissed without any income.

Defenselessness almost automatically generated workers' reaction. The 24-year-old Friedrich Engels, who spent a lot of time in Manchester's textile factories, described his experiences of the situation of the early British working class in his book of 1844: "the earliest, crudest, and least fruitful form of this rebellion was that of crime. The working man lived in poverty and want ... Want conquered his inherited respects for the sacredness of property, and he stole ... As a class, they first manifested opposition ... when they resisted the introduction of machinery ... Factories were demolished and machinery destroyed."[45] It happened first in England before 1758. Machine-breaking, however, became a capital offense, and 18 workers were executed in York in 1813. During the eighteenth century, more than 400 labor disputes occurred in Britain, and sometimes there was "little to separate the strikes and the riot."[46] The Lyon silk workers and Silesian weavers rebelled in 1831 and 1844, respectively.

The spontaneous rebellion was soon replaced by organizations for worker self-defense. The London shoemaker, Thomas Hardy, founded a Corresponding Society, and within a few years, 10,000 workers had joined. Nevertheless, even in the Gironde period of the French Revolution, a 1791 decree banned all workers' and artisans' associations. Unions and other workers' organizations were banned for decades. In England, workers' organizations were illegal until 1824, when the "Combination Act" was repealed.

When laborers' unions and associations became legal, the Grand Union of Spinners, the National Association for the Protection of Labour, and the Grand National Consolidated Trades Union were established in just a few years. The workers' movement and the vigorous Chartist years of the late 1830s and 1840s, forced some social concessions in Britain, among them the introduction of the ten-hour workday in 1847.

Early continental European working organizations, self-help, cooperative associations, and Friendly Societies appeared in several countries between the 1820s and 1840s. Several were founded by artisans who organized self-help. Industrialization gained momentum from the 1860s on in continental Western Europe, and, as a symbolic turning point, the first workers' revolution erupted in Paris in 1871. Although it was suppressed by a bloodbath, the early restrictions and bans on workers' organizations were gradually abolished on the continent. It happened in Germany and Austria in 1869 and in France in 1884. The 1892 Halberstadt congress of the German trade unions decided to form a well-organized, centralized, nationwide union. At that time they had only 300,000 members, but this had doubled to 600,000 by 1899. Unions were organized and national federations were founded throughout Europe: it happened in 1873 in Switzerland and in 1898 in Sweden. Similarly, the National Federation of Trade Unions was founded in France in 1886. In 1906, the National Federation of Labor joined the General Confederation of Labor (Confédération Générale du Travail, or CGT), which soon had one million members. Here too, social legislation and workday limitations soon followed, and then comprehensive social insurance for miners was introduced in 1892 and 1894, and accident insurance and compensation rights for victims of industrial accidents were introduced in 1898.

During the last decades of the nineteenth century, the European labor movement picked up Marxist ideas, and in some countries the trade union movement built close connections with the newly founded social democratic parties. The Second International introduced a Europe-wide campaign to fight against the unfair system, to defend workers' interests, including female laborers, and to fight for universal male suffrage, to ban child labor, and to organize and regulate the labor market.

However, only part of the labor movement and trade union organizations was socialist. Christian trade unions and the so-called yellow unions were also established, and they often had equally huge or even larger memberships. The "yellow unions" preached peace and cooperation with the employers. Paternalism equally characterized several British, German, and French giant companies. Le Creusot Company in France, among others, provided schools, houses, cheaper company stores, clinics, and pension funds for its workers. The giant Siemens Company built an entire district in Berlin for its workers, and the Krupp Company in the Ruhr region built 6,000 employee dwellings. Revolt against the employer risked the loss of those privileges. Many workers thus joined company unions. Britain's case well characterized the European situation: in 1892, more than 1,200 trade unions existed, and they concentrated 11% of the labor force. By 1913, their membership represented 23% of the workers. By 1975, for the first time in Britain, the less than 500 existing unions had 12,000,000 members, more than half of the workers. However, the Owenite Friendly Societies and Benefit Societies in Britain had 4.4 million members in 1872 and 7 million by 1914. Various workers' cooperative organizations had another 2.5 million members by 1905.

The history of the unions, at a certain point, was marked by the revolutionary syndicalist movement, which maintained that unions would introduce socialism by using the general strike as a weapon. In reality, trade unions became an integral part of the capitalist system while opposing its several "deformations" and organizing workers' self-defense efforts. Marx considered the unions to be organizations that would strengthen workers' class consciousness and lead to a political movement and the formation of a workers' party. At a certain period, mostly in Germany and partly in France in the late nineteenth century, this road was seemingly opened, but in the long run, it essentially failed. As it happened, unions separated themselves from the socialist parties, as happened in 1894 at the Nantes conference of the French trade unions.

Workers revolutionary attempts were also discouraged by brutal reprisals for workers' actions by entrepreneurs and the state. Troops were often used, and they even opened fire and killed strikers. Sometimes huge armies attacked the workers, such as in the case of France in 1906 when 95,000 troops invaded mining villages to suppress the rebellion following the Courrières pit disaster. Companies locked out workers and hired and transported strike-breakers. Though general strikes remained a weapon of the unions from the late nineteenth century, and even in 1968 in France, they led to the threshold of revolution only in Russia in 1905. Workers' self-defense was sometimes quite violent, using the weapon of strikes and sometimes even the occupation of factories, such as in Italy after World War I in Torino, or in France in the 1930s. However, the main practical weapon was and remained their collective bargaining power to achieve better wages and work conditions.

The Italian nationalist movement before and after World War I established the ideology of unifying nationalism and syndicalism to subordinate trade unions to the national goals, including expansionism and colonialism. Mussolini, who banned the unions, established his own fascist labor organization within the framework of the corporative system. In the Soviet Union and later in the entire Soviet Bloc, trade unions were "nationalized" and served the state in the role of intermediary between the government and the workers. In post-World War II Austria and Germany, corporatism created the collaborative system of *Sozialpartnerschaft* in a democratic and voluntary way, in which unions joined the government and employer organizations to reach joint agreement reducing wage demands and price increases to stop a dangerous wage-price spiral and to assist in the reconstruction of those countries.

The integration of these labor organizations into the democratic and market economic system was connected with an early bureaucratization of the organization. Once the trade union movement contained millions of workers, spontaneous organization and leadership was replaced by paid union employees and hierarchically organized leadership. Although democratic rules remained intact, including voting and elections, the leadership often actually hijacked the organization. This trend was connected with the traditional leading role of artisans (in the early stages) and well-paid skilled workers, who formed a so-called "labor aristocracy." Trade unions excluded unskilled workers for a long time, and the labor leaders and highly skilled, well-paid workers developed a strong middle-class identity. The term and concept of an "aristocracy of labor" already appeared in the early nineteenth century. William Thompson, in his 1826 *Labour Rewarded*, criticized this "class" of workers, the labor aristocracy, for being "full of unsocial antipathies to those less remunerated then themselves."[47] Friedrich Engels also wrote in an 1858 letter to Marx about the Manchester entrepreneurs who were using "prosperity ... in order to buy the proletariat," referring to a workers' elite who founded schools and libraries for themselves.[48] Karl Marx also stated that British capitalism was able to "castrate" the working class, and in 1870, at the London conference of the International, he maintained that the trade unions were organizations of the "aristocratic minority." Mikhail Bakunin used the term of "bourgeoisified workers" for the privileged upper layer of the workers.[49]

Nevertheless, trade unions continued to successfully fight for workers' interests in contemporary Europe. In the late 1960s, they achieved major social concessions and a rapid increase in the living standard of workers when their position was very strong in Western Europe during the decades of virtual full employment. The British miners' union's extremely long fight in the 1970s was, however, ruthlessly defeated by Margaret Thatcher. Successful and unsuccessful strikes, and even general strikes, signaled the road and history of the trade unions to the present. However, in contrast to the expectations of Marx and the revolutionary labor movement, trade unions mostly lost connection with socialist goals and sometimes became the representatives of narrow special interests. From the 1970s, organized West European workers often turned against immigrants and discovered their enemies in the underclass. Huge swathes of blue collar workers voted for racist right-wing parties. In 2010, the major and violent union rebellion in France against the government's plan to increase the retirement age from 60 to 62 also definitely represented short-sighted views.

Altogether, the trade union movement became an important institution for workers' interests that, in the long run, significantly contributed to the moderation of capitalism and the emancipation of the workers, and thus, to the renewal of capitalism.

Renewal of capitalism: the welfare state[50]

Early industrial capitalism was cruel and highly exploitative. Industrial workers labored in inhuman, uncontrolled working conditions, and they lived in miserable, unhealthy workers' slums. The first generations of workers worked 12 to 16 hours daily. Female and child labor was widespread and strongly underpaid. Injured workers or those aged over 50 often lost their jobs and declined into deep poverty. The British Poor Law of 1834 sent tens of thousands of paupers into prison-type, inhuman workhouses. Their miserable life was excellently described by Charles Dickens.

In Britain, Robert Owen advocated the eight-hour work day in 1817, but at that time it still belonged to the ideas of utopian socialism. Indeed, the

Factory Act in 1833 limited the workday for 9- to 13-year-olds to eight hours, but the workday of children between 14 to 18 was only limited to 12 hours. In France, workdays were limited to 12 hours by 1848. After the period of spontaneous riots between 1810 and the 1840s, and short-lived organizations such as the Chartist movement, workers' self-defense organizations, trade unions, the socialist movement, and strong parties gained ground in the last third of the century. At its Geneva Convention in 1866, the International Workingmen's Association demanded an eight-hour workday as part of the "emancipation of the working class." The Paris Commune in 1871, the first workers' revolution, although bloodily suppressed, signaled a turning point. Socialist parties were founded throughout Europe during the 1870s–80s. As universal male suffrage gradually gained ground, the socialist parties enjoyed their first relative electoral successes, gaining 30–40% of the votes.

Chancellor Bismarck of Germany pushed through anti-socialist legislation, banning and suppressing the socialist movement. This turned out to be counterproductive and led to the continued strengthening of the Social Democratic Party. Bismarck changed tactics during the 1880s: "borrowing" from socialist programs he introduced welfare institutions such as accident and sickness insurance, and a general workers' pension scheme for old age and invalidity. The Vatican joined the war against socialism. In 1891, Pope Leo XIII published his unprecedented encyclical on the conditions of labor, the *Rerum Novarum*. The wording of certain parts—although explicitly against a socialist solution—was not so very different from Friedrich Engels' description of the workers' conditions in 1844. "Some opportune remedy must be found quickly for the misery and wretchedness pressing so unjustly on the majority of the working class ... [The] working men ... isolated and helpless, to the hardheartedness of employers ... a small number of very rich men have been able to lay upon the teeming masses of the labouring poor a yoke little better than that of slavery itself."[51]

The Scandinavian countries also took the initiative: the Commission on Workers' Conditions started working in Denmark and in 1878 recommended a mostly state-funded, but voluntary, pension system. Denmark and Sweden made the first significant steps towards a universalist, basically tax-financed welfare system that covered the entire society. Sweden introduced the first compulsory and universal pension system in the world in 1913. The first welfare institutions, pension plans, and insurance schemes were introduced in France in 1910 and in Britain in 1911. Austria, the Netherlands, Finland, Italy, and Norway followed with partial insurance schemes. Capitalism responded to the challenge of socialism. The seeds of the welfare state, however, fell on dry soil, and the idea required another third of a century to come to fruition.

In the interwar decades, especially during the Great Depression, new welfare institutions were enacted in several European countries. The eight-hour workday slowly became general, first in Russia after the Bolshevik Revolution and then—after long general strikes—in Spain, but the Accords de Matignon, the Matignon Agreements in France under the Popular Front government enacted legislation establishing the 40-hour work-week in 1936. In the 1930s, even strongly conservative Hungary enacted an eight-hour workday law. These institutions, however, did not yet become Europe-wide. Some countries introduced unemployment benefits, and Sweden, after the social democratic victory in the 1932 elections, began methodically building up a complex welfare state. Before World War I, only 10–12% of GDP in Western Europe went towards public expenditures, including welfare, but by 1935, 20–33% of GDP did so.

However, in another half century, the share of public expenditures doubled as a percentage of the GDP, and it jumped to 50–60% in various European countries by 1980. This dramatic change was the consequence of building up European welfare states after World War II. The wartime Churchill government established a Social Insurance Committee under the leadership of William Beveridge who presented a complex social security plan in 1942. Thomas Humphrey Marshall introduced the concept of social citizenship, reinterpreting citizenship rights by including the right to a job and social security. Ludwig Erhard, Chancellor of West Germany and architect of the German post-World War II economic miracle, established the social-market system under the slogan of *Wohlstand für Alle*, well-being for all. Full employment became an official policy of most of the European countries.

Two main driving forces pushed the building of modern welfare states in Europe: on the one hand, the shock of World War II and the recognition of the importance of communal solidarity, and, on the other, the emerging Cold War and the required response to the communist challenge. Capitalism was reinvented with a strong human face. However, there were not only outside stimuli to change. The Austrian-American economist Joseph Schumpeter called attention to the fact "that social legislation or, more generally, institutional change for the benefit of the masses is not simply something which has been forced upon capitalist society ... the [rationalizing] capitalist process also provided for that legislation the means and the will ... The fundamental impulse that sets and keeps the capitalist engine in motion comes from the new consumers' goods, the new methods of production or transportation ... the new form of industrial organization ... Capitalism, then, is by nature a form or method of economic change and not only never is but never can be stationary ... [that inner character of the system] revolutionizes the economic structure from within, incessantly destroying the old one, incessantly creating a new one."[52]

The inner renewal mechanism of capitalism renewed not only the economic structure, but the system as well. One of the most spectacular renewals was the rise—with national differences—of a fairly uniform Western European social model. This model was characterized by state-financed pensions and health insurance; free education at all levels; paid holidays (that gradually increased to 5–6 weeks); maternity leave for mothers (and later parental for fathers) to stay home with new babies with full or partial salaries for between

16 weeks to 16 months; as well as other welfare institutions such as slum clearance, low-rent housing, child benefits for everybody, and home care for disabled and very old people. Per capita social security expenditures increased ten-fold between the 1930s and 1957 in Western Europe.

The redistributing state required high taxes. In 2004, tax revenue in the United States and Japan reached 26% of GDP, while in the European Union countries it was 40%. As a survey showed, the population in Europe accept high taxation because the "core services of the welfare state—health, education, housing, and provision for old age, illness and unemployment—are regarded as a government responsibility by more than 90% of the population."[53] Welfare expenditures, indeed, mean that "in most countries, one-fifth to one-fourth of private consumption is financed by public budgets through social transfer payments."[54]

The welfare states strongly decreased income differentiation, not allowing people to drop out from the society. A large part of the redistributed income, however, is life-cycle redistribution, i.e., taking a part of the income from families when they earned the most, but giving it back to the same families as a pension in old age, or free education for the next generation. At least half, and in some cases two-thirds, of welfare spending is life-cycle redistribution.

According to a report of the Organisation for Economic Co-operation and Development (OECD) in 1981, the welfare state was challenged and declined into crisis around the turn of the twenty-first century. This evaluation was repeated by the director of the International Monetary Fund (IMF) in 1998. Some elements of the system were, indeed, changed and expenditures cut, especially the pension schemes, which were radically rearranged and stopped being fully financed by the state. Moderate university tuition fees and co-payment at doctors' visits were introduced, and some services were abolished, but the extremely popular welfare state was basically preserved. In the spring of 2010, the world media reported the sensational news: Antonio Tajani, European Union commissioner for enterprise and industry, initiated a new welfare institution declaring that "tourism is a human right" and pensioners, youth, and poor people have to get subsidized travel. The project was planned to be piloted until 2013 and then established on permanent basis.[55] Welfare expenditures actually increased by more than 9% in the European Union countries between 1990 and 2003. The deepening economic crisis of 2008–12, however, led to the introduction of austerity measures in several countries that endanger the welfare state. Capitalism, nevertheless, is indeed a "relentless revolution."[56]

Renewal of capitalism: the regulated market system[57]

A self-regulated market system that—as Karl Polanyi put it[58]—subordinates the society to the economy is evidently in the self-interest of big business. There is no doubt about its positive outcomes for economic activities and economic growth. Its social outcomes, however, are in sharp contrast with the "trickle down" argument that, at the end of the day, everybody profits from such a system. A growing gap between rich and poor both in national and international contexts clearly proves that is not the case. Moreover, although a self-regulated market, in which the market and only the market regulates itself, is advantageous in the short run, it unavoidably leads in the long run to speculative bubbles and major depressions, a decline of production and income, and to a dangerous rise in unemployment. Accordingly, just like the cycles that characterize the market economy, cycles of policy change and the renewal of the market system, and of the replacement of the self-regulated market economy by a regulated one, also accompanied the modern history of the European economy.

After the first period of laissez-faire economy in Europe from the 1860s–70s to the First World War, a backlash followed and characterized the interwar decades. The German war economy generated new ideas about the advantages of state intervention for the economy and society. John Maynard Keynes, the most influential economist of the age, argued as follows in his 1924 Oxford University lecture entitled *The End of Laissez-Faire*: "The world is not so governed from above that private and social interests always coincide. Many of the greatest economic evils of our time are fruits of risks, uncertainty, and ignorance ... [B]ig business is often a lottery, that great inequalities of wealth come about; and these factors are also the cause of the unemployment of labour ... The cure lies outside the operations of individuals ... I believe that the cure for these things is partly to be sought in the deliberate control of the currency and of credit by a central institution ... [Savings and investments should be regulated]. I do not think that these matters should be left entirely to the chances of private judgement and private profit."[59]

The famous British historian Edward Carr analyzed the interwar decades and concluded: "Laissez-faire, in international relations ... is a paradise of the economically strong. State control is the weapon of self-defence invoked by the economically weak ... The assumption that no natural harmony of interests exist and that interests must be artificially harmonized by state action, became the practice ... of almost every state."[60]

Regulations spread in the chaotic and, in many countries, miserable post-World War I years, but the real turning point arrived with the Great Depression of 1929–33. That was history's greatest economic disaster in terms of its duration, intensity, and worldwide scope.[61] State intervention was unavoidable and indeed, happened worldwide. President Franklin D. Roosevelt's New Deal created jobs by public works financed by the state, and also introduced the Social Security system. Britain's "cheap money" policy generated a construction boom, and several boards and commissions were established to control various fields of the economy and regulate competition. State subsidies of £30–40 million per year helped agriculture. In France, the state became a shareholder in several companies and introduced price controls in 1933. Public works were financed to the tune of 3 billion francs, and other measures stimulated an increase in consumer demand. A Banking Regulation Act introduced state control over private banks in 1934. After Hitler's rise to power, Germany introduced the Autobahn construction program and initiated a Four-Year Plan of war preparation. Moreover, state planning, state financing, and state ownership became an everyday phenomenon in peripheral countries such as Poland and Hungary.

In 1936, the theory of a regulated market was also born: Keynes published his landmark *General Theory of Employment, Interest and Money* and changed the paradigm of economics. The "supply side" idea of classical economics was replaced by the concept that supply and demand are not balanced in the market system, that supply does not automatically create its demand, and that the state has to increase demand to establish prosperity. While a regulated market system became the norm in the interwar and war years, it became partly internationalized at the end of World War II by the Bretton Woods agreement that introduced the fixed international exchange rate policy and control of the financial markets. The Keynesian regulated market system dominated post-World War II recovery and prosperity for a quarter-century. The European mixed economy was not only strictly regulated, but the state also owned 20–50% of the economy throughout Western Europe. France carried out nine Four-Year Plans, and planning appeared in several other countries, including Japan.

In mid-October 1973, a dramatic oil crisis ended Europe's most prosperous quarter-century. Growth stopped, inflation became uncontrollable, and the new phenomenon of stagflation dominated the next decade. The system no longer worked as usual, and Keynesian demand-side economics could not cure the ailing economy. A *structural crisis* emerged, caused by a major technological-communication revolution[62] that had started at the end of World War II and reached its turning point in the mid-1970s, gradually transforming the economy.[63] Parallel with these, another new trend, globalization, emerged in the international economy. Multinational companies became the main players, monopolizing 75% of the world's trade of manufactured goods. The Western countries assured markets and cheap labor forces by outsourcing investments and the production of goods to less-developed, low-wage regions.

In the era of globalization, international trade increased by more than three-and-a-half times, but daily financial transactions increased even more steeply and came to total more than 50 times the value of world trade.[64] Outsourcing the production of goods allowed advanced countries to concentrate on service and high-tech industries, as well as on research and development. In other words, globalization was the way out of economic crisis and into a new paradigm for economic development in Western Europe. In 2004, Europe had become the most globalized region in the world.[65] In this new situation, neo-liberals emerged triumphant and started an ideological war in favor of deregulation, privatization, and free markets as the only solutions for free societies in the grip of cut-throat global competition. They argued that state intervention was the real cause of economic troubles, because it disturbed market automatism and undermined freedom.

During the 1980s, proponents of the neo-liberal ideology challenged both of the peculiar postwar institutions that distinguished the European economic model: the mixed economy and the welfare system. Privatization became a universal agenda. Margaret Thatcher took the first decisive steps in Britain, followed by France, Italy, and post-Franco Spain. Thus, Europe mostly eliminated the mixed economy. The welfare system was saved, so the European social model was preserved, despite having been seriously curbed and having had the pension system radically reorganized. Europe also abolished its Keynesian regulated market regime, controls over financial markets, and several other forms of state interference that dominated the entire period of postwar prosperity. The advanced countries deregulated their banking systems. Deregulation increased flexibility for relocating resources from crisis-ridden areas to emerging sectors of the economy. The entire banking and financial industry changed radically. The separation of commercial and investment banking—a regulation introduced during the Great Depression—was abolished. Banks increased their liabilities (loans) far beyond the value of their assets (deposits). Their capital was insufficient to repay deposits if a financial panic had pushed people or institutions to withdraw their deposits. Insurance companies also performed banking activities, and the most flexible financial entities, hedge funds, began to play a crucial role in investment actions. In 2006, 370 new hedge funds were established in Europe. As of 2008, more than 120 of the big hedge funds (members of the "billion dollar" club) were headquartered in New York and 65 in London.

One of the most flexible financial innovations that were made possible by an unregulated market was the *securitization* of credits. Creditors (who provided mortgage loans, credit card loans, student loans, corporate loans, car loans, etc.) performed securitization by pooling their assets, issuing securities, and selling their existing loans to an investor. In this way, the lending companies transferred their risk to other companies. Deregulated financial markets offered the advantage of more flexible and risky financial activities, which resulted in higher profits and cheap credit for the economy. However, deregulation had a dangerous side effect: lender–borrower relations lost transparency and stability. Another new characteristic of the financial market was the *derivatives* business. Traders—predominantly commercial and investment banks and insurance companies—bought and sold future contracts, future commodity trade, and future options on shares, bonds, currencies, and interest rates. The derivatives business served as risk management, but the practice itself was also a major risk because it involved speculation about future prices and future exchange and interest rate movements. In other words, the derivatives business became a way to gamble on assumed future price movements, which might result in huge profits or huge losses. The world's derivatives trade increased from $75 trillion in 1997 to $600 trillion by 2008. To put these astronomical figures in perspective, it is important to note that the 1997 figure was already two-and-a-half times larger than the world's aggregate GDP. It thus became impossible for any single country to handle the potentially huge losses.

Deregulation and the flexible financial market undoubtedly contributed towards coping with the economic crisis in the early 1980s. Economists and governments did not worry about the potential for loss or collapse because they blindly believed in the self-correcting mechanism of the unregulated market and the monetary maneuvering. In 2008–10, however, a global crisis and the collapse of the financial systems on a scale unheard of since the Great Depression arrived. The crisis hit the advanced West strongly; growth slowed down dramatically, and unemployment skyrocketed. Hedge funds lost 57% of their invested money in 2008. German banks alone held $1.15 trillion in troubled assets. According to the IMF's estimation in April 2009, the European banking system still needed $375 billion to cover losses.[66] The circle was closed, and the return to a regulated market economy became unavoidable. The European Union turned to new rules for the over-the-counter derivative market to cut risks and introduced a standardized contracting system and transparency. A European Systemic Risk Board will monitor and signal the build-up of risk, and a new European supervisory authority will control cross-border financial activities. Banks were forced to meet liquidity requirements, hold more buffer capital, and limit their borrowing. Hedge funds and equity funds are facing "heavy-handed regulations."[67] For the first time in history, common European regulations will reorganize the financial markets. A new orientation and adjustment, especially the return to a regulated market economy, was needed and has begun.

The European Union's redistributive system: towards a homogenous Europe[68]

The market system is competitive, and competition is usually won by the stronger and better. This is true for companies and countries alike. When the six founding countries established the European Common Market, later the European Union (EU), they abolished protective tariffs, quotas, and other weapons of market protection that were broadly used from the 1870s on, and free competition became dominant in the large, united market of the member countries. However, the EU began accepting new members in 1973, and, by 2007, it became a union of 27 member states, with five candidate countries from the Balkans and Turkey, and several further applicants.

In 1973, Ireland joined the EU, the first time a less-developed country had done so. Its income level was only 55% of the old members' standard. Additional less-developed countries joined during the 1980s, when Greece, Spain and Portugal were accepted. In the first decade of the twenty-first century, ten former Soviet Bloc countries became members of the EU, with per capita GDP levels only about 40–45% of that of the EU-15 countries. In other words, unlike in the first period, severe income inequality and differences of economic advancement level characterized the EU after 1973. Besides relatively backward peripheral countries, even highly developed countries had less developed regions such as the so-called "rust-belt," as well as declining manufacturing areas with high unemployment rates. The advanced Nordic countries had low-population, sub-Arctic regions, some isolated islands, and certain agricultural areas, etc. Within the EU-15 countries, the ten richest regions had income levels that were 2.6 times higher than in the ten poorest regions. In 2008, within the EU-27, the difference between those two most and least developed regions grew to six-fold. Unemployment differences between these two areas also showed a marked difference of 2.3% and 19.7%, respectively, before the 2008 crisis.

The integrated single market of the EU, due to the characteristics of free competition, gave the advantage to the stronger and better companies and countries. It strengthened the danger of further income polarization within the EU. Another important element of potential income polarization was the typical agglomeration type of modern industrial-economic development: new investments are strongly attracted by areas with existing well-advanced infrastructure and services, and where a well-trained, even specialized, labor force is concentrated. Consequently, a "Silicon Valley" type of advanced regional agglomeration emerged, while agricultural or otherwise less developed areas were not magnets for investments.

The EU realized the danger here and decided to establish some institutions and policies to counterbalance the impact of market competition. Indeed, the founding fathers of the EU had already declared in 1957 in the preamble to the Treaty of Rome that the community "is anxious to reduce the differences existing between the various regions and the backwardness of the least-favoured regions." Until the early 1970s, however, real actions to realize this goal did not happen. Ireland was probably the first member to prompt the introduction of an assistance policy. In 1975, the European Regional Development Fund was established to assist and stimulate faster development in backward regions. Backwardness was defined as less than 75% of the EU's average per capita income level, or higher than average unemployment rate and agricultural occupations. Regional policy was revised several times, especially in 1989, when assistance was doubled. In the end, resources were increased from €1 billion per annum in the first years to €25 billion per annum in the early twenty-first century.

Financial assistance was provided from the EU's budget. Although that budget is relatively small, totaling only 1.2% of the aggregate GDP of the member countries (while national budgets, as an average, concentrate about one-third of the GDP of a country), it is a huge amount in absolute numbers. The EU used roughly one-third of its budget for that policy. Between 1989 and 2006, €382 billion, or nearly half a trillion dollars, were spent on helping declining industrial and urban regions and disadvantaged agricultural areas, on supporting the education and retraining of the local population to reduce unemployment, and on developing remote regions. The efficiency of the policy was increased by the introduction of multi-year subsidies and the requirement of matching money that each beneficiary country was required to add to the EU money. Altogether, 58% of the EU's population in those regions profited from the redistribution of income.

According to well-based calculations, if relatively backward regions reach 1.3–1.8% higher annual economic growth than advanced regions, a catching-up process may level the economic standard in 15–20 years. The sixth periodic report of the EU announced that by 1996, the 25 poorest regions had risen from 52% to 59% of the EU's average. The policy worked for countries that were considered entirely backward, rather than just some of their regions, and that thus received huge amounts of assistance. Ireland, whose per capita GDP in 1990 represented 74% of the EU average level, reached 141% of that level by 2004. Spain's GDP per capita was 77% of the EU average level in 1990, but it reached 99% by 2004. Portugal elevated from 61% to 73% (calculated in purchasing power parity). Even the former Soviet Bloc countries started a catching-up process. The EU started assisting development even before the acceptance of new countries, during the process of joining: four advanced former Soviet Bloc countries increased from 56% to 64% of the EU average GDP per capita between 1995 and 2005.

It has never before happened in history that rich countries sacrifice a part of their income on a permanent basis to assist less developed areas to catch up with them. The cohesion policy of the European Union reflects a unique understanding of long-term interest. The European economic disparity was historically large and permanent. From early modern times, the southern and eastern peripheries of the continent were backward and hardly reached or surpassed half of the income level of the advanced core. Moreover, the gap between the advanced core and the less developed peripheries did not narrow during the nineteenth and twentieth centuries. For the first time in history, the gap started narrowing in the last decades of the twentieth century, as a consequence of European integration. The EU's main recognition was that a more even income level increases the market power for the entire community and at the end of the day is good for both advanced and less developed countries and areas. They were also convinced that, for social as well as political reasons, they had to counterbalance the market advantage of the more developed countries by income redistribution to the less developed ones. In an integrated market, only a relatively equalized level of development leads to balanced labor and capital movement. In the end, assisting the less developed by targeted funds elevates the entire European Union. This process is in the making.

Globalization: its winners and losers[69]

Globalization is one of the terms that is frequently used nowadays, reflecting the fact that a new chapter of history, the age of globalization, was opened during the last quarter of the twentieth century. The process itself, however, has had a longer history. The half century before World War I was already a period of globalizing, but not yet of a globalized world. This trend—after the severe backlash in the interwar decades—reemerged after World War II, and then culminated beginning in the 1970s–80s. Economic interactions between various countries and continents—trade, capital investment, the establishment of subsidiaries, production abroad, and financial transactions—all existed before and characterized modern capitalism. However, in the last quarter of the twentieth century, a further dramatic quantitative change of these interactions transformed the world economy.

Trade, pushed by international agreements, developed by leaps and bounds. The postwar General Agreement on Tariffs and Trade (GATT), with its multi-lateral, non-discriminatory character, played a positive role in ending interwar protectionism, economic warfare, and hostility. The Tokyo Round, concluded in 1979, and most importantly, the Uruguay Round, launched in 1986, led to the Punta del Este declaration, which led to the foundation of the World Trade Organization (WTO) and the opening of a multitude of markets. This process was assisted by the spectacular decline in the cost of communication and transportation. The value of exports increased from \$0.3 trillion, 9% of the GDP of the Western world in 1950, to \$5.8 trillion, or 30% of it, by the 1990s.[70]

Foreign direct investment (FDI), a phenomenon well-known since the second half of the nineteenth century, also increased in an unparalleled way, growing four times faster than foreign trade. The major players behind this tremendous increase in economic transactions are multinational companies— those that have operations in two or more countries. Multinationals, although they appeared nearly a century before, became dominant in the world economy in the last quarter of the twentieth century. In the early 1970s, they numbered around 7,000. At the turn of the twenty-first century, they totaled nearly 50,000, with roughly 300,000 foreign subsidiaries, producing one-quarter to one-third of world industrial output. By the mid-1990s, their global sales represented 40% of world trade and 75% of trade in manufactured goods. Economic interactions, however, not only increased but also changed the traditional international division of labor. Multinationals established subsidiaries in highly sophisticated branches of industry in other *advanced* countries. This trend was closely connected with the new phenomenon of specialization within industries, rather than between them. Intra-industry trade steeply increased and represents two-thirds to three-quarters of total industrial trade in Germany, Britain, France, and Belgium.[71]

The typical pre-globalization investment in developing, agricultural, and raw-material-producing areas shifted more and more toward investment in other highly developed countries: three-quarters of the stock of the world's FDIs are located in advanced countries. American subsidiaries in Europe produce one-third of European imports from the United States, and European subsidiaries in the US are responsible for 38% of American imports from Europe.[72] The new division of labor also changed the traditional economic connections between the advanced core and the less developed peripheries. Dutch multinationals employ three-quarters of their labor force abroad. As a consequence of this phenomenon, a strong trend of deindus-trialization became characteristic in the most advanced countries. Industrial labor force sharply declined: in Britain, the Netherlands, Italy, and Sweden, it dropped from between 40% and 48% to between 16% and 20% in the period from the mid-1960s to around the end of the century. Nevertheless, the research and development (R&D) capacities, as well as the top, science- and knowledge-intensive processing branches, remained on the territory of the advanced West. Multinationals account for roughly three-quarters of R&D expenditures for the entire advanced (OECD) world, and they are thus the prime movers and monopolists of the new technology.

Globalization dramatically increased foreign exchange transactions. Cross-border transactions of bonds and equities amounted to 10% of the aggregate GDP of the most advanced G-7 countries in 1980, but 15 years later it was 140% of aggregate GDP. The transactions have reached unparalleled proportions, going from $15 billion a day in 1973, to $1.3 trillion daily already by 1995, more than 50 times the total value of world trade. International financial markets, where trillions of dollars flow in and out of various countries, undermining currencies, have little to do with productive activities. Less than one-fifth of foreign exchange transactions support international trade and/or investment. More than four-fifths is speculation.[73]

Globalization went hand in hand with the emergence of neo-liberal economics, laissez-faire individualism, and postmodern cultural nihilism. When Keynesian economics failed, globalization globalized the ideological concept of "market fundamentalism." The neo-liberal school launched an ideological war in the mid-1970s, advocating deregulation, privatization, and the free market as the only solutions to cut-throat global competition in a free society. This ideology certainly helped pave the way for uncontrolled international activity by multinationals and financial capital. As George Soros put it, neo-liberal policy "has put financial capital into the driver's seat."

As Joseph E. Stiglitz, the former chief economist of the World Bank and a Nobel laureate economist, stated in 2002, "the most dramatic change occurred in the 1980s." The leading economic powers of the world, and the international monetary institutions they created and financed, most of all the IMF, were also champions of "market supremacy with ideological fervor."[74] "Big government" and "tax and spend" policies were attacked, and drastic tax cuts and the privatization of key public services followed. The international monetary system of Bretton Woods created after the war in response to the lessons of previous economic instabilities, introduced the strict control of capital movements. However, this system collapsed in 1971 along with all of its regulations. The goal of Bretton Woods, as Henry Morgenthau, the American Treasury Secretary, characterized it in biblical terms, was to "drive the usurious moneylenders from the temple of international finance."[75] With the collapse of Bretton Woods, money-lenders now reoccupied "the temple." In 1975, the New York Stock Exchange was deregulated, followed by the London Stock Exchange in 1986. A "competitive deregulation race" began: Australia, New Zealand, France, Germany, and then practically the entire European community had abolished capital controls by 1988, with the Mediterranean and Scandinavian countries following soon thereafter.

According to globalization enthusiasts, everybody is profiting from globalization, because in the age of the new technological-communication revolution "the nation state has become an unnatural, even dysfunctional, unit for organizing human activity and managing economic endeavor in a borderless world."[76] In the globalized system, they argue, the social and political trends of the more advanced countries will also be globalized: social convergence will take place, a global civil society will rise, and global democratization will follow. Free movement of capital and goods will produce a much more efficient allocation of resources and more efficient production and distribution of goods and services. Capital will be invested where it is most profitable and thus will flow into low-wage-level developing countries. Former categories such as "Third World," and "core and periphery" will become meaningless. In general, they strongly and one-sidedly stressed the assumed overall positive impact of globalization.[77]

Globalization, nevertheless, has a many-colored, strong opposition, which speaks about globalization as a "betrayal" and "treason" to the national cause, the "death of the nation-state" and "embryonic institutions of world government" where "faceless foreign bureaucrats" will decide on national issues. At a time when global financial markets are not regulated, "there are practically no institutions for rule making on an international scale. Collective decision-making mechanisms for the global economy simply do not exist ... financial markets are inherently unstable ... To put the matter simply, market forces, if they are given complete authority ... produces chaos and could ultimately lead to the downfall of the global capitalist system."[78] Others warn that market forces will increase initial inequalities and the poor countries will become poorer.[79]

In reality, globalization is a double-edged sword, neither good nor bad in itself, and globalization has both winners and losers. Income disparities between the poorest and richest countries had a 1:10 ratio in 1913 and a 1:26 ratio in 1950, but at the end of the century this ratio had increased to 1:40. Income differences among various world regions went from a 15:1 ratio in 1950 to a 13:1 ratio by 1973, but then broadened during the decades of globalization in the last quarter of the century to 19:1.[80] After the collapse of communism, the former Soviet Bloc countries were virtually forced to liberalize and deregulate their economy by IMF conditions for loans that led to a severe temporary decline. The bloc as a whole needed the two decades until 2010 to reach the pre-collapse level of GDP.

Even taking into account all the dangerous consequences of globalization—the polarization, a growing core–periphery disparity, etc.—it still not true that all the advantages go to rich countries and all the negative consequences hit poor ones. Several backward regions and countries have profited from globalization. A group of backward countries attained an annual average of 3.5% growth, and during the entire last quarter-century, Asia achieved the highest growth rate: it grew at 5.46% per annum, or 2.5 times more than Western Europe, even on a per capita basis (3.54%), which led to a near doubling of per capita income. Several developing Asian countries that had a stagnating peripheral economy for a century (-0.11% between 1820 and 1870; 0.38% between 1870 and 1913; -0.02% between 1913 and 1950, measured in per capita GDP) became "small tigers," or rapidly developing countries, in the second half of the century, with annual growth of 2.95% between 1950 and 1973, and 3.54% between 1973 and 1998.[81] Foreign investments and multinational companies played a decisive role in generating this spectacular catching-up process. European experiences reflect a similar disparity in peripheral reaction to globalization. The traditional West European core countries had an annual 1.8% growth rate during the last quarter of the twentieth century, while Ireland, a former periphery of Britain, had a growth rate that was 2.33 times higher. A part of the former Mediterranean periphery gradually caught up with the Western core, increasing from half of the core's income level in 1950 to 80% of it at the end of the century.

In other words, peripheral countries by no means reacted uniformly. Some seemingly profited from globalization, which in the Mediterranean region and Ireland generated a significant catching up process until the 2008 financial crisis.[82] Globalization, especially the activities of the multinationals, played the decisive role in introducing modern technology to newly establish modern export sectors in the former Soviet Bloc countries as well. The European Union also played an important role in homogenizing economic levels by assisting backward regions within itself.

When political stability exists, where domestic infrastructure is relatively well-developed, the educational system is good, and trained engineers, computer experts, and skilled workers are available, and when local value systems and religion do not work against international adjustment, globalization might have positive impacts. Domestic abilities and actions play an important role. Certain geopolitical advantages and physical proximity also have a role and can make countries or regions politically and economically more attractive. The infiltration of multinationals, investment from abroad, and the broad market opportunities made possible by free trade agreements may make a difference in these cases. They may mobilize domestic resources and forces generating high prosperity and a catching-up process vis-à-vis the core. Globalization is thus a mixed blessing or a mixed curse. In the last century, huge portions of the former periphery became parts of the European core. Further peripheries might be incorporated into the flourishing core during the first half of the twenty-first century.

Notes

1 John Maynard Keynes, *The End of Laissez-Faire*, London: Leonard and Virginia Woolf, 1927.
2 Douglas North, *Institutions, Institutional Change, and Economic Performance*, Cambridge: Cambridge University Press, 1990, 3.
3 Douglas North and Barry Weingast, "Constitutions, and Commitments: The Evolution of Institutions Governing Public Choice in 17th-Century Britain," *The Journal of Economic History*, Vol. 49, No. 4, 1989, 803–32.

4 Avner Greif, *Institutions and the Path to the Modern Economy*, Cambridge: Cambridge University Press, 2006, 3–4.
5 Dan Bogart, M. Drelichman, O. Gelderblom, J-L. Rosenthal, "State and Private Institutions" in S. Broadberry and K. O'Rourke (eds), *The Cambridge Economic History of Modern Europe: 1700 to the Present*, Cambridge: Cambridge University Press, 2010, 71.
6 Sheilagh Ogilvie, "Whatever is, is Right? Economic Institutions in Pre-Industrial Europe," *Economic History Review*, Vol. 60, No. 4, 2007, 649–84, quote 651.
7 This essay is based on Karl Polanyi, *The Great Transformation: The Political and Economic Origins of Our Time*, Boston: Beacon Hill, [1944] 1964; Keynes, 1927; Eduard Heimann, *History of Economic Doctrines*, New York: Oxford University Press, 1964; Ivan T. Berend, *An Economic History of Twentieth Century Europe: Economic Regimes from Laissez Faire to Globalization*, Cambridge: Cambridge University Press, 2006.
8 This essay is based on John A. Hobson, *Imperialism: A Study*, London: James Nisbet, 1902; Eric Hobsbawm, *The Age of Extremes. The Short Twentieth Century, 1914–1991*, London: Michael Joseph, 1994.
9 Eric Hobsbawm, *The Age of Empire, 1875–1914*, New York: Vintage Books, 1989.
10 Hobson, 1902, 85.
11 Ibid, 51–52.
12 Heinrich von Treitschke, *Politics*, Vol. I, London, [1898] 1916, 115–16.
13 Mauro Marsella, "Enrico Corradini's Italian Nationalism: The 'Right Wing' of the Fascist Synthesis," *Journal of Political Ideologies*, Vol. 9, No. 2, 2004, 208–9.
14 Rosa Luxemburg, *Gesammelte Werke*, Band 5, Berlin, [1913] 1975, 299.
15 Vladimir I. Lenin, *Imperialism, the Highest Stage of Capitalism: A Popular Outline*, Moscow: Foreign Language Publisher, [1917] 1974.
16 Karl Kautsky, "Der Imperialismus," *Neue Zeit,* II. 1914, II. 921.
17 John Kenneth Galbraith, *A Journey Through Economic Times: A Firsthand View*, Boston: Mariner Books, 1995.
18 This essay is based on Philip E. Cleator, *Weapons of War*, London: Robert Hale, 1967; Siegfried Breyer, *Battleships and Battlecruisers of the World, 1905–1970*, London: Macdonald and Jane's, 1973; Berend, 2006.
19 Keynes, 1927, 5.
20 This essay is based on Benito Mussolini, *Fascism: Doctrine and Institutions*, Rome: Ardita Publisher, 1935; James A. Gregor, *The Ideology of Fascism: The Rationale of Totalitarianism*, New York: Free Press, 1969; Salvatore Saladino, "Italy," in Hans Rogger and Eugen Weber (eds), *The European Right: A Historical Profile*, Berkeley: University of California Press, 1974; Roland Sarti, *Fascism and the Industrial Leadership in Italy, 1919–1940*, Berkeley: University of California Press, 1971; Vera Zamagni, *The Economic History of Italy 1860–1990*, Oxford: Clarendon Press, 1993.
21 Mussolini, 1935, 10–11, 26–27.
22 Gregor, 1969, 300, 388–89.
23 William G. Welk, *Fascist Economic Policy: An Analysis of Italy's Experiment*, Cambridge, MA: Harvard University Press, 1938, 250.
24 This essay is based on Karl Marx, *Selected Writings*, Oxford: Oxford University Press, 2000; Karl Marx and Friedrich Engels, *Selected Works*, Vol. 2, Moscow: Foreign Language Publishing House, 1955; Evgeny Preobrazhensky, *The New Economics*, Oxford: Clarendon House, 1965; Alexander Erlich, *The Soviet Industrialization Debate, 1924–1928*, Cambridge, MA: Harvard University Press, 1967; Berend, 2006.
25 Marx, 2000, 261.
26 Marx and Engels, 1955, 433–38.
27 Marx, 2000, 593.

28 Marx, 2000, 614–15.
29 Karl Marx and Friedrich Engels, *The German Ideology*, New York: International Publisher, 1970.
30 Leon Trotsky, *1905*, London: Pelican Books, 1973, 333; Robert S. Wistrich, *Trotsky: Fate of a Revolutionary*, New York: Stein and Day, 1982, 62.
31 Vladimir I. Lenin, *Selected Works*, New York: International Publisher, 1971, 417, 443.
32 Joseph Stalin, *Problems of Leninism*, Peking: Foreign Language Press, 1976, 672.
33 This essay is based on *Documents on German Foreign Policy*, Series C II, Washington, DC: Government Printing Office, 1950; Hans Ernst Posse, "Möglichkeiten der Grossraumwirtschaft," *Die nationale Wirtschaft*, Vol. 2, 1934; Ivan T. Berend and György Ránki, *Magyarország a fasiszta Németország életterében*, Budapest: Közgazdasági Kiadó, 1960; Jenny J. Brine, *Comecon: The Rise and Fall of an International Socialist Organization*, New Brunswick, NJ: Transaction, 1992; Sándor Ausch, *Theory and Practice of CMEA Cooperation*, Budapest: Akadémiai Kiadó, 1972.
34 Posse, 1934.
35 Hannah Arendt, *The Origins of Totalitarianism*, Cleveland: World Publishing Co., 1966.
36 *Deutsches Zentral Archive*, Potsdam, Auswärtiges Amt, Abteilung 2, January 1934, 41288.
37 Ivan T. Berend, *Decades of Crisis: Central and Eastern Europe Before World War II*, Berkeley: University of California Press, 1998, 276.
38 This essay is based on Tom Clarke and Laurie Clements (eds), *Trade Unions Under Capitalism*, Stanford Terrace, Sussex: The Harvester Press, 1978; Wolfgang Abendroth, *A Short History of the European Working Class*, New York: Monthly Review Press, 1972; Dick Geary, *Labour and Socialist Movements in Europe Before 1914*, Oxford: Berg Publishers, 1989.
39 Catharina Lis, Jan Lucassen, and Hugo Soly (eds), *Before the Unions: Wage Earners and Collective Action in Europe, 1300–1850*, Cambridge: Cambridge University Press, 1994, 8.
40 Sydney and Beatrice Webb, *The History of Trade Unionism*, London: Longman, Greens, 1894, 1.
41 Lis et al., 1994, 7.
42 Karel Davids, "Seamen Organizations and Social Protest, c. 1300–1825," in Lis et al., 1994, 146, 167.
43 Jan Lucassen, "Seasonal Labourers and Miners," in Lis et al., 1994, 179, 181–82.
44 Anders Florén, "Social Organization of Work and Labour Conflicts in Proto-Industrial Iron Production in Sweden, Belgium and Russia," in Lis et al., 1994, 100.
45 Friedrich Engels, "The Condition of the Working Class in England," in Karl Marx and Friedrich Engels, *Collected Works*, Vol. 4, London: Lawrence and Wishart, 1975, 502.
46 Geary, 1989, 16.
47 William Thompson, *Labour Rewarded*, New York: Kelley, [1826] 1969, 32.
48 Marc Linder, *European Labor Aristocracies*, Frankfurt: Campus Verlag, 1985, 49.
49 Ibid, 65–66.
50 This essay is based on Ludwig Erhard, *Wohlstand für Alle*, Düsseldorf: Econ Taschenbuch Verlag, 1990; Peter Baldwin, *The Politics of Social Solidarity: Class Basis of the European Welfare State 1875–1975*, Cambridge: Cambridge University Press, 1990; Sir William Beveridge, *Social Insurance and Allied Services*, London: His Majesty's Stationery Office, 1942; Nicolas Barr, *The Welfare State as Piggy Bank: Information, Risk, Uncertainty, and the Role of the State*, Oxford: Oxford University Press, 2001; Peter Flora and Arnold J. Heidenheimer (eds), *The Development of the Welfare States in Europe and America*, New Brunswick: Transaction Books, 1981; Ivan T. Berend, *Europe Since 1980*, Cambridge: Cambridge University Press, 2010.

51 Rerum Novarum, www.vatican.va/holy_father/leo_xiii/encyclicals/documents//hf_I-xiii_enc_15051891_rerum_novarum_en.html.
52 Joseph Schumpeter, *Capitalism, Socialism and Democracy*, London: Allen and Unwin, 1976, 82–83, 127.
53 Mark Kleinman, *A European Welfare State? European Union Social Policy in Context*, Houndmills: Palgrave Macmillan, 2002, 18–19.
54 Flora and Heidenheimer, 1981, 317.
55 *The Sunday Times*, April 18, 2010.
56 Joyce Appleby, *The Relentless Revolution: A History of Capitalism*, New York: W.W. Norton & Co., 2010.
57 This essay is based on Keynes, 1927; Edward H. Carr, *The Twenty Years' Crisis*, New York: Harper and Row, 1964; Berend, 2006.
58 Karl Polanyi, *The Great Transformation: The Political and Economic Origins of Our Time*, Beacon Hill: Beacon Press, 1964.
59 Keynes, 1927, 35, 39, 47–49, 52–53.
60 Carr, 1964, 60, 51.
61 The industrial output of the world declined by 30%, coal and iron production by 40–60%, grain prices fell by 60%, and European trade dropped nearly two-thirds. Thousands of banks collapsed and unemployment reached tragic proportions.
62 Schumpeter, 1976, 67–68.
63 After World War II, the revolution in electronics was advanced by the invention of the transistor, and then by the first silicon integrated circuit in 1958. From the mid-1970s, a ceaseless communications revolution emerged (with its milestones, the computer, the internet, and the cellular telephone).
64 Angus Maddison, *World Economy: A Millennial Perspective*, Paris: 2001, 127, 362; OECD, *Structural Adjustment and Economic Performance*, Paris: OECD, 1987, 273.
65 According to the Swiss KOF Index of globalization, which assesses the economic, social, and political aspects of 122 countries. The first 16 most globalized countries are European.
66 "Europe Tests Banks, and Worries," *The New York Times*, July 4, 2009.
67 Ibid.; "European Union Proposes to Police Derivatives Trading," *The New York Times*, July 4, 2009; "Reforming Finance: The EU's Proposals: Divided by a Common Market," *The Economist*, July 4–10, 2009.
68 This essay is based on Willem Molle, *The Economics of European Integration: Theory, Practice, Policy*, 5th edition, Aldershot: Ashgate Publishing, 2006; Ali M. El-Agraa, *The European Union: Economics and Politics*, New York: Prentice Hall, 2004.
69 This essay is based on Joseph Stiglitz, *Globalization and its Discontents*, New York: W.W. Norton, 2002; Mark Rupert, *Ideologies of Globalization: Contending Visions of a New World Order*, London: Routledge, 2000; George Soros, *The Crisis of Global Capitalism*, New York: Public Affairs, 1998; Ivan T. Berend, "Globalization and Its Impact on Core-Periphery Relations," in Peter H. Reill and Balázs Szelényi (eds), *Cores, Peripheries, and Globalization*, Budapest: Central European University Press, 2011.
70 Maddison, 2001, 127, 362.
71 OECD, 1987, 273.
72 Mark A. Pollack and Gregory C. Shaffer, *Transatlantic Governance in the Global Economy*, Lanham, MD: Rowman & Littlefield, 2001, 12–14.
73 Rupert, 2000, 79.
74 Stiglitz, 2002, 12–13.
75 Eric Helleiner, "From Bretton Woods to Global Finance: A World Turned Upside Down," in Richard Stubbs and Geoffrey R.D. Underhill (eds), *Political Economy and the Changing Global Order*, New York: St. Martin's Press, 1994, 164.
76 Kenichi Ohmae, quoted by Rupert, 2000, 78.

77 See for example: John Dunning, *The Globalization of Business: The Challenge of the 1990s*, London: Routledge, 1993; Deepak Lal, *A Liberal International Economic Order: The International Monetary System and Economic Development*, Princeton: Princeton University Press, 1980; James H. Mittelman, "Rethinking the International Division of Labour in the Context of Globalization," *Third World Quarterly*, Vol. 16, No. 2, 1995.
78 Soros, 1998, xx, xxiii, xxvii.
79 Shahid Alam, *Poverty from the Wealth of Nations: Integration and Polarization in the Global Economy since 1760*, Houndmills: Macmillan, 2000, 63.
80 Maddison, 2001, 126.
81 Ibid.
82 Ibid, 185–87.

3 The power of ideas and inventions

Introduction

Economic development has its own inner rules and laws. Economists discovered and began analyzing several of them in the late eighteenth century. Nevertheless, it is only an abstraction to separate economic life from other spheres of life and action in human societies. The economic area is only an interrelated part of a complex that includes social, cultural, and political activities. These areas strongly influence each other and are interrelated.

Culture—in a broad sense that includes social values, behavioral patterns, and ideas—strongly influences the economy. Ideas, whether based on superstitions or on knowledge and science, are central factors in economic success or failure. Knowledge and knowledge-based ideas create a social capacity to handle the economy well, to create rules and institutions, and to form human behavior into the basis for successful economic development. Ideas and knowledge about the universe, nature, and their physical characteristics, as well as knowledge about the animal and human world and its biological laws, all led to major inventions. Scholars and their books, such as Newton's and Darwin's, changed the world. Modern agricultural and industrial technologies were born, new materials were discovered. Building engines and machines made possible successive industrial and communication revolutions. Causes of diseases were discovered and this contributed to curing sicknesses and extending life expectancy.

Ideas and inventions were equally important regarding social and political life and institutions. The spread of liberalism and the secularization of the European societies and states became major prerequisites of transformation. The Enlightenment and Romanticism changed human behavior and society. The role and power of ideas became crystal clear if one looks to those countries and regions that were not conquered by and remained outside of the reign of Enlightenment and secularization. The peripheral regions exhibit the areas of preserved premodern culture and behavioral attitudes. These cultural-social factors blocked the road of modern transformation. New ideas, new social attitudes, new machines, and new skills belong together and determine the economy. The power of ideas is the engine of human development and the cradle of both social and technological inventions and renewal. New society and dominant culture, together with new technology and skills are the most important growth factors, and their importance has steeply increased in modern times.

The essays in this chapter present several case studies and examples of the power of ideas and of crucial inventions in modern Europe. The role of the Enlightenment and Romanticism as they transformed the way of thinking and led to the spread of liberalism and secularization introduces the *leitmotif* of the power of ideas. As a counter-point, the Balkans and other peripheries are presented with their long preserved pre-modern culture. These major social-cultural factors are connected with technological ideas and inventions. The revolutions that reinvented agriculture, and the new way of building roads and revolutionizing transportation are illustrated by case studies. Milestone inventions of vaccinations and antibiotics, synthetic dyes, and the endless applications of electric power, up to the present-day computer and internet age are the most important examples. The essays help the understanding of the decisive role of ideas and inventions in human life.

Enlightenment and Romanticism: the ideas of modern society and the nation-state[1]

The rise of the modern economy and society in northwestern Europe during the seventeenth and eighteenth centuries was accompanied by a revolution in science and philosophy, which evolved into a new *zeitgeist*. This development had roots in several West European countries, including the Netherlands, England, France, Germany, Italy, and Switzerland. A new conception of human society and the universe, a new value system, and a new way of thinking began to spread throughout the West. Increasing numbers embraced an unquestionable belief that reason and experience can reveal the laws of nature and facilitate the just reorganization of society. Secularized science and political theory replaced religion and thus became the basis for the most fundamental intellectual transformation of the modern world.

These radical changes in ways of thinking, together with the spread of a commercial spirit that gradually appeared in Europe's late medieval centers, had a centuries-long history and were closely connected with the Renaissance that challenged medieval religious bigotry. Men looked for God in themselves, became fascinated with the human body, and began to establish a new materialistic and rationalistic society. Renaissance individualism and *joie de vivre* created an intellectual ferment that became the forerunner of the Reformation.[2]

The Reformation of the sixteenth century represented the "triumph of the commercial spirit over the traditional social ethics of Christendom … trade and tolerance flourished together."[3] The Reformation paved the way for the scientific revolution between the mid-sixteenth and seventeenth centuries. Copernicus, Pascal, Kepler, Galileo, Descartes, and Newton revolutionized human awareness. This was a "seismic shift in understanding of the natural world."[4]

The long march from the Renaissance, via the Protestant Reformation and the scientific revolution, had its crescendo in the seventeenth- and eighteenth-century Enlightenment. The forerunners of the latter trend included Joost Lips in Leiden and Antwerp, whose translations of the classics induced a fundamental change in the European worldview. René Descartes presented the first modern concept of the universe operating under mathematical laws in his *Discours de la méthode*, published in 1637. Descartes and subsequently Benedict (Baruch) Spinoza emerged as the philosophers of rationalism and natural law. Spinoza developed the concept of social contract, majority rule, and individual freedom, and rejected religion as the product of human fear of the unknown forces of nature.

The philosophy of the Enlightenment gradually emerging from Holland paved the way for a revolution of thought in Britain and France. Isaac Newton's rigorous experimentation and scholarly methodology to explain the laws of the physical world presented a unified view of the universe. The Newtonian scientific *Weltanschauung* transformed the way people thought about nature and society. It was the rock-hard foundation of the Enlightenment.

Thomas Hobbes was preeminent among seventeenth-century pioneers of thought as the first plebeian English philosopher and the founder of modern political philosophy. In *Leviathan* (1651), Hobbes challenged basic feudal concepts, such as the ancient bonds of loyalty to sovereigns, and replaced them with the notion of individualism: "The condition of man ... is a ... condition of war of everyone against everyone ... everyone is governed by his own reason and every man has a right ... of doing anything he likes."[5] John Locke, the most popular philosopher of the late seventeenth century in the age of the "Glorious Revolution" in Britain, went even further. His *Two Treatises on Government* (1689) posited the central role of laws as the most important "guarantor of freedom," and called for a social contract between kings and commoners that limited governmental power and made it constitutional. "All men by nature are equal ... being born ... with a title to perfect freedom and an uncontrolled enjoyment of all the rights and privileges of the law of Nature ... It is evident that absolute monarchy ... is indeed inconsistent with civil society, and can be no form of civil government."[6] Locke also propagated the separation and mutual limitation of legislative and executive powers. He became one of the most influential apostles of the modern *Rechtsstaat*, the state ruled by laws and the parliamentary system.

These innovations of British philosophy had a strong impact on the French Enlightenment. François-Marie Arouet, who adopted the name Voltaire, traveled to England and lived there for three years. He was impressed by the intellectual freedoms and was inspired by the teachings of Newton and Locke. In his *Letters Concerning the English Nation* (1733), he exudes admiration for Britain, and Voltaire became one of the most powerful proponents of natural law and tolerance. He therefore passionately called for an intellectual revolt against the antiquated Church and state.

The French Enlightenment showcased the wit, sarcasm, and lucidity of a legion of writers and philosophers. Charles-Louis de Secondat, Baron de Montesquieu, idealized the British parliamentary system and attacked absolute power. Political liberty, he insisted, cannot exist "when the legislative and executive powers are united in the same person or in the same body ... [T]here is no liberty if the judiciary power [is] not separated from the legislative and executive."[7] Here, the ideas of a revolutionary social and political system were clearly germinating. Diderot's *Encyclopedia* spread knowledge of the world and views on society and political systems. The Geneva-born Jean-Jacques Rousseau, who moved to Paris in the mid-eighteenth century, expressed the aura of revolution most eloquently. The very first sentence of his *Social Contract, or Principles of Political Right* (1762) reads like a declaration of war against the *ancien régime*: "Man is born free and everywhere he is in chains." Whereas every philosopher before him appealed to elites, and the entire movement of the Enlightenment was an intellectual revolt that attracted the elite, Rousseau addressed the masses. He defined an entirely new concept of legitimate power: "Each, while uniting himself with all, may still obey himself alone, and remain as free as before ... [Only the] State that is governed by laws ... [and] the public interest ... [has a] legitimate government."[8]

The Enlightenment was a fundamentally West European phenomenon. One of its greatest representatives in the German principalities was Immanuel Kant, professor at Königsberg University. In his 1784 essay, *"Beantwortung der Frage: Was ist Aufklärung?"* ("Answering the Question: What is Enlightenment?"), Kant declared that enlightened mankind was beginning to emerge from its self-incurred immaturity. The leading and most celebrated philosopher of the post-Kantian generation, Georg Wilhelm Friedrich Hegel, was mesmerized by Napoleon, and welcomed the arrival of the new world order, the end of history embodied in the *Weltseele* (Absolute Spirit) and "reason" of Napoleon.

The ideas they espoused were not obscure or inconsequential in the western half of Europe. The new and liberating values of the Enlightenment held tremendous appeal for the elite and the educated throughout the region. "The religion of liberty took hold on the European continent ... England, France, and Germany exemplified the evolution of the religion of liberty in Europe."[9] This "religion" made liberalism the dominant political trend in the nineteenth century. It was genuinely cosmopolitan and internationalist and it guaranteed individual freedoms under the law. Equality, freedom of belief, the inviolability of private property, and popular sovereignty became the leading ideas. The values of the Enlightenment had become institutionalized by the American Declaration of Independence and the Bill of Rights, and by the French Revolution and the Right of Man and of the Citizens. The newly created legal systems and the Code Napoleon that became the basis of modern legal systems in Europe created and institutionalized the new norms of a modern society. The Enlightenment—or, as it was often called, the Age of Reason—also influenced ardent representatives of the *ancien régime*, including several autocratic rulers in Central Europe such as Frederick the Great in Prussia,

Maria Theresa of Austria, and her son and successor, Joseph II, all of whom instituted reforms following some ideas of the Enlightenment.

In the footsteps of the Enlightenment, a new artistic-ideological current, Romanticism, became the most influential propagator of liberty, personal freedom, and the brotherhood of people in Britain and France, and also a yearning for change beginning half a century before the French Revolution. This gained new impetus during the nineteenth century on the continent, especially in Germany. "Man wished to be free from restrictions imposed by religious traditions, political absolutism and a hierarchical social system in order to express and determine himself and create the kind of order in which he wished to live."[10] Unlike the strictly rational Enlightenment, Romanticism wanted to liberate emotion, sentiment, and instinct. Romanticism passionately called for the freedom of man to create his own values.[11] French Romanticism, meanwhile, was sensitive to social problems, and the German Romantic movement included the idea of freedom of national individuality as well. Cultivating national culture and languages, so-called linguistic-cultural nationalism emerged as a powerful movement in countries and regions that lacked the genuine nation-building process that took place within the borders of the absolute state in Britain and France. Romantic nationalism targeted the creation of a national self-identification and will among peoples and groups of peoples to create the nation.

Romanticism was an intoxicating dreaming, an "artistic Protestantism and liberalism" or, as Victor Hugo, the French Romantic writer, defined it in his *Hernani*, Romanticism was "liberalism in literature ... liberalism in art, liberty in society," a war against the rules of convention and existing, unacceptable reality. Isaiah Berlin equated the impact of Romanticism with the most important historical events of the age: it was "no less far-reaching," he affirmed, than the British industrial revolution and the French Revolution.[12] The new credo was popularized by poets, writers, composers, and painters.

Romantic artists became national heroes who addressed not only the small educated elite, but the nation as a whole and mankind in general. The art of the century became pan-European. Romantic arts were able to mobilize the masses and indoctrinate them with new values and ideals. Nineteenth-century novels, the discovery of history and the powerful historicism, operas, symphonies, and the newly invented Romantic musical genres such as symphonic poems and program music, which contained literary and philosophical messages, became effective promoters of a new *zeitgeist*.

Romanticism, however, was not just a continuation of the Enlightenment, but in a way, "an intellectual reaction against the eighteenth century ideals of order, discipline and reason."[13] As Peter Reill maintains, Romanticism found a solution to the real problem of the Enlightenment, how to deal with the senses and how to evolve a theory of knowledge that would include sensation, the passions, and habits into their scheme. The Romantic *Naturphilosophen* believed that absolute knowledge can indeed be obtained, and mind and matter are the same, hence the laws of the mind reveal nature's laws. In this sense, Reill concludes that the romantics were more "rationalistic" than enlightened thinkers.[14]

The eastern and southeastern parts of Europe were not deeply touched by these intellectual currents. In that region, Romanticism carried the ideas of the Enlightenment as well, a kind of religious belief in progress and human action. Romantic passion was connected here with national cataclysm and oppression. "Romantic longing conjured up a glorious past and a victorious future, stirring desire to rejuvenate the ailing nation." Messianistic Romanticism penetrated the arts, intellectual life, and politics in Central and Eastern Europe, and became a century-long movement. "Heroic advocacy of freedom and social justice, rebellion against an obsolete and unjust society, revolt against all kinds of oppression … with passionate subjectivism" paved the way for independent nation-building. Nations subordinated to the Habsburg, Ottoman, and Russian multinational empires, or nations that lacked unity and were divided into smaller units such as Germany and Italy, became mobilized by these intellectual trends.[15]

The Enlightenment and Romanticism transformed Europe's way of thinking, creating a dream and a model of a rational, free, and just society and independent nationhood. These ideas were embodied in the French Revolution, and the "Spring of the Nations" in 1848, the building of liberal states, and paving the way for democratic-parliamentary systems and the *Rechtsstaat* in the West. German unification and the Italian *Risorgimento*, and the struggle of independent nationhood in Central and Eastern Europe were all connected with those ideas. Powerful ideas mobilized the people and transformed history.

Liberal and secular values that formed the modern capitalistic attitude[16]

The road of the gradual rises of modern capitalism—first in its merchant variety, and then in its industrial guise—was paved by liberal and secular ideas. They gained ground first in northwest Europe, and then in the western half of the European continent. The Low Countries and Britain experienced the earliest "bourgeois revolutions" in Europe, which cleared the way for social-institutional transformation and eliminated feudal obstacles. The new societies put major political turmoil behind them. The Netherlands established its independence through the Eighty Years' War against Spain (1568–1648) and the Dutch Revolt became an early bourgeois revolution that transformed Dutch society and created a new attitude toward life and business that was also influenced by Protestantism. Opposed to the dogmatic Catholicism of their Habsburg and Spanish enemies, the United Provinces found their identity in the Protestantism that was born in Germany and Switzerland. This was a new religious ideology that created a deeply reformed Church. The radical Anabaptist legacy, with its stance on the separation of Church and state, and Calvinist anxieties stemming from a belief in predestination that was thought to establish certain people's worldly success as a sign of their heavenly salvation, contributed to the creation of an ethos of hard work, thrift, self-discipline, and the rejection of luxury as sin. Puritan Calvinist thinking created a new attitude and lifestyle.

Max Weber, the founder of modern sociology, maintained in his famous 1905 work, *The Protestant Ethic and the Spirit of Capitalism* that the Protestant ethic created the spirit of capitalism. However, this claim is more than questionable, and a corresponding question may be also asked: what created the Protestant ethic? A silent and gradual social-economic transformation generated the new ideas and the rejection of religious bigotry, embodied by the Catholic Church.[17] A close interrelation between social transformation and religious-ideological changes slowly started eliminating the obstacles that blocked the way to capitalism.

The Low Countries evolved into the most democratic and tolerant region based on, and governed by, constitutions. Provincial charters had to be respected by the sovereign as early as the fourteenth century. The region became a flourishing center of arts and sciences at the time, reflecting rising prosperity. Like in Britain, a few Swiss cantons, German free cities, and the Low Countries developed a new social pattern fundamentally different from that in other parts of the continent: prestige and autonomy for merchants and financiers, and free rein for economic and technological innovation.

The most crucial cultural-institutional transformations emerged as a broad European process. Reformation, scientific revolution, Enlightenment, and the ideas of the French Revolution and Romanticism were widespread European trends impacting the Netherlands, Britain, and France, with especially deep roots in and influences on Germany, Switzerland, and Scandinavia. From the late eighteenth and during the nineteenth century a common West European *zeitgeist* emerged and penetrated the region. Based on structural and cultural similarities, the common West European *zeitgeist* became the prime mover of Western transformation.

The barriers to spreading the new *zeitgeist* were severe in most of continental Europe because the *ancien régime* survived the eighteenth century and remained strong in the first half of the nineteenth century. With the defeat of Napoleon, the new *zeitgeist* also met its Waterloo. In France's neighbors, which were occupied and reorganized/modernized by Napoleon, the new ideas and institutions were considered to be "French," and thus hostile, and so they generated resistance and the regimes of restoration began eliminating them. The Bourbon restoration also rushed to destroy what remained of the Revolution and the Napoleonic era in France.

Nevertheless, the era following the Congress of Vienna (1814–15), though it was able to restore several major elements of the *ancien régime*, turned out to be unable to eliminate the impact of the Revolution. The Napoleonic Codes, the first codification of a comprehensive modern legal order that established the modern "rules of the game," became the basis or foundation of nineteenth-century law throughout Europe.[18] Property became sacred and free, defended by law. Business was also freed but under new regulations. The secular state was also an important legacy of the Enlightenment and Revolution and its Napoleonic realization, but it took an entire century before it really penetrated the West European states and societies. Freemasonry became a Church of Enlightenment throughout the continent.

The new, liberating values of the Enlightenment were tremendously attractive and its ideals penetrated borders and recruited a part of the elite and educated people with ease. The carrier of the new ideas in the early nineteenth century became the new urban bourgeois, middle-class elite that gradually emerged. Merchants, industrialists, bankers, managers of companies, professionals, teachers, doctors, engineers, freelancers, artists, and writers formed this social stratum. A new layer of society elevated in social status by higher education, a layer that the Germans call *Bildungsbürgertum*, became a special and important element in the rising new elite. In the mid-nineteenth century all of these layers together represented about 5–15% of the societies of the West.[19]

As heterogeneous as they were, they shared common interests and ideas. They had the same enemies in the form of the *ancien régime* and its social pillars. They were strongly urban and highly critical of the aristocracy and absolute monarchy. They shared a similar culture, rooted in the Enlightenment, and their lifestyles exhibited similar characteristics. They became much less church-going and religious. The modern bourgeois society gained ground in Western Europe from the 1840s to the 1870s and became the carrier of liberalism. As the French republican politician, Léon Gambetta, maintained, the "new social stratum" was liberal, republican, and anti-clerical; it provided the basis for the new order. Church-going sharply declined after the 1848 revolution in Britain, France, and Germany. As Friedrich Nietzsche noted in 1886, German Protestants in the middle classes were religiously indifferent.[20]

A complex change stood behind this declining religious involvement. Urban and modern economic development played an important role. National euphoria and nationalism were elevated to a level of substitute religion and also contributed to dwindling church attendance. Modern materialist science played a major part, too. Theories about the origins of the planets and stars, and inventions in chemistry and electricity dramatically broadened knowledge about nature. As the French biologist Jean-Baptiste Lamarck stated: "How little the idea of those who attribute to the globe an existence of six thousand and a few hundred years duration."[21] Darwin played the most important role in undermining religious beliefs. His *On the Origin of Species* was published in 1859 and immediately made a big splash.

Political and social thought, economic theory, and philosophy summarized and spread the new way of thinking. Political liberalism, the carrier of the ideas of the Enlightenment and the French Revolution, when turned against the *ancien régime* and conservatism, turned also against the Church as its main representative. The state in the *ancien régime* was a confessional state and religion governed private and collective life. The struggle against the *ancien régime* or its restoration and remnants, the struggle for modernity, had to be combined with the struggle against the Church. "In the *Syllabus errorum* of

1864, the papacy itself defined Catholicism as the antithesis of modernity ... The two religions [Protestantism and Catholicism] seemed to have positioned themselves in pro- and anti-modern camps ... The liberals ... were convinced that the Catholic Church, as a conservative force, was blocking the breakthrough to a modern industrial society ... Across Europe, the emergence of constitutional and democratic nation states was accompanied by intense conflict between Catholics and anticlerical forces over the place of religion in modern polity."[22]

The campaign for the secularization of the state became a pan-West European trend from the mid-nineteenth century. Unified Germany launched a series of laws to neutralize Catholicism as a political force. Secularization penetrated practically all of social life and the public sphere. Confrontations became sharper because of the Catholic Church's attempts to keep and even strengthen its position in European social and political life. In 1870, the provocative declaration of papal infallibility generated a bitter reaction throughout Europe.

Against the medieval ideas of the Vatican and the straitjacket of Catholic Church policy, even the illiberal German state of Otto von Bismarck launched its famous *Kulturkampf*, a secularization campaign. Most of the other states, practically the entire "common European political-cultural place,"[23] launched its *Kulturkampf* during the 1860s–1880s. In Belgium the *Kulturkampf* was called the "school war" in 1879–84; there were violent confrontations in the Netherlands, and demonstrations in Spain in 1878. Italy initiated a campaign for the victims of the Church and established a statue for Giordano Bruno at the spot where he was burned under the watch of the Pope. Switzerland experienced one of the most drastic *Kulturkampf* in Europe. Berne radically decreased the number of religious holy days and expelled the religious orders from schools. The canton appointed "state-priests," and the parochial councils that refused to accept them were disbanded.[24]

The widespread secularization campaigns in Western Europe were accompanied by an intellectual movement at universities that spread to the press and to homes. Enlightenment ideas became the belief of many via the secularization of states and minds. Secularization, however, was a gradual process that "first brought about the dissociation of church and state, then separated religion from society, spanned a period that varied from one country to another; in any case never less than some hundred years."[25]

Liberal politics conquered Western Europe between 1848 and 1870. In the changing public spirit, civil organizations played an important role. Numerous reading clubs, debating clubs, singing and literary societies emerged throughout Western Europe. Urban societies held various cultural and leisure activities and organized political civil associations. In Austria alone, 85,000 civic associations were in operation in 1910. These self-organized associations became the main networks of a gradually emerging self-organizing civil society.

Liberalism became the dominant ideological and political trend, carrying the central ideas. The essence of the French Constitution of 1793 and the "Declaration of the Rights of Man and of the Citizen" became common values in Western Europe. Civil liberties, sacrosanct property rights, individual freedom, tolerance, equality under the law, free markets, limited government, and the secular state became the new values and the international doctrine. The common cultural space of Western Europe was cross-fertilized by the new *zeitgeist*. The bourgeois middle-class became the dominant social and political force. This new cultural-social-institutional development opened the gates for economic transformation.

Pre-modern culture that blocked the road to the modern capitalist transformation[26]

The *ancien régime* that was swept away in the West remained virtually intact on the European peripheries until the 1860s–1870s. Revolutions that aimed at creating radical social-political changes either did not happen or were defeated. Modern social-legal and institutional systems were not in place before 1870. The dominant role of the Church survived for a long time and feudal institutions, serfdom, and noble privileges existed in peripheral regions for another 70 to 80 years after the French Revolution. The legacy of the past heavily burdened the present.

History, indeed, did not spoil the peripheries. They suffered from foreign invasions and sometimes long-lasting occupations by non-European powers. The transforming, rejuvenating movements of the Reformation and Enlightenment did not influence them. Bad historical experiences generated negativism and a lack of energetic response to major challenges. From time to time, desperate helplessness was, all of a sudden, replaced by bitter heroism, fighting ultimately hopeless battles and then declining even deeper into desperation and self-pity after the defeat. They developed the habit of valuing those who fought hopeless fights and lost, but rejected those who were ready to compromise and achieve results.

The population of the backward and uneducated peripheries conserved traditional values and social behaviors. The noble mentality, the hidalgo attitude in Spain, combined with the suppression of secular-scientific thinking and the heavy legacy of the Inquisition since the sixteenth century, did not disappear with the feudal institutions and remained a strong obstacle to modernization during the eighteenth and nineteenth centuries. At the end of the eighteenth century, "practicing industry or commerce still seems incompatible with the status of nobility ... the ideal of aristocratic life impregnated the mentality of all strata of Spanish society in the Old Regime and was solidly rooted in the lower layers, so much so that work on some trades was socially rejected." In 1906, the economic attaché at the British Embassy in Madrid, reported, "Spaniards are not enterprising in business, and few care to venture on a new industry or undertaking." "The heavy hand of the Inquisition, the interference of the Church with learning, was at its worst in Spain."[27]

The similar value system of the nobility dominated the Eastern peripheries as well. An entrepreneurial attitude was mostly lacking. The elite, followed by large parts of the population, looked down on business as an ungentlemanly activity, alien to a Pole and a Magyar. A contemporary Russian, Baron Nicholas E. Wrangel, made a sarcastic remark: "You want to work? How odd! Don't you know that ... [he] who works is a lost man? ... There are gentlemen, who don't do anything ... and in a few years become State Councilors, and who can get anything they want."[28]

An indigenous entrepreneurial class was barely present in these regions and most of the early entrepreneurs belonged to minorities who were mostly considered non-indigenous, or had arrived from abroad. In the case of Spain, foreign, mostly French entrepreneurs established the entire banking industry and, together with Brits, opened the mines. Gabriel Tortella concluded: "A society that was frozen in orthodoxy, that repressed original thought ... since the late sixteenth century, found itself three centuries later without a competitive and inventive entrepreneurial class."[29]

In Moscow and St. Petersburg, respectively, 40% and 30% of the entrepreneurs were "German-speaking foreigners" in 1869–70.[30] In Belarus in 1897, 90% of merchants were Jewish. In Vitebsk and Wilna, the share of Jewish merchants reached 85% and 98%, respectively.[31] In Łódź, the "Polish Manchester," the most advance textile center of the country, 67% of the inhabitants were German, and nearly 20% were Jewish in 1864.[32] The majority of the Hungarian and Romanian business elite were Jewish and German. The capital cities of these countries, in which the bulk of modern economic sectors were concentrated, were strongly minority populated: one-quarter of Budapest's and one-third of Bucharest's inhabitants were Jewish.

An anti-Western and anti-capitalist attitude, similar to the one in Spain, ruled the large majority of the elite in Central and Eastern Europe, and in many senses, an ethos of "elegant gentlemanly" behavior penetrated the entire society. Bolesław Prus, the Nobel Laureate Polish writer, rejected that nobleman's ethic in his novel of 1890: "He who makes a fortune is called a miser, a skinflint, a parvenu, he who wastes money is called generous, disinterested, open-handed ... Simplicity is eccentric, economy is shameful."[33]

These characteristics were extremely traditional and marked in Poland. *Glos Szlachcica Polskiego* (*Voice of a Polish Gentleman*), an anonymous pamphlet published in 1880, rejected the idea of nation-building via commerce and industry. "[The Polish noblemen] lived according to the customs of their forebears and not the customs of shopkeepers ... [The nobility rejects] the worship of the golden calf and utilitarianism ... [they are] the exclusive heir to the entire historic national past ... Religion, Motherland, Family and Tradition."[34]

Maria Bogucka characterized the Polish noble value system thusly: "engaging in urban occupations was shameful and dishonest by their very nature."[35] Gyula Szekfű, the leading Hungarian historian of the interwar decades, when discussing the nineteenth century history of the country in 1920, spoke of the "anti-commercial and anti-capitalist talents of the Hungarian race." He continued: "The principle of trading and producing for profit disagreed with the Hungarian nature ... Bourgeois characteristics were quite far from the mental habit of Hungarians, nobility and peasantry alike ... Undoubtedly, the Hungarians may be listed among those peoples that have the least inclination to develop in a capitalist direction."[36] Similar views were articulated about the Romanian noble elite: "Educated Romanians have shown a tendency to avoid following a commercial career, leaving this field of activity to alien elements ... The country ... is thus deprived of the opportunity of building up an independent middle class."[37]

Under the rigid autocratic traditionalism of Russia, an immobile and uneducated society did not even long for modernization. Religious fatalism, a fear of innovation, and resistance to monetized market relations were deeply embedded in Russian peasant society. From the 1870s on, the populist *Narodnaya Volya* (People's Will) group dreamed about the liberation of the peasantry from tsarist oppression, idealized the "uncorrupted peasant virtue," and denied the need to industrialize on the grounds that it destroys the natural egalitarian values of villages. In this view, Western capitalism is degrading and destructive. Populist intellectuals prophesized an independent "Russian road" based on cooperation and avoiding capitalism.

The conservative-nationalist Slavophiles celebrated the unspoiled Russian values of common ownership and a "real and concrete equality." In 1895, the German Ambassador summarized anti-Western views in Russia: "Western Europe is rotten ... it is a moral danger to Russia, and therefore she must prevent close contact with the West as much as possible. Nihilism and all revolutionary ideas are ... the product of European civilization. I would not have believed it possible that such intense fanaticism could rule in Russia."[38] Giorgio Mori also spoke about the "radical anti-industrialism, latent or explicit, of a large part of economic thought and of the culture of the ruling classes of the southern Italian states."[39]

Illiterate peasant masses in Russia, the Balkans, southern Italy, and Spain preserved pre-industrial behavioral patterns. The famous Russian populist economist, Alexander V. Chayanov, explained that peasant families did not follow the Western standard and worked on different principles that were understandable only in their own terms. If their income was sufficient to meet their usual consumption needs, they decided to take more time in leisure instead of exploiting the prosperity and working and earning more when their labor input would generate higher outcomes.[40] Krzysztof Zamorski spoke about an anti-modern peasant mentality, where "in the common value system money was never of utmost importance ... peasant merchants as well as producers directed their fortune towards the institutions which were not connected with production ... They remitted to church all their capital for religious reasons." In some cases 20% of the deceased's wealth was spent on a fancy funeral.[41] Mass illiteracy, deep poverty, superstition, and extremely traditional ways of thinking and values made the peripheral societies unprepared for the modern capitalist transformation. In other words, the human-cultural factor of modernization was mostly absent or extremely weak on the peripheries.

The two books that contributed the most to creating the modern world: Newton and Darwin[42]

Landmark ideas are not born from nothing. The development of ground-breaking thought always has a long prehistory. In the late medieval era, the north Italian city-states and Flanders became cradles of modern capitalism, and long-distance and maritime trade, and saw the beginning of modern banking activities. This development strongly influenced ways of thinking. The spread of a commercial spirit that gradually appeared in the late medieval centers was closely connected with the Renaissance. The reclaiming of ancient arts and scholarship was a tacit challenge to medieval religious bigotry. Men looked for God in themselves, and Renaissance individualism created an intellectual ferment that became a forerunner of the Reformation.

The Reformation of the sixteenth century broke the rigid bigotry and strong control of the Catholic Church, thereby paving the way for the scientific revolution. The giants and pioneers of scientific discoveries in astronomy, physics, and anatomy between the mid-sixteenth and seventeenth centuries—the Polish Copernicus, the German Kepler, the French Descartes, the Italian Galileo, among others—also revolutionized human consciousness. The invention of the telescope and the microscope assured a deeper understanding of nature.

Science broke through and got its own cathedrals: the academies of sciences in England and France. In the 1660s, the Royal Society, the Académie Royale des Sciences, and several other private societies and associations were established that inspired and cultivated science and its practical application in the form of industrial and agricultural innovations. This generated a "monumental change in the realm of learning ... a seismic shift in understanding of the natural world ... [that led to the] crucial transition in the formation of the modern world."[43]

The towering figure of the scientific revolution was Isaac Newton, who was born in Lincolnshire, England, in January 1643. In the most symbolic way, he was born within a year of the death of Galileo. Isaac was born three months after the death of his father, an illiterate but well-to-do English yeoman with 100 acres of land. His mother remarried and left the three-year-old Isaac in his grandmother's care. This experience made him a loner and a withdrawn, meditative character. He was enrolled in King's School, Grantham, where he studied the Bible, Greek, and Latin. At the age of 15, his mother, widowed again, returned and took him from school to continue his father's trade as a farmer. Isaac resisted, and spent his time reading. In the end, his former headmaster convinced his mother to send him back to school. At the age of 19, Newton was accepted by Trinity College, Cambridge, where he studied Aristotle and Plato, but he also read Descartes, Copernicus, and Kepler, and self-educated himself in mathematics and natural philosophy (physics).

By the mid-1660s, based on his readings, Newton had developed a strict conception of the universe as governed by rational mechanical laws, but he was also convinced that behind it all lay the presence of an "intelligent design." He earned his BA and a Master's Degree, and then became Fellow of Trinity College in 1667, and soon he was the most important scholar of the age. Typical for the time, he was also an alchemist who made one of his last failed experiments to produce gold in the early 1690s. As a religious man he wrote more on theology than on science. His work, however, became the watershed separating the old and the new world by establishing the base of modern mathematics and physics. The best mathematician of the age, he developed the differential and integral calculus, the concept of universal gravitation, the basic laws of motion, the basic characteristics of light and optics, i.e., all the solid bases of modern science.

Newton published his *Philosophiae Naturalis Principia Mathematica* in London in 1687, the "capstone of the Scientific Revolution of the sixteenth and seventeenth centuries and ... often said to be the greatest work of science ever published."[44] In this and his next three works of the early eighteenth century, Newton utilized rigorous experimentation and scholarly methodology to explain the laws of the physical world. He presented a "grand unified vision of the universe ... [and] provided a rational mechanics for the operations of machines on earth."[45]

The Newtonian concept of the universe was one of a secure and harmonious system. A wide array of lectures and publications, including Voltaire's, popularized Newton's theories and gave rise to a number of practical works on applied mechanics and machine building. The Newtonian scientific *Weltanschauung* transformed the way people thought about nature and society. It was the foundation not only of Enlightenment scholarship, but of civil engineering as well.

The scientific revolution turned people's interest from metaphysical issues to physical problems, and to applied science. Important links developed between renowned philosopher-scientists and instrument-makers. As A.E. Musson and Eric Robinson have shown, mathematics became a practical tool for artisans in the early seventeenth century. Traders, merchants, seamen, and carpenters used and developed it. The newly founded Royal Society—Newton became its president in 1703—"was actively concerned with the practical applications of natural philosophy," and its members sought to improve "mechanic arts" such as building, metal-smithing, shipbuilding, and agriculture. Beginning in the sixteenth century, inexpensive textbooks were published in Antwerp in Dutch, French, English, and German. Francis Walkinghame's bestselling textbook *The Tutor's Assistant* (published later in the eighteenth century) appeared in 18 editions of 5,000–10,000 copies each.[46] The *Dictionnaire Universel des Arts et des Sciences* was first released in 1690, and the *Lexicon Technicum* was published in 1704. A flourishing encyclopedic culture emerged, embodied in Diderot's *Encyclopédie*. Among its 72,000 entries, rich and precise technological descriptions facilitated everyday industrial practice.[47] The new *Weltanschauung* became increasingly accessible and served as a guiding compass for thousands of entrepreneurs.

Newton's discoveries strongly influenced philosophical thinking as well, and became one of the initiators of Enlightenment philosophy. The newly born economics of Adam Smith proposed the same harmony and automatism, the rule of an "invisible hand" in the world of the market economy, as in Newton's physical world. Isaac Newton was knighted, became a Member of Parliament at the time of the Glorious Revolution, and he was appointed Master of the Mint with an office in the Tower of London. After his death in 1727, he was buried in the main sanctuary of Westminster Abbey.

Not quite two complete centuries after the publication of Newton's landmark *Principia*, another book with a long title, *On the Origin of Species by Means of Natural Selection, or the Preservation of Favoured Races in the Struggle for Life*, was published in 1859.[48] This work put the 50-year-old author, Charles Robert Darwin, next to Newton. Darwin's father and grandfather were both medical doctors. His father wanted him to continue in his footsteps and sent Charles to study medicine at the University of Edinburgh. When his interests attracted him in other directions, his father sent him to Christ's College, Cambridge, to learn Anglican theology and become a clergyman.

Like the young Newton, the young Darwin was also influenced by geniuses before him. Three major books had an especially formative influence on him: Paley's *Natural Theology*, Herschel's *Natural Philosophy*, and Alexander von Humboldt's personal reports on his scientific travels. Darwin was not the first to establish the concept of evolution. Some of his predecessors included the French biologist Georges-Louis Leclerc, Comte de Buffon, Jean-Baptiste Lamarck in his *Zoological Philosophy* in 1809, Robert Chambers in 1844, and—precisely during the years when Darwin was feverishly working on his *Origin of Species*—Alfred Wallace published on the problem of transmutation and evolution. However, virtually everyone accepted the religious concept of creation. None of them went so far as Darwin.

Before starting work as a clergyman at the age of 22, one of Darwin's Cambridge professors recommended that he participate in a discovery boat tour along the Latin American seashore. His father did not want to allow him to go, but his famous uncle, Josiah Wedgwood, convinced the elder Darwin that the tour will not be "in any degree disreputable to his career as a clergy-man."[49] The trip on the HMS *Beagle* was planned to take two years, but it actually took nearly five years. They visited a great number of places, among them Cape Verde Island, the Falklands, the tropical forests of Brazil, Tahiti, and New Zealand. His 19-day stay on the Galapagos Islands had a special impact on him. Darwin collected fossil bones and studied marine inverte-brates. In his *Autobiography*, Darwin noted "The voyage of the Beagle has been by far the most important event in my life, and has determined my whole career."[50] He studied geology, biology, anthropology, made zoological notes, and in 1839 he published his findings and experiences in his *Journal and Remarks, 1832–1835*, which established his fame.

It took another 20 years, and endless studies and experiments, to develop his theory of evolution, which he presented in his *On the Origin of Species*. The lengthy work's first outline was written in 1842 as a 35-page sketch in pencil. In two years, he developed a 230-page essay with the description of the natural selection mechanism.

Originally a religious man, Darwin's experiments and learning led him to become critical about the creation and a designed hierarchy in nature where humans are unrelated to animals. His scientific knowledge and religious belief struggled with each other. As he described in one of his letters, "I remember well how many years it cost me to go round from the old beliefs."[51] Consequently, according to some experts, "the *Origin* is the last work of natural theology as much as the first of modern evolutionary biology."[52] He concluded that all organic forms had probably "descended from some one primordial form into which life was first breathed."[53]

On the Origin of Species shocked Victorian England and the world. Vitriolic attacks were launched against it, such as the "Monkeyana" in the May 1861 issue of *Punch*, which was signed "Gorilla." The book irritated traditional religious believers, and several maintained that it undermined the basic moral values of Western civilization.[54] The endless attacks hurt Darwin who wrote in one of his letters in January 1863: "I could not get to sleep till past 3 last night from indignation."[55] Darwin, however, had a tremendous impact on science and people's way of thinking. The book demonstrated the "ability to penetrate areas of knowledge once obscured by religious dogma ... The discovery of natural selection marks a turning point in the development of modern science."[56] Several experts stated that the *Origin* became "the most important book of the century." Because of the book, Darwin "took [his] place along with Galileo and Newton ... those who have altered the entire mentality of civilization."[57] As in the case of Newton, Darwin and the scientific advances he made possible strongly influenced philosophy as well. As the outstanding twentieth-century biologist Julian Huxley concluded, "Newton's great generalization of gravitational attraction made ... [it] necessary to dispense with the idea of God guiding the stars ... Darwin's equally great generalization of natural selection made ... [it] necessary to dispense with the idea of God guiding the evolutionary course of life."[58] Besides creating the foundations of modern biology, Darwin played the most important role in secularizing science and gradually, during the second half of the nineteenth century, society and the state. When he died, he was buried near Newton in Westminster Abbey as a national hero.

Inventing and reinventing agriculture[59]

Agricultural performance in Europe did not change much in the millennium after Roman times. In the early medieval centuries, the two-field rotation system used half of the cultivated land for grain and the other half remained fallow to recover and for grazing. The soil was plowed by digging-sticks or scratch-plow, pulled by family members or oxen. Harvesting was performed by sickles, and the quantity of the harvest was 2–3 times the sown seed. In later medieval centuries, three-field rotation systems used two-thirds of the arable land for winter and spring crops, and left one-third of it fallow. Heavy plows were pulled by oxen or horses, and the harvest increased to 3–4 times the seed.

An agricultural revolution began to transform Flemish, Dutch, and later British agriculture from the late Middle Ages on, and particularly during the eighteenth century. In Flanders and Holland in the seventeenth century the revolutionary four-field rotation was introduced. This system did not require fallow land for soil recovery, but a rotation of different plants, including turnip and legumes that fixed nitrogen in the soil. In north Italy and the Low Countries, irrigation systems were built. Seed-drills and iron plows that turned the soil much better were already used in the early eighteenth century.

This did not happen without major social change in those societies. Revolutionary reforms replaced feudal institutions with modern ones, serf labor was supplanted by free farmers and/or mobile wage labor. The government confiscated Church land and sold it to private farmers. In some countries, such as Holland and France, an owner-entrepreneur farmer economy was created, while in other places, such as Britain, Eastern Prussia, and Austria-Bohemia, big estates turned into modern capitalist enterprises.

Both peasant farms and capitalist big estates adopted modern rotation systems in the place of the traditional three-field rotation, and they radically decreased fallow land from 33% to 3–5% of the arable area by alternating their planting of legumes, turnips, and clover with grain. Corn and potatoes from the Americas became common and produced twice as many calories per land unit as wheat. In many places, from Flanders to Ireland, potatoes replaced nearly half or even more of the wheat consumption. Scientific experimentations led to the introduction of sophisticated rotation systems such as the Norfolk rotation of 17 kinds of crops. These methods improved the soil without leaving it fallow. The cultivated land of the continent had increased by 38% between 1800 and 1910.

The new rotation system also produced fodder and helped introduce stall-feeding animal husbandry instead of grazing. Animals now survived the winter and early spring; prior to this, a great part of the stock had to be slaughtered because of a lack of grazing possibilities. Consequently, cattle and pig stocks roughly doubled in the second half of the nineteenth century. The period also saw the introduction of new, mostly science-based nineteenth-century innovations. One was animal breeding. The British breeder Robert Bakewell founded the science of animal breeding in the late eighteenth century by "breeding the best with the best." Selective line breeding and cross-breeding of livestock effected vast improvements. In 1780, the development of artificial insemination led both to an increase of animal stocks and a refinement of animal types. New breeds of cattle produced better quality and increased quantities of milk and meat. Improved pig stocks produced leaner meat (bacon and ham). At that time, plant breeding, an applied academic science, also appeared and contributed to increasing yields.

The appearance of new inventions that are emblematic of the nineteenth century—advanced tools such as cast-iron moldboard plows, and machinery such as horse-driven drills, reapers, cultivators, and grain- and grass cutters—increased labor productivity from five- to ten-fold. The milking machine became available in the 1870s, the corn-picker in 1900. Full mechanization, however, was characteristic of one agricultural activity alone: the use of steam-threshers, especially portable models that enabled its rapid adoption after the middle of the century. Still, the steam engine had only limited applicability in agriculture: besides threshing, the steam-plow was introduced in big estates for large parcels of land.

The introduction of new animal husbandry helped raise production. Stabling the animals made it possible to collect manure and use it, on average, at least every fourth year to improve soil quality. More advanced countries began importing nitrates from Chile and guano from Peru. The most revolutionary innovations, however, came from modern science-based chemical industry. The German Justus von Liebig was the founder of organic chemistry in the 1830s: his 1840 work *Chemistry in its Application to Agriculture and Physiology* became the foundation of scientific agriculture. Laboratories and factories began producing organic substances based on von Liebig's discoveries. The commercial production of phosphate took off in 1840, followed by potash, artificial nitrogen fertilizer, and ammonium sulfate. West European agriculture began using artificial fertilizers around 1880 and increased their use 5.5-fold by 1913. Pest control chemicals appeared in the first half of the nineteenth century, and they were crucial in combating vine parasites.

However, it was not until the invention of the internal combustion engine that a new wave of mechanization took hold. The revolutionary tractor contributed to an increase of productivity and output at the turn of the century, but its proliferation in Europe occurred only after World War I. Machines started replacing man- and animal power and more and more activities were mechanized. The harvester-thresher combined with a truck behind it rationalized one of the most burdensome tasks on the field.

The "industrialization" of agriculture, however, became most characteristic after World War II. During the first postwar decade the number of tractors increased four-fold in Western Europe. From the 1960s to the 1980s, almost all agricultural activities became mechanized, including sowing, hoeing, and harvesting potato, sugar beets, grapes, and fruits. Another major element of industrialization was the dramatic increase in the use of chemical agents. Although they appeared around the turn of the century, their use hardly developed in the interwar decades. In the second half of the twentieth century, the use of artificial fertilizer increased in the European Union from a few dozen kilograms, to 300–500 kilograms per hectare. A similar breakthrough characterized the use of pesticides. Plant-breeding reached its zenith in those decades, and hybridized seeds increased yields steeply. In 1968, the term "green revolution" was coined to describe the worldwide spread of basic Western inventions to revolutionize agriculture.

A series of agricultural revolutions in this complex sense emerged in Western Europe, but modern methods slowly and gradually spread to the less developed peripheral regions of the continent from the late nineteenth and throughout the twentieth centuries. Agricultural labor productivity increased by leaps and bounds, e.g., by 3–5% per annum in the post-World War II period, and altogether by 7–8 times. Two centuries ago, 60–80% of the active population in most of Europe was engaged in agriculture. At the end of the twentieth century, their share declined to 3–5%.

Until the eighteenth century, agriculture was a built-in brake on population growth. Thomas Malthus, a British clergyman and scholar at the turn of the nineteenth century, published his *Essay on the Principle of Population*. Based on the experience of previous centuries, he maintained that agriculture and food supply increase only arithmetically—1, 2, 3, 4—while the human population increases geometrically—1, 2, 4, 8, 16, 32—such that agriculture establishes a strict limit on population growth. According to the so-called Malthusian check, the shortage of food—because of faster demographic than agricultural growth—causes famine and population decline from time to time. Malthus, working in the time of the British agricultural and industrial revolutions, did not think about a revolutionary technology that would change the historic trend. When he published his work, a demographic revolution had actually started. During the nineteenth century, Europe's population increased by three times and was not checked by a lagging agriculture. Between 1700 and 2000, Europe's population increased by more than six times and agricultural output by much more. Famine never returned to Europe after the mid-nineteenth century (except for a few years during the devastating world wars). Moreover, Europe became a net food exporter.

Revolutionizing transportation with the steam engine[60]

The steam engine has a long history. The first steam pump engine, Thomas Savery's "The Miner's Friend," was invented in 1698. In 1712, Thomas Newcomen, a blacksmith, patented his fire machine. This was still a pump engine, incapable of continuous movement and extremely ineffective because of its tremendous loss of steam and huge consumption of coal. Nevertheless, his engines were used in mines for 60 years.

James Watt was the inventor of the first modern, efficient steam engine, the new power source of the industrial revolution and the basis of various applications. At the age of 18, he went to London to learn the skill of instrument-making and finished his training in one year, instead of the official seven-year apprenticeship. In 1756, at the University of Glasgow, Watt set up his shop as "Mathematical-Instrument Maker of the University." In 1763, Watt was commissioned to investigate the severe steam loss and high coal consumption of the university's Newcomen model. In two years, at the age of 29, he found the solution. He realized that the main source of energy loss was the alternate heating and cooling of the cylinder of the Newcomen engine. The cooled cylinder had to reheat again and this procedure hindered continuous operation and caused a tremendous loss of energy. His idea was to make the condensation of the steam separately in a condensing vessel that was kept cool, while the cylinder might be kept hot all the time, avoiding the cyclical cooling and reheating process. In 1769, Watt patented the separate condensing chamber. It took six months for Watt to build the model, and 11 years until a functional machine was ready. Dozens of "minor" problems had to be solved, among them the appropriate isolation of the cylinder, oil lubrication, etc. In 1775, the engine was proved. James Watt, however, continued his research. It took 15 years until the Watt engine was ready. In 1781 and 1782, Watt replaced the reciprocal engine motion with a rotating motion, and then a double-acting engine. Watt also turned out to be a good practical business-man by finding rich business partners to collaborate with. With Matthew Boulton, Watt established the Boulton & Watt Co. to produce steam engines. Eventually, this company produced all of the steam engines that were in operation in Britain before 1800. For a century, James Watt's steam engine served as the main energy source of the mechanization of industry.

This landmark invention of the British industrial revolution played an equally decisive or even more important role in revolutionizing transportation. The possibility of applying the steam engine to transportation was evident, but it required dozens of new innovations until it succeeded. It happened first through the invention of the steamship. The huge size and weight of the first steam engines and the very heavy coal consumption created an enormous deadweight to carry. That made the steamship uneconomical and not competitive with sailboats. Smaller size and weight, as well as a much more efficient fuel consumption, were the prerequisites of application. The French pioneers of the steamship created the first steamboat in 1775, sailing on the Seine.[61] In 1783, a 182-ton paddle-wheel steamer, the *Pyroscaphe*, was launched on the river Saône. The British William Symington built a horizontal double-acting cylinder paddle-wheel boat, the *Charlotte Dundas*, and the American Robert Fulton continued in these footsteps and made new progress with his *Clermont* in 1807. The engines became smaller, more adjustable to the ships, and gradually more efficient as well. James Watt continued with his experiments and new innovations, his much more efficient "trunk engine" reduced the deadweight of the engine and fuel. The technological develop-ment of steamers continually advanced between 1770 and 1820, but the real breakthrough was Robert Fulton's steamship in 1807.

New innovations continued to improve the steamships. The propulsion system was discovered in 1808.[62] In 1819, the *Savannah* was the first steam-boat to cross the Atlantic Ocean. The first commercially successful steamboat in Europe started service in 1812. In the 1830s, so-called steeple engines were used, and in 1837 the direct-acting vertical engines appeared, followed in a few years by oscillating engines. The invention of the turbine-propelled ship, and then paddle-wheeled, screw-propelled, and twin-screw-propelled ships, offered further advances.

Altogether, 40 years of experimentation led to the success of the 237-ton *Archimedes* in 1838, the first impressive screw-steamer. At the end of the century, 28,000-horsepower and bigger engines served the giant steamers and cut transportation expenses to one-fifth of the 1820 cost by 1910.[63] Until the mid-nineteenth century, the steamship was still not competitive with sailboats. Steamers represented only 15% of the capacity of sailboats. By 1880, it increased to 40%, but by 1914, 90% of shipping capacity was represented by steamers.

Pioneered by the application of the steam engine to ships, the railroad followed. This also required the solution of special problems. Here, too, French experiments are among the very first: Nicolas-Joseph Cugnot constructed a steam road carriage in 1769. However, a kind of breakthrough is connected with the name of the British mine engineer, Richard Trevithick, who built a high pressure steam engine and used it for an efficient steam road carriage, the "Puffing Devil," in 1801. He became the first person in history to use the steam engine for a railroad locomotive in 1804. Mines used rail transportation that was powered by mules or horses, and there were horse-driven railroads as well. Several minor innovations such as the Frenchman Marc Seguin's new boiler and Henri Giffard's injector, along with other experiments and innovations—especially George Stephenson's *Locomotion No. 1* in 1825 and, four years later, his most successful *Rocket*, the first modern locomotive with a direct drive between piston and driving wheels—opened the railway age.

Britain opened the world's first short railway line between Stockton and Darlington in 1825. Stephenson's first locomotive pulled 34 wagons and transported goods and passengers at a "speed" of 4 miles (6.5 kilometers) per hour. His subsequent "Rocket" carried 13 ton loads and covered 12 miles (20 kilometers) per hour. Transportation fees soon dropped from 18 to 8 shillings per ton. Between 1830 and 1850, Britain built nearly 10,000 kilometers of railroads. At the same time, continual improvements were made on the steam locomotive that guaranteed faster and safer service: innovations such as the railway switch, patented in 1832, and the Morse telegraph lines, introduced on the Paris–Rouen line in 1845.

By 1910, the total length of British railway lines was 32,182 kilometers. In 1830, 165 kilometers of railway lines were in operation in Europe. By 1870, it had increased to 104,900 kilometers, but the most exuberant railroad boom took place during the half-century prior to World War I, when the length of railroads had reached 362,700 kilometers by 1910. Western Europe attained a density of 10.14 square kilometers of land for each one-kilometer line, and 90.2 kilometers of railway line per 100,000 inhabitants. The railways transported 800,180 tons of goods per inhabitant each year; and each inhabitant, on average, traveled 22 times by rail per year.

Railroad transportation continued developing. Larger and faster locomotives were produced from the 1880s on, and then the diesel engine and the electric locomotive started their triumphant conquest before World War I. Nowadays the European railway system is renewed and the fastest French railways run at 400 and even 500 kilometers per hour.

Killing the killers: from vaccinations to antibiotics[64]

The population of Europe has increased dramatically during the past two centuries. Between 1800 and 2000, Europe's population increased by five times. The average life expectancy at birth jumped from 25 in some parts of Europe to 80 years. What were the causes of this spectacular demographic revolution? The modernization of agriculture and a similarly revolutionized increase in output and the food supply was definitely a significant factor. The first, second, and third industrial and communication revolutions, as well as the gradually but also radically improved welfare institutions, improved the standard of living. Workdays and weeks became much shorter, housing more comfortable and healthier.

Besides all of these factors, the rise of modern healthcare and the pharmaceutical industry played a central role in drastically cutting death rates and infant mortality. An endless chain of medical and scientific discoveries gradually controlled and even eliminated the mass killers of human society. The first major step on this road was the killing of the main medieval killers: smallpox, cholera, and the plague that from time to time decimated the population of the continent. Just as the demographic revolution was an all-European phenomenon, so was the invention of the miracle vaccinations and medicines. The pioneers were mostly British, French, and German scientists.

One of the very first steps was made by the British Edward Jenner, a practicing doctor in Gloucestershire. He heard talk about milkmaids who did not get the smallpox infection, and as a passionate observer he began studying the problem. In 1778, and then in 1798, smallpox returned to his township. He realized that peasant women who milked cows and got the so-called cowpox disease, a mild infection stemming from a common cow disease, developed immunity against the deadly smallpox. Jenner, like all of his contemporaries, did not know anything about microbes and viruses, but he used the secretion from the cowpox rash to inoculate people against smallpox. He called the procedure "vaccination," using the Latin word for cow (*vacca*). The experiment succeeded. The relatively harmless microbe, the cowpox virus, provoked the human body to produce antibodies and provided immunity against smallpox. Jenner published his *Inquiry into the Causes and Effects of the Variola Vaccination*, and it became a worldwide sensation.

The scientific basis for vaccination, which paved the way for the discovery of further vaccines, was revealed much later, through the work of the Frenchman Louis Pasteur. He was the first in his peasant family to go to high school, and he then studied at the Écôle Normale Supérieure in Paris and became a research chemist. He learned about Jenner's discovery and assumed that other vaccines might also be possible. His historical discovery was that micro-organisms and microbes exist in the air and cause diseases.[65] That was the birth of bacteriology. The scientific base for research was established. Pasteur became the founder of microbiology and the germ theory of diseases. He also realized that some of the small creatures kill each other and, as he noted, "life hinders life." In 1877, together with Jules François Joubert, Pasteur discovered that certain kind of molds destroyed bacilli. The door was opened and hundreds of scientists and chemists started working on the problem. "Small" discoveries paved the way for the founding of antibacterial agents.

In 1867, with public money, a laboratory was built for him that became the Pasteur Institute. He started working on vaccinations. In 1880, as often happens, an accidental discovery—using 14-day-old, and thus weakened germs, in an experiment—illuminated the fact that weakened microbes and viruses are the best sources to provoke the body to produce antibodies and provide immunity. In 1881, with weakened anthrax germs, he produced a vaccine against anthrax, the widespread animal disease. Five years later, he discovered the vaccine against rabies, and, without human experiment, in an emergency case, he used it on a young boy who had been bitten by an infected dog. It worked.

As Pasteur gained the initiative from Jenner, he inspired several other scholars. Among them was the British Joseph Lister, a practicing surgeon. He experienced the dramatic 50% death rate of patients operated on in hospitals. Pasteur's discoveries, including the existence of microbes in the air, led Lister to discover the cause of sepsis. He sprayed carbolic acid into the wound and used carbolic acid dressing on the operated part of the body after operation, and sepsis disappeared. Lister also experimented with molds, and in 1891 he discovered that penicillium luteum eliminated other molds.

In the late nineteenth century, the antibiotic effect of fungi was already reported. The Frenchman Ernest Duchesne realized that penicillium glaucum fungus killed E. coli bacteria in 1897. L. Rosenthal's research led to the recognition that bacillus subtilis killed colonies of pneumococcus bacteria that cause pneumonia. Antibiotic science was gradually born. All these discoveries, nevertheless, did not lead to a breakthrough, but their publications influenced new generations of researchers.

Another follower of Pasteur, the German medical doctor Robert Koch, started studying the causes of diseases, and in 1882 he established the methodology for further research and experiment. He also discovered the germs that caused two of the main killers of the age, tuberculosis and cholera. By 1900, as the fruit of 21 years of research, 21 disease-causing germs were identified. Koch also discovered that certain tar-based aniline dyes—the main discovery of organic chemistry and the superb German chemical industry—which he used to color bacteria for better visibility in research, also kill bacteria. However, it required painful, meticulous research to discover which types of dyes are good and not poisonous for people. A younger German co-researcher, Paul Ehrlich, who started working in Koch's institute, continued the work in his own institute, and discovered the causes of and vaccinations for diphtheria, malaria, and syphilis, a sexually transmitted mass killer of the age. In 1911, his arsenic-based drug, commercially called Salvarsan, was used successfully for the first time.

During the first half of the twentieth century, a huge further jump in science led to the discovery of several miracle drugs to kill mass killer bacteria. One of the most important lines of research continued analyzing the hidden properties of dyes. The German Gerhard Domagk, in the Bayer Dye Work, became the most successful researcher to produce various sulphonamides, synthetic anti-microbial agents. In 1933, he patented the first medicine synthesized from red dye, named Prontosil, which was effective against streptococci. He "produced important chemo-therapeutic substances one after another and potent drugs in the fight against bacterial infections."[66] The sulfa drugs were synthetic chemical substances, effective against certain bacterial diseases that served very well in World War II against wound infections, but did not work against all kinds of bacteria.

Another line of research, finding effective fungi against bacilli, became even more successful. The breakthrough occurred in the 1920s. A Scottish researcher, Alexander Fleming, working in St. Mary's Hospital in London, made extensive experiments to find antibacterial agents. His first success was the discovery of what he called the lysozyme, an enzyme existing in the white blood cells (and in human tears, and the white of the eggs) that destroyed less virulent bacteria. He made endless experiments with fungi and various kinds of dangerous bacteria such as coli, staphylococci, streptococci, gonococci, diphtheria, and influenza bacilli. The real watershed discovery in medical history happened six years later in his laboratory. An accident helped him: having returned from a month-long vacation, he found a culture plate on which staphylococcus had remained uncovered, and a blue-green mold—penicillium notatum, as identified by Charles Thon—had developed in it. Fleming realized that the mold released a substance that repressed the growth of the bacteria. He published this result in the *Biochemical Journal* in 1932 with the title: "Penicillin, the Antibacterial Substance of Fleming," but did not continue the work for years.

However, he met with the Australian Howard Florey at a medical meeting, and they talked about Fleming's discovery. More importantly, Florey had an excellently equipped laboratory at Oxford University with 20 researchers and technical assistants. Among them, a refugee from Hitler's Germany, Dr. Ernst B. Chain, who read Fleming's article, ordered penicillin notatum culture from Fleming's laboratory and started his experiments. It took several years and the painstaking work of the entire Oxford laboratory until penicillin was ready for use in August 1943. It was a miracle drug: "it destroyed no less than eighty-nine different pathogenic bacteria, and in addition there were sixteen others which were favourably influenced by it to some degree."[67] The new medicine was successfully tried with mice, but in an urgent case, was first used on a London policeman, and two other patients. Mass production was still unsolved. In 1945, Dorothy Crowfoot Hodgkin determined the chemical structure of penicillin and mass production became possible. In 1945, Fleming, Florey, and Chain were awarded the Nobel Prize in Medicine. Fleming already forecast that microbes would adjust and became resistant after a while. That really happened, but the research has produced several different types of antibiotics in an endless struggle against sicknesses.

The creation of synthetic dyes[68]

Like several major inventions, the breakthrough of modern chemistry and the chemical industry was also a product of international cooperation. The story starts in France and Germany. The first name to mention is definitely Justus von Liebig, the father of organic chemistry. He started his studies at the University of Berlin and continued in Erlangen. At the age of 19, he continued his studies in Paris under the towering French scientist, Joseph-Louis Gay-Lussac. In two years, he was appointed professor at the University of Giessen, and, based on his experience in France, he was the first to establish a university laboratory. In 1852, he moved to the University of Munich and became the founder of the first major school of chemistry.

One of his students, August Wilhelm von Hofmann, a native of Giessen, studied under Liebig at Göttingen and then at the University of Giessen. He was a privatdozent at the University of Bonn when he received an invitation in 1845 from Prince Albert, husband of Queen Victoria of Britain, to teach at the Royal College of Chemistry in London. Hofmann was already conducting research on coal-tar in Liebig's laboratory. He never stopped research in that area, analyzing the nature of aniline and introducing molecular models and color schemes into his teaching. During his stay in England, the 15-year-old William Henry Perkin became one of his students. Perkin, the son of a carpenter-builder, enrolled in the City of London School where Thomas Hall, an enthusiastic teacher, conducted laboratory experiments during lunch breaks. The young Perkin fell in love with laboratory work, and he enrolled in the Royal College of Science. Here he met Hofmann who impressed him tremendously. The passionate young student built his own laboratory at his parents' home and made such progress that Hofmann made the then 17-year-old student his assistant.

Theoretical chemists in the first half of the century studied substances found in living organisms and soon recognized that the overwhelming majority of those substances are compounds of carbon. "Carbon is unique in the facility with which its atoms will join together to form chains and rings ... the compounds of carbon are numbered in millions."[69] Liebig and Hofmann were convinced that coal-tar had a huge potential to produce various chemical products. The Frenchman Antoine Béchamp, another genius scientist, had already discovered in 1853 how to produce nitrobenzene from coal-tar and convert it to aniline. In 1859, he also synthesized atoxyl, another product from aniline that later became the base for Salvarsan.

The second generation of chemists strongly focused on that area. Perkin was among the very first of them. During Easter vacation in 1856, he tried to follow Hofmann's instruction and synthesize quinine at his home laboratory. His point of departure was coal-tar. This material, mass produced by the rising gas industry, was a waste product, but now became the point of departure for chemists. After several distillations, benzene, toluene, naphthalene, and anthracene were produced. Perkin's experiment failed and instead of white powder, a black jumble was the result. Perkin, however, was not discouraged and continued analyzing the product, and he accidentally produced an aniline purple stuff, later called mauveine. He recognized the importance of the new product, actually the world's first artificial dye, and sent it to the silk factory of Perth to try coloring silk with it.[70] The experiment succeeded and the factory was able to produce different shades of purple.

The 18-year-old Perkin turned out to be not only a scientific but an entrepreneurial genius as well. With the financial assistance of his family, he founded a factory in Middlesex and started producing his patented artificial dyes in 1857. The world's first coal-tar-based chemical factory was established. During the 17 years his factory was in operation,[71] he also solved the major problem of how to produce and industrially use alizarin, another coal-tar (via anthracene) product, a red synthetic dye that was first produced in 1868 in the laboratory of two German scholars, Carl Gräbe and Carl T. Liebermann. The very expensive method, however, blocked the road for the industrial use of alizarin. Perkin solved the problem by a new method—using bromine—and patented it in 1869. This led to cheap, industrially useful synthetic dyes.

Until the mid-nineteenth century, only natural dyestuffs were used, produced from various plants and vegetables. Several of them were imported from India and other parts of the world. When the scientific foundation was prepared by Liebig, Béchamp, Hofmann and others, and when Perkin discovered the first artificial dyes and started their industrial mass production, the road was opened for the production of cheap artificial dyes, and the modern chemical industry emerged. If the first steps were the achievement of German, French, and British cooperation, the next ones were mostly made in Germany. The superior German higher education and specialized technical-technological training produced dozens of outstanding talents and hundreds and thousands of superb technicians and skilled workers who established the world's leading chemical industry that was number one in synthetic dyes. Among several pioneers, two men towered as central figures in the rise of the German chemical industry: Johann Friedrich Wilhelm Adolf von Bäyer and Heinrich Caro.

Bäyer studied mathematics and physics in Berlin and then in Heidelberg, received his PhD in 1858, and in 1871 became professor at the Université de Strasbourg, and he later succeeded Liebig in the Chair at the University of Munich. At his university laboratory, Bäyer produced breakthrough results in chemistry. He discovered the phthalein dyes and barbituric acid, the parent compound of barbiturates in 1864, and most of all, synthetic indigo in 1867. In 1871, he produced synthetic phenolphthalein. Bäyer received the Nobel Prize in 1905, and his discoveries strongly assisted the rise of the dyes and pharmaceutical industries.

Among many others, the Badische Anilin- und Soda-Fabrik (BASF) AG, established in 1865 by Friedrich Engelhorn for the production of dyes, became a leading producer of synthetic dyes, including Bäyer's indigo blue. Another major German chemist, Heinrich Caro, played a central role in the rise of BASF. Caro studied in Berlin at the Friedrich Wilhelms Universität, and then continued for two years in England. His first job was at Robert, Dale & Co. in Manchester. In 1866, however, he returned to Germany and became the director of the laboratory at BASF. He initiated alizarin production, realized synthetic indigo production in 1878, and he himself discovered several synthetic dyes, among them the methylene blue and naphthol yellow. The modern chemical industry, and almost the entire German one, produced various kinds of cheap artificial dyes, acidic, azoic or naphtal, chrome or mordant, disperse or acetate, fiber-reactive and others. "By 1900 the center of activity had been decisively transferred to Germany. The number of patents relating to dyes [in a five-year period] filed in Britain … was 52 … the figure for Germany was 427."[72] Altogether about 10,000 synthetic dyes were discovered and produced, most of them from coal-tar.

Heinrich Caro, a major figure of the German chemical industry, contributed to the elevation of BASF. Since artificial dyes, artificial fertilizer (sulfuric and nitric acid and caustic soda), and explosives all belonged to the same family of chemical products, BASF, beside dye production, also introduced artificial fertilizer manufacture in its newly opened Oppan factory in 1913, and in 1916, started producing explosives for the army. Together with five other major chemical companies, BASF founded I.G. Farben, a giant chemical company that played a criminal role during Nazi times and consequently was dissolved by the Allies in 1945.

Nevertheless, the re-established BASF continued, becoming the largest chemical company in the world. During the 1960s, BASF established production in Argentina, Australia, Brazil, India, Japan, Mexico, and the United States as well as in several European countries. In the end, it owned subsidiaries and participated in joint-ventures in 80 countries with 360 production sites in three continents. By 2009, the company employed 104,000 people, about half of them in Germany.

Electrical power and its applications[73]

One of the most important landmark inventions of the second industrial revolution, which transformed the industrial landscape and people's lives, and eventually established the twentieth century's revolutionary technology, was the generation of electrical power. This enabled the widespread use of electricity in transportation, metallurgy, chemical, and other industries. It made possible the mechanization of areas, such as households and offices, that was impossible before, and also the illumination of homes and cities. This fundamental scientific discovery had a centuries-long history, including William Gilbert's *De Magnete*, probably the very first description of magnetism in the age of Queen Elisabeth I. The "Elektrisiermaschine" of Otto von Guericke, the Mayor of Magdeburg and a scientist, produced a continuous supply of electricity in 1660. In the early eighteenth century, Stephen Gray discovered the difference between materials that conduct electricity and others that were non-conductors.

The early nineteenth century was a period of scientific breakthroughs. The chemical battery of Count Alessandro Volta, the Italian physicist (1800), the electric circuit of the German high school teacher Georg Simon Ohm (1827), and most of all the electromagnetic induction of the English chemist-physicist Michael Faraday (1831), gradually laid the scientific groundwork. Faraday's discovery of the interaction between electrical and magnetic fields that can produce mechanical motion became the starting principle of the first electrical engine, and the point of departure for converting mechanical into electric power. The French instrument-maker Hippolyte Pixii exhibited his first mechanical generator in Paris a year later. Dozens of "minor" innovations such as those of the British Humphry Davy, the Danish Hans Christian Ørsted, the French R.L.G. Planté, Émile A. Faure, and Georges Leclanché, the German Siemens brothers, the Hungarian Ányos Jedlik, the Americans George Westinghouse and Thomas Alva Edison, and many others contributed to the practical implication of electricity. The *Annals of Electricity*, the first journal in that field, was published in Britain in 1836.

A completely new power source, electric power, became available and had started closing the age of the steam engine. Electric power was clean and could be used much more flexibly. However, at first there was no solution to the problem of transporting electricity even over short distances. The power of transported electricity invariably dissipated. Discovering how to transform low voltage into high voltage and back again was the achievement of several inventors, three engineers of the Hungarian Ganz factory, the Serbian-American Nikola Tesla, and the German Siemens brothers. In doing so, they made the transportation of electricity possible from the 1880s on. Transformers were the key to such transport, as well as to electricity's unlimited application on any scale by reducing voltage for low-voltage circuits.

The construction of hydroelectric power stations began in Europe in 1881, when the Siemens Brothers built the Godalming power station in Britain. In 1889, the British electrical engineer Sebastian Ziani de Ferranti, who himself patented 176 inventions, built power stations that became the prototype for modern electric power stations. The world's first hydroelectric power station was built at Niagara Falls in 1881. Countries lacking sufficient coal resources, such as Italy, Norway, Sweden, and Switzerland, rushed to tap their abundant water power resources by building power stations. The Swiss Brown Boveri Company, founded in 1891 in Baden, became Europe's leading turbine producer for electric power generation and erected efficient electric transformation networks throughout Europe.

The window of opportunity for industrial use of electricity was opened. Applications were numerous, including—to mention only a few of the first— the telegraph and telephone systems and the various kinds of electric engines, especially after Nikola Tesla produced the first alternating-current motor in 1888, manufactured by Westinghouse. In 1879, the Siemens brothers exhibited the first electric locomotive in Berlin, and the first electric tram began operation in that city in 1884. The London electric tram network expanded to

3,533 kilometers of track by 1906, and the Paris network was 2,000 kilometers long by 1912. The Paris electric metro network opened in 1900, and the inner circle of the London subway was electrified in 1905.

The refrigerator, electric iron, and vacuum cleaner signaled the beginning of the mechanization of households, and electric lighting emerged onto its triumphant path. First came the so-called arc-lamp, the first form of electric illumination, especially after the Russian-French Paul Jablochkoff's improved version, and then the incandescent-filament light bulbs that were invented and then improved upon from the 1840s and 1880s, mostly by Joseph Swan and Thomas Alva Edison. The two competitors at last established the Edison & Swan United Electric Light Company in 1883. Several micro-inventions improved the bulb and made it better and more affordable. By 1903, nearly all of the cities in Britain with more than 100,000 inhabitants already had an electric energy supply, though only 6–7% of the urban population used electric lighting. In 1906, 3,000 communities got electric energy in France.

Shockingly enough, the late-nineteenth- and early-twentieth-century story of electricity turned out to be only the very beginning of the twentieth-century triumph of electricity, established by the invention of the transistor and the chip after World War II, the rise of electronics, and the computer and cellphone revolution. This century-long story is not ended yet.

From the macadam road to the autobahn[74]

Road construction is almost as old as human history. Already in ancient times, durable stone-paved roads were constructed that are visible even today in Rome—the Via Appia Antica—and in Pompeii and Herculaneum. In Britain, the old Roman roads were used as a solid rock base for modern road construction. As a country with an advanced economy, Britain launched an extensive road construction program in 1705, when Parliament enacted a law to establish trusts and build a toll-road system, the turnpike roads. Wide-ranging construction took place over the next three decades, with a yearly investment of £1.5 million. In 1770, 24,000 kilometers of turnpike roads connected cities in England and Wales, and 35,000 kilometers by 1835. By the early twentieth century, 370,000 kilometers of first class roads were already in operation.

There were 42 regular coach service routes in existence by 1797. It took 43 hours to go from London to Edinburgh. Regular stagecoach service began as early as 1640, and mail-coaches ran between London and Bristol beginning in 1784. In the early nineteenth century, regular carriage connections were established on surfaced roads between London and Manchester. In contrast to the British private toll road system, France established a central civilian authority, the *Corps des Ponts et Chaussées*, in 1716. It opened a special school for the training of road and bridge engineers in 1747, and they built 130 cable bridges in the 1830s and 1840s. In the first years of the nineteenth century, more than 500 engineers oversaw the road-works. In 1841, nearly 700 engineers, 3,000 foremen, and 15,000 permanent workforces built, improved, and maintained the national road system. At that time, France could boast the largest road network in Europe: the 33,000-kilometer long *routes royales*, completed in 1824. Local and regional roads spanned similar distances and made the network markedly denser. Traveling now became a great deal faster: a trip from Paris to Lyon, which took 4–5 days in 1816, took only two days in 1848.

New road construction technologies began to be introduced in the late eighteenth century. The French engineer Pierre Trésaguet built modern roads on large stone sub-bases, covered by a layer of gravel and a smooth surface, and framed by deep side ditches for drainage. The British Thomas Telford and John McAdam emulated his technique and developed road construction further. Strong and long-lasting roads were created on a base of large stones and crushed stone bound with gravel, covered by cobblestones, and built in a slightly convex shape for rapid drainage of the road surface.

By the end of the nineteenth century, most European roads used the macadam technology. Until the 1830s, however, only France and the Netherlands had a real road network on the continent, followed by the German Rhine region. In time, a similar network was introduced throughout Europe. Roads connected Berlin and Breslau, Vienna and Prague. In the latter case, the coach trip took 28 hours in 1807. Emperor Joseph II initiated an impressive con-struction program in the Habsburg Empire that was realized after his death in the 1790s, and linked Vienna via the Semmering Pass to the Adriatic ports. By 1818, in the Bohemian province alone, a 1,755-kilometer road network assured faster transportation. Regular express carriages operated between Vienna and Prague, and between Vienna and Trieste. By 1885, a network encompassing more than 61,000 kilometers of roads served North Italy, i.e. nearly 5 kilometers per 1,000 inhabitants.[75] "In general, the road system was most satisfactory where industrialization had proceeded fastest; the road map of Europe corresponded to that of the industrial revolution."[76] In the latter part of the century, the northern countries adopted the British organi-zational system of road construction, while most of the others followed the centralized French pattern. In the Netherlands, an institution, founded in 1894, oversaw the maintenance of the 2,300 kilometers of primary roads and the nearly 30,000 kilometers of secondary and tertiary roads.

Road construction often required extensive tunnel-building. One of the modern forerunners of European tunnel construction was the Bridgewater Canal Tunnel, built in Manchester in 1761. From the mid-nineteenth century on, major Alpine tunnels, among them the St. Gotthard and Simplon tunnels, were constructed. The Mont Cenis Tunnel (1857–71) was 13.6 kilometers long, and the Simplon Tunnel (1898–1906) 20 kilometers.

By the early twentieth century, a vast road network of 1.6 million kilometers existed in Europe, which effectively connected local communities to water and rail transport. In the early twentieth century, the Permanent International Association of Road Congress was established in Paris; by 1913, 50 nations had become members in an effort to standardize road construction and maintenance systems. However, road transportation began to lose its importance when the railroads took over. From the 1860s on, roads supplied mostly short-distance transportation and transportation to the railroads and ports.

Although the macadam technology predominated until the turn of the twentieth century, the need for smooth surface roads became important because of the appearance of the bicycle and, more importantly, the car. In 1820, Britain already constructed roads combining the macadam technology with the use of hot tar to bind and flatten the surface. Asphalt-paved roads appeared in the 1870s, and the "tarmacadam" technology was patented in 1910. At that time refined petroleum asphalt was already available, instead of the natural asphalt that did not exist in Europe and was an expensive import item. That made its use widespread. The stone-gravel base was covered by an asphalt-mix surface and steam-rolled. Almost in parallel from the 1890s on, a new road construction technology started using a concrete foundation, covered by sheet asphalt pavement, or rigid concrete roads without asphalt cover.

As in many other areas, World War I, the first mechanized war in history, offered some lessons for road construction as well. Belligerent countries recognized the importance of fast troop movements that was first assisted by trains and trucks. From the early twentieth century, the car symbolized modernity, speed, a new lifestyle, and the future. Although car density was still very low, it was easy to envision a new age with hectic automobile traffic. The idea of expressways was born, nurtured certainly by several people in various countries. These roads would avoid cities and settlements and have two lanes of divided traffic in both directions, roads without sharp curves and crossings, and would be accessible by special entrance and exit lanes. This was probably the idea of some military personnel, but also of civilian visionaries.

The first attempt to realize this vision goes back to 1909, when a private company, the *Automobil-Verkehrs- und Übungsstraße*, was established to build a 10-kilometer-long autobahn between Charlottenburg and Wannsee in Berlin. Although this road was completed only after the war, it is still considered to be the earliest example of expressway construction. During the 1920s, various visions emerged about future expressways in Europe. Albert Thomas, the head of the International Labor Organization in Geneva—a branch of the League of Nations—was asked to be the main speaker at the first International Congress on Expressways at the end of the summer of 1931. He proposed the construction of expressways to create jobs. The Technical Commission, headed by the most active proponent of expressway creation, the Italian Pietro Puricelli, suggested the building of a 14,000-kilometer-long European network. The following year, when the second International Congress held its session in Milan, the participants were able to make an excursion to see the world's first expressway in northern Italy.

Italy, indeed, became the pioneer of highway construction. Puricelli, a Milan-based building contractor, had not only the vision to build expressways, but he was able to fund the realization of his ideas by mobilizing private money, and, after the takeover of the fascist regime, he presented his plan to

Mussolini in October 1922. The dictator enthusiastically supported it. "The development of Italy's Southern Alps chain for motorized traffic expressly incorporated defense-enhancing features. This effort was born out of World War I experiences and explains the backing that this project received in Italy."[77] The Italian project was not a plan for a road network, but for single, unconnected expressways. The construction of the first one between Milan and the Lake area started in 1923. Between that year and 1933, express roads were built between Milan and Bergamo, Bergamo and Brescia, Milan and Turin, Naples and Pompeii, and Florence and Viareggio. Altogether, in the decade after 1923, about 400 kilometers of expressway were put into operation in north Italy. The first Italian autostrada, although junction-free, was not yet built according to later norms. They were three-lane roads without a middle divide. The central lane served as a passing lane for cars in both directions.

Germany in the 1920s also became the cradle of the idea of expressways or, as it was called, autobahn construction. Several initiatives were discussed on various local levels. The Leipzig–Halle road with links to Heidelberg and Mannheim, the Düsseldorf–Cologne–Bonn road, and the Berlin–Leipzig–Munich expressway were not only discussed, but associations were founded for their realization. In the town hall of Frankfurt am Main, the Association for the Preparation of the Autobahn of Hanseatic Cities–Frankfurt-Basel was founded in November 1926. On the board of the Association, Puricelli represented the connection with the Italian enterprise. Although the original idea was the construction of a north–south expressway from Hamburg to Basel, the association presented a plan for an autobahn network for the entire country in 1927. In its altered version of 1931, the association recommended a norm of two-lane road for both directions, with a width of 20.5 meters and a separating strip of 3.5 meters.

From the various plans, at last, the 20-kilometer long Cologne–Bonn autobahn was opened on August 1932. The Mayor of Cologne, Konrad Adenauer, stated at the opening ceremony: "That is what the roads of the future will look like."[78] This happened a few months before the Nazi takeover in Germany. The country was hit by the Great Depression, industrial output declined by 40%, and 6 million people became unemployed. The deep crisis helped Hitler win the elections. Somewhat before that, in December 1932, the Nazi engineer, Fritz Todt, presented a plan in his memorandum to Hitler, the *Braunen Denkschrift*, with the recommendation to create a German autobahn network.

Hitler immediately recognized the importance of the autobahn project as a major job creation program to realize his political promises to elevate Germany out of the crisis. After the *Machtergreifung*, taking over the government in January 1933, one of his very first steps was the foundation of the *Gesellschaft Reichsautobahnen* in the summer of 1933 to prepare and start construction work under the direction of Todt. This idea was immediately combined with Hitler's other pet project, the motorization of the German masses, announced at the Berlin Auto Show three months after having been appointed Chancellor of Germany. Ferdinand Porsche, an Austrian-German engineering genius, made his first design for a cheap people's car in 1931. That car later became the "Beetle." After the Nazi takeover, Porsche realized the unique possibility and within a few weeks, Hitler, indeed, received him. That was the birth of the Volkswagen program that was put in motion by state investments in 1936 by building the new factory that started producing cars at the turn of 1938–39 with 3,000 workers. The two smartly combined projects, the motorization plan by producing cheap cars (Volkswagen) and the construction of autobahns, established Hitler's great popularity and political success in Germany.

They did not lose time. In the spring of 1934, autobahn construction began simultaneously at 15 locations with 15,000 workers. The first 22-kilometer-long stretch between Frankfurt and Darmstadt was opened in May 1935, followed by the Munich–Holzkirchen and the Darmstadt–Heidelberg sections. Every small section opening was connected with major festivities, Hitler was celebrated as the "Father of the Autobahn," statues were erected, and by the fall of 1936, 1,000 kilometers of autobahn were completed. By the end of 1941, a 4,000-kilometer-long autobahn network was in operation with 9,000 bridges. The very first expressway network in the world was created. That served as a model for President Eisenhower when the Federal Aid Highway Act was enacted in 1956, and the construction of the vast American freeway network system began. Europe also followed. In 1970, more than half of the European freeways were still in Germany and Italy, but the Declaration on the Construction of Main International Traffic Arteries, signed in Geneva in 1950, called for the construction of an internationally connected European highway system of 75,000 kilometers. By 1975, a 22,000-kilometer-long freeway network connected 17 West European countries; a decade later the length of the network had increased to 37,000 kilometers. From the 1990s on, countries without significant freeways, such as Finland, Ireland, Greece and Portugal, started extensive construction and their freeway systems increased by 6% per year. In 1996, the European Union issued guidelines for the development of a trans-European freeway system, and the connection of the former Soviet Bloc countries gained a major incentive. By 2005, the European freeway network totaled 89,000 kilometers. Germany has the world's third largest system, while Switzerland has the highest freeway density.[79] Like railways in the nineteenth century, freeways with car traffic became the symbol and vehicle of modernization in the twentieth and early twenty-first centuries.

The birth of the movie[80]

In the twentieth century, going to the movies and watching films became an important form of entertainment. Nowadays, people watch movies at home, sometimes several of them a day, often in their bedroom on a TV screen, through movie channels, or via house-delivered discs. Movies have become an integral part of everyday life. The movie industry is one of the world's biggest industries. In 2012, the highest American film prize, the Academy Award or Oscar, was given to a newly made silent movie, recollecting the memory of the 1920s.

Like many other integral parts of everyday life in the early twenty-first century, the basic inventions of film are rooted in the nineteenth century, the greatest period of discontinuity in human history. Various histories of technology go back centuries searching for the origins of film in Ptolemy's second book on optics in 130 CE and in Arab writers on optics at the end of the first millennium. On the way towards the movie, the seventeenth-century *camera obscura* and the recognition of sunlight's effect on silver salts also played a role. In the early nineteenth-century, the "Thaumatrope" of the British J.A. Paris, and then the "wheel of life" demonstrate film's true origins. These were the first instruments to give the illusion of movement through a progressive series of drawings.

The real turning point that led to the movie, however, was the beginning of photography in the work of the French physicist Joseph Nicéphore Niépce, who made the world's first photograph in the 1820s with an eight-hour exposure. Nearly two decades later, the Frenchman Louis J.M. Daguerre developed the daguerreotype photography process, which he presented at the French Academy of Sciences in 1839. It still took about 15 minutes of sitting motionless in sunshine to take a portrait photo. That was the starting point, followed by hundreds of innovations that improved the technology of photography. Among many others, the key advances included the replacement of the silvered copper plate used by Daguerre, and then the replacement of the later glass plate, after various steps, by rolls of film, and also a significant reduction in the size of the camera.

The genuine incentive to photograph movement led to several experiments. Among the first was when the French astronomer Pierre J.C. Janssen, using a revolving photographic plate, a clock mechanism that rotated the plate, and his telescope, made photos of the movement of the Venus around the sun, which he recorded in a series of 48 pictures in 1874. Two years before, Eadweard Muybridge used 24 cameras and a complicated exposure system to make a series of photos of a galloping horse. Ten years later, the Frenchman Étienne-Jules Marey constructed his chronophotographic gun that was able to make 24 photos on a rotating glass plate in one second with an exposure of 1/720 of a second. Several photos made in very rapid progression series tried to capture movement. His 1888 demonstration at the French Academy of Sciences already exhibited the basic principles of modern cinema photography.

Nevertheless, a further series of numberless innovations improved the process. Among them was William Friese-Greene's patent of his "chronophotographic" camera that was able to make ten photos in a second on prepared (perforated at the sides) celluloid film. The forerunner of a movie theater, the Kinetoscope Parlor, based on Thomas Alva Edison's invention, was opened on Broadway in New York in 1894, where the audience, sitting one by one in a wooden box, could see 46 pictures a second through a peephole. However, Edison's camera weighed nearly one ton. One of Edison's collaborators, William K.L. Dickson, introduced the 35-millimeter celluloid film that became the norm.

In 1895, real movies were at last born: the French brothers, Louis and Auguste Lumière, who were photographic manufacturers in Lyons, created the modern cinema-camera that made 16 pictures a second. They opened the world's first real public cinema in a Paris café, visited by 2,000 people per evening. The first movies were very short and mostly presented movement, such as *Arrival of a Train*. The last decade of the nineteenth century was the time of several further practical innovations. Georges Méliès built the first full-glass film studio, founded Star Films, and produced a combination of entertainment and art. One of the Lumières' cameramen made films from a moving train, replacing the fixed camera in 1896, and the next year the first rotating camera was invented in London. Hand-colored films were already being made, and the basic inventions behind the sound film, which appeared decades later, became available around this same time and awaited application: namely, Emile Berliner's disc-recording gramophone and the Dane Valdemar Poulsen's magnetic sound recordings.

Between 1895 and 1906, the first decade that the technology was available, a large entertainment industry already emerged. Charles Pathé ran the largest film company, movie theaters opened throughout Europe, and silent films were screened, accompanied by live music. The 1920s were characterized by several experiments with sound film, but dozens of new innovations were needed before the first fully sound feature film, *The Jazz Singer*, was screened in 1927. However, the real appearance and spread of sound film that elevated Hollywood to a world-leading position took place only in the 1930s. The endless history of moving pictures, the post-World War II French, Italian, Swedish, Hungarian, and other art movies, and the supremely influential Hollywood film industry, the greatest entertainment industry ever, continued and further continues on its way.

Women in work and on the labor market[81]

Women have always worked, and often more than men. During the time of the gradual rise of the capitalist market economy in the seventeenth and eighteenth centuries, most women had a triple work burden. First, during their reproductive years, they gave birth—to 8–18 offspring on average. They took care of the children who survived, while also running the household, doing tasks such as washing laundry, cooking, baking bread, preserving fruits and vegetables for the winter months, and sewing clothing for the whole family. They also took care of the animals around the homestead and milked the cows, goats, or sheep. They worked on these household and child-rearing tasks from early morning to dusk. But, since agriculture was the main source of family income, women also worked in the fields from spring through fall, helping their husbands with sowing, cultivating, weeding, and harvesting. They had the additional task of caring for the small kitchen gardens that supplied their families with produce. This labor of women, joined together with that of husbands and sons, made peasant families almost wholly self-sufficient. However, to supplement their income and provide a kind of insurance against crop failures or other disasters, peasants, and especially women, additionally participated in what came to be known as cottage industry—the application of their skills to the production of goods for local markets.

The emergence of cottage industries is a particularly significant example of the changes in the "structure and behavior" of households in the seventeenth and eighteenth centuries that transformed supply and demand in what Jan de Vries has called "the industrious revolution."[82] The increasingly affluent upper and middle classes, as well as the upwardly mobile peasant families of Western Europe created increasing demand. The effects can be seen in probate inventories, for example, where the value of wardrobes rose between 1700 and 1789, even in poor households, to represent 8–16% of the total. Expenditures for clothing, including those of wage-earning families, more than doubled. European watch production jumped from a few thousand to 400,000 in just one year in the late seventeenth century, with 38% of inventories being sold to poorer families. Expensive furniture, tapestries, and tiles adorned ever greater numbers of homes in the Netherlands in the 1660s. Towards the end of the eighteenth century, Dutch consumption was two- to four-times greater than the European average, and British consumption several times more than that. Consumption of colonial luxuries, such as coffee, tea, sugar, cocoa, and distilled spirits spread but did not surpass that of the various consumer goods produced domestically in peasant homes. To boost their own incomes so that they too could buy "luxuries," peasant households increased labor input by having women and children work in household industrial activities. The success of this proto-industrializing activity, of this industrialization before the industrial revolution, was, therefore, strongly reliant on female work.[83]

Merchants began playing a role rather early in the organization of cottage industries. They began by buying up cottage industrial production and selling the goods on markets, sometimes even on foreign markets. They inserted themselves further into the organization of cottage industries when they began also to supply raw materials to the peasant households whose products they were also selling on the markets. This putting out system, a hallmark of the seventeenth- and eighteenth-century era of proto-industrialization, became extremely widespread, especially in areas with poor soils unable to sustain agriculture, or in regions with ready access to ports and rivers. The famous textile and silk industries of the seventeenth and eighteenth centuries, the former in Alsace, the latter in Lyon, and the textile-producing complex in Languedoc, the largest in pre-industrial Europe, all arose within this system. Industry in Carcassonne and Clermont-de-Lodève, the principal towns of the Languedoc production area, enjoyed great prosperity until 1750. The total labor force of Clermont-de-Lodève in 1732 was 5,649. Figures for 1754 show that cottage industrial workers in 56 villages and towns were doing the carding, spinning, and weaving that supplied this urban center with raw materials for its textile industry. In Carcassonne, the number of villages involved in the cottage industry was 81.

In eighteenth-century Central European regions, similar patterns can be seen. Export-oriented rural textile and iron industries flourished in the German towns of Krefeld, Elberfeld, Barmen, Zwickau, and in the Aachen-Stollberger region. In 1800, approximately 900,000 cottage workers held contracts in the putting out system in German states. In mountainous Switzerland, a strong cottage industry still contributed significantly to the economy in the nineteenth century. Lace-making, the production of linen and cotton fabrics, calico-printing, and watch-making comprised the leading industrial sectors. Linen production in the Schaffhausen and St. Gallen areas, as well as lace-making in Neuchâtel, thrived in the eighteenth and early nineteenth centuries, with some merchant-industrialist families employing 500–600 cottage workers. The trademark export-oriented watch-making industry was organized as a putting-out cottage industry until the last third of the nineteenth century. Watches had been produced by means of this system in Geneva since 1550 and in Neuchâtel since 1680. The roughly 100 different small parts comprising the mechanical watch were produced by peasants working at home, with final assembly occurring in a merchant-industrialist's factory. The first modern watch factory was established in Geneva only in 1840.

Proto-industry, based on the peasant household and especially on female labor, remained dominant in less developed peripheral countries—among them Bulgaria and Russia—until the later part of the nineteenth century. In the West, however, the British industrial revolution began to undermine and destroy most cottage industries much earlier. As a consequence, women started seeking employment outside the household. Female employment in rapidly industrializing Britain became dominant in textiles, the leading industry. Between 1850 and 1870, the portion of women employed outside the home reached 40% and comprised some 30% of the British workforce. By 1880, women made up 34% of that force. In non-agricultural employment, the comparable figure was 40% in Norway and 50% in Denmark, but only 18% in Germany and Sweden. In France, women comprised 40% of the workforce in the middle of the nineteenth century. By 1910, female employment in Western Europe generally stood at about 30% of the labor force. This figure, actually a slight decline from the earlier period, was caused by the spread of a new social norm and model, that of the family in which the male head-of-household functioned as the sole breadwinner. Women nevertheless played important roles in rising twentieth-century industries, but they were not the equals of their male co-workers: for example, women sometimes earned only 50% of the salary of males holding the same kind of job.

The nineteenth century, therefore, became a turning point in the history of female work, with the traditional pattern of women working in two or three different kinds of occupation giving way to modern structures.[84] It was not a rapid and complete change, however, but a gradual one with strong elements from the previous centuries persisting alongside the major innovations of the new age. During this century, a great percentage of working middle-class women would become self-employed in retailing, turning that sector into a strongly "female realm" that gave "recognized social status" to women. In Sweden, one-quarter of urban retailing was controlled by women. In Belgium in 1900, nearly 36% of merchants in retailing were women, and this share increased to more than 42% by 1930.[85] In Vienna before World War I, 62% of food and beverage retailers were women. Their shares in the grocery and restaurant businesses were 36% and 32% respectively. Small-scale handicraft industries in areas such as tailoring, steam-stressing, and embroidery-making were also female-dominated in Europe. In 1910, women self-employed in these three trades represented 43%, 93%, and 88%, respectively, of all European self-employed workers. In Vienna, "self-employed tailors and seamstresses were often married, petit-bourgeois women who worked as small subcontractors from home. … In 1869 each independent garment worker still employed, on average, 5.4 paid workers." By 1910, women working for themselves in industry, trade, and commerce totaled 35% of all self-employed in the city.[86]

During the last decades of the nineteenth and the first ones of the twentieth century, new opportunities opened for women in white-collar jobs. In Germany, by 1907, 30% of such workers were female: 22% of office personnel and 80% of retail employees. In France, 40% of bank, insurance, and retail employees were women. In Britain, the share of female civil service employees was 27% of the total before war broke out in 1914, while nearly three-quarters of teachers and most nurses were women. Female medical doctors, in contrast, were slow to appear.[87]

The twentieth century brought tremendous changes in the status and situation of women in society, equally affecting family, politics, education, and the workplace. Though gradual, they were virtually permanent. They culminated at the turn of the millennium with the emancipation of women and the establishment of legal gender equality. Transformations brought about by demographic trends and by structural changes in the economy contributed to the process of change. First of all, the traditional family structure of the nineteenth century broke down. Beginning in the 1970s, birthrates began dropping below the population replacement level until by 2005—except in the Nordic countries—the rate was only 1.5 children per family. People married much later, at an average age of 29.5 and 26.5, for men and women respectively. A great many people did not marry at all, and one-third to one-half of all marriages ended in divorce. Single-person households represented about one-quarter of the total in Europe overall, although in Germany and Denmark, the figure reached 30%. Secondly, the portion of people living in the countryside and working in agriculture dwindled to 4–5%. In several Western European countries 80% to 90% of the population lived in urban settlements. With removal from the agricultural sector, the dual and triple occupational burden associated with status as a woman in a peasant family disappeared. Then too, the heavy toil associated with caring for a family significantly decreased, in large part due to generous child allowances, maternity leave (later expanded to parental leave for fathers as well), and other services for families provided by the postwar welfare state. Finally, deindustrialization destroyed large numbers of industrial jobs, replacing them with positions easily filled by females in a vastly expanded service sector. Together these transformations liberated women and made them equal members of society.

Today, in the second decade of the twenty-first century, the consequences of these changes in female status can be seen in several statistical measurements. The employment level of the population as a whole has increased to about 50% in most countries, with exceptions in the Mediterranean and Balkan regions. This percentage holds, even for female employment levels, at least in Scandinavian and Baltic countries: there 49–51% of the labor force is female. The European Union, at its Lisbon meeting in 2000, set the goal of 60% employment for women, although this has yet to be achieved. Gender integration has made impressive progress in several areas of life. Finland enacted an Equality Act in 1995 and Sweden has established a ministry for gender equalization. The centuries-old pattern of wage discrimination—the lower wages paid to women working in the same positions as men—is gradually disappearing. In Sweden, women's salaries were equal to 92% of men's in 2007. However, in the advanced EU-15 countries, the average wage gap is still more than 14%, and in Germany and Britain 20%. In some Central and Eastern European countries the salary gap has even increased during the transformation to the market economy after 1989: in Bulgaria, Estonia, and Slovakia, for example, women's salaries today are 25–30% less than men's.

Despite the still significant differences separating the Nordic countries from their Mediterranean neighbors, women are generally becoming equal, and ever more equally paid, members of the European labor market. Top business positions may still be out of reach in many cases, but women are much more equally represented in intellectual, medical, legal, and artistic fields. The crushing burdens that characterized women's work in earlier periods have eased everywhere, and have virtually disappeared in the most gender-egalitarian countries.

Wernher von Braun: the visionary pioneer of the missile technique—and an "apolitical" war criminal[88]

The von Brauns were a traditional Prussian Junker military and landowner family whose members had for generations spent lives in high-ranking army and state positions. Into this family Wernher Magnus Maximilian Freiherr von Braun was born in 1912. His father was a civil servant, and later a cabinet minister. As a young boy, Wernher was fascinated by the science fiction of Jules Verne and H.G. Wells, as well as the 1923 book of Hermann Oberth, *Die Rakete zu den Planetenräumen*. Although he was not a good student, he started studying physics and mathematics to understand Oberth's book, and he made such progress that he soon substituted for the math teacher, teaching students who were a year older.

His mind was preoccupied by dreams of space travel. At the age of 15, he joined the *Verein für Raumschiffahrt* (Society for Space Travel) in Silesia. A year later, Wernher von Braun modified his wooden children's car by attaching half a dozen large firework rockets to it and running zigzag on the street until he was arrested by the police. His obsession with rockets and space travel brought him to the Berlin-Charlottenburg Institute of Technology, one of the best schools in that field in Europe. He got his pilot's license at the age of 19. While studying at the university, he also started working with a young group of rocket enthusiasts in a rented abandoned ammunition storage depot, the *Raketenflugplatz Berlin*. The team sent a memorandum to the *Reichswehr* about building long-range rockets. The army was interested, because the Versailles Treaty that harshly restricted German armament had no clause about rockets.

That was the beginning of von Braun's connection with Captain Walter Dornberger (later Colonel, and then Major-General), who aimed to build a bombardment rocket carrying a ton of explosives up to 160 miles. They worked together until the end of the war. In 1932, the army invited von Braun to work on the project, which he accepted, realizing that this was the only way to get enough money for his experiments. One of his biographers asked the question: "had he not made a Faustian bargain, a pact with the devil, when he had aligned himself with the German army and ultimately with Hitler? Was he not bothered by the moral implication of ... building weapons while wishing to go into space?"[89]

Von Braun, in one of his later interviews maintained: "the Army was desperate to get back on its feet. We didn't care much about that ... We felt no moral scruples about the future use of our brainchild."[90] He often stated later that he was naïve, not interested in politics, and did not follow closely what happened in Germany. Did he live in his space dreams? Probably. Meanwhile, however, he focused on his career in Nazi Germany and enthusiastically helped Hitler to realize his obsession. He had, indeed, made a pact with the devil.

The Dornberger team, with von Braun playing a leading role, diligently worked on the bomb-rocket project, and in December 1934 they launched the first two A-2 rockets, the first in history to fly over two kilometers. That was ideal timing because Hitler started German rearmament in 1935. From that year on, von Braun became a permanent employee and, with a few dozen engineers, technicians, and workers, started working on the A-3 project, a huge rocket weapon with an engine that generated 1,500 kilograms of thrust. He was very enthusiastic and recruited talented scholars and engineers to work with. By 1937, the team already had 80 members. Von Braun, who was strongly interested in the power of a nuclear explosion, visited Professor Werner Heisenberg, the leader of the German atomic program, a couple of times before 1942.

After 1936, the failed A-3 program was followed by the A-4 project to build the world's first ballistic missile to cover 275 kilometers, carrying one ton of explosives. Its engine was 17 times bigger than the A-3 rocket's. This weapon, to which wings were later added to cover a much bigger distance, was named V-2, or *Vergeltungswaffen* (retaliatory weapon). Attempts to launch the V-2 began in 1942, and the third attempt was successful in October: the first man-made object touched the edge of the space.

In 1939, on the Baltic seashore at Peenemünde, a rocket production plant was built. After the occupation of Prague, Hitler visited the rocket team. Von Braun explained the technical achievements, but Hitler asked how many years they needed to be ready. Hitler was certainly influenced by the success of the Heinkel-He176 program that had constructed the world first rocket plane that year, and he did not believe in the timely success of the rocket-weapon program, so he rejected giving preference to it. The team, however, worked hard, and, as one of his colleagues stated, von Braun was "creating enthusiasm by his own enthusiasm." In the 1930s, to pave the way for the progress of his project, von Braun joined the Nazi Party, and he entered the SS as an *Untersturmführer* (second lieutenant) with membership number 185,068. "Es geht nicht anders [There is no other way]," he said to some of his co-workers. When Himmler visited Peenemünde in the summer of 1943, von Braun, already an SS *Hauptsturmführer* (captain), appeared in his black SS uniform. Soon he became an SS-*Sturmbannführer* (major).

In August of that same year, Hitler wanted to hear a report about the rocket program, and he ordered the leaders of the rocket team to the *Wolfschanze*, his headquarters, where his top military aids, headed by Marshal Wilhelm Keitel and General Alfred Jodl, were present. Von Braun screened and narrated a film about the rocket, and talked about the production of 5,000 rockets per year. Albert Speer, Hitler's right-hand man in armament, later described the 31-year-old von Braun as a man "without a trace of timidity and with a boyish enthusiasm."[91]

Hitler, depressed by the lost battle of Stalingrad—and the second crucial battle of that year at Kursk was soon also lost by the Germans—became enthusiastic and said "this development is of revolutionary importance for the conduct of warfare in the whole world. The deployment of a few thousand devices per year is therefore unwise. If it is deployed, hundreds of thousands of devices per year must be manufactured and launched ... A strange fanatical light flared up in Hitler's eyes ... But what I want is annihilation—annihilating effect!"[92] The importance of the "miracle weapon" increased day by day and top military leaders became regular visitors at Peenemünde, including Admiral Karl Dönitz, Luftwaffe Field Marshal Erhard Milch, and Armament Chief General Friedrich Fromm.

Von Braun, who met Hitler a few times during the war, was deeply impressed by him. As he later described: "My impression of him was, here is a new Napoleon, a new colossus ... [with] astonishing intellectual capabilities ... [and] hypnotic influence of his personality on his surroundings."[93]

Building hundreds of thousands of rocket weapons, however, was impossible. The labor shortage was severe, and Allied bombing of Peenemünde started in the summer of 1943. Nevertheless, concentration camp prisoners were ordered to work, and a new establishment was created in caves in the south Harz Mountains, using about 10,000 slave laborers, partly from the Buchenwald camp. In the end, tens of thousands of slave laborers were used for construction and production. The weapon, ready to launch, was not completed according to the hoped-for schedule. Thousands of new problems had to be solved. A desperate and nervous Himmler ordered the arrest of von Braun in March 1944, but released him in two weeks, and the first rocket weapon was launched from northern France against London in June 1944, landing at a railway bridge.

From that time on, 70 flying bombs landed on Britain every day, more than 9,000 in all. This jet-propelled rocket, the 8-meter-long V-1, carrying an 850-kilogram warhead, was far from perfect, however. Its speed was only 580 kilometers per hour, and about 2,000 were destroyed by anti-aircraft guns and fighter pilots. Only about 2,500 reached their targets. In September 1944, the first 14-meter-long, 13-ton V-2 rocket, using burning alcohol and liquid oxygen, was launched against London. Its peak altitude was 80 kilometers, touching space. It was followed by about 5,000 rocket bombs of which 1,100 reached their targets, killing several thousand people (different calculations put the number killed between 5,000 and 7,000), and causing severe destruction in several British cities. The V-2, which could travel 3,500 miles in a few seconds with a 750-kilogram warhead, was a destructive but ineffective weapon. In the last phase of the war, after the Allied landing, the Germans also used it against Antwerp, Lille, Arras, Brussels, and other cities on the continent. They could launch the rockets from mobile launchers from virtually everywhere. The last V-2 landed in London in March 1945.

The rocket was mostly ineffective at its early stage of production. According to some estimations it caused more death by its production than its deployment, because probably around 20,000 concentration camp inmates died working in construction and production facilities. In the underground rocket assembly facilities at Nordhausen, prisoners lived in underground tunnels, sleeping on straw or just on the rocks, or in four-story bunks. The sleeping tunnels "quickly became contaminated with excrement, lice, and fleas; there were no sanitary facilities … only oil barrels cut in half, and virtually no drinking water."[94] As one of the survivors, the French resistance leader Jean Michel, described the slave laborers' situation: "Some deportees are too weak and collapse. They have dysentery … no longer have the strength to sit over the barrels, even to get to them. The SS beat them. The blows are useless, they do not get up. They will suffer no more."[95] Two hundred were executed for sabotage and altogether 350 were hanged. Thousands died because of starvation, exhaustion, and disease.

Wernher von Braun, who often visited the facilities both in Peenemünde and in the Harz Mountains, and had seen the prisoners in work, maintained that he did not know about any abuse. "It naturally left on me an extraordinarily depressing impression each time that I went into the underground plant and had to see the prisoners at work." Later he said: "I never knew what was happening in the concentration camps. But I suspected it, and in my position I could have found out."[96] He subordinated everything to the success of his rocket, and he excluded human considerations for the sake of his career. Later, with his selective memory, he did not remember disturbing facts, including the anti-Jewish atrocities. Moreover, even in retrospect he did not reconsider his attitude towards serving Hitler's war: "But war is war, and because my country found itself at war, I had the conviction that I did not have the right to bring further moral viewpoint to bear. My duty was to help win the war."[97]

The genius and "apolitical" rocket-builder successfully served Hitler to create the "miracle weapon." He became a war criminal, but he belonged to the group that did not have to pay for it. At the end of the war, with his team of 500 top scientists and engineers, and with packed plans and test vehicles, von Braun escaped and surrendered to the American army. He was only 33 years old. The US army confiscated and delivered about 300 train-loads of V-2 rockets, parts, and equipment, and transported them to the United States. The Soviet Union also captured V-2 rockets and 250 German engineers who worked for the first Soviet R-1 missile, an exact copy of the V-2. In the emerging Cold War, von Braun and his team were sent to the United States and continued working for the American army at Fort Bliss, Texas. Later, when NASA was established, von Braun became the director of the Marshall Space Flight Center, building Saturn and Apollo rockets. Realizing his childhood dream, he played a central role in launching the first American satellite in 1958, and a decade later he made a central contribution to sending men to the moon. In the second half of his life, Wernher von Braun became the most active advocate of the American space program, its most creative and successful celebrity space engineer, an American citizen, and author of several books.

When Congress established the Office of Special Investigation of the US Department of Justice in 1979 to discover and deport former war criminals, von Braun was already dead. He died of cancer in 1977. His close friend and old rocket teammate, Arthur Rudolph, was interrogated and signed an agreement to renounce his American citizenship and go back to Germany. "We are lucky," some investigator said, "von Braun isn't alive."[98]

The computer, the internet, and the world wide web[99]

The invention of the computer, which opened a new technological age and transformed everyday life, belongs to the greatest chapters of history. As in the case of every major new invention, including the steam engine and the various applications of electricity, it has a centuries-long history and was the result of hundreds and thousands of inventions and innovations. Hundreds of great talents from various countries were the midwives of the newcomer and worked on its realization. Theoretical mathematicians played a pioneering role. The Englishman Charles Babbage's "Analytical Engine," a calculating machine he began designing in 1840, definitely belongs among the pioneering work, along with that of Ada Lovelace Byron—the poet Byron's daughter—who created the first program for Babbage's machine. In 1886, the first mechanical adding machine was built, and the Hollerith tabulating machine was patented three years later. Before and during the first years of World War II, the German Konrad Zuse and the American IBM Company built program-controlled automatic calculators independently of each other in Berlin and in the United States.

The real breakthrough, however, happened during World War II, urged—as so often in the history of technology—by military needs. At the University of Manchester in Britain and the University of Pennsylvania in the United States, several scholars and engineers worked on a computing machine, not least to decode coded German military communications. The American Mark I, the first electro-mechanical computer, started work for the US Navy. The central role was played by two congenial mathematicians, the British Alan M. Turing in the 1930s, and the Hungarian born John von Neumann, whose so-called EDVAC Report in the spring of 1944 solved the central problem and established the concept of the modern universal computer with stored programs. The first two computers based on this principle were built in Britain at Manchester University and Cambridge University. The British Colossus, a five-ton giant computer successfully decoded Nazi military messages.

Each part of the computer and each piece of the program and software—actually hundreds and even thousands of them—are connected but independent inventions. The second breakthrough was prepared in the late 1940s and 1950s in the United States by the invention of the transistor by John Bardeen, William Shockley, and Walter Brattain in 1947–48, and then a decade later when the group led by Jack Kilby invented the integrated circuit with thousands of transistors on a single silicon chip.

The transistor—the name is an portmanteau of "transfer resistor"—is a semiconductor that can amplify and switch electronic signals, and it revolutionized electronics. One of the great advantages of the transistor is that its mass production is easy and cheap. By the early twenty-first century, 60 million transistors were produced for every living human being on the globe. The way was paved for miniaturization. On the other hand, programming was also established by the American Grace Hopper's innovation. She developed a program for translating programming languages for computers in 1952. The first pioneering computer programming language, FORTRAN, was introduced in 1954.

The revolutionary outcome of these technological inventions led to the production of the world first personal computers in the 1970s. France produced its own system very early, followed by several improved versions, among them the Apple and the Commodore in 1976–77. This opened an endless series of newer and newer, and more and more powerful, personal computers. A series of further inventions followed. Among them, the creation of networks should be mentioned. Networks that connected computer systems—Janet, Arpanet, Csnet and others—were introduced first for the military and then for research purposes. The first European Information Network was created by CERN, the European Organization for Nuclear Research in Geneva, by the French Louis de Broglie. By the end of the 1980s, the internet became the world's standard network, connecting various networks as an "international communication freeway system." It was first used in Europe to monitor Soviet nuclear tests. By 1990, 30,000 internet sites existed in Europe, but two years later there were already 500,000, and since that time the number has increased exponentially.

During the 1960s, the hypertext systems were also created and were demonstrated for the first time in 1968 by Douglas Engelbart. The hypertext produced references to other texts that are immediately accessible at the computer. The Xanadu, HES, FRESS, and other systems made it possible to store thousands of documents. ORACLE's innovations made it possible to download information. All of these made possible the invention of a "truck service" carrying information on a communication freeway system, the world wide web. This was invented in 1990 by a 25-year-old Oxford graduate British researcher, Tim Berners-Lee, with the help of the Belgian computer engineer, Robert Cailliau at CERN. Instead of a hierarchical storage system, Berners-Lee created a link that worked as free association opening windows and keeping several texts in line. He rejected patenting the web to help its fast and cheap spread. In a year, web traffic carried information at a rate of 400,000 bytes/second, equal to the length of a novel each second. Commercial use started in 1994. The next year, Microsoft created its Internet Explorer and offered newer and newer versions of it. By 2012, Explorer 10 was already in operation.

The speed of the use and spread of the web produced unbelievable numbers. In 1994, there were 10,000 web servers. At the end of the 1990s, 10 million web servers were in operation and used by 150 million people. Between 2005 and 2010, the number of global web users doubled, and, by 2010, 2 billion people were using it. At that time, about 110 million websites were in operation, and 26 billion webpages existed in 75 languages (an increase of more than ten times since 2001). The computer, the internet, and the web became the prime movers of the communication revolution, offering an unlimited, easily accessible pool of knowledge, culture, and information that changed the world and became a central instrument of its globalization.

Notes

1 This essay is based on: Jacob L. Talmon, *Romanticism and Revolt: Europe 1815–1848*, San Diego: Harcourt, Brace & World, 1967; Isaiah Berlin, *The Roots of Romanticism*, edited by Henry Hardy, Princeton: Princeton University Press, 1999; Isaiah Berlin, *The Power of Ideas,* edited by Henry Hardy, Princeton: Princeton University Press, 2000; Ivan T. Berend, *History Derailed: Central and Eastern Europe in the Long Nineteenth Century,* Berkeley: University of California Press, 2003; Ivan T. Berend, *An Economic History of Nineteenth-Century Europe: Diversity and Industrialization*, Cambridge: Cambridge University Press, 2013.

2 William N. Parker, *Europe, America and the Wider World: Essays on the Economic History of Western Capitalism, Vol. I: Europe and the World Economy*, Cambridge: Cambridge University Press, 1984.

3 Richard H. Tawney, *Religion and the Rise of Capitalism: A Historical Study*, Holland Memorial Lecture, 1922, New York: Mentor Books, 1954, 17.

4 Peter Harrison, "Was there a Scientific Revolution?" *European Review*, Vol. 15, No. 4, 2007, 446.

5 Thomas Hobbs, *Leviathan*, Chicago: Gateway, [1651] 1956, 122–23.

6 John Locke, *Two Treatises on Government*, New York: Hafner, [1689] 1947, 801.

7 Charles-Louis de Secondat, Baron de Montesquieu, "The Spirit of Laws," in *Introduction to Contemporary Civilization in the West: A Source Book*, New York: Columbia University Press, [1748] 1946: 936, 938.

8 Jean-Jacques Rousseau, "The Social Contract," in *Introduction to Contemporary Civilization in the West*, [1762] 1946, 957, 965.

9 George L. Mosse, *The Culture of Western Europe: The Nineteenth and Twentieth Centuries*, 3rd edition, Boulder, CO: Westview Press, 1988, 119, 130.

10 Talmon, 1967, 136.

11 Berlin, 2000, 9–10.

12 Berlin, 1999, xiii.

13 Eugen Weber, *Path to the Present: Aspects of European Thoughts from Romanticism to Existentialism*, New York: Dodd, Mead, 1960, 13.

14 Peter H. Reill, *Vitalizing Nature in the Enlightenment*, Berkeley: University of California Press, 2005.

15 Berend, 2003, 44, 46.

16 This essay is based on: René Rémond, *Religion and Society in Modern Europe*, Oxford: Blackwell, 1999; Christopher Clark and Wolfram Kaiser (eds), *Culture Wars: Secular-Catholic Conflict in Nineteenth-Century Europe*, Cambridge: Cambridge University Press, 2003.

17 Barry Supple, "Institution and Economic Development: Economic History and Human Arrangement," in W.R. Garside (ed.), *Institutions and Market Economies: The Political Economy of Growth and Development*, Houndmills: Palgrave Macmillan, 2007.

18 The *Code civil* (1805), *Code de procédure civile* (1806), *Code de commerce* (1807), *Code d'instruction criminelle* (1808), and the *Code pénal* (1810).

19 John Breuilly and Jürgen Kocka (eds) "Bürger und Bürgerlichkeit im 19. Jahrhundert," Bulletin of the German Historical Institute, Vol. X, No. 3, 1988, 13.

20 Hugh McLeod, *Secularisation in Western Europe, 1848–1914*, New York: St. Martin's Press, 2000, 94, 100–101.

21 Roland N. Stromberg, *European Intellectual History Since 1789*, 5th edition, Englewood Cliffs, NJ: Prentice Hall, 1990, 118.

22 Clark and Kaiser, 2003, 221, 59, 1.

23 Ibid, 3.

24 Ibid, 103, 109–13, 124, 130–31, 255–67.

25 Rémond, 1999, 127.

26 This essay is based on: Maria Bogucka, "Social Structures and Customs in Early Modern Poland," *Acta Poloniae Historica*, Warsaw, No. 68, 1993; Zsigmond Pál Pach, *Hungary and the European Economy in Early Modern Times*, Aldershot: Variorum, 1994; Gabriel Tortella, "Patterns of Economic Retardation and Recovery in South-Western Europe in the Nineteenth and Twentieth Centuries," *Economic History Review*, Vol. XLVII, No. 1, 1994; Ivan T. Berend, *An Economic History of Nineteenth-Century Europe: Diversity and Industrialization*, Cambridge: Cambridge University Press, 2013.

27 Quoted by Gabriel Tortella, "Economic Entrepreneurship: A Scarce Factor in Spain: The Banking Sector, 1782–1914," in Paul Klep and Eddy Van Cauwenberghe

(eds), *Entrepreneurship and the Transformation of the Economy*, Leuven: Leuven University Press, 1994, 190.

28 Quoted by Sidney Harcave, *Count Sergei Witte and the Twilight of Imperial Russia: A Biography*, Armonk, NY: M.E. Sharpe, 2004, 35.

29 Tortella, 1994, 192.

30 Ditmar Dahlmann, "Religion und Geschäft: Deutsche Unternehmer in Moskau und St. Petersburg von der Mitte des 19. Jahrhunderts bis 1914," in Jörg Gebhard, Rainer Lindner, and Blanka Pietrow-Ennker (eds), *Unternehmer im Russischen Reich: Sozialprofil, Symbolwelten, Integrationsstrategien im 19. und frühen 20. Jahrhundert*, Osnabrück: Fibre Verlag, 2006, 169.

31 Andrej Kištimau, "Jüdische Unternehmer in Weissrussland: Zeitgenössische Wahrnehmung, Sozialprofil und Wirtschaftsformen," in Gebhard, Lindner, and Pietrow-Ennker, 2006, 222.

32 Andreas Kossert, "Gelobtes Land? Religiosität und Unternehmer in der Industriegesellschaft Lodz und Manchester in langen 19. Jahrhundert," in Gebhard, Lindner, and Pietrow-Ennker, 2006, 150.

33 Beth Holmgreen, *Rewriting Capitalism: Literature and the Market in Late Tsarist Russia and the Kingdom of Poland*, Pittsburgh: University of Pittsburgh Press, 1998, 70–77.

34 Quoted by Jerzy Jedlicki, *A Suburb of Europe: Nineteenth-Century Polish Approaches to Western Civilization*, Budapest: Central European University Press, 1999, 218–19.

35 Bogucka, 1993, 110.

36 Gyula Szekfű, *Három nemzedék: Egy hanyatló kor története*, Budapest, 1920, 291; Gyula Szekfű, *A magyar bortermelő lelki alkata: Gazadságtörténeti tanulmány*, Budapest: Minerva Társaság, 1922, 81–82.

37 George Clenton Logio, *Rumania: Its History, Politics and Economics*, Manchester: Sherratt & Hughes, 1932, 115, 118.

38 Quoted by Theodor H. von Laue, *Sergei Witte and the Industrialization of Russia*, New York: Atheneum, 1969, 120–21.

39 Giorgio Mori, "Industry Without Industrialization: The Italian Peninsula from the End of French Domination to National Unification, 1815–61" in Jean Batou (ed.), *Between Development and Underdevelopment: The Precocious Attempts at Industrialization of the Periphery 1800–1870*, Geneva: Librairie Droz, 1991, 328–29.

40 Alexander V. Chayanov, *The Theory of Peasant Economy*, New York: R.D. Irwin, 1987.

41 Krzysztof Zamorski, "Necessity of Freedom: Economic, Social, and Political Consequences of Late Industrialization in Poland in the 19th Century," in Pasquale Fornaro (ed.), *Transizione e sviluppo: Le Periferie d'Europa (secc. XVIII-XIX)*, Catanzaro: Rubbettino, 1998, 44.

42 This essay is based on: Gale E. Christianson, *Isaac Newton*, Oxford: Oxford University Press, 2005; Patrick H. Armstrong, *Darwin's Luck: Chance and Fortune in the Life and Work of Charles Darwin*, London: Continuum, 2009; Peter J. Bowler, *Charles Darwin: The Man and His Influence*, Oxford: Blackwell, 1990; Frederick Burkhardt, Duncan M. Porter, Sheila Ann Dean, Jonathan R. Topham, and Sarah Wilmot (eds), *The Correspondence of Charles Darwin*, Vol. III, Cambridge: Cambridge University Press, 1999; Berend, 2013.

43 Harrison, 2007, 446, 450.

44 Betty Jo Teeter Dobbs and Margaret C. Jacob, *Newton and the Culture of Newtonianism*, Atlantic Highlands: Humanities Press, 1995, 10.

45 Ibid, 38, 44.

46 Albert Eduard Musson and Eric Robinson, *Science and Technology in the Industrial Revolution*, Manchester: Manchester University Press, 1969, 12–25.

47 Joel Mokyr, *The Gift of Athena: Historical Origins of the Knowledge Economy*, Princeton: Princeton University Press, 2002, 68–69. Mokyr's list also contains the

Encyclopaedia Britannica (1771), the *Allgemeines Lexicon* (1721), the *Oekonomische-Technologische Encyklopädie* in 221 volumes (1796), the *Brockhaus Enzyklopädie* (1809), and the *Dictionary of Arts, Manufactures and Mines* (1839)
48 Later a shorter version of the title – *On the Origin of Species* – was used. By 1872, the sixth edition came out and Darwin made continuous corrections and additions based on his continued research and experiments.
49 Armstrong, 2009, 41–42.
50 Charles Darwin, *The Autobiography of Charles Darwin*, edited by N. Barlow, New York: Harcourt Brace, 1958, 76.
51 Burkhardt et al., 1999, 39.
52 Armstrong, 2009, 22.
53 Charles Darwin, *On the Origin of Species*, London: John Murray, 1859, 484.
54 These attacks continued during the twentieth century as demonstrated by the infamous "Scopes Monkey Trial" in the United States in the 1920s. Even around the turn of the twenty-first century, religious fundamentalists in the United States do not allow their children to attend public schools and prefer home-schooling to avoid Darwin. They maintain that evolution is only another concept and demand teaching of the creation as well.
55 Burkhardt et al., 1999, 7.
56 Bowler, 1990, 2–3.
57 Roland N. Stromberg, *European Intellectual History Since 1789*, 5th edition, Englewood Cliffs, NJ: Prentice Hall, 1990, 123.
58 Quoted by Stromberg, 1990, 127.
59 This essay is based on Mark Overton, *Agricultural Revolution in England: The Transformation of the Agrarian Economy 1500–1850*, Cambridge: Cambridge University Press, 1995; Jan de Vries and Ad Van der Woude, *The First Modern Economy: Success, Failure, and Perseverance of the Dutch Economy, 1500–1815*, Cambridge: Cambridge University Press, 1997; Berend, 2013.
60 This essay is based on: T.K. Derry and Trevor I. Williamsons, *A Short History of Technology*, London: Oxford University Press, 1975, 326–35; B.E.G. Clark, *Steamboat Evolution: A Short History*, London: Lulu Enterprises, 2007; Angus Sinclair, *Development of the Locomotive Engine*, New York: Angus Sinclair Publishing, 1907; Berend, 2013.
61 The very first experimental steamship used a far-from-efficient Newcomen steam engine in 1736.
62 The propulsion machine produces thrusts to push an object forward. It may drive a paddle wheel or a propeller.
63 In sea-going ships, to illustrate the importance of further "minor" innovations, the boilers were filled with sea water that led to strong deposition of salt and corrosion. In 1834, Samuel Hill produced a surface-condenser that made distilled water for the boiler.
64 This essay is based on: Arthur Allen, *Vaccine: The Controversial Story of Medicine's Greatest Lifesaver*, New York: W.W. Norton, 2007; Patrice Debré, *Louis Pasteur*, Baltimore: Johns Hopkins University Press, 2000; Thomas D. Brock, *Robert Koch: A Life in Medicine and Bacteriology*, Washington, DC: ASM Press, 1999; Helmuth M. Böttcher, *Miracle Drugs: A History of Antibiotics*, London: Heinemann, 1959.
65 As early as 1837, the German Friedrich Gustav Jacob Henle discovered the existence of microscopic "small living creatures" in diseased tissues and hypothesized that they may cause diseases.
66 Böttcher, 1959, 135.
67 Böttcher, 1959, 170.
68 This essay is based on: Carsten Reinhardt and Anthony S. Travis, *Heinrich Caro and the Creation of Modern Chemical Industry*, Dordrecht: Kluwer Academic Publisher, 2000; www.madehow.com/inventorbios/87/William-Henry-Perkin.html;

T.K. Derry and Trevor I. Wiliams, *A Short History of Technology from the Earliest Time to A.D. 1900*, London: Oxford University Press, 1975.

69 Derry and Williams, 1975, 542.

70 In 1704, a synthetic dye, called Prussian blue, was already accidentally produced without understanding the principles and, consequently, without any continuation. This was used to dye the uniform of the Prussian army.

71 Perkin sold his factory in 1874 and continued as a researcher. He became Fellow of the Royal Society in 1866 and received the Royal Medal from the Royal Society in 1870. He discovered the first artificial perfume, and pioneered research on the relationship between the physical properties and the chemical constitution of substances.

72 Derry and Williams, 1975, 546.

73 This essay is based on: Derry and Williams, 1975; Berend, 2013.

74 This essay is based on: L. Girard, "Transport," in H.J. Habakkuk and M. Postan (eds), *The Cambridge Economic History of Europe*, Vol. VI, Cambridge: Cambridge University Press, 1965; Richard Vahrenkamp, *The German Autobahn 1920–1945: Hafraba Visions and Mega Projects*, Lohmar: Josef Eul Verlag, 2010; Ivan T. Berend, *An Economic History of Twentieth-Century Europe*, Cambridge: Cambridge University Press, 2006.

75 Albert Schram, *Railways and the Formation of the Italian State in the Nineteenth Century*, Cambridge: Cambridge University Press, 1997, 97.

76 Girard, 1965, 220.

77 Vahrenkamp, 2010, 15.

78 Ibid, 74.

79 *OECD Factbook*, Paris: OECD, 2007, 235.

80 This essay is based on: Derry and Williams, 1975; Marta Braun, *Picturing Time: The Work of Etienne-Jules Marey (1830–1904)*, Chicago: Chicago University Press, 1992.

81 This essay is based on: Rachel G. Fuchs and Victoria E. Thompson, *Women in Nineteenth-Century Europe*, Houndmills: Palgrave Macmillan, 2005; Robert Beachy, Béatrice Craig, and Alastair Owens (eds), *Women, Business and Finance in Nineteenth-Century Europe: Rethinking Separate Spheres*, Oxford: Berg, 2006; European Commission, *Eurostat, the Life of Women and Men in Europe: A Statistical Portrait*, Luxembourg: Office for Official Publications, 2008; Lynn Abrams, *The Making of Modern Women*, London: Longman, 2002.

82 Jan de Vries, *The Industrious Revolution: Consumer Behavior and the Household Economy, 1650 to the Present*, Cambridge: Cambridge University Press, 2008.

83 Franklin F. Mendels, "Proto-industrialization: The First Phase of the Industrialization Process," *Journal of Economic History*, No. 32, 1972.

84 Lynn Abrams (2002, 175) calls attention to two different approaches in historiography: one stresses the "strong and enduring continuity in women's work," the other "stresses change in women's experience of work."

85 Tom Ericsson, "Limited Opportunities? Female Retailing in Nineteenth-Century Sweden," in Beachy et al., 2006, 144, 150; Valérie Piette, "Belgium's Tradeswomen," in Beachy et al., 2006, 131.

86 Irene Bandhauer-Schöffmann, "Businesswomen in Austria," in Beachy et al., 2006, 116–17.

87 Abrams, 2002, 205–6.

88 This essay is based on: Michael J. Neufeld, *Von Braun: Dreamer of Space, Engineer of War*, New York: Knopf, 2007; history.msfc.nasa.gov/vonbraun/index.html; www.battlefield-site.co.uk/V2cutaway.gif; www.ww2aircraft.net/forum/stories/vergeltungswaffen-10368.html.

89 Neufeld, 2007, 4,

90 Daniel Lang, *From Hiroshima to the Moon: Chronicle of Life in the Atomic Age*, New York: Simon & Schuster, 1959, 183.

91 Albert Speer, *Inside the Third Reich*, New York: Avon, 1970, 101.
92 Neufeld, 2007, 128, 147, 151.
93 Bob Ward, *Wernher von Braun Anekdotisch*, Esslingen: Bechtle, 1972, 28, quoted by Neufeld, 2007, 64.
94 Neufeld, 2007, 360.
95 Jean Michel with Louis Nucera, *Dora*, New York: Holt, Rinehart and Winston, 1979, 70.
96 Neufeld, 2007, 145. 161.
97 Ward, 1972, 31.
98 Neufeld, 2007, 475.
99 This essay is based on: James Gillies and Robert Cailliau, *How the Web was Born: The Story of the World Wide Web*, Oxford: Oxford University Press, 2000.

4 Pioneering companies

Introduction

The modern economy was built by the human knowledge that was the main factor behind technological and managerial inventions. As the economist Joseph Schumpeter put it, the entrepreneur became the central figure in modern economic growth. In many cases, several generations of entrepreneurs and managers worked continuously and formed leading companies that had a permanent role in their fields of activities. The history of companies presents a variety of company forms. In the eighteenth century, the long-existing cottage industry still dominated. Besides urban guilds, peasant households were the basis of the bulk of industrial production, and merchants provided them with raw materials and bought their products to sell them, sometimes on foreign markets. While this type of proto-industry persisted for a long time, it was sometimes already combined with the newly invented factory system. The final procedure of the industrial production process, i.e., the assembly of the parts produced by cottage industries, was sometimes finished in a non-mechanized factory where hundreds of workers often worked under one roof.

The British industrial revolution made the factory system dominant in industry. Most of them were owned and managed by one family or a family with a partner. In some areas of business, such as coal-mining, shipping, and canal-building, the joint stock company system dominated. Joint stock companies already existed in earlier centuries as well. They enjoyed state monopolies, as in the cases of the British, Dutch, and French East India Companies. These company empires owned huge colonial territories, armies, and navies. The joint stock form was legally banned after the so-called "South Sea bubble" of 1720, which was the bankruptcy scandal of the British South Sea Company, a monopoly joint stock company for South American trade. The joint stock form, however, became dominant in the entire industrial and transportation world in the last third of the nineteenth century. Private or state-owned companies that built international waterways or railroads remained profit-oriented companies, while also serving the colonization attempts of certain countries.

In the early nineteenth century, industrial firms were relatively small, and the working conditions in them were subhuman, with cheap child and female labor being made to serve 12- to 16-hour workdays. During the second industrial revolution in the second half of the century, the size of companies significantly increased. Industrial laboratories were attached to industrial firms to promote innovation. It often went hand in hand with the separation of ownership and management. Companies with tens and hundreds of thousands of workers employed an army of top- and medium-level managers. The companies became scientifically organized. Workdays and weeks shortened. Some of the firms introduced major welfare institutions and built factory cities to provide housing for the workers.

In small countries, several modern, high-tech companies immediately started business abroad and became multinationals. In the last third of the twentieth century, multinational companies operating at least in two countries and that established subsidiaries abroad became dominant and monopolized three-quarters of the trade in manufactured goods. Research and development work became an inseparable part of the activities of those large multinational companies. Today we still have hundreds and thousands of companies that were established in the nineteenth century, became pioneers in a certain branch of production, and still preserve their leading role.

This chapter introduces a number of European companies that were long-time leaders in their fields. The various East India Companies, themselves empires with a navy, army, and colonies, represented the very first modern joint-stock organizational form. Companies with worldwide importance such as the German Thyssen, the British Vickers-Armstrong, the Swiss Rolex, or the Dutch Philips, as well as the Italian Gucci and the airlines Air France, KLM, and Lufthansa, were pioneers and dominant in the steel, armament, watch, electrical, electronics, fashion, and air transportation industries. The case studies on these companies help to understand how they emerged and rose to dominance. Another set of case studies represents different types of companies. The German Orientalische Eisenbahnen and the French Suez Ship Canal companies equally served the usual profit orientation and colonial aspirations. Some essays present companies with European importance in peripheral countries such as Hungary and Ireland. The case studies cover the story of famous companies from their foundation to the present.

The empires' companies and the companies' empires[1]

During the sixteenth and seventeenth centuries, merchant capitalism and leading merchant countries emerged. The tremendous development of ship-building and great discoveries inspired trade with far away continents to buy and sell exotic new spices and other products. However, trade with the Orient and Asia, which involved going around the Cape of Good Hope at the southern tip of Africa, was a risky and very expensive venture. This was far beyond the capacities of one merchant. This situation led to the foundation of big companies and the invention of the joint stock enterprise. In the seventeenth century, the three leading European powers, England (in 1600), Holland (in 1602), and France (in 1664) all established their East India Companies.

England established this kind of organization as far back as the mid-to-late sixteenth century. The "Russia Company," certainly the first example, got a royal charter in 1555. London merchants petitioned Queen Elizabeth in 1580 to receive an exclusive monopoly for the Near East trade, and the joint stock "Levant Company" established trading centers (called "factories") in Aleppo, Constantinople, Alexandria, and Smyrna.

From the early seventeenth century, sharp competition for the Asian trade emerged between the pioneering and monopolistic Portuguese, the strong and quickly ascending Dutch, and English merchants. This situation inspired a group of English merchants to ask for monopoly rights for trade east of the Cape of Good Hope. In December 1600, a royal charter established and authorized with exclusive privileges the English East India Company with 219 original shareholders. During its first 20 years, the company established more than a dozen trading stations and a chain of supply-points, among which the two most important were Surat in northwest India and Bantam in Java. They owned two shipyards on the Thames and 76 ships. Royal control was strict and permission was needed for each voyage, but the Royal Navy offered defense for the merchants. "During some three hundred and fifty years of its existence it not only proved to be the greatest of the joint stock companies ... but also a valuable instrument in the creation of English colonial and imperial system."[2]

The company revolutionized foreign trade by building up a supra-national, worldwide multilateral trade system. Before its activity, English foreign trade served specific needs of domestic consumers. Trade had a rather one-sided direction, with Holland as the main partner. Trade with continental Europe, however, met with unbreakable obstacles, in the form of Spanish and Portuguese restrictions and Dutch competition that endangered the English Levant spice trade. London merchants experimented with breaking through by sending ships to the East Indies as early as 1591. Members of the Levant Company also turned to the East Indies. To overcome these barriers, the East India Company was established, and it created a triangle structure of trade: bilateral trade between England and India, an intra-European trade that re-exported colonial goods to the continent, and last but not least, trade transactions within Asia. This meant the building up of huge commercial links. English export was almost solely woolen manufactured products that were exchanged for Mediterranean wine, oil, fruits, and linen, and Asian commodities that were re-exported to the continent. Re-export became the most dynamic element of English trade in the seventeenth century. Trade was assisted by a multilateral financial system within the trade triangle that made it possible to balance a trade deficit in one relation with a trade surplus in another.

The company's organization was a regulated joint stock enterprise. In its *Laws and Standing Orders*, a strict structure of governance was created. The executive body was the Court of Committees, headed by the governor, with his deputy, a treasurer, secretary, auditors, and accountants, altogether comprising 24 members, while the General Court consisted of all the stockholders who controlled the activity. The company was in very close relations with the state that granted privileges and offered assistance to it. The Royal Navy had a permanent role in defending the English trade routs against Portuguese and Dutch attacks. Hostility and confrontations were fellow travelers of trade. In 1618–19, sharp confrontation exploded between the Dutch and English merchant companies around the Indonesian trade. The Dutch captured 11 English ships loaded with silver. The conflict was ended by direct royal involvement and an agreement between the two states in 1619. Potential Portuguese attacks were an everyday threat. Conflicts also erupted when the English company captured Ormuz from the Portuguese in 1622. Military force was thus indispensable and required a large and heavily armed navy to provide protection. The huge capital requirements were also connected with the military function of the trading companies. The royal charter provided huge privileges to the company that "made them look almost like subordinate departments of the State but at the same time they remained self-interested groups with private rights."[3] On the other hand, the company was a financial resource for the state partly by paying customs. In the 1820s, tea duties alone totaled nearly £3 million. The company became also a banker by providing loans to the court.

When Britain gradually gained the upper hand in the competition with her rivals in the eighteenth and early nineteenth centuries, the English East India Company increasingly became a military and colonizing partner of the state. The company waged wars and conquered territories in India in the 1770s and 1780s. True, the royal army and navy often had to intervene to defend the new conquests of the company. "The Company's own military resources [were regarded] as an important supplement to national strength in the struggle against France, Spain, and the Dutch, and ... the deployment of Company's men, ship, and equipment alongside Crown forces in the broader Indian Ocean region [became more common] ... By 1805 the Company's three Indian armies numbered almost 200,000 men."[4] The company's naval power was so significant at that time that it was the third largest in Europe, ahead of several countries. A similarly significant contribution to empire-building was provided by the company's administration and information systems. From the 1760s on, and especially after the establishment of the Board of Control in 1784, the company became a kind of information and administrative agency of the imperial state by sharing its information with Parliament. As a contemporary stated in an article in the *Edinburgh Review* in 1810: "Among all the visionary and extravagant systems of policy ... no one has been absurd enough to maintain that the most advisable way of governing a mighty empire was by committing it to the care of a body of merchants."[5] The British Empire had a company that itself ruled an empire.

Probably no other company had such a huge role in empire-building as the English East India Company. In the golden days of Dutch power, the Dutch *Vereenigde Oostindische Compagnie* (United East India, or Dutch East India

Company) founded in 1602, which was the world's second most powerful multinational corporation after England's, also played a somewhat similar role, at least in the seventeenth century.[6] It was established to compete with England, and similar to the English pattern, it secured a monopoly for Asian colonial trade. This company also acquired quasi-governmental powers, including the power to wage wars, sign treaties, and establish colonies, as well as to imprison and even execute people. During the nearly two centuries between 1602 and 1797, this company sent about one million Europeans to work in Asian trade and plantations, owned altogether nearly 5,000 ships, and carried one-fifth by tonnage of the trade in Asian goods. It established outposts in Banten, occupied the Spice Island of Maluku by defeating the Portuguese in 1605, and, in 1619, it attacked Jayakarta, destroying it and establishing Batavia (now Jakarta). Dutch settlers established coffee plantations on the island. The company also established outposts in Malacca (Malaysia), Persia, Bengal (Bangladesh), and Formosa (Taiwan). It conquered Ceylon from the Portuguese, and in 1652 it established a settler base—Cape Town—halfway to India at the Cape of Good Hope. Like the British, they also launched trade within Asia between Japan, China, India, and Indonesia.

By 1750, the company had 25,000 employees in ten Asian countries, and huge warehouses for European trade in the safe Batavia and Galle (Sri Lanka). At the end of the seventeenth century, it was the wealthiest company in the world, with 150 merchant ships, 50,000 employees, 40 war ships, and a private army of 10,000 soldiers. For 200 years, the company paid 18% dividends. However, at the end of the eighteenth century, the company declined, together with Dutch power, and became almost bankrupt in 1799. The territories it conquered became the Dutch East Indies, and the company was dissolved.

French merchants launched their first adventure to the Indies in 1603, and Henry IV authorized the *Compagnie des Indes Orientales*, a state company with a 15-year monopoly. From three existing companies, Jean-Baptiste Colbert, the father of French mercantilism, founded the French East India Company in 1664. Like its competitors, the French state granted concessions and monopoly to the company, including the concession of Madagascar, and all potentially conquered territories. Although the company established itself in India in 1719, it had a shorter and more troubled history, was abolished a century after its foundation in 1769, but then reconstituted again. However, the French Revolution rejected giving monopolies, and the company was liquidated for good in 1794.

The three East India Companies, the biggest joint stock companies in history, were closely connected to their states—or, better yet, were states within states—and contributed to trade expansion, the enrichment of their country, and colonial conquest.

The port of Rotterdam—"port of Europe"[7]

The Rotterdam port emerged in the 1960s as the world's largest and busiest seaport, handled 300 million tons of cargo per year. In the mid-1960s,

Rotterdam became the most important container port as well, the "port of Europe." During the four decades between 1966 and 2006, 85 million containers passed through the port. In 2010, 400 million tons of cargo was delivered by 33,000 seagoing vessels and 110,000 inland navigation vessels. The port, with its connected industrial sites, occupies a 40-kilometer long, 10,000-hectare area, and it is equipped with the most advanced high-tech traffic guidance and service systems. Goods are transported to and from Europe, and to and from America and Asia. The goods are transported to and from huge cargo ships via coastal shipping, inland waterways, railroads, pipelines, and roads. Rotterdam's position was partly granted by its outstanding geographical location. The deep waters of the North Sea, and the 24-meter depth of the port, are able to accommodate the largest ships and tanker vessels. The rivers Meuse and Rhine lead to the large German, French, and even Swiss hinterlands.

However, the port of Rotterdam would never have been elevated to its position of importance without human work and innovation. The seagoing Dutch people built the first harbor of Rotterdam, *Onde Haven*, in 1325. The world famous Dutch water engineers connected Rotterdam with the River Schie in 1340, the very year in which Rotterdam gained city status. The importance of the port was elevated during the Dutch Golden Age when the northern Low Countries, later the Netherlands, became the first dominant naval power, and had by far the largest merchant fleet. Dutch merchant capitalism reached its peak in the seventeenth and eighteenth centuries. One of the leading institutions and symbols of Dutch naval and merchant-colonial power, the Dutch East India Company, had operated partly from Rotterdam since 1602.

The most important turning point, however, was the building of the *Nieuwe Waterweg*, or New Waterway, in 1872. That was a time of unique continental modernization and industrialization. This canal connected Rotterdam with the North Sea and the Meuse and Rhine rivers and opened access to inland Western Europe. The 6.5-kilometer-long canal was navigable for seafaring ships as well. From the 1870s on, the importance of the Rotterdam Port increased dramatically because of spectacular German industrialization, especially in the nearby Ruhr area, and increasing foreign trade. Rotterdam virtually became a German port for Britain and the United States.

The city of Rotterdam started growing rapidly. In the eighteenth century, it had 50,000 inhabitants, by the mid-nineteenth century it increased to 90,000, and by 1940, to 600,000. World War II and the devastating German bombing of Rotterdam in 1940 and later—after the German occupation of the Netherlands— Allied bombing, virtually eliminated the center of the city and severely damaged the port. Postwar reconstruction, especially between 1950 and 1970, not only rebuilt the city and the port, but significantly modernized it as well. A brand new skyline was created, and the port became the first automated terminal. In 2010, nearly two million people were concentrated in the greater Rotterdam-Rijnmond agglomeration.

The most important novelty was the containerization of Europe that started in Rotterdam. About ten years after the containerization of the United States,

Rotterdam followed suit. Strangely enough, it is almost impossible to give the exact date when container transportation was invented. It actually existed as early as World War I, when the American army delivered munitions to Europe in containers. Some European companies, such as the Dutch Van Gend and Loos, introduced door-to-door container delivery service in the late 1920s. However, containers were not standardized, some of them were wooden, and they did not yet change the transportation system. Containerization broke through after World War II, and its pioneer was an American trucker, Malcom McLean, who founded the Sea-Land Company in 1956, which became the first company to deliver cargo entirely in containers. His container ship *Fairland* arrived in Rotterdam in May 1966 and, with three sister ships, delivered 226 containers.

The Sea-Land Company had weekly transatlantic operations, and Rotterdam emerged as the leading container port. Five Rotterdam companies founded the Specialized European Container Terminus. The containerization of transportation was revolutionary. "The advent of the container during the final quarter of the twentieth century could be analogous to the transition ... to coal ... Like steam shipping, containerization drastically altered cargo handling in seaports and revolutionized the whole concept of transport."[8] Containers were moved from railways, to trucks, and to ships without unpacking and repacking the entire cargo. Transportation became more efficient, cheaper, and faster.

These changes were connected with technical innovations that transformed the container ships: they were equipped with bridge cranes; their size was standardized by international agreements.[9] Bigger and bigger container ships were built: the first, 4,500 twenty-foot equivalent unit (TEU) ships were replaced by 6,000 TEU ones and then, around the turn of the century, by 10,000 TEU vessels. Giant tanker vessels were also introduced. In a decade, Rotterdam sent and received 6,000 containers in a year. The port was automated and computerized. Measured in TEU terms, Rotterdam was the seventh largest container port in the world in 2006. Its leading position as the largest port was taken over by Singapore in 2003 and then Shanghai by 2006. In 2006, however, the European Investment Bank provided a €100 million loan to the *Havenbedrijf Rotterdam NV*, the Rotterdam Port Authority, and a major further enlargement began by constructing a second Maasvlakte, a new harbor and industrial site. The mega-project will cost more than €1,570 million and it enlarges the port by 2,000 hectares, basically by reclaiming land from the ocean. It will be a 20% enlargement of the port and connected industrial spaces. As the report in May 2010 maintained, half of the coastal sand needed for the first phase of land reclamation, 120 million cubic meters, has been sprayed on and has enlarged the peninsula by 3 kilometers. The first containers will arrive at the expanded and largest port of Europe in 2013.

Rolex—one of the most successful Swiss watch-makers[10]

Swiss watch-making is legendary and has a long history. Horology began with the production of mechanical town clocks. From the sixteenth century, personal watches became popular among certain urban layers of the population. Around 1550, Geneva established itself as the leader of Swiss watch-making. While deluxe watches were mostly produced there, industrialists of the Jura Mountain region produced less expensive solid watches. The business, as usual in the early modern times, was based on peasant cottage industry and the Verlag, or putting-out system. A merchant-industrialist provided the material for the peasant households where the various parts were produced, and, at the end, in a centralized workshop, the parts were assembled.

Several exceptional talents and companies established the fame of the Swiss watches. Abraham-Louis Breguet at the turn of the nineteenth century was one of the greatest among them. He worked for 30 years producing his Marie-Antoinette watch, and was appointed watch-maker to the Navy in 1815. According to Jean-François Bergier, "there is no doubt that in his lifetime – he died at the age of 77 in 1823 – Breguet advanced watchmaking by two centuries ... [He was] the genius of watchmaking industry ... as over 80% of the discoveries in the precision watchmaking industry have been attributed to him."[11]

The Breitling Company, established in 1884 in the Neuchâtel region of the Jura Mountains, introduced the wristwatch in 1914, although the Cartier Company already had a design in 1904. Another pioneer of the wristwatch was the Rolex Company, which started its spectacular career in the early twentieth century. Hans Wilsdorf and Alfred Davis established the Wilsdorf and Davis Company in London in 1905. They produced only the quality cast and imported the mechanisms from Switzerland. In 1919, the company, which at that time was already called Rolex Watch Company, moved to Geneva, Switzerland. In the mid-1920s, they produced the "Oyster" case, the first really waterproof wristwatch that was tested for three weeks under water. Later, Jacques Piccard tested it at a depth of 11,000 meters. In 1931, Rolex came out with the "forerunner of modern automatic watches, the perpetual self-winding rotor mechanism based on storing energy from the natural movements of the wearer's wrist."[12] In 1945, they produced the first wristwatch that displayed the date.

The years between 1960 and 1980 became a critical time for Swiss watch-making. A new technological war shocked the traditional industry and undermined the Jura watch industry. Competition from the American Timex and, most of all, the Japanese Seiko and Citizen, the introduction of the quartz watch, Japanese miniaturization, and the appearance of "Delirium," the world's thinnest watch, opened a new chapter in the watch industry. How to answer the challenge? Several Swiss elite companies remained in the field of producing very expensive luxury and jewelry watches. The Breguet company, for example, preserved the old handicraft tradition and produced watches in the old handicraft way: one single watch-maker started and finished the work. Each worker studies for four years and works another five to ten years to become qualified to work for the company. Another kind of answer was the foundation of the Swiss Corporation for Microelectronic and Watchmaking Industries in Neuchâtel in 1982 to take up the challenge and compete with the Japanese in the new technology field. This company renamed as the Swatch Groups, started producing simple, plastic watches with half the components of a usual watch. The first products were sold in 1983 and opened a new successful road for the Swiss watch industry. Swatch became the largest watch-making company in the world.

Rolex continued its road as one of the technology leaders and remained prominent in both areas: the luxury watch and the less expensive, modern watches. Its trendy, partly gold, platinum, and diamond watches, the Yacht-Master, Day-Date, Daytona, Datejust, Explorer, Submariner, and others became status symbols. By 1975, Rolex produced a quartz version of Oysters and, under the brand name of Tudor, also sold less expensive watches until 2004. At the turn of the twenty-first century, Rolex produced 2,000 watches per day and represented 20% of the value of Swiss watch exports.

Small is beautiful: "Fabriques collectives" in the Lyon silk industry[13]

The nineteenth century was the period of the rise of big industry and mass production. Some pioneering companies and entrepreneurial talent changed the economy for ever. The traditional Lyon silk industry, based on highly developed, small-scale craftsmanship, did not follow the general pattern of industrial development, but preserved its small-scale, craft-oriented character in the age of industrialization. The alternative system of the Lyon silk industry paved the way for the exceptional development of the fashion industry in modern times. Lyon had a long history in silk production and design. In the fifteenth century, a royal decree established silk manufacturing, but the attempt failed. Its real career began as a marketplace for imported Italian silk products in the sixteenth century. Various privileges attracted Italian weavers who settled in Lyon, and by the mid-seventeenth century they produced silk using 14,000 hand looms, employing one-third of the inhabitants of the city. In 1775, Basile Bouchon and Jean-Baptiste Falcon's punched card loom, an early forerunner of modern machines, was being used there. Based on its long legacy, the small-scale silk-producing workshops flourished and 28,000 craftsmen represented the Lyon silk industry before the French Revolution.

Based on that legacy, the Lyon silk industry preserved its pre-industrial revolution character for a long time. Small-scale workshops produced and processed the silk and big firms and mass production did not emerge in Lyon until the late nineteenth century. The traditional merchant-manufacturer from the early modern centuries continued to run the silk business. In this structural framework, small companies produced certain processes of the silk manufacturing as weaving, dyeing, and polishing, thus the end product was the result of the organized cooperation of a network of small producers. This phenomenon was named *fabriques collectives*, and was able to produce a great variety of relatively small quantities of various assortments of products. For the silk industry, which targeted a small, rich layer of society with its luxury product, this organizational form was the most advantageous. It made possible frequent changes to the production lines, following changes in taste and fashion, and also made it possible to modify products to create new markets.

The technological base for remaining competitive and for producing high-quality products in a small-scale process was provided by the invention of the Jacquard loom in 1801, which was a much more sophisticated version of the previous punch-card loom. The new miracle machine was exhibited at the Invention Exposition in Paris. Using perforated cards, programming and reprogramming the Jacquard loom was very easy. By 1834, nearly 2,900 Jacquard looms were in operation in Lyon. That made it possible to produce small quantities of new patterns and colors and also to combine differently dyed threads and even different materials. Lyon preserved the hand-looms for a long time: even in 1875, only 7,000 looms, or 20% of the total, were mechanized. The small, traditional workshops were able to change their production methods and print dyes onto the woven silk.

Another important technical development, however, played a crucial role in turn-of-the-twentieth-century Lyon: small electric engines provided the required cheap and mobile energy sources to mechanize small-scale firms. Between 1870 and 1914, the number of mechanical looms increased by eight times, and the silk industry achieved very fast growth rates. Even embroidery became mechanized. In 1884, the invention of viscose, or artificial silk, by Hilaire de Chardonnet, and the beginning of its mass production in 1891, gave a new impetus to the silk industry in France. The difficulties of coordinating a great number of small firms were solved by municipal and state regulations. State involvement included guaranteed access to required resources, assistance in training and providing certified skilled workers, and the allocation of credits to weavers in difficult times. Lyon had learned the lessons of the famous 1831 and 1834 weavers' uprisings and founded the *conseil de prud'hommes*, a forerunner of corporative organization to settle disputes between workers and employees. The state also provided funds to create mutual aid societies by the workers. Another secret of Lyons' success and competitiveness was the combination of high-quality silk production with the fashion industry, especially from the 1870s and 1880s on.

From the turn of the twentieth century, the traditional character of the silk industry started changing and later declined. At the end of the twentieth century, China regained its leading position in silk production—as in many other fields—and produced 58,000 tons, or 72%, of the world's 81,000 tons of total silk output. The Lyon silk industry, however, created an alternative pattern for modern mass production in the special, strongly fashion-oriented luxury consumer industries. This remained characteristic of the French and later Italian fashion industries in clothing, shoes, and other products. Some of the small-scale workshops gradually enlarged and even became multinational companies, such as the Italian Benetton that started as a small family business, involving home production and door-to-door selling by the two Benetton siblings. From modest beginnings in the early 1960s, within a quarter of a century Benetton was coordinating 250 outside suppliers and owned 5,000 retail outlets in 60 countries. However, most of these fashion industries, especially in Italy and France, remained small-scale in a time of mass production and globalization, though they represented a significant part of the value of industrial output until the twenty-first century.

The Ganz Works: a cutting edge engineering company in a less developed country[14]

Hungary entered the age of industrialization as the bread-basket of the Habsburg Empire. In the mid-nineteenth century, the Austrian-Czech half of the Empire had already made impressive progress in modern industrial development, and it met the limited demand for industrial goods in the agrarian provinces of the monarchy. In Hungary at that time, there were nine steam engines in operation, totaling 100 horsepower, and only half of that capacity served the industry. The industrial sector was represented by a few flour mills and mostly non-mechanized manorial works that processed raw materials, coal, iron, wood, and wool from the big estates using serf labor.

Social mobility was extremely limited in this uneducated peasant country, and entrepreneurial attitude was mostly missing in the noble society where business activity did not belong to a "gentleman's" lifestyle. Trade became a Jewish business, and merchants slowly invested in the food processing industry from the 1860s on. Immigrants, although small in numbers, also played an important role in initiating modern sectors. One of them was a Swiss iron founder. Abraham Ganz was born in Unter-Embrach, Switzerland, the youngest son of a large family. Due to guild traditions, he wandered Europe to learn his foundry skills, working in various countries. He arrived in Hungary in 1841 when he started working in the foundry of a mill. He recognized the business possibilities and settled there, founding a small iron foundry in Buda with seven workers in 1844.

During the 1850s and 1860s, two booming sectors—railroad construction and the export-oriented flour mill industry—offered a special opportunity for the embryonic iron and engineering industries in Hungary. Ganz jumped into these businesses. With the new method he invented and patented, he started producing chilled cast iron railway wheels, which he exhibited at international exhibitions in London and Paris. The rapidly developing Hungarian railroads— 6,000 kilometers of track were laid between 1844 and 1973—turned out to be a huge and stable market, but Ganz was also able to export his products for 60 railway companies in Europe. By 1867, 100,000 railroad wheels had already left the factory, which employed 400 workers.

In 1859, Ganz invited the Bavarian Andreas (András) Mechwart, who was educated at the Augsburg Engineering School, to join the factory. The talented engineer had patented a breakthrough invention. He changed the porcelain roller in the roller frame for flour mills in favor of chilled cast iron rollers that made it possible to grind wheat much finer, and also made it possible to produce various kinds of grinds. This patent gave the Budapest flour mill industry, the second biggest in the world after Minneapolis, a great advantage in international competition, and led to a boom for the Ganz factory.

In 1867, when Abraham Ganz committed suicide, Mechwart became the managing director of the firm, which was transformed into a joint stock company, and in 1868 he built up contacts with Hitelbank (Creditbank), a big, Rothschild-founded bank in the country. Mechwart recognized the potential and future of the newly born electric industry at the right time. In 1878, he established an Electrotechnical Department that, in 1906, became an independent company, the Ganz Electric Company, with close connections to the German AEG that owned 45% of its stock. Hungary had a better position in the new industries of the second industrial revolution than in the traditional branches of the first one, such as textiles. Austrian competition was not overwhelming in the new branches.

The good technical education available in Hungary also contributed. The Budapest Technical University trained excellent engineers. One of them was Károly Zipernowsky, who was invited to join the Ganz Works from university and became the head of the electric department of the factory. In the first half of the 1880s, three more exceptionally talented engineers, most of them graduates of the Budapest Technical University, joined the factory: Kálmán Kandó, who worked in France first; Ottó Bláthy, a graduate of the Technical University of Vienna; and Miksa Déry, who studied both in the Budapest and the Vienna Technical Universities. This group of electrical engineers made breakthrough inventions. Zipernowsky himself received 40 patents while he worked for Ganz. Their patents gave the factory a significant advantage. Zipernowsky's idea of a transformer that was able to transform electrical currents from high to low voltage, was a major invention that solved the problem of the transportation of electricity, and it was realized by Bláthy and Déry in 1884–85. The Ganz factory delivered transformers to power stations of Luzern, Rome, and Vienna. The company introduced electric lighting, and in 1882 the National Theater of Budapest became the world's third theater with electric lighting. The Ganz engineers, unlike their Western counterparts, recognized the potential of alternating current technology. Kálmán Kandó developed a high-voltage, three-phase alternating current engine for electric trains, and the Ganz Company won the contract for the electrification of Europe's first main railroad line, the north Italian Valtellina railroad, in 1897.

Several other inventions and patents led to the unique growth and all-European importance of the Ganz Works, which employed nearly 6,000 workers in 1910. Before and during World War I, Ganz began airplane production for the Austro-Hungarian air force, and it produced warships (after its fusion with the Danubius Ship and Crane Factory). In a mostly agricultural country, the Ganz Works emerged as one of the technology leaders of Europe. In the interwar decades, however, Ganz lost its all-European status, although it remained one of the most important factories in Hungary. The country returned to protectionism, and Ganz lost its decisive international connections. The domestic market was shrinking, and it did not offer new possibilities. Before World War II, 62% of the company's production was sold abroad. Only two significant new results should be mentioned: the development of the 220-horsepower diesel locomotive by György Jendrassik in 1928, and the building of river- and oceangoing 1,200-ton ships from 1933. The Ganz Work sold two diesel locomotives in Hungary and about 500 in Latin America and Africa. The electrical engineering products lost their cutting-edge position. Ganz still sold power stations to Turkey and produced its old products, dynamos, transformers, and turbo generators, and it sold most of them in the Balkans. The number of employed workers did not even reach their 1910 levels.

In 1946, as part of the gradual communist takeover, the factory was nationalized and separated into six independent companies, and later, in 1959, it merged with the State Wagon and Locomotive Factory (MAVAG). In 1980, reorganization followed and seven companies and three joint ventures were created. The former crown jewel of the Hungarian engineering industry declined into merely local importance. After the regime change in 1989, Ganz was privatized again, this time by foreign investors. The British Telfos Holding gained a majority in the Ganz Railway Vehicle Factory, but it later sold its shares, and, in the end Ganz became part of an Austrian company. The Italian giant, Ansaldo, bought 51% of the Ganz Electric Works in 1991 and then the rest in 1998, but it sold Ganz again in 2000. The other parts of the company became Ganz-Škoda, which was mostly German-owned. The Ganz complex, like in Hungary and several other post-communist countries, was swallowed by multinational companies in the strongly globalized European economy.

The Thyssen empire: from local to global[15]

This is a story of three generations of family business and far beyond. We know about Thyssens[16] from the seventeenth century, but their first steps towards building an industrial empire begin in the early nineteenth century. Johann Friedrich Thyssen, born in 1804, was a self-made man. Orphaned at the age of 13, he became director of the English-founded Draht Fabric Company in 1822. In 1861, with his accumulated capital, he opened an exchange and bank business in Eschweiler. He and his wife had nine children, and Friedrich later involved two of his sons, August and Joseph, in the business.

From this well-to-do family, August, born in 1842, got a good education at the Politechnische Schule Karlsruhe, and then at a commercial school in Antwerp. After working in his father's bank for two years, he and a partner founded and managed the iron works Thyssen & Foussel in Duisburg in 1866 and employed 130 workers. After four years, with the financial assistance of his father, he became independent and, with 70 workers, established his Walzwerk Thyssen & Co in Mülheim in 1871. After the death of his father and some other family members, August and some of his sisters inherited and invested relatively huge amounts into his business. His brother, Joseph, also joined with his inheritance.

These were the years of the birth of the modern steel industry in Germany. The location of the company in the Ruhr area, offered great opportunities in the form of nearby raw material resources. "That [was the] time, [when] steel became the symbol of technological and economic progress."[17] August Thyssen, although he was already a second-generation entrepreneur, had a typical first-generation founder-industrialist attitude: his company was his life. He did not accept different views and was the almighty commander of his army. The authoritarian *pater familias* had virtually no time for his young wife, and later for his children. His marriage was ruined and soon ended with divorce. His relations with his children remained cold and unfriendly during his entire life. However, he built his empire with limitless energy.

Thyssen recognized the advantage of vertical integration, and in 1880 he bought coal mines and then iron ore resources in countries as far away as France, North Africa, and Russia. An endless expansion made him the ruler of the Ruhr iron, steel, and coal industries; he also incorporated engineering and construction businesses. He bought majority shares in the Bremer Vulkan Schiffbau- und Maschinenfabrik and Flensburger Schiffbau-Gesellschaft and produced ships. Incorporating a mining company, Gewerkschaft Deutscher Kaiser, offered good coal resources. Several smaller iron and steel works, such as the Press- und Walzwerk AG, also became part of the Thyssen empire. His son, Fritz, continued the expansion and bought majority shares in the Geisweider Eisenwerke and the Gewerkschaft Lohberg in Hamborn. Later the empire also incorporated the Krefelder Stahlwerk. Meanwhile, the company itself established new branches, such as a new steel mill in Buckhausen in 1889, with six Siemens-Martin furnaces and rolling mills.

At the time of World War I, Thyssen had five major iron and steel works in the area. Already the biggest in Germany, Thyssen produced 700,000 tons of steel. When August Thyssen died in 1926, the empire had 12 huge units and employed 40,000 workers. They owned a bank in Rotterdam and built 10,000 apartments for workers, doubling the Hamborn city limits. *The New York Times* reported on the front page of its April 5, 1926 issue, a day after the death of August, that the Thyssen empire's value reached $100,000,000.

From 1926, the third generation took over. Fritz Thyssen, born in 1873 had already been trained to lead the company. He studied mining and metallurgy in London, Liège, and Berlin, and he joined the board of his father's company in 1897. In 1926, Fritz took over the company, and reorganized the Empire of the Ruhr steel works by founding the Verenigte Stahlwerk AG in 1926.

Fritz was a good entrepreneur, and he launched a major rationalization by shutting down the less efficient plants of the company. By 1934, the number of the company's iron and steel works decreased from 145 to 66, its blast furnaces from 23 to nine, and its rolling mills from 17 to ten. Productivity increased, and the output per workers increased by nearly 50%. However, Fritz Thyssen's interests, especially in the difficult and confusing time after the lost war, turned towards politics.[18]

The third-generation syndrome characterized the Thyssen family as well. After the founders' hard drive, the grandchildren of the first founding generation grew up in richness, often lost interest in business, and turned towards other entertainments. Fritz, an ardent German nationalist who was arrested by the French authorities during the French occupation of the Ruhr area after World War I, met with Hitler in 1923, and started financing the Nazi Party. Moreover, he mobilized his big business partners to do the same. In 1933, he joined the Nazi Party, and became a member of Hitler's Reichstag. His company served Hitler's war preparations well. At that time the Thyssen empire was the largest coal-iron-steel conglomerate in the world, owning 75% of the German iron ore resources and employing 200,000 workers.

Fritz Thyssen, however, did not like the harsh Nazi violence, became deeply disappointed by the infamous *Kristallnacht*, and opposed the war. He left Nazi Germany for Switzerland and then France. His company was confiscated by the Nazis and renamed Rheinisch-Westfälische Beteiligungs AG in 1940. During the last phase of the war, he was captured and arrested by the Nazis. It did not help him much after the war because the Allies liquidated his company as one that was responsible for Nazi war crimes. Fritz Thyssen left Germany and died in Buenos Aires in 1951.

One of his brothers, Heinrich Thyssen, studied science and art history in Munich, London, and Berlin, and received his doctorate in Heidelberg in 1899. He married the daughter of a Hungarian aristocrat, Margit Bornemissa de Kászon et Impérfalva, and settled in Hungary in 1906. His father-in-law adopted him, but after the Hungarian communist revolution in 1919 they left Hungary and moved to the Netherlands. Heinrich Thyssen-Bornemissa became a major art collector and established one of the greatest private art museums for himself in Lugano. His son, whose full name was Hans Henrik Ágost Gábor Tasso Freiherr Thyssen-Bornemissa de Kászon et Impérfalva, was born in the Netherlands, became a citizen of Switzerland, and was a resident of Monaco, Britain, and Spain. This branch of the family manifests the characteristics of the German bourgeoisie that tried adjusting to the aristocracy, buying or building castles as August Thyssen did in Landsberg, where the family has a mausoleum. They believed in elevating their social status by initiating marriages with old aristocratic families. Actually Heinrich was not the only one among the Thyssens. The only daughter of Fritz Thyssen, Anita, married another Hungarian aristocrat, Count Gábor Zichy, and Heinrich's son, Stephan, married a member of the leading Hungarian aristocratic family, Ilona Andrássy. Part of the family, meanwhile, also turned its back on business.

In 1953, however, the family, together with the Commerzbank and the Allianz AG, regained the company and the August Thyssen Hütte AG was reestablished. By the mid-1960s, managed by Hans-Günther Sohl, the company became Europe's biggest crude steel producer again and the fifth largest in the world. From the 1970s on, the company started diversifying its production under the new manager, Dieter Spethmann, buying high-tech engineering groups, starting to produce rapid trains, and the company was renamed Thyssen Industries AG. During the 1980s, the Thyssen company started adjusting to the globalization process and wanted to get the advantage of even larger scale and capital strength. This attempt led to a new merger with another giant, the Krupp Company. After some initial cooperation, the merger was realized in 1999 and the ThyssenKrupp AG was established with five main divisions. The new company produced iron and steel, had a large automotive section, and in a separate unit it produced elevators and escalators. The company's construction and engineering unit built chemical and cement plants. ThyssenKrupp also had a trading and service branch.

The world giant built up a huge network of subsidiaries, in 18 European countries, and in virtually all post-communist countries after 1989. It had shares or full ownership in several companies in 18 Asian and Near-Eastern countries, including China where ThyssenKrupp had 42 subsidiaries. They were present in 12 Latin American countries, Australia, New Zealand and Canada. In the United States, their subsidiaries employed more than 12,000 workers. In its large area of production, ThyssenKrupp AG rules the world.

The Universal Suez Ship Canal Company[19]

The Suez project was a typical child of mid-nineteenth-century European capitalism. On its bright side it embodied superb entrepreneurship and organization, the new steam technology of the first industrial revolution, and outstanding engineering work. This belonged among the most spectacular and grandiose investment projects of the age. On its dark side, it was a typical example of adventurist colonial-imperialist policy forcing lavish concessions from a dependent country and even using cheap colonial forced labor.

On November 16, 1869, the Suez Canal was opened with a high-flying celebration. With Empress Eugénie and the builder of the canal and hero of the day, Ferdinand de Lesseps, on board, the French imperial yacht *L'Aigle* entered the newly built waterway, followed by other ships. Among the celebrity participants were Franz Joseph, Emperor of Austria-Hungary, Friedrich Wilhelm, Royal Prince of Prussia, the Prince and Princess of the Netherlands, and the representatives of Queen Victoria of Britain and Tsar Alexander II of Russia. The next day a pompous party was arranged in Ismailia where the 5,000 guests were received in 1,200 tents. Hundreds of buffets, two suppers, and a spectacular ball were held in the Khedive's new palace, crowned with fireworks. The convoy continued the trip on November 20, arrived at Suez, and dropped anchor in the Red Sea.

These events were the culmination of a decade of heroic work from March 25, 1859, when the digging started—the Universal Suez Ship Canal Company was founded four months before—to the November celebration of 1869. The story of the Suez Canal, however, is much longer. Did it start in 1826, when the young Ferdinand de Lesseps started his diplomatic career as assistant consul of France in Alexandria, Egypt? This was definitely an important date.

De Lesseps gradually rose to the rank of consul, and in the 1830s he established a friendship with Mohammed Sa'id Pasha, the son of the Viceroy—of the Ottoman Port—who himself became the Viceroy, ruling Egypt as a quasi-independent unit in 1854. De Lesseps, as a son of his age—some later called him an American-type "robber baron"—used this connection, and as a result of his meeting with Sa'id on November 15, 1854, he gained the concession for construction ten days later. As the chronicle of the Suez Canal phrased it: "The financial and technological pressure of the North on the South, of the powerful on the weak, had resulted in an exceptional contract, a long-term concession (1858–1968) which deprived Egypt of the massive revenues generated by this hugely successful waterway ... Lesseps took full advantage of a weak Khedive to extract an unfair contract ... The French entrepreneur made the most of the ruler's lack of foresight and his blindness regarding his own financial and territorial motives."[20]

The story of the canal, however, has even deeper layers in history. According to some chronicles, two millennia before Christ, the pharaohs already connected the Mediterranean to the Red Sea via the River Nile. This canal was abandoned and rebuilt several times until the seventh century, but then disappeared. Napoleon's Egyptian expedition in the last years of the eighteenth century offered an opportunity to make discoveries in Egypt: the French also found some signs of the ancient canal, and Napoleon asked Jacques-Marie Le Père to study the possibility of cutting a canal at Suez. His report appeared in 1808 with the results of his measurements. In 1808, Jean-Baptiste Lepère and the Egyptian expedition already initiated the building of the canal, but failed. However, the idea was taken over by the utopian Saint-Simonians, personally Saint-Simon's best follower, Barthélemy Prosper Enfantin, who dreamed about spreading industrial civilization "to rejuvenate Asia." In August 8, 1833, he wrote in a letter to Barrault: "We cut through Suez and Panama – this ancient continent would very soon turn into ravishing spectacle! ... It is for us to create one of these two new routs ... [one] which would open the way to India and China ... Suez is the heart of our life and endeavors."[21]

Enfantin was not only a dreamer. He convinced rich French businessmen, F.B. Arlès-Dufour and the Talbot brothers to establish the *Société d'Études*, the Suez Canal Study Society, in 1846. Measurements and preparation of a detailed plan for a 400-kilometer-long canal from Alexandria to Suez started. An Egypt mania flooded France. The nine-volume *Description de l'Égypte* appeared between 1809 and 1825, and the obelisk of Luxor was erected in Paris in 1836. In 1850, François Auguste Mariette traveled to Egypt to enrich the collection of the Louvre Museum and discovered a subterranean tomb-temple complex. Half of his findings were transported to Paris, the other half remained in Egypt and Ismail Pasha invited Mariette to conserve monuments. He became the director of the Cairo Museum of Antiquities.

In those decades, the industrial revolution gained ground in Europe, including in France, and was combined with a transportation revolution led by steam shipping and the railways. Canal-building also achieved a new boom throughout the continent. Between 1822 and 1848, the French canal network was enlarged by three times. France led the modern educational revolution by training thousands of engineers who led road, bridge, port, and canal constructions throughout Europe. Egypt started nurturing the dream of modernizing the backward country. Big public works became everyday phenomena: in 1818, Alexandria was connected to the Nile by the 80-kilometer-long Mahmoudieh Canal that was dig by 300,000 fellahin, Egyptian peasants. Steamboat service started from Suez to India and the railroad arrived in Cairo in 1856. At the mouth of the Nile delta, two French engineers, Linant de Bellefonds and Eugèn Mougel, started building dams in the 1840s, and they presented a plan for the Suez Canal with locks in the spring of 1855.

By the mid-nineteenth century, the dream of a Suez Canal became realistic and moreover, a requirement. In this environment, the energetic Ferdinand de Lesseps was able to realize his gradually built-up plan, establish the company, mobilize French entrepreneurs and financiers, employ French engineers, and exploit the possibility of the concession he had gained. He formed an International Technical Committee, which presented its report in January 1856; a final version was ready by 1858. De Lesseps contracted Alphonse Couvreux, the famous entrepreneur and railroad-builder, who actually invented a digging excavator comprising a chain with buckets that was carried by rail alongside the canal. More than 100 highly educated engineers started working for the company.

The gigantic work included the building of landing ports, housing for the workforce, a food supply, a fresh water canal, and medical service, especially after cholera and typhus epidemics visited the site. Several towns or bases were established for the workers along the planned canal, and 1,500 private merchants delivered food. During the building years, 8,000 to 15,000 workers were recruited, but it was difficult to guarantee the required labor force. The problem was solved by well-known colonial methods that were "natural" in mid-nineteenth-century capitalism: the Viceroy ordered forced labor from 1862: each village got a contingent and 12,000 to 22,000 villagers worked in a quarterly rotation paid by the company. They were two-and-half times cheaper than unforced labor. They dug a 4–5-meter-wide trench southward by hand and moved the earth in baskets. Nevertheless, canal construction used the modern technology of the industrial revolution: 13 45-ton bucket excavators. In the end, three-quarters of the excavated earth was removed by steam power. Huge, 10,000-horsepower machines were replacing thousands of workers. In 1862, the Suez Company established an assembly plant for the delivered parts and repair, foundries, saw mills, and various workshops with about 850 technicians and workers.

The enormous organization worked as a well-oiled mechanism because of de Lesseps' unlimited energy, enthusiasm, and organizational talent. As a later biographer noted: "Lesseps was everywhere ... at Paris and London, at Constantinople and Cairo ... Constantly in the move, in two decades he crossed ... the Mediterranean 99 times ... Single-handedly pursuing and conducting all negotiations, he remained in constant and direct contact with his engineers and laborers ... He traversed the desert from one end of the proposed canal to the other ... he oversaw every detail, supporting, encouraging, galvanizing."[22]

At last, after ten years of hard work, the canal was ready: 21 meters deep, 300 to 365 meters wide at water level, and 193 kilometers long, the longest lockless canal in the world. This shortened the shipping routes from Europe and America to Asia significantly. The ships did not have to go around the Cape of Good Hope, thus shortening the distance from Liverpool to less than 4,000 miles from nearly 11,000, a decrease of 63%. From Rotterdam, the distance decreased by 41%, from Marseille by 56%. World trade became faster and much cheaper.

The further history of the Suez Canal already belongs to political chronicles. During the post-World War II decades, colonialism declined into a deep crisis and the colonies started liberating themselves. The colonial-type of the Suez Treaty was also questioned by an awakening Egyptian nationalism. In 1952, the Egyptian revolution abolished the monarchy, and a military-nationalist regime was established. The second—and first elected—president of the country, Gamal Abdel Nasser, took over in July 1956. Four weeks later, Nasser declared the nationalization of the Suez Canal Company. A combined British-French-Israeli attack followed to occupy all strategic points along the canal. The military intervention was one of the last colonial military actions. This coincided with the 1956 Hungarian Revolution and the Soviet military intervention, a major political world crisis. "President Eisenhower had an uncomfortable course to steer. In condemning the aggression of the Soviet Union in Hungary, he lost most of the potential tactical advantage due to him as the Anglo-French moves unfolded in Suez."[23] The Eisenhower administration condemned the action and succeeded in achieving a United Nations ceasefire resolution. In spite of their quick military success, the allied forces had withdrawn in March 1957. The Suez Canal was reopened under Egyptian control in April.

The Orientalische Eisenbahnen company and German colonization plans[24]

The old leading economic powers of Europe had already built up huge colonial empires during the early modern centuries, and their colonization drive culminated during the second half of the nineteenth century. At that time, however, new players entered the game. Latecomer Germany, which started its modern industrial transformation mostly after the mid-nineteenth century and especially after unification in 1871, soon took over industrial leadership as a leading country in the second industrial revolution. Nevertheless, the German political elite considered their country a second-rate power without colonies. Germany occupied some still-available left-over territories in Africa. In 1884, they occupied Kamerun and Togo and some territories in East Africa, such as Ruanda-Urundi and Wituland.

The rising German power was not satisfied with those chunks of colonies and the old, traditional *Drang nach Osten* politics gained a new content: expansion towards the East of Europe or, as Hannah Arendt called this attempt, "continental imperialism." Via that area, Germany sought to compete with Britain in the Middle East and even India. The declining Ottoman Empire attracted all of the great powers to try to conquer parts of the vast Empire that ruled Asia Minor, most of the Middle East, huge part of North Africa, and the Balkans. A series of wars with the participation of Britain, France, and Russia signaled the Western and Russian hunger for those territories. It was quite evident that Germany recognized the possibility of successfully competing with the other Western powers for territory. That was the idea behind the construction of the Berlin–Baghdad railway.

The great powers initiated a trade and transportation connection with the Ottoman Empire in the 1860s and 1870s. A British consortium already gained a concession and built a rail line from Varna to Ruschuk along the River Danube in the 1860s. A French-Austrian group started constructing the 2,500-kilometer-long line from Varna to the Austrian border in 1870. Only small, unconnected parts of lines were completed until the Balkans gained independence. Baron Hirsch established the *Orientalische Eisenbahnen* in the 1870s and three parts of the Vienna–Constantinople line, which was 1,400-kilometer-long, was accomplished before 1888. Meanwhile new agreements became necessary with the Ottoman port and the independent Balkan countries that agreed about the completion of the railroad line. In Serbia and Bulgaria, respectively, 460-kilometer and 697-kilometer parts of the Vienna–Constantinople line became national trunk lines to which only side-lines were added under the aegis of the new states.

In 1886, the Ottoman Ministry of Public Works initiated a trunk line from the Bosporus to the Persian Gulf, a line that connected Constantinople to Syria and Baghdad. Sultan Abdul Hamid, a late modernizer, offered huge subsidies for the construction. The opportunity was seized by a German bank consortium of the Württembergische Vereinsbank and Deutsche Bank, and it gained the concession in 1888 with a guaranteed minimum interest of 15,000 francs per kilometer; it also established the Anatolian Railway Company. Deutsche Bank established a holding company for its railway enterprises, the *Bank für orientalischen Eisenbahnen*, with a Zürich headquarters, but only with 6% Swiss participation. The new company bought the Vienna–Constantinople line and began rapid construction work in Anatolia.

Urged on by colonial ambitions, the right-wing German intellectual elite nurtured grand colonial dreams. Professor A. Sprenger called attention in his 1886 pamphlet to "Babylonia" as a potential German colony since the "Orient" was not occupied yet by great powers, and Germany may "not miss the opportunity before the Cossacks arrive." In 1892, Dr. Kartl Kärger called Asia Minor a "deutsches Kolonisationsfeld." The hyper-nationalist and expansionist *Alldeutsche Verband*, published pamphlets in 1896 urging the colonization of Ottoman Turkey by redirecting emigration from Germany to

Asia Minor—instead of America—and establishing German colonies there. The president of the organization, Ernst Hasse, worked out a plan for the division of the Ottoman Empire. According to these colony-hungry dreams, "The entire Asian Turkey, with the exception of Armenia, would be taken over by Germany."[25]

The young Emperor, Kaiser Wilhelm II, visited Constantinople in 1889 with his wife on the imperial yacht *Hohenzollern,* at the time when the first kilometers of track were being laid down for the railroad line in Anatolia towards Baghdad. The Kaiser visited again in 1898. The construction of the Berlin–Baghdad railway progressed successfully. By 1892, the line was completed to Ankara and by 1896 to Konya, the first two sections of the Constantinople–Baghdad line. The Ottoman government backed the construction as a bulwark against potential danger from the Russians, while the Germans had a complex interest to compete with the colonial powers, avoiding their Suez Canal towards the Middle East and India, and even to the African colonies. In 1901, the Germans discovered a "lake of petroleum" around the Tigris and Euphrates rivers that gave them further incentive to go on. "Thus the Baghdad Railway was an imperial enterprise ... Its success was associated with the national honor, to be defended, if needed be, by military force ... The Railway was no longer a railway alone, but a state of mind ... the specter of the twentieth century."[26] Of the 1,600-kilometer-long line through Turkey, Syria, and Iraq, only 480 kilometers remained to be completed when World War I stopped construction.

In his annual report on Turkey, the British Ambassador stated in 1907: "The policy of Germany ... secured them the concession of the Baghdad Railway, the monopoly of all orders for military munitions for the Turkish army, and a privileged position for all industrial and commercial concessions which were in the power of the Sultan."[27] In August 1914, the German–Turkish Alliance was signed. Germany lost the war and Article 231 of the Versailles Treaty put blame for the war entirely upon Germany and the Central Powers. Germany lost the Berlin–Baghdad Railway and its colonies. The *Drang nach Osten* policy became history and colonial dreams were eliminated. From the desperation of the lost war and crashed dreams, the phoenix of German expansionism started rising again in the 1930s before crashing again in 1945. Germany was renewed and became one of the founders of the European Union. The Orient Express, however, continued operation. But in 2009, the luxury train lost its attraction in the face of air travel, and the famous Express stopped running.

Vickers-Armstrong: the multi-arms military giant[28]

In the last years of the British industrial revolution, an ambitious miller, Edward Vickers, established a steel foundry in Sheffield, the heart of the world's steel industry at that time. His family was relatively well-to-do from the iron and steel trade, and his brother operated a rolling mill. More importantly, he married the daughter of George Nylor, the rich owner of an iron and steel mill. However, the Nylor and Sanderson Company closed its business and was taken over by two independent firms. One of them was Nylor, Hutchinson, Vickers and Company, owned by the son of George Nylor and the brother of Edward Vickers.

From successful investments, Edward accumulated enough capital to take over the company in the 1840s, and in 1854, he got his two sons, Tom, an officer and technological genius, and Albert, a great business talent, involved in the family business. Both of his sons received their technical education in Germany. Tom took over the technical controls of the operation and patented several innovations, among them a method of constructing railway engines and carriage wheels of cast steel. Steel casting became one of the company's specialties secured by Tom's various patents. None of the Vickers was a genuine all-round autocratic managerial genius like the famous captains of industry who populated the history of nineteenth-century industrialization. However, as Clive Trebilcock, one of the chroniclers of the company, stated, "they functioned as an unusually complementary entrepreneurial partnership." They also had the ability to select "talented subordinates ... [and] put together a board of directors which operated as a genuine and brilliant team." Their special "directorial system" that became dominant during the twentieth century, was rare before World War I. The huge and growing empire was governed by the board of directors, "with a central group of only seven key figures."[29]

The company went public in 1867 under the name Vickers, Sons & Co. The factory was first of all a steel-making firm that introduced the most modern technology. Retrospectively it looks pretty paradoxical that one of their first successful products was church bells. Soon, the company gradually emerged as Britain's, and probably the world's, number one armaments combine. The first steps towards this direction were taken in 1868 when the company started producing marine shafting and, in another four years, screw propellers. They also started delivering armament parts and armor for ordnance work. The idea to produce guns was a natural step to make, especially because the 1880s became a period when military technology, static for decades, started to revolutionize. Britain started producing much bigger 16-inch and 80-ton guns. Warships became also much bigger, with thicker armor and more and bigger guns.

The Vickers brothers, especially Albert, dreamed about transforming the steel factory, already connected to the armament industry, into a naval armament factory that produced ships, armor, and guns. The easiest way to realize the dream was to buy and merge competing armament factories. Parallel with the Vickers, a few leading companies emerged. Among them were W.G. Armstrong and Co., Naval Construction and Armaments Co., Charles Mitchell and Co., and last but not least, the Maxim Gun Co., based on Hiram Maxim's major invention, the machine gun.

In 1897, as the first breakthrough, Vickers purchased the Naval Construction's Barrow-in-Furness shipbuilding factory, which employed 5,500 workers and occupied 25 acres. The new owners soon increased the number of employees to 10,000. In the same year, they bought the small Maxim Gun Factory, and also enlarged it. A few years later, this unit of Vickers already employed 4,000 workers in an 18-acre factory. In 1902, as the next step in expansion, Vickers bought Beardmore and Co., the number one armor factory in the country. In 1911, the Whitehead torpedo factory was also incorporated into the Vickers empire.

The dramatically enlarged firm entered the naval revolution of the turn of the century. Those years were characterized by rapid military preparations and an arms race, most of all between Germany and Britain. The crown jewel of British military might was the navy, and naval competition introduced the Dreadnought-type warships, a devastating weapon with ten 12-inch and 27 12-pounder guns, and five torpedo tubes. In 1909, Tom Vickers offered to construct three Dreadnoughts in three years "without going outside its own factories."[30] Small wonder that Vickers had become the preferred child of the British Admiralty before World War I. Vickers paid back: in 1901, the factory produced its first submarine, Holland 1, and a decade later launched aircraft production.

Among several new elements of the armament revolution, three new weapons demand special attention: the submarine, the airplane, and the tank. Vickers played a pioneering role in the production of all three. The first small, steam-propelled submarines were already produced in the 1880s. Two companies played a special role in that development, but in 1900, Vickers signed an agreement to take over the submarine project, and they built what were, at that time, enormous submarines, 257 feet in length with a 3,700-horsepower engine. They added the periscope, designed by Howard Grubb, and started producing two types, a coastal and an overseas. By buying a torpedo factory, Vickers also established torpedo production.

The arms race with Germany soon turned attention to the possibility of aerial warfare. The first step by Vickers in Britain was to buy the German patent in 1910, and to produce a German Zeppelin-type airship, the Rigid Naval Airship, called Mayfly. The first Vickers monoplane was ready in 1911, but in the few years before the war the company tested eight new types. The Fighting Biplane 2 became the "world's first real fighting airplane, and improved versions of it ... were to be built in large numbers [actually altogether 26] for the Royal Flying Corps, which called them all the Gun-bus."[31] During the war, Vickers started producing a twin-engine (two 360-horsepower Rolls-Royce engines) night-bomber, the "Vimy," due to a 350-piece order from the Air Board. It was able to carry six tons of payloads at 100 miles an hour. The modern air industry was born. During World War I, Vickers became one of the most important military industrial bases in Britain.

One of the revolutionary new weapons of World War I, the tank, was not among the Vickers-produced weaponry. Producing battleships, submarines, guns, munitions, and airplanes at full capacity made the company unable to participate in tank production. The brand new weapon was produced by one of Vickers' main competitors, Armstrong. Nevertheless Vickers created the potential to join this business in 1901 through its subsidiary, the

Wolseley Tool and Motor Car Company. During the 1920s, Vickers indeed became the only producer of the new weapon, but orders from the War Office or abroad were limited until the 1930s.

A new chapter opened in the history of the company after the war. Peace-time production was not a great challenge since decimated navies and merchant fleets had to be replaced. Commercial air traffic was also one of the outcomes of the development of aviation during the war. Several newly independent countries started building up their military forces and bought weaponry. Vickers did not suffer from lack of orders for long.

The interwar years, as Marshall Foch prophesized at the time of the peace treaty in 1920, were more of an armistice for 20 years than a real peace. Some historians introduced the idea of the "thirty years' war of the twentieth century" that included both world wars and the troubled armistice in between. Vickers definitely calculated in this way and continued its expansion to incorporate most of its rivals. The most significant step towards this direction after World War I was the incorporation of its most important rival, the Armstrong Whitworth Company, in 1927. Armstrong was a major military producer in the same areas as Vickers, especially artillery and shipbuilding. The next year, they developed a 7.2-ton tank and sold them throughout the world. The Soviet Union bought it and produced a version of it under the name of T-26. In 1928, Vickers took another bold step and bought up the Supermarine Company, one of the aviation pioneers, and transformed it into The Supermarine Aviation Works (Vickers) Ltd in 1931. Vickers-Armstrong's 12- to 13-ton tanks and the Vickers-Supermarine fighter planes, the world's fastest and most efficient Spitfire, elevated the company to the status of leading Britain's rearmament drive during the 1930s. In the single year from 1936 to 1937, the Vickers-Armstrong workforce increased from 47,000 to 67,000, and they prepared to employ 10,000 more and to provide armaments during the life-or-death struggle of World War II.

Three generations of the Vickers family—Edward, his two sons Tom and Albert, and then Tom's son, Douglas—ran the ever-enlarging company from its foundation until 1926, when Douglas Vickers became the president of the company and the first non-family member, General Herbert Lawrence, took over the chairmanship of the board of directors. Douglas Vickers died in 1937.

Vickers' 2,000-horsepower, 500-mile-an-hour fighter planes and four-engine bombers contributed to Britain's victory in the war. By 1942, 20,000 workers produced more than 700 war planes per month in the two Vickers airplane factories. Between the outbreak of the war and the end of 1941, Vickers produced about 40% of the British tanks. By 1942 and 1943, respectively, Britain was producing 7,500 and 8,500 tanks a year, and Vickers delivered one-third and then one-quarter of them, respectively. Vickers also delivered large artillery pieces: in the first years of the war, Vickers contributed two-thirds of national production. In the Vickers-Armstrong shipyards, roughly 40,000 workers supplied the navy with powerful warships. The company significantly contributed to the victory in the war against Nazi Germany.

The post-World War II history of the company became very stormy. They continued producing for the military and launched the first British nuclear submarine, and the first British V-bomber. Their famous tanks had a huge foreign market. However, Vickers had to diversify and broaden their production lines in various areas, with a much stronger commercial direction. Besides their traditional steel, aircraft production, shipbuilding (during the 1960s, the company also became part of the British Hovercraft Corporation), and engineering businesses, Vickers began producing tractors, moved into chemical and medical engineering, and produced printing machines. Nevertheless, these new endeavors failed. In some other areas, however, such as office equipment, bottling machinery, machine tools, and others, they succeeded. Those same decades became the period of a widespread nationalization wave in Britain and several branches of the Vickers-Armstrong company such as their steel, shipbuilding, and aircraft sectors were nationalized in 1977 under the aegis of the Aircraft and Shipbuilding Industrial Act of 1965, which created the state-owned British Shipbuilding and Engineering and British Steel companies. However, during the 1980s, Margaret Thatcher reprivatized most of the state-owned companies, among them the former Vickers branches. In 1986, for example, from the Royal Ordnance Factory the Vickers Defence System was formed and Vickers Shipbuilding and Engineering was also reprivatized. The Vickers name remained a major trademark in Britain until the end of the twentieth century.

The Dutch Philips: from the electrical to the electronic age[32]

The Netherlands, a world economic leader in the seventeenth and part of the eighteenth centuries, lost its leading position to Britain, and it could not follow its competitor's footsteps in industrialization. The Dutch path to the modern industrial age was unique: it led via innovative food processing. The flat country, with its very advanced agriculture, lacked any of the industrial raw materials that were a decisive factor at the time of the first industrial revolution. However, the Netherlands built up the most advanced and innovative food processing industry, including the processing of imported sugar, tobacco, and other goods from the colonies. In the latter part of the nineteenth century, however, rich merchants established some industries to supply the country with consumer goods, and, at the very end of the century, they jumped on the bandwagon of the second industrial revolution and created the most modern high-tech industries. Two main prerequisites were present: huge amounts of capital in one of Europe's richest countries, and probably the best-educated population.

The most important step on the road towards the establishment of high-tech industries was made by Gerard Philips, a talented engineer and businessman. The Jewish Philips family emigrated from Prussia to tolerant Holland in the eighteenth century. Philip Philips became a tobacco merchant, and his son, Benjamin, continued that business in Zaltbommel. The family assimilated and even became baptized. One of Benjamin's eight sons, Lion, a tobacco and coffee merchant, continued the family business. By marriage he became the uncle of Karl Marx, who sometimes visited the Philips family in the Netherlands.[33] Three of Lion's five children continued the family business. Among them was Frederik Philips, a rich tobacco and coffee merchant, who established a mechanized cigar factory and also became a banker. Frederik had five children: one was a lawyer, another one a chemist, but the other three remained in the family business. His elder son, Gerard, was born in 1858, studied at the Delft Polytechnic, and graduated as an engineer in 1883. He started working at a shipbuilding factory, and then moved to Glasgow to work in the most advanced shipbuilding industry. Lighting ships became a major issue at that time, and the young engineer also read *The Electrician* and became informed about the manufacture of incandescent lamps. Electricity intrigued him so much that he enrolled as an evening student at the Glasgow College of Science and Arts where he studied and worked with one of the greatest experts of electric studies. After his graduation he joined the American Brush Electric Light Company in London. The young electric engineer worked for five important years in England and Germany, built up a valuable network of electric engineers and companies, and became the Dutch agent of the German AEG.

This was the period when electric lighting started conquering Europe. Between two major exhibitions, the International Electricity Exhibition in Paris in 1881 and the International Electricity Exhibition at Frankfurt am Main in 1891, the spread of electric lighting in public buildings and streets throughout Europe's capital cities clearly signaled the future of electric lighting. The latter exhibition presented the new heavy electrical engineering products. The very first lighting companies were already founded in the Netherlands from the late 1870s. Electricity was in the air of Europe.

Gerard Philips returned to the Netherlands at the end of 1889 and worked for a concession of AEG for lighting Amsterdam, a project that created a market for tens of thousands of light bulbs. He was well trained, connected, and informed, and he decided to establish his own company. The situation was outstanding in the Netherlands since the lack of patent legislation offered a great business opportunity. His family wealth solved the problem of investment capital. Gerard made an agreement with his father, and Frederik joined the business. Later his brother Anton did so, too. Gerard employed a manager and carefully prepared everything. In 1891, he established his factory in Eindhoven. The township was small, but the surrounding villages and townships had altogether 20,000 inhabitants. In 1892 they produced 11,000 light bulbs, but in 1893 they produced 45,000, the result of mass consumption and production. By 1913, 6.4 million bulbs were sold, produced by 2,500 workers. The pioneering company became Europe's third-largest electric company. Next year, Philips established its own chemistry and physics research laboratories and the company continued along its triumphant path.

The secret of its success was its exceptional engineers and researchers. From its foundation until 1939, Gerard and then Anton Philips managed the factory, and the family still controlled management under Frits Philips during the 1960s. They employed excellent experts and good, loyal workers. The company had a strong social policy orientation, and it built a workers' village in the city with more than 1,000 houses. The workers' village was enlarged from time to time. Four different types of houses, all with a garden of 80 to 100 square meters offered housing for the entire workforce. Cultural and sports activities were also offered.

From the very beginning, the company produced top electrical products. The bulb made permanent progress from its early stages through the invention of new and more efficient filaments. The carbon filament was replaced by various metal filaments and the vacuum by gas. During World War I, the company established a glass factory to assure self-sufficiency in a time of uncertain supply. Philips coped with the intense competition from the top Berlin electrical companies and the American General Electric Company. From time to time, Philips made cartel and patent agreements and became a major player in the new technology. Beside the bulbs, they immediately experimented with electrical equipment, and from the 1920s they produced vacuum tubes for radios. In 1927, the Philips radio became one of the leading trademarks throughout the continent. In 1939, Philips introduced the electric razor.

More importantly, the company led the industry from the turn-of-the-century electrical age to the post-World War II electronic age. In 1953, they started producing semiconductors that became the essence of several of their new products. Their semiconductor division became an independent unit in 2005. They pioneered recording technology, produced audio compact cassettes with recorded music, introduced the first portable radio and cassette recorders, and answering machines, and their C-cassettes became the first storage device for personal computers in the 1970s. In 1972, Philips introduced home video cassette recorders, and in the early 1980s, in cooperation with Sony, it produced the compact disc (CD), then the DVD in 1997, and the Blu-Ray disc in 2006. The company has various sectors and branches for health instruments, lighting, electric consumer goods, dictation systems, and lighting control systems, etc.

As one of the leaders of the international electrical and then electronic industries, Philips became a multinational company from the very beginning. The small Dutch market was not sufficient for such a firm that played a leading role in the European and international cartel organizations, and it soon established subsidiaries all over the world—in Brazil in 1924, Australia in 1927, India in 1930, Hong Kong and Israel in 1948—and it gradually developed a Philips empire with subsidiaries in France, Britain, the United States, China, Mexico, and Poland. In 2009, the huge company empire had 116,000 employees, directed by 8,000 managers in more than 60 countries, and their annual sales reached €23.2 billion.

"Guinness is good for you"[34]

One of the most peculiar and popular beers, the "black stuff," Guinness started its career as a homemade beer in the eighteenth century, and it became a major export item of the world's biggest brewery before World War I. The story starts in Celbridge, Ireland with Richard Guinness, father of six children and the steward of the Archbishop of Cashel, Arthur Price. Among his duties was to brew beer for the household, which was a usual custom. The Archbishop died in 1752 and left £100 each to Richard and his 27-year-old son, Arthur. The young man, with his inherited money and knowledge of brewing, moved to Leixlip and established his small brewery. In 1759, Arthur Guinness decided to move to Dublin, where he bought an old, out-of-business brewery at St. James's Gate. The business started flourishing and in 1873 he bought a huge plot of land between James's Street and the River Liffey to build several additional buildings and a port on the river to transport beer by boat.

In 1761, Arthur Guinness married Olivia Whitmore, who brought her inheritance of £1,000 and a useful connection to the Dublin elite. The family rapidly rose up the social hierarchy: in 1763 Arthur became warden of the brewers' guild, and in the 1870s, he represented it at the City Council. In 1780, in partnership with his brother Samuel, he founded Dublin's first insurance company, the Hibernian Insurance, and two years later he built the Hibernian Flour Mill just outside the city. Arthur Guinness's son, also called Arthur, became the director of the Bank of Ireland and, in 1820, its governor. The Guinness family rose to the highest echelons of Dublin society. Arthur Guinness II's son, Benjamin, became Lord Mayor of Dublin in 1851, before he took over the factory in 1855. The Guinness factory already had 600 employees at that time. Benjamin's son, another Arthur, was a talented and successful businessman, and was more than ambitious in social and political fields as well. In the 1870s, he became a Member of Parliament and was then ennobled as Lord Ardilaun. When Arthur died in 1803, Arthur II, took over the factory, assisted by his brother Benjamin. The latter had already become Sir Benjamin, and Edward Cecil Guinness of the fourth generation became the first Earl of Iveagh in 1919.

Guinness beer, thanks to its special feature, became the most popular alcoholic drink in Ireland, and soon in England, too. It was a so-called porter type of beer that gets a special black color and burnt dry taste from the roasted, unmalted barley. The fresh brew was always blended with aged brew as well, and mixed with nitrogen when poured to make a thick, creamy head. In the middle of the nineteenth century, the company produced 100,000 barrels of beer a year, but by 1868 it was already producing 350,000 barrels, which more than doubled in the next decade, totaling 2,652,000 barrels by 1914. The Guinness factory was the biggest brewery in the United Kingdom, twice as big as the second biggest brewery in Ireland, and it provided 60% of the Irish beer output and covered about one-quarter of the Irish, and one-tenth of total British beer consumption.

Until the late 1880s, brewing was traditional, based on experience that was inherited by successive generations. From the 1880s, however, the scientific inventions of the second industrial revolution started influencing production methods. A small laboratory was established with microscopes and other equipment. The company employed Oxford- and Cambridge-trained chemists, the first one in 1893, who became assistant managing director, and later managing director. The old apprenticeship training, often from father to son, was changed and science graduates took over as brewers and managers.

One of the chroniclers of the Guinness company speaks about "a monarchical succession of four: the first Arthur Guinness, the second Arthur, Sir Benjamin Lee, and Edward Cecil."[35] Indeed, the company was and, in some ways, remained a family company. Edward Cecil Guinness—after having spent almost a quarter-century at the company from the age of 15—longed for an aristocratic luxurious lifestyle, and he decided to transform the family business into a public, joint stock company in 1886 with the contribution of the Baring Bank. Nevertheless, he bought up the majority of the shares and remained at the company until his death in 1927. "Guinness, the public company, was run essentially as a gigantic family firm."[36]

The successive generations of the Guinness family continued the feudal-rooted paternalistic British tradition and sought to gain workers' loyalty by taking care of the factory's employees. In 1886, the number of employees was 1,680, already one of the biggest industrial firms in Ireland, but by 1913, they totaled 3,500. Although the workers of the company worked 64 hours a week until nearly the end of the century, and although their hours were limited to 54 and even 48 hours per week only in 1897, the company built comfortable low-rent housing for about one-seventh of the employees in the early 1870s, and 6,000 people lived in company apartments by 1886. The company offered work for the workers' wives and daughters by buying the Kingsbridge Woollen Factory in 1881.

In case of sickness, married workers received three-quarters of their wage and two-thirds if they were hospitalized. In 1869, a medical officer was employed and regular medical service was provided, including for family members, medicines were prescribed, and homes were inspected to investigate living conditions. In 1894, the enthusiastic Dr. Lumsden, a young physician, launched a campaign to prevent illnesses. From the 1870s, workers' widows got pensions, and from 1891, compulsory retirement was introduced at the age of 60 with a guaranteed pension for the retirees. The company established a Savings Bank for its employees, established a club, called the Workmen's Hall, organized cooking classes for wives, made physical exercise arrangements, and then paid for technical education for children. Organized excursions and free-time programs helped to build a "company family."

The interwar years and the tragic Great Depression slowed down the development of the company. The 1914 level of output was never achieved again: by 1930, it rose to three-quarters of the prewar level, but it then declined again until 1939 when it was only two-thirds of the prewar level. Exports became increasingly important: the domestic market consumed only somewhat more than half of the company's production even before the war, and the company targeted the English and other foreign markets. As part of this effort, in the summer of 1934, the construction of a Guinness factory was begun at Park Royal in London, and the first brewing began in February 1936. By 1939, the London factory produced 28% of the total Guinness output and covered nearly half of the sales in Britain. About six decades later, at the end of the twentieth century, the British market was bigger than the Irish one, and 40% of Guinness beer was sold in Africa and other continents. Subsidiaries were built, and Guinness is produced under license in Nigeria, Ghana, Malaysia, Canada, the Bahamas, and Indonesia. In 1973, the original St. James's Gate factory dismissed several thousands of its employees, and the first strike in the history of the Guinness factory erupted the following year. Further reductions of employees followed in the 1980s, but the remaining labor force received company shares as an annual bonus.

At the bicentenary celebration of the foundation of the company in 1959, the members of the Guinness family, Lord Iveagh and Lord Moyne, were still present, but the last Guinness to work at the company was the Third Earl of Iveagh, Benjamin Guinness, until his death in 1992. After that, family members remained involved only in the Family Foundation's activity. The company, no longer connected with the founder family, merged with Grand Metropolitan and the multinational giant Diageo was formed. In 2005, the London factory was closed, but construction of a new big brewery started next to Dublin, to be opened by 2013. Guinness beer is still one of the most popular alcoholic drinks in several countries.

The first airlines: Air France, KLM, and Lufthansa[37]

The dream of flying, as the Greek legend of Icarus and Daedalus demonstrates, is as old as humankind. At the beginning of the sixteenth century, Leonardo da Vinci designed an airplane, and various attempts accompanied the early modern centuries until the modern combustion engine and several other inventions made flying possible. In December 1903—after having built three gliders and perfected the controls between 1900 and 1902—the American Wright brothers' 12-horsepower combustion engine airplane made the first sustained and controlled air flight. On December 17, "on the fourth flight that morning, he flew the aircraft for a distance of half a mile in 59 seconds. After that day, the world was never the same place again."[38] Further pioneering breakthroughs followed, such as Louis Blériot's 1909 crossing of the English Channel, but airplanes and flying were still in an experimental stage. Nevertheless, the idea to use airplanes in war was born and even tested in 1911, when the Italians bombed Ottoman trenches by throwing hand grenades from planes in their colonial war in North Africa. Eventually, World War I transformed the flying toys into solid airplanes. As in the case of several other prewar inventions, the commercial use of the airplane started immediately after the war.

In 1919, France and the Netherlands founded their first airlines in virtual parallel. The Lignes Aériennes Farman, renamed as Société Générale de Transport Aérien, was founded in 1919. With the merger of four more small companies, it became Air France in 1933. The Koniklije Luchtvaart Maatschappij voor Nederland en Koloniën, or KLM, also started its sparkling career in 1919, and it had regular flights to London, Copenhagen, and Hamburg a year later. Air France and KLM merged 85 years later to form the world's largest airline company. Germany had an advantage because Rathenau's AEG electric company already founded the Deutsche Luftreederei GmbH, the world's first air company, in 1917. As a defeated and militarily controlled country, however, Germany suffered a few years' delay, but in 1926, it also established its trademark carrier, Deutsche Luft Hansa AG. At the time of the Air France–KLM merger, the Lufthansa Group was the second largest in the world.

These giant airlines had a modest start. KLM carried 345 passengers in the first year of its existence. True, in 1924, it was the very first in the world to introduce regular intercontinental flights to the Dutch East Indies, Batavia (Jakarta). The small aircraft carried four passengers and flew 81 hours in ten days to cover the distance. The decade of the 1920s was still a period of experiment and innovation. In 1926, a Junker G-24 Lufthansa aircraft had leather-covered seats and a toilet. Two years later, a Lufthansa flight covered the 12,000-kilometer roundtrip to Irkutsk in three days. For the first time, stewards served a freshly-prepared meal made in the small kitchen of the aircraft. During the 1930s, the all-metal, three-engine German Junker aircrafts, the Dutch-made Fokkers, and soon the American-made Douglas DC-2, first bought by KLM, became better and bigger aircrafts that reached 200 kilometers per hour and even higher speeds, and carried more and more passengers. KLM offered regular services to Australia, India, and South America, and its flights carried 160,000 passengers in 1939.

Air traffic became regular during the interwar decades, and new infrastructure, including modern airports, was built: Le Bourget in Paris and Tempelhof in Berlin in 1926, while the military airfield of Croydon was rebuilt and opened to civilian traffic in 1928 and Gatwick in 1936. But air traffic was still in its infancy. The new turning point arrived again with war. By World War II, aircraft had become a major weapon, and tremendous efforts were made to develop them. In Britain, war preparation programs from 1934 first aimed to produce 2,000 aircraft in a year. The next year, it was increased to 8,000 in three years, but the famous "Harrogate Program" already sought to reach an output of 2,550 planes per month. British aircraft production totaled 26,500 planes by 1944. In Germany, 40% of total armament production was aircraft production. In 1941, 11,000 airplanes were delivered to the air force, and 40,000 by 1944. The Messerschmidts, Heinkels, and Junkers became more and more efficient. The major powers produced 39,000 airplanes in 1939, but more than 235,000 by 1944.[39] The aircraft industry made fantastic progress and introduced mass production. Moreover, the Hermann Göring-led Nazi Air Ministry initiated a rocket program in 1935, and the Heinkel-176, the world's first rocket aircraft, and the Heinkel-178, the world's first turbojet airplane, were tested in 1939. In the summer of 1943, Hitler ordered the mass production of already tested ballistic rockets: 263 of them were shot at Britain between September of 1944 and the end of the war. Brand new air technology was available.

After the war, a new, triumphant chapter of air traffic was opened. Air France was nationalized in 1945 and the state's share remained dominant, 54%, until 2002. The company had 130 aircraft in 1948. From 1946, intercontinental flights were opened: in 1947 the Paris–New York line, followed by Paris–Montreal in 1950, and by 1956, Air France had 275,000 kilometers of regular flight service to 73 countries, carrying 180,000 passengers and employing 16,000 people. From 1953, Havilland Comets jets, Caravelle, Boeing, and Lockhead airplanes were in operation. In cooperation with Britain, the supersonic Concorde started its regular flights in 1976, and they continued until 2003, covering the distance from Paris to New York in three hours and 23 minutes. By the mid-1980s, with a 634,400-kilometer network and 150 destinations, 34,000 employees elevated Air France to the top in Europe.

Meanwhile KLM, with its 117 aircraft, carried 15 million passengers to 90 countries and 500 cities at the end of the twentieth century. The gigantic progress of Air France and KLM was crowned in 2004 by their merger. The new company, Air France-KLM was 81% French-owned—with a decreased, 20% state share—and 19% Dutch-owned. By 2007, the giant company already employed 103,000 people. Measured by regular operating revenues, the new company became number one in the world. Measured in passenger-kilometers it was first in Europe, but third in the world.

Parallel with the French–Dutch development, Lufthansa was reorganized in 1953, started buying the new Boeing aircrafts in the 1970s, and by the early twenty-first century 710 of its aircraft were in operation. Lufthansa built up a huge Lufthansa Group with 117,000 employees, carrying 90 million passengers to more than 200 international destinations in 78 countries; and the Lufthansa Group became the second largest in the world. In the gradually progressing European integration, one cannot exclude the possibility of further future merges and, probably, the foundation of a European Union Airline.

Gucci[40]

In the late 1890s, millions of Italians escaped unemployment by emigrating, mostly to the United States. One of the emigrants, a 17-year-old Florentine man, whose father's small straw-hat factory had just become bankrupt, landed in London. His name was Guccio Gucci. He did not speak English, but he found a job washing dishes in the new Savoy Hotel's basement. The ambitious young man learned English and soon was promoted and became a waiter, serving millionaires from all over the world. The world of wealth and glamour made a strong impact on the young Italian. After a few years, Guccio, unlike most of his compatriots, returned to Florence in 1901. The following year he married Aida Calvelli, a young and pretty seamstress from his street, who had a son. Guccio adopted her son, who was probably his from an affair before he left to London. From their marriage, five children were born, one daughter and four sons, one of whom died at a young age.

Guccio started working in an antiques shop, and then at a leather factory. During World War I, he served in the army as a driver throughout the war. In the early 1920s, he found a job in the Franzi leather factory, which produced high-class leather wares. Guccio already had an idea and wanted to establish his own leather wares business, producing the highest quality luxury leather products for the rich, who he learned to admire in the London Savoy Hotel. A fast learner, he learned all the basics and became manager of the company's Rome branch in a year. He, however, had no capital to establish his own leather wares business yet. In 1923, with a business partner who provided the money, Gucci established his shop in Florence to produce and sell the highest quality, art-type leather wares. His sister, Grimalda, sat at the cashier box. He employed one sales assistant and a few local craftsmen who worked in a small workshop behind the shop. After a year in business, Gucci opened a small factory in a converted warehouse. Guccio Gucci was a nineteenth-century-type entrepreneur. He wanted to keep the business strictly in family hands, and he bought out his business partner as soon as he could. His two sons, Aldo and Vasco, joined the family business with great enthusiasm. The third son, Rodolfo, although he became a minor movie star in the silent film period, also joined the family business in 1948.

From that time on, the energetic Aldo, a visionary businessman, turned out to be the real engine of expansion and development. Vasco, much less ambitious, directed the factory. Guccio was cautious, sometime even overly cautious, and he opposed any kind of enlargement, including opening shops in other cities but Florence. Aldo, however, broke through, and the Gucci family opened shops in Rome and Munich. Before World War II, Gucci rose to be an international trademark with luxurious shops and celebrity clientele. The real history of the Gucci house, however, started after the war.

As a chronicler of Gucci history, Gerald McKnight, stated, "the new post-war Gucci set an uncompromising standard of luxurious excellence down to its smallest detail."[41] The three flagship shops in the most elegant districts—in Florence on via Tornabuoni, run by Guccio; in Rome, Aldo's shop on via Condotti, and in Milan in the via Monte Napoleone, managed by Rodolfo—reached world fame and rank. In the early 1950s, the third generation of Guccis entered the business as well. First, Aldo's two sons, Giorgio and Paulo, and then the much younger Maurizio, the only son of Rodolfo. The founder, Guccio Gucci, died in 1953. At that time the Gucci empire was worth about $1 million. The entrepreneurial Aldo virtually took over the entire business, although his brothers, sons, and nephew were all members of the board of directors and had leading roles in the large family business.

Aldo succeeded in opening shops in New York, Chicago, Philadelphia, San Francisco, Beverly Hills, and Palm Beach. World-famous celebrities visited the shops and made the Gucci trademark a sign of elegance, fame, and wealth. The GG trademark sign on luggage, belts, shoes, and various accessories, such as the silk scarf—made famous by Grace Kelly—signaled elegance and high social status. Princess (soon Queen) Elizabeth of England, Eleanor Roosevelt, Elizabeth Taylor, Bette Davis, Katharine Hepburn, Sophia Loren, Audrey Hepburn, Princess Margaret, Imelda Marcos, Jacqueline Kennedy-Onassis, John Wayne, and many others visited and shopped at Gucci. The Gucci empire flourished, and a new, bigger factory on a 150,000-square-foot lot was established on the outskirts of Florence in 1967. They also bought a Scottish tannery. Several other firms delivered half-finished leather products that were finished in the Gucci factories. A perfume branch was also established and became one of the most profitable parts of the Gucci empire.

In the 1970s, however, when the family company reached its peak, with 1,000 employees and thousands of part-time workers in various places producing the luxury Gucci products, internal fighting among the family's second and third generations, and between the members of the third generation, started undermining the family. The third generation actually destroyed the family. It happened in a different way than the usual, commonplace story of a lack of business interest on the part of the spoiled third generation that turns its back on the family business. The third generation of the Gucci family was just the opposite. Overambitious young people, especially Paolo and Maurizio, fought against Aldo and Rodolfo, and then against each other. In the 1980s, the fourth generation entered the family business when Aldo's grandson, Umberto, became vice-president of the perfume branch. Several other grandsons of Guccio followed. Just as Aldo had fought against Guccio's conservatism, Paolo and Maurizio blamed Aldo's conservatism and wanted to transform the family business into a public, multinational company. Paolo pushed the idea of selling licenses for selected shops to market Gucci products.

Unlike the second generation, however, the third generation was ruthless in their fight within the family. Paolo discovered some tax evasion by the American Gucci business, and he blackmailed his father into giving him the leading role and realizing his own ideas and initiatives. When he was rejected, he turned to the courts, and Aldo Gucci was arrested, tried, and imprisoned in 1986 at the age of 82. His two brothers, Vasco and Rodolfo, were dead. Although the Gucci empire became much larger and even more popular, with shops in London, Tokyo, Hong Kong, and 278 shops throughout the world with half-a-billion dollars in income, the overambitious brothers and cousins of the third and fourth generations, fighting for their leadership position, fired, sued, and in the end totally ruined each other and ended the family's ownership. In 1995, the Gucci empire went public and, in the end, became owned by the French Pinault-Printemps-Redoute Company. By 2008, from the small Florentine shop of Guccio Gucci, the huge empire had €2.2 billion revenue from its worldwide business.

Notes

1 This essay is based on: K.N. Chaudhuri, *The English East India Company: The Study of an Early Joint Stock Company 1600–1640*, London: Frank Cass, 1965; H.W. Bowen, *The Business of Empire: The East India Company and Imperial Britain, 1756–1833*, Cambridge: Cambridge University Press, 2006; Albert Hayma, *The Dutch in the Far East: A History of Dutch Commercial and Colonial Empire*, Michigan: George Wahr Publisher, 1942; Glenn J. Ames, *Colbert, Mercantilism, and the French Quest for Asian Trade*, DeKalb, IL: Northern Illinois University Press, 1996.
2 Chaudhuri, 1965, 3.
3 Ibid, 31.
4 Bowen, 2006, 45, 47.
5 Ainslie Thomas Embree, *Charles Grant and British Rule in India*, London: George Allen & Unwin, 1962, 262.
6 The founding capital was 6.4 million guilders.
7 This essay is based on: Ferry de Goey (ed.), *Comparative Port History of Rotterdam and Antwerp, 1880–2000*, Amsterdam: Aksant, 2004; Reginald Loyen, Erik Buyst, and Greta Devos (eds), *Struggling for Leadership: Antwerp-Rotterdam Port Competition Between 1870–2000*, Heidelberg: Physica Verlag, 2003; container50.org.uk/rotterdamHistory.pdf; www.3PLNews.com/ocean-freight/port-of-rotterdam-construction-of-maasvlakte-2-enters-new-phase-html.
8 Loyen et al., 2003, 2.
9 The so-called "twenty-foot equivalent unit" (TEU) was introduced as a measure. One TEU was 20x8x8 feet.
10 This essay is based on: Jean-François Bergier, "Horology, Luxury Goods, Precious Metals," in *The Swiss Economy: A Trilogy*, St. Sulpice: SQP Publication, 1991; James M. Dowling and Jeffrey P. Hess, *The Best of Time: Rolex Wristwatches: An Unauthorized History*, Atglen, PA: Schiffer Publisher, 2001.
11 Bergier, 1991, 494–95.
12 Ibid, 514.
13 This essay is based on: Giovanni Federico, *An Economic History of the Silk Industry, 1830–1930*, New York: Cambridge University Press, 1997; Josette Gontier, *La Soierie de Lyon*, Paris: C. Bonneton, 1978. The paper of my research assistant, Hannah Butler, *The Silk Industry of Lyon: An Anomaly of Success in the 19th-Century World of Mass Production*, 2010, also contributed to this essay.
14 This essay is based on: the archive of the Ganz Company in the Hungarian National Archive, Jubilee Files; Ivan T. Berend and György Ránki, *Magyarország gyáripara, 1900–1914*, Budapest: Kossuth Könyvkiadó, 1955; Ivan T. Berend and Miklós Szuhay, *A tőkés gazdaság története Magyarországon*, Budapest: Kossuth Könyv Kiadó, 1978.
15 This essay is based on: Horst A. Wessel (ed.), *Thyssen & Co. Mülheim a.d. Ruhr: Die Geschichte einer Familie und Ihrer Unternehmung*, Stuttgart: Franz Steiner, 1991; Helmut Uebbig, *Wege und Wegmarken: 100 Jahre Thyssen*, Berlin: Siedler, 1991; Stephan Wegener (ed.), *August und Joseph Thyssen: Die Familie und ihre Unternehmen*, Essen: Klartext Verlag, 2004.
16 The Thissen family moved from the Netherlands to the Aachen region and changed the spelling of their name.
17 Uebbig, 1991, 7.
18 David S. Landes, *The Unbound Prometheus: Technological Change and Industrial Development in Western Europe from 1750 to the Present*, Cambridge: Cambridge University Press, 1969, 465.
19 This essay is based on: Hubert Bonin, *History of the Suez Canal Company, 1858–2008: Between Controversy and Utility*, Genève: Libraire Droz, 2010; Jules Charles-Roux, *L'Isthme et le canal de Suez*, Paris: Hachette, 1901.

20 Bonin, 2010, 8–9.
21 Charles-Roux, 1901, 198–99, quoted in Bonin, 2010, 49–50.
22 Georges Edgar-Bonnet, *Ferdinand de Lesseps, le diplomate, le créateur de Suez*, Paris: Perrin, 1998, quoted by Bonin, 2010, 41.
23 Sami H. Dessouki, *Suez Canal: Changing World 1956–2000*, London: Heinemann, 1982, 16.
24 This essay is based on: Manfred Pohl, *Von Stambul nach Bagdad: Die geschichte einer berühmten Eisenbahn*, München: Piper, 1999; Edward Mead Earle, *Turkey, the Great Powers, and the Baghdad Railway: A Study in Imperialism*, New York: Russel & Russel, 1966; Bekir Sitki, *Das Bagdad-Bahn-Problem 1890–1903*, Freiburg: Rudolf Goldschagg, 1935; Paul K. Butterfield, *The Diplomacy of the Bagdad Railway 1990–1914*, Göttingen: Georg August Universität, 1932.
25 Sitki, 1935, 153–58.
26 Earle, 1966, 142.
27 Butterfield, 1932, 78.
28 This essay is based on: J.D. Scott, *Vickers: A History*, London: Weidenfeld & Nicolson, 1962; Clive Trebilcock, *The Vickers Brothers: Armament and Enterprise, 1854–1914*, London: Europa Publications, 1977; Harold Evans, *Vickers: Against the Odds, 1956–1977*, London: Hodder and Stoughton, 1978.
29 Trebilcock, 1977, 27, 51.
30 Scott, 1962, 57.
31 Ibid, 75.
32 This essay is based on: A. Heerding, *The History of N.V. Philips' Gloeilampenfabrieken*, Cambridge: Cambridge University Press, 1988.
33 Marx in one of his letters called Lion's daughter, Nannette, "our Dutch secretary." She received membership card number 1 issued by the Dutch branch of Marx's First International. Heerding, 1988, 56, 58.
34 The title of the essay comes from one of the best-known Guinness advertisements. The essay is based on: Derek Wilson, *Dark and Light: The Story of the Guinness Family*, London: Weidenfeld & Nicolson, 1998; Tony Corcoran, *The Goodness of Guinness: The Brewery, Its People and the City of Dublin*, Dublin: Liberties Press, 2005; S.R. Dennison and Oliver MacDonagh, *Guinness 1886–1939: From Incorporation to the Second World War*, Cork: Cork University Press, 1998.
35 Dennison and MacDonagh, 1998, x.
36 Ibid, xi.
37 This essay is based on: Helmut Trunz, *Die Geschichte der Lufthansa: Luftfahrtlegende Seit 1926*, München: GeraMond, 2008; Ronald E.G. Davies, *Lufthansa: An Airline and Its Aircrafts*, New York: Orion Books, 1991; Philippe-Michel Thibault, *Le roman d'Air France*, Paris: Gallimard, 2003.
38 Niall G. Weldon, *Pioneers in Flight*, Dublin: Liffey Press, 2002, 15.
39 György Ránki, *The Economics of the Second World War*, Wien: Böhlau, 1993.
40 This essay is based on: Gerald McKnight, *Gucci: A House Divided*, New York: Donald I. Fine, 1987.
41 McKnight, 1987, 76.

5 From the rise of industrial cities to post-industrial suburbanization

Introduction

Modern economic development transformed the settlement structures of Europe. The overwhelmingly rural population of earlier centuries started concentrating into urban centers. A new type of industrial city emerged with a huge absorption of industrial companies and workers. Manchester and Birmingham in England, the big industrial cities of the Ruhr area and Westphalia in Germany, and Brno in Moravia serve as great examples. Even in less developed and only partially industrialized countries such as Poland and Hungary, some industrial cities such as Łódź, or a strongly industrialized suburban network around the capital city as in the case of Budapest, illustrate this new development. Urbanization became a 200-year-long trend that culminated around the turn of the twenty-first century when, in some of the most developed West European regions, more than 90% of the population became urban inhabitants.

The beginning of this process led to the rise of overcrowded, unhealthy, and strongly polluted cities that often still preserved their medieval physical characteristics, with narrow streets and a lack of sanitation systems. After a few decades, a modernization trend took place, and the city centers were rebuilt. Slums were also cleared, as well as some old medieval districts, new wide boulevards were cut, and ring-roads were created in place of the old city walls. Large green areas and parks, with a kind of suburban "garden city," were planned and realized.

However, the late twentieth-century chapter of urbanization saw a new development: de-urbanization, or better to say, suburbanization. Millions of people started moving out from the traditional compact cities, away from the central parts of the old towns, and moving to newly developing suburbs to establish a new form of life. This trend is closely connected with a new change in the European economy: the breakthrough of the service revolution and the rapid growth of the white-collar population. Old, previously crowded downtown areas became places for office buildings, banks, shops, and other services, and they lost a great part of their population. In comfortable suburbs, families built big houses with gardens and combined urban life with the advantages offered by the countryside. Modern transportation systems made it easy to commute a few dozen kilometers to work, and to go to downtown restaurants and theaters. In several countries, a whole chain of suburban-type settlements occupied long stretches of seashore, such as in Spain and Portugal. An international trend, often called "losangelesization," i.e., building a garden-city type of settlement with relatively small local centers in urban areas, became dominant around the turn of the twenty-first century in Europe.

The case studies in this chapter offer a comprehensive picture of urbanization from its beginning in the rise of industrial cities, such as Manchester in England, Lyon in France, and Turin in Italy. Besides the advanced, industrialized West, this type of city also became characteristic in Poland, Hungary, and Moravia, as shown by the cases of Łódź, Budapest, and Brno presented in this chapter. Special examples of late industrial cities created by the Soviet-type of twentieth century industrialization are presented here in the stories of Stalingrad in the Soviet Union, and Stálinváros in Hungary. The studies also present the interesting stories of urban rebuilding and modernizing in the mid- to late nineteenth century, as illustrated by the examples of Paris and Prague. The successful attempt to humanize urban settlements, through the Garden City movement and later by spreading suburbanization combined with de-urbanization of the old city centers, expands the story of urban development during the entire two centuries under discussion.

The world's first industrial city: Manchester[1]

Before the industrial revolution, Europe's settlement structure was entirely traditional. The huge majority of the population lived in rural areas, in small villages and townships. Very few big cities existed, and only London had more than one million inhabitants, while Paris had half a million. From the late eighteenth century on, a new type of city began to emerge: the industrial city. The first among them was Manchester, the heartland of the British textile industry. Manchester had already existed for centuries, however. Sources at the turn of the fourteenth century speak about 2,000 inhabitants who lived on the land of de Grelley, the Baron of Manchester, the first lord of the manor. This small village started growing during the sixteenth and seventeenth centuries and became a flourishing market town. A highly sophisticated putting-out system developed, based on the surrounding villages' cottage industries, which focused mostly on wool, silk, and cotton production. Flemish refugees settled there and introduced the weaving industry. The population of the city reached 10,000 in the early eighteenth century when a flourishing proto-industrialization made England into the "workshop of the world."

On this base, the eighteenth century became the scene of a unique and spectacular textile boom with its center in Manchester, which got the nickname of "Cottonopolis." At the end of the century, the city had 70,000 inhabitants, but by 1831, it had 142,000, and by the mid-century 186,000 people, mostly working in the rapidly rising cotton industry, the leading sector of the British industrial revolution. Why Manchester?

There were several factors behind the city's amazing growth. One certainly was its status as a flourishing market town with a large textile proto-industry. Natural resources were also extremely favorable. During the first decades of the industrial revolution, the most important energy source was still water. The breakthrough new textile machine, the first spinning jenny, was operated by water power. When the pioneering inventor Richard Arkwright built his first cotton factory in Manchester, he based it on the rich water resources of the city, offered by the Irwell and Mersey rivers. When the Quarry Bank Mill was established in 1784 in neighboring Styal, it installed Europe's strongest water wheel to move the machinery. By the 1850s, more than 100 cotton factories were in operation in the city.

James Watt's steam engine, however, gradually replaced water power. The coal-hungry machines, especially in the first decades, consumed a huge quantity of fuel. This change did not make any difference in Manchester. In nearby Worsley, huge coalfields produced the required quantities, and the Duke of Bridgewater started to deliver coal to Manchester in the 1770s. Transportation became a crucial problem of industrialization. The pioneering countries invested a lot in building canals, and England had an exceptional natural advantage because it was an island with easy coastal shipping, and it could use the natural waterways to reach the nearby seashore. British talent and entrepreneurship, however, helped nature with extensive canal-building activity. In 1761, the Bridgewater Canal connected the coalfields with Manchester. In later decades, a whole network of canals connected the city to other parts of the country, and in 1894, the Manchester Ship Canal connected the city to the sea, 40 miles away, and the city became a major inland port.

With the invention of railroads, however, the industrial revolution produced the most modern transportation system. In 1825, England became the first country in the world to open a railroad. The very first main line, the Manchester–Liverpool railway that opened in 1830, and the first railroad passenger station in Manchester broadened the opportunities. Indian cotton arrived at the Liverpool port and was cheaply and quickly delivered to Manchester's factories. Railroad connections to London and Birmingham were also created by 1838, and Manchester's textile industry skyrocketed. The population grew rapidly and reached about half a million before World War I, the peak of Manchester's development. At that time, a whole network of industrial satellite villages and cities—Blackburn, Bolton, Burnley, Oldham, Wigan, Rockdale, Salford, and others—surrounded Manchester and virtually became part of a Greater Manchester that was created administratively only a century later in 1970.

In 1771, the first bank opened its doors in Manchester, and in 1826, the Bank of England opened a branch in the city. Several other industries settled there, among them engineering factories to produce textile machinery serving the textile industry, the most important export sector of Britain. The city itself gradually transformed and modernized.

At the beginning of the textile boom, workers—almost one-third of them children—were accommodated in poorhouses, which were overcrowded, miserable living quarters, with a great many in one-room cellar dwellings. It was not rare that ten to 12 people, who worked in shifts, shared one bedroom, and in the worst part of the workers' slum, 100 houses had one common "toilet," a big hole at the corner of the yard. Even in 1907, only one-third of toilets were modern water-closets, but the sewage ran directly into the river that produced drinking water for the city. Small wonder that in 1832, a terrible cholera epidemic decimated the population. The factories and coal heating polluted the air, and in general the city was an extremely unhealthy place to live. The young Friedrich Engels gave a dramatic description of the living conditions and lack of hygiene and sanitation in the first industrial city.

Modernization was signaled by the supply of running water and the installation of gas street lights in the 1810s and 1820s, the opening of the first omnibus line in the city in 1824, the first public park in 1846, the first public library in 1852, and a new town hall in 1877. Manchester received the status of a city in 1853. The health reform of 1868 led to the closing of the cellar dwellings and the opening of public baths, and the gradual destruction of the slums, which was actually finished only in the early twentieth century when council houses were built to replace them. Irish workers moved in and represented about 15% of the population. In the ghetto of "Little Italy," Italian immigrants and about 40,000 Jewish immigrants from Eastern Europe settled in Manchester and contributed to its gradual transformation into a cosmopolitan city.

The peak of the rise of Manchester before World War I, when 65% of the world's processed cotton was manufactured there, was followed by a steep decline in the twentieth century. By 1960, the Manchester textile industry, the crown jewel of the industrial revolution, disappeared and the population decreased. Nevertheless, a modern services and financial industry, and an important research and development center started forming the new character of the city that actually played an important role in the computer revolution. Manchester University, established in 1903, was the home of mathematician Alan Turing, the inventor in 1949 of stored-program software for computer, called Manchester Mark 1, a major turning point of the computer revolution. In 2001, the city had less than half a million inhabitants, but nearly 6 million people lived in the larger Manchester agglomeration, one of the most densely populated regions of Britain, now an important cultural and scientific center.

Lyon: the silk center of Europe[2]

The Lyon agglomeration, with its more than 1.7 million inhabitants, is the second largest urban center in France. Meanwhile, Lyon is one of the oldest cities, established by a lieutenant of Julius Caesar in 43 BCE as Lugdonum. It was an important Roman city where two later emperors, Claudius and Caracalla, were born. Christianity arrived here with Greek settlers in the second century. Between the eleventh and thirteenth centuries, Lyon was an independent city ruled by the Primate of the Gauls (as the French were called at that time), but in 1312, Philip the Fair incorporated it into the French Kingdom.

The rise of modern Lyon started in the fifteenth century when annual fairs were established and made the city a kind of European trade center. The strategic geographical location of the city, on a peninsula that was already important for the Romans between France's two navigable rivers, the Saône and the Rhône, along with the good road network connection to Paris and Provence and to northern Italy, became crucially important factors of prosperity. At that time Italians introduced the silk trade and industry that gained further impetus after François I granted the weaving right—until that time an Italian privilege—to the city. Printing and publishing industries also settled there. During the early modern centuries, Lyon's position was strengthened as an important silk center. Merchants introduced the putting-out system, and the silk cottage industry gradually became the main occupation of the city's population.

In those early modern centuries, famine periodically visited Europe. One hit Lyon in 1662 and another in 1694, but the worst of them hit in 1709, when a terrible winter destroyed the crops and famine raged in the city. This caused a mortality crisis: in the second half of the year, 1,644 people died, twice as many as the average number of deaths per year between 1703 and 1715. The part of the population hit hardest were the silk craftsmen and especially their children.[3] However, at the end of the eighteenth century, Lyon's population totaled 150,000. Lyon and silk became synonymous at that time. About 30,000 people worked with 15,000 looms. During the eighteenth century, the silk industry developed a special capitalist-handicraft character. About 400 very rich *marchands-fabricants* subordinated the previously independent craftsmen, who became wage-earners, paid on a piece-work basis by the merchants. They worked at home with their own looms, and the merchants supplied them with raw silk. The weavers also employed *compagnons* and apprentices, who almost belonged to the family.

The weavers of the Lyon cottage industry preserved their independent spirit, and stood up for their rights. They organized a two-week strike in 1744 supported by a strike fund. A similar revolt occurred in 1786, when they struggled for higher wages with a long strike, which ended in harsh repression, even hanging and imprisonments. During the French Revolution, the rich entrepreneurs of Lyon preferred to protect their property, which in the end led to a civil war and to the city's revolt against the Jacobin terror. In October 1793, a nine-week siege by the Convention's army of 20,000 occupied the city, which was followed by 1,900 executions. Later, after the Revolution, a white terror massacred those who took public office during the Revolution.[4]

After the Revolution and the Napoleonic wars, Lyon continued to emerge as one of France's most important industrial centers. By 1848, the number of looms increased to 60,000. About half of Lyon's population earned their living in the silk industry. At that time, the industry was owned by 1,400 merchants and bankers. The entire silk industry remained a traditional handicraft sector, and only one real factory with 600 workers was in operation in the city. The weavers (canuts) were well organized. They founded a cooperative grocery shop in 1806 and a mutual support society in 1825. When salaries were cut in 1831, the craftsmen initiated an agreement to introduce a fixed rate mediated by the authorities. More than 100 manufacturers rejected the agreement, which led to a revolt in November and a confrontation with the National Guard. With about 600 casualties, including the deaths of 100 soldiers and 69 workers, the canuts occupied the city. The Lyon uprising became a major event in labor history as the very first workers' revolt.

King Louis-Philippe ordered 20,000 troops to attack and reoccupy Lyon, which happened in December, followed by 90 arrests and the abolition of fixed rates. In two years, however, a new salary conflict generated a second canuts' uprising. Barricades were built again, and the craftsmen and their employees confronted the army. During the "bloody week," hundreds died and, after the army had reoccupied the city in April, 10,000 workers were arrested and tried. Lyon's name became eternally connected to the dawn of the age of a new kind of social conflict. The old social conflict between the feudal nobility and the bourgeoisie was replaced by the confrontation between the bourgeoisie and the workers.

Revolutionary traditions not only survived, but the suburbs, with their overwhelmingly working-class population, remained a hotbed of radicalism. The 1848 revolution led to the election of a Central Committee. More than half of its members belonged to illegal secret associations before the Revolution that announced an artisan republic. Old and new radicalism, however, were mixed. Luddites, especially during the June 1849 insurrection, destroyed machines, while the most radical and best-organized group, the so-called Voraces, were called communists. "The clash between silk merchants and their dependent weavers lay at the heart of Lyonnais radicalism."[5] Retribution was harsh again, and martial law was prolonged for two and half years.

The nineteenth century became the crucial period of the explosion of the silk industry. The leading industry of the British industrial revolution was cotton textiles, with Manchester as its capital, and this made competition difficult for continental European countries. France began specializing in labor-intensive luxury silk products. The country retained and even strengthened its leading role in the silk business, producing 20% of Europe's silk output. The traditional northern Italian silk industry declined at that time and began to produce and sell silk thread to Lyon. As a unique phenomenon, the Lyon silk and garment industry still preserved its small-scale manufacturing, cottage industry, and handicrafts character until the 1880s. In 1856, 20% of the city's population were operating 110,000 hand looms and 60,000 mechanized looms, and 90,000 people worked in the silk business. At that time, 25% of French exports were silk products.

Mechanization, however, began with the French invention in 1807 of the mechanized Jacquard loom that increased productivity by four times. New inhabitants moved in during those decades and founded industrial suburbs around Lyon. These suburbs, such as Croix-Rousee and Guillotière located on the opposite bank of the two rivers and on the northern plateau, were thus physically separated from the city. The city and the suburbs were also strictly separated socially, since most of the workers lived in the suburbs. Their population increased from four to seven times in the first half of the century. The silk industry spread to five surrounding departments where the number of looms doubled in one decade after the mid-1830s. By the mid-nineteenth century, one-third of the looms were already modern Jacquard looms. Mechanization continued, and at the end of the century 310 mechanized silk factories employed 210,000 workers.

At the end of the nineteenth century, the Lumière brothers pioneered the cinema industry. A century later, Lyon, still the second largest city in France, already had a very complex economy. It became a banking center and the headquarters of modern chemical, pharmaceutical, and biotechnical industries. The communication revolution led to the foundation of a strong software industry as well. Most of all, historic Lyon became a tourist attraction, especially its Roman district, Renaissance district, and silk district. Lyon was also considered to be the capital of gastronomy. Lyon and silk, however, remained synonyms.

Turin: the industrial capital of Italy[6]

Turin, the northwest Italian city, the third Italian economic center after Rome and Milan, and the world's 78th richest city, has 900,000 inhabitants, or 2.2 million counting its entire agglomeration. It was the "industrial capital" of Italy and part of the so-called industrial triangle of Turin–Genoa–Milan. The city's history, however, stretches over 2,000 years. It was established by the Romans as Augusta Taurinorum in the last decade of the first century BCE at the banks of the river Po, surrounded by the fertile land of the Po valley, the Alps, and the Ligurian Apennines. The nearby passes are a traditional strategic point for crossing the Alps—as did Charlemagne in 773 to conquer Italy—and nowadays carry the main road and railroad link to France. This is also the place for an easy crossing of the upper Po River. The river also offers excellent transportation possibilities. Rivers run from the Alps to the Po, which was used for centuries to build canals and a sophisticated irrigation system in the surrounding Piedmontese plain.

Turin had a rather eventful, troubled, but mostly successful history. A small provincial town until the late Middle Ages, Turin did not outgrow its ancient Roman walls. In Roman times, it had about 5,000 inhabitants, and it still only had 8,400 in 1510. In the twelfth century, Turin became a self-governing city-state like Milan, Venice, and Florence, but it never expanded so successfully and could not compete with its north Italian rivals. The city was ruled by the Prince-Bishop, but the commune developed its own political power. After having been conquered by the Count of Savoy at the end of the thirteenth century, Turin soon became the capital city of the principality of Piedmont, mostly occupied by the Savoyards.

During the fifteenth and sixteenth centuries, silk production gained ground and Lombard merchants settled in the city, which also had a relatively large self-governing Jewish community of about 800 people, the largest in Italy. A university started flourishing, and one of the most precious Christian relics, the Holy Shroud, the sheet in which legend says Jesus Christ was buried, was moved into the city by the Savoyan ruler from France and exhibited in a special chapel that made Turin a pilgrimage place. By 1571, the population of Turin already totaled 14,000, but by 1702, it has grown to nearly 44,000, and to 78,000 by 1796, with another 5,000 people living in the industrial suburbs and working in 56 spinning plants and in a more widespread cottage industry.

The city was extended by the Città Nuova outside the ancient walls, followed by new settlements in the east and west of the old city. Artisans and workers moved in from nearby villages and worked in the local textile industry of wool, linen, and silk spinning and weaving. A state bureaucracy was also built up around the Savoyan court, led by 300 noble families, while the largest single group, totaling 10% of the population, was domestic servants. Turin became famous, and in 1753, the first guidebook was published for visitors.

The still rigid *ancien régime*, however, was overthrown by the revolutionary French army, led by Napoleon in 1796. The 18 years of French rule thoroughly modernized Turin. With the first edict of Napoleon, the old city wall was destroyed, the Church's rule was severely curbed, and 29 convents and monasteries were closed and their properties auctioned. The juridical system was changed by the introduction of the Napoleonic Code. Modern commercial code, the abolition of guilds, removal of tariff barriers, and the foundation of stock exchanges and chambers of commerce paved the way for the modern capitalist economy. This was also helped by modern law enforcement, standardized central administration, emancipation of Jews, the introduction of modern healthcare, directed by a Superior Council of health, hygienic control of shops and markets, and the introduction of vaccination (which was opposed by the Church). The rising bourgeoisie gained equal rank with the previously dominant noble elite.

Although the restoration of the House of Savoy in 1814 led to the arch conservative regime of Victor Emmanuel I, it was impossible to turn back the clock to the pre-revolutionary era. The restoration regime, especially after the Piedmont Revolution in 1821 that led to the abdication of the king—in spite of its military defeat by the Austrian army at Novara—had to modify its policies "in recognition of the changes that had taken place during the previous decade and a half ... and many of the French ... [measures] remained in force."[7]

The following decades elevated Turin into the center of Italian politics. After the American and French Revolutions, the new concept of nation and nationalism emerged and the period of nation-building dominated European politics. As in the case of Germany, the idea of unification and the creation of a united Italian nation—the *Risorgimento* or revival—became the most decisive question in Italy. Giuseppe Mazzini, Giuseppe Garibaldi, and the composer Giuseppe Verdi became the best-known and most dedicated fighters for unification. The son of one of the leading aristocratic families in Turin, Count Camillo di Cavour, emerged into a leading role in this struggle after 1848. In post-1848

Italy, Turin and the Piedmont Kingdom remained the only constitutional monarchy of any kind, and Cavour launched a successful diplomatic campaign in various posts, but mostly as Prime Minister, and in a crucial time, even launched a military campaign that made Turin the nucleus and leader of unification. When it happened, after the victory of the Piedmont army against the Vatican, Victor Emmanuel II became the king of united Italy in 1861. Turin became the capital city of the united country, but not for long. A few years later it was shifted to Florence, and then in 1871 to Rome.

Before the unification, Cavour, who clearly recognized the importance of the British industrial revolution and its impact on agricultural countries such as Italy, initiated modern infrastructure building, especially railroad construction and port modernization for transatlantic shipping, and the development of the banking industry. At the time of unification, 40% of Italian railroads were located in Piedmont. Local industries flourished and trade trebled. The city hosted engineering, chemical, and textile industries. The population soared and by 1880, totaled 250,000 in Turin, which "consolidated its position as the top financial and banking center in the country."[8]

When the National Exposition of 1884 was opened in Turin, the city was a vibrant, modern economic and cultural center that boasted the Royal Polytechnic of Turin, which provided the best engineering education in the country and introduced the teaching of electric engineering, among other firsts. From the late nineteenth century until World War I, Turin was emerging as the industrial capital of Italy. Based on the rich new hydro-energy source of northern Italy, the most modern steel, chemical, metallurgical, and engineering industry mushroomed in the city and its surroundings, which had the fastest economic growth rate in the country. Between 1905 and 1911, the industrial population more than doubled.

The focal point of Turin's industrial development was the automotive industry. Its beginning is connected with a family that moved in 1853 to Villar Perosa, near Turin. Here Giovanni Agnelli was born in 1866. He later became a cavalry officer, but after his very early resignation, the family moved to Turin, and in 1899, four years before Henry Ford did so in America, established his *Fabbrica Italiana de Automobili Torino*, or Fiat, with 50 workers. By 1914, Fiat employed 4,000 workers and produced 4,000 cars a year. At the end of the war, producing for the army, the firm became the third largest in the country, with 10,000 employees. Turin soon became a Fiat city. This company employed one-third of the industrial population of the city even before the war. The exploding automobile industry led to the foundation of several supply and service companies, 61 already in 1907. Agnelli introduced the most modern management system and continued a consistent policy of vertical integration to incorporate rivals and supply companies, such as providers of ball bearings, radiator and motor-makers, and several others. In the two decades before the war, Turin's population increased by nearly 50%, but the spreading industrial suburbs grew by 500%.

Turin became the cradle of the organizations of entrepreneurs by launching the Industrial League of Turin that soon became the Italian Confederation of

Industry. On the other hand, the city also became the birthplace of the Italian labor and socialist movement. Turin University educated Antonio Gramsci and Palmiro Togliatti, the founders of the Italian Communist Party after the war. During the fascist regime of Benito Mussolini, Agnelli joined the Fascist Party and became a senator for life; moreover, during the war years and German occupation, he worked for the Nazi army. Turin, however, became the center of anti-fascist resistance. The communist Garibaldi brigade, with nearly 15,000 fighters, liberated the city from German occupation.

On the foundations of the early twentieth century, the most sparkling period of Turin's history emerged after World War II as it became a main participant of the postwar Italian economic miracle. One of the core players in the economic boom that at last elevated Italy to the seventh largest economic power in the world was the Turin industry, and in the first place the Fiat company. In the mid-1960s, the company employed 130,000 workers, controlled 95% of the Italian car industry, and became Europe's second biggest car manufacturer. The grandson of the founder, Gianni Agnelli, elevated the company to a multinational giant with subsidiaries from Monte Carlo to Pakistan, Turkey, the Soviet Union, Poland, Spain, and Argentina—altogether 569 subsidiaries, 190 associated companies in 50 countries throughout the world, generating $33 billion in income. The per capita income of the city increased by three times and became one of the highest in Italy. The company owned one of Italy's leading newspapers, *La Stampa*, and one of the most popular professional soccer teams in the country, Juventus.

The other star company of the city, Olivetti, which had begun by producing typewriters, now became a high-tech giant, and Turin became the real industrial capital of the country. This led to an enormous enlargement of the population: from 719,000 in 1950 to 1.4 million during the 1980s. An endless wave of immigration from the south led to the creation of new districts. Turin became the third largest "southern city" behind Naples and Palermo. This situation created a hotbed for social conflict. The new immigrants lived in terrible situations, much like the infamous Manchester situation in the early period of the industrial revolution in Britain. Most of the inhabitants from the south lived in attics, cellars, and improvised barracks. Workers shared beds in shifts, three-quarters of them did not have a bathtub, and dozens of families shared one bathroom.

In the 1960s, workers' militancy re-emerged, and Turin became the scene of cooperation between radical students and organized workers. The "Hot Autumn" of 1969 raged with terror acts by the Red Brigade and neo-fascist organizations. Twenty-seven Fiat managers were killed or wounded. The turmoil of the late 1960s was followed by the economic crisis of the 1970s, and Turin never recovered from those shocks. Fiat shifted a great part of its operation to other places and countries, and employed only 30,000 in and around Turin. The city lost nearly 100,000 jobs, and the population of the city lost half a million people and declined to 900,000. Turin, however, reinvented itself as a post-industrial city with small and medium-sized companies and a flourishing tourist industry, but it did not return to such a role as it played before the 1880s.

The emergence of the largest urban industrial agglomeration: the *Ruhrgebiet*[9]

Germany was a latecomer to industrialization. The main drive began only around the mid-nineteenth century when the country gradually became a leader of the second industrial revolution. Natural resources, one of Europe's richest coal and iron reserves, and a superb higher scientific and technical education played important roles in this development. In Prussia, and later in unified Germany, several industrial centers emerged. One of the most peculiar, however, was the *Ruhrgebiet*, or Ruhr area of about 4,500 square kilometers around the rivers Ruhr, Rhine, and Lippe. That area had superb agricultural land, with 11 small medieval cities and villages such as Dortmund, Essen, Duisburg, Bochum, Gelsenkirchen, and Oberhausen. Essen's history goes back to the eighth and ninth centuries when abbeys were founded on the place, but the settlement received a town charter and built the city walls in the thirteenth century, and it became a free imperial city in the fourteenth century. Duisburg built its city walls in the early twelfth century and became a member of the Hanseatic League. Dortmund, later also a Hanseatic city, became the seat of Frederick I (Barbarossa) in the mid-twelfth century. Bochum was the seat of Charlemagne's royal court in the ninth century, and it gained the official town charter in the fourteenth century.

Nevertheless, these medieval townships remained small and relatively unimportant until the nineteenth century. Bochum and Gelsenkirchen had 4,500 and 6,000 inhabitants, respectively, in the mid-nineteenth century. From that time on, however, they became one of the most important centers of German industrialization. Two reasons for the rise of the Ruhr area stand out. First, one of Europe's largest coalfields was discovered here in the 1840s, although the first coal mine was opened in Essen in the sixteenth century. Coal was available in huge quantities, in some places reaching the surface, and was of outstanding quality, good for producing coke, the fuel for the modern iron and steel industries. Second, the dense network of natural waterways offered excellent and cheap transportation possibilities. In the mouth of the Rhine, Duisburg became one of the biggest inland harbors in the world, while Dortmund, after the building of the Dortmund–Ems Canal, became the largest canal port in Europe. The *Ruhrgebiet* was connected to the North Sea.

The industrial revolution, all of a sudden, led this area to fast and unique urbanization: the 11 cities of the Ruhr heartland, although they preserved administrative independence, in a unique way, virtually formed one single enormous polycentric urban-industrial agglomeration. From the later eighteenth century, coal mines—in 1850 there were already 300—and iron works were established. The two super-giants, the Krupp and Thyssen companies, nowadays the unified ThyssenKrupp, started their business here and created

Europe's largest iron and steel center. Engineering industries, oil refineries, and chemical companies also settled in the area. The Ruhr agglomeration became the center of the German military industry even before World War I. The huge industrial complex attracted tens of thousands of workers from Germany and even from other countries. From the eastern part of Prussia, half a million Poles and Silesians moved here, and workers arrived from more than 100 countries. The population increased by leaps and bounds. Bochum and Gelsenkirchen offer good examples: they had, respectively, 4,500 and 6,000 inhabitants in 1850, but their numbers increased to 100,000 and 140,000, respectively, by 1904. Essen itself became the headquarters for 13 of the largest 100 German corporations, and the small medieval city attracted 580,000 inhabitants.

From a few tens of thousands in the mid-nineteenth century, the Ruhr agglomeration had 3.8 million inhabitants by 1925, and about 7.3 million by 2010. Counting the so-called Bergisches Land at the southwest border of the *Ruhrgebiet*, the Ruhr industrial agglomeration concentrates 12 million inhabitants.

The region, just because it was the heart of the German military industry, suffered a lot after World War I, when the French army occupied the area for years. During World War II, very heavy Allied bombing destroyed a great part of the industrial and residential quarters alike. In Essen, 270 air raids destroyed the center and 60% of the suburbs. In Duisburg, the June 1941 and the May 1943 bombings, and altogether 299 air raids, destroyed or heavily damaged 80% of the buildings and made 96,000 people homeless. Similar destruction destroyed Bochum and Gelsenkirchen where 38% and 75% of the buildings, respectively, were eliminated. In the first postwar years, 706 plants were also removed by the Allied forces. However, the deindustrialization and de-Nazification of Germany stopped in the 1950s when the Cold War confrontation led to a new policy of strengthening and even rearming Germany.

The incredible potential of the Ruhr agglomeration led to a shockingly rapid recuperation. Moreover, the *Ruhrgebiet* survived the death of the coal industry, its god-given base of prosperity. After World War II, a major structural renewal, among other things, ended the era of coal as the most important energy source. From the 1960s on, more and more coal mines were closed. The last coal mine was closed in Duisburg in 2009. By the turn of the century, the coal industry belonged to history. As part of the German economic miracle and the rapid adjustment to the new structural crisis in 1973–85, new modern industries settled in the agglomeration. Gelsenkirchen became the center of the German solar power industry. In Bochum, coal was replaced by the automotive industry, several medium-sized information technology industries settled in Dortmund, and Essen became the location of the country's second largest electric utility company, as well as of the largest construction company in the country. The logistic division of the German Railroads is in Essen. The Duisburg harbor receives 20,000 ships and 40 million tons of goods every year. Essen became a city of trade fairs: 50 of them were organized in 2003. The entire region became the center of a new service industry.

The polycentric urban agglomeration became a first-class cultural center as well. The devastating impact of nineteenth-century industrial pollution was gradually eliminated; so-called brownfields were restored such as in the case of the Emscher Landscape Park along the river Emscher, formerly a virtual sewer. Half of Duisburg became a green area and woodland. In 1965, Ruhr University was founded in Bochum, and in 1972, two universities were established in Essen and Duisburg that later merged into one, with campuses in each city and with 33,000 students. Essen's flourishing cultural life was honored in 2010 when it became one of the Cultural Capitals of Europe. One of Europe's most interesting urban agglomerations, a child of the nineteenth-century industrial revolution, and the center of the coal and steel industries gradually became diversified and home to modern medium-high and high-tech industries and services, with a strong cultural life.

Budapest: an old capital city becomes a new industrial center[10]

When industrialization belatedly and partially began in late nineteenth-century Hungary, Budapest, the capital city had already an 800-year-long history. Moreover, the first significant settlement, Aquincum, the capital of the Roman province of Pannonia at the Danube-Limes of the empire had already 20,000 inhabitants in the first century BC. In medieval times, three independent cities on the two shores of the Danube River, next to each other, Buda, Pest, and Óbuda had altogether about 25–30,000 inhabitants. In the late fourteenth century, a university was founded there. In 1848, it was in this area that the Hungarian revolution exploded and the first railroad construction started.

The turning point of the history of the city, however, happened after the Austro-Hungarian compromise in 1867, that established Hungarian autonomy with independent government and parliament. In 1873, the three independent cities were merged and named Budapest. At that time the population of the settlements was 300,000.

After 1867, an American-style robust and rapid development characterized Budapest. During the last three decades of the nineteenth century, the population of the city trebled, in one single decade of the 1890s the population increased by nearly 50%, and by 1910 it reached 1,000,000. Budapest became the eighth largest city in Europe surpassing Rome, Milan, and Madrid. This spectacular development was closely connected to the beginning of modern social and economic transformation. As a capital city, Budapest became the center of a country with 20 million inhabitants, the partner capital of Austria-Hungary. Although the country remained agricultural— even by 1910, nearly two-thirds of the population was engaged in agriculture— Budapest became a Western-type modern middle-class city. Two-thirds of the Hungarian middle class lived in Budapest, which had a strongly Jewish character. Although only 5% of the population of the country was Jewish, about one-quarter of the capital's population belonged to a strongly assimilated Jewish community.

Big banks and merchant houses settled here, and when railroad construction began before industrialization started—as happened in most of the peripheral, less developed countries of the continent—especially from the 1860s onwards, the railroad network was built like a spider's web, with Budapest at the center. Water and rail transportation to Vienna, only 260 kilometers away, was simple and cheap. The central location of the city, the presence of the railroads, and the city's proximity to the River Danube attracted the first big industrial companies. This development was also assisted by the nearby rich coalfields of Dorog and Tatabánya, 30 and 80 kilometers away respectively, and the unlimited water resources of the Danube. Besides, a dense network of local transportation was created as well. Trams connected the suburbs and local trains ran even to the outward ring of the more than 20 settlements around the capital city.

Budapest soon became the center of the dramatically emerging food processing industry. On the Pest side of the city, very near to the center, huge flour mills were established next to the Danube. Hungary, with its one-sided grain economy, and the bread basket of the Habsburg monarchy, uniquely among the agricultural exporter countries exported two-thirds of its grain in processed form. In the southern part of Buda and Pest, beer and distillery industries were settled. Food processing became the leading branch of the Hungarian industry with Budapest at its center, and the city became the world's second largest flour mill center after the American Minneapolis. In north Pest, leather and engineering industry started developing and Budapest became the real industrial center of the country, concentrating 54% of Hungary's industrial workforce. In sharp contrast to the overwhelmingly peasant character of the country's population, 44% of the inhabitants of the capital city were blue-collar workers.

The rapid rise of Budapest went hand in hand with the development of an industrial suburban ring around the city. While the city's population grew three times until 1910, the suburban ring's inhabitants increased by ten times. Hundreds of thousands of migrants settled in the neighboring villages that partly became dormitory cities for commuting workers, and half of them commuted daily to Budapest factories. The rents in the suburbs reached one-quarter to one-half of the level of the rents in Budapest. By 1900, the population of the suburban ring reached 14% of the population of Budapest, but its share jumped to 26% by the end of the war.

More and more settlers, however, found jobs within those suburbs, especially in the north (Ujpest or New-pest) and the south (Kispest or Small-pest, and Pesterzsébet, or Pest-Elisabeth) of the Pest-side that became a new industrial belt. Before World War I, three of the five largest industrial cities in Hungary were located in the inner ring of the Budapest agglomeration, and already 40% of the industrial workers of the agglomeration worked in the suburbs. The real turning point arrived in 1914, when the city decided to move out the industry from the center of the capital. A new regulation—following the European pattern—divided the city into eight zones and banned the foundation of factories in the inner six zones. In the interwar years, all the big flour mills were removed from the center and the new textile industry established its headquarters in the southern suburbs. Electrical engineering and several other branches of the heavy-industries concentrated into Csepel, Kispest, Ujpest, and other settlements of the suburban ring. The interwar decades, without an administrative unification, closely integrated the suburbs into Nagy-Budapest (Great-Budapest) with joint urban planning and a joint master plan for further development. In Csepel Island, south of the center, a modern port was built that could receive 3,000-ton Danube-seagoing ships. The suburban ring doubled its population to nearly half a million during World War II, and three-quarters of the workers of the Hungarian manufacturing industry worked in the Budapest agglomeration.

The de facto integration definitely took place in the interwar years, but the administrative unification of Budapest and 21 suburban settlements—the de jure integration—happened only in 1949. Budapest's inhabitants increased to two million by 1944, and after the severe war destruction, reached this level again by the 1970s and stabilized at that level, concentrating one-fifth of the country's population. The state-socialist industrialization drive, although targeting the industrialization of the countryside and the building of new industrial cities, further strengthened the industrial sector of the enlarged capital city. A new, large suburban region of 44 settlements emerged around the unified Budapest that already swallowed its former suburbs.

The regime change in 1989 opened a new chapter in the history of Budapest: the period of de-industrialization and declining population. In 1990, the city had 2.02 million inhabitants, but by 2003, only 1.72 million. The industrial population declined even more dramatically from 350,000 to less than 130,000. Industrial employment declined to less than one-quarter of the inhabitants while banking, real estate, and other service industries increased their employment to three-quarters of the workforce of the city. This went hand in hand with the development and transformation of suburbia: while Budapest's population dropped by 4.4%, the inhabitants of a new suburban ring of 44 settlements around the city increased by 4%. Meanwhile the suburbs, a former working-class residential and industrial zone, became more and more middle-class residential areas with huge shopping malls and gated communities.

The rise of Brno (Brünn), Central Europe's foremost industrial city[11]

The industrial city, a new phenomenon from the late eighteenth and nineteenth centuries, was first a British historical product, but later characterized the entire European urban development. The area of Central and Eastern Europe was a latecomer and was relatively backward in industrialization, thus very few industrial cities emerged in that area. Brno was among the very first, followed by Poland's Łódź, and Hungary's Budapest.

Brno was not a new settlement. People settled in early centuries at the rivers Svratka and Sviteva, and the old Czech word for the muddy, swampy area became the name Brno. The settlement became a walled and fortified city only in 1243, and it increased its population to 11,000 inhabitants by the end of the fourteenth century. Germans, Flemish, and Jews settled here in medieval times. The city was besieged several times in the troubled centuries: Hussites attacked twice in the fifteenth century, Swedes did so in the seventeenth century during the devastating Thirty Years' War, and the Prussians came in the eighteenth century, but the well-fortified city successfully defended itself. The extraordinary loyalty of the city to Emperor Ferdinand III, during the 60-week Swedish attack in the mid-seventeenth century, was a kind of turning point in Brünn's history. The emperor gave various privileges to the city and established regional offices there. During the eighteenth century, the Habsburg rulers turned towards a mercantilist (in Austria it was called *Kameralist*) economic policy, characterized by strong and complex state interventionism to support industrial development. Protective tariffs, direct state subsidies, and state ownership of factories served modern transformation in this enlightened absolutist state.

The small and—after the Thirty Years' War—baroque city's modern history began with industrialization. In Bohemia-Moravia, several aristocratic landowners—Count Kinsky, Count Kaunitz, Count Waldstein and others—founded industrial factories, mostly producing textiles. The absolute state, especially after the wars of the 1740s and the loss of Silesia to Prussia, aimed to found a "military-industrial complex"[12] and establish self-sufficiency. As a historian of the city maintained, "strong government intervention was unquestionably the catalyst"[13] of the rise of Brünn as an industrial city.

Brünn was certainly one of the beneficiaries of Maria Theresa's industrialization policy. In 1764, the *Kaiserlich Königliche Privilegierte Feintuch Fabrik zu Brünn*, a fine-woolen cloth factory, was established. Together with other state-owned factories, its goal was to replace the fine-cloth imports of the country to save about a million florins per year. This factory, originally on the Emperor's estate in Kladruby, was actually established under the auspices of Franz Stephan of Lorraine, the husband of the Empress. After 14 years, this factory was moved to Brünn. Forty skilled textile workers were invited from Verviers in the Low Countries, and a state contract guaranteed special privileges for the firm. Within a decade, a second woolen factory opened in the city, and during the following 30 years, 17 others emerged.

A horizontal and vertical chain reaction followed. A school was established in 1765 to train skilled workers. Based on smuggled British machinery, Count Hugo von Salm-Reifferscheidt established a factory for the production of spinning machines in 1804. A merchant and shopkeeper established another machine factory. By 1814, the steam engine was introduced in the city. Around the medieval, fortified city, 32 independent industrial settlements were established. In contrast to the German majority of the old city, the industrial suburbs became mostly Czech populated. In 1849, 42 factories were already in operation, mostly in the textile industry (30 wool, linen, and spinning mills), tanning, and food processing. In that first phase of industrial development of the Czech lands, textiles were the leading sector, and in Brünn, the woolen industry flourished most of all. By 1865, 21 major woolen mills produced and exported fine woolen fabrics. In 1850, the 32 neighboring communities were administratively united with Brünn. The old city walls and fortifications were demolished; a city ring-road and green areas were created. The city's territory increased from 349 to 4,486 acres. Several city-zoning plans served for the rebuilding of modern Brünn. The first plan was accomplished in 1847, and then other ones in 1863 and 1901. The latter was made by the Viennese architect F. Fassbinder.

In the enlarged, modernized city, textile prosperity ended in the late nineteenth century. The industrialization of the Czech lands exhibited the development of a strong engineering industry, and Brünn became its center. From two small factories, the First Brno Engineering Work was established and started producing steam engines, boilers, and pumps, and later turbines as well. In 1864, the former Bedrich Waniek Company was also merged into First Brno Engineering, and the variety of products enlarged with the production of the famous diffusers for sugar factories. Their products won the Gold Medal at the Paris Exhibition in 1896, and the number of employees increased to 1,000 in 1902, and to 3,000 by 1915. Other major engineering companies such as Brand & Lhullier and Lederer & Porges produced water turbines, steam rollers, various other kinds of machines, and iron bridges. From the 1880s, the most modern electrical engineering took roots as well. By 1902, nearly 4,000 factories employed more than 50 employees each in Brno. The textile industry employed nearly 13,000, the garment industry more than 6,000, and food processing about 3,000 workers. Brünn's population surpassed 200,000 at the end of World War I, and neared 300,000 before World War II.

Industrialization went hand in hand with the creation of a modern transportation system. Brünn was connected to the rapidly growing railway network of the Austro-Hungarian Empire in 1839. Public city transportation emerged from 1869 when the first horse-driven tram appeared. In 1884, steam locomotives ran on a 10.4-kilometer-long network, with nine junctions for major factories. In 1896, the Austrian *Union-Elektrizitäts-Gesellschaft* bought the entire network and started its electrification. By 1906, a 22.5-kilometer-long electric tramway system was in operation. Modern transformation was also signaled by the introduction of gas lighting in 1847. In 1882, the Municipal Theater was lit by electric lamps. The first electric power station of Brno was built in 1898, and the electric lighting of the streets started with Liberty Square.

Brünn emerged as an important cultural center as well. Gregor Mendel, the German monk in Brünn's Augustinian Monastery of St. Thomas made his groundbreaking experiments in plant breeding (inheritance) and established modern genetics. His first paper was read in the Brünn Society of Natural Science in 1865. Brünn resident Leoš Janáček's famous opera *Janufa* was performed first here in 1904. The Masaryk University was established in

1919. Roman Jacobsen, the world-renowned linguist worked in Brünn for years, and Milan Kundera, one of the best Czech writers, was born here.

Until World War I, Brünn, as in many Central European cities, was strongly German, and the city administration was also in German hands. Before the war, 46 German elementary schools were in operation, but only eight were Czech; while the first German secondary school was established in 1778, the first Czech one was established only in 1869. The famous Technical College educational institutions, except the Agricultural College (1899), were only established after World War I when Czechoslovakia became independent. Ethnic cleansing, however, made Brünn a Czech city: The Jewish community, 12,000 people in 1938, was eliminated by the Nazi German occupants during World War II, and the roughly 3 million-strong German population of the country, including the Germans in Brünn, was expelled from the entire country after the war. Brünn continued developing after World War II, and its population in the 29 districts of the city numbered more than 400,000 by 2010.

Łódź—the "Polish Manchester"[14]

The name of a small village, Łodzia, first appeared in written documents in 1332. Ninety years later, the small marketplace received a town charter. Centuries began and ended, but it hardly changed. In the sixteenth century, the town still had only 800 inhabitants; by 1810, less than 200. Around the turn of the nineteenth century, the township, along with the rest of Poland, had a stormy history because, in the second partition of Poland, it became part of Prussia. The city was named Lodsch in 1793, but in 1806, Napoleon attached it to his newly created Duchy of Warsaw. Nine years later, after the defeat of Napoleon, the Congress of Vienna created Congress Poland (or the Kingdom of Poland) and the small agricultural settlement on its territory became part of the Russian Empire. The same generation of the city's inhabitants became Prussian, Polish, and then Russian subjects. In a surprising and paradoxical way, the spectacular rise of Łódź began in one of the politically oppressed autonomous Polish provinces of one of the most backward Tsarist Empires of Europe.

On September 18, 1820, Rajmund Rembieliński, speaker of the autonomous Polish Kingdom's *Sejm* (Parliament), enacted a decree transforming five small townships, Łódź among them, into industrial cities. In the Łodka district of the city, linen and cotton industry took roots. Rembieliński invited entrepreneurs and craftsmen from abroad by offering tax concessions. In 1825, when Tsar Alexander I visited the city, which had 1,000 inhabitants at that time, he also encouraged industrialization, and the first cotton mill was founded that year. In 1839, the Berlin-born Ludwig Geyer's White Factory, one of the first mechanized cotton factories—actually, the first in Poland and, moreover, in the Russian Empire—started production. Immigrants arrived from Silesia, Germany, Bohemia, and even from Western Europe. The number of inhabitants increased from 4,000 in 1830 to 13,000 by 1840, and

80% of them were German. During the 1840s, Jósef Richter founded a cotton-weaving mill, while Dawid Lande, Abram Prussak, Ludwik Grohman, and others opened new textile factories. Entrepreneurial Jews started settling in the city from the later 1840s as well.

In 1831, the second unsuccessful Polish uprising was defeated by Russia, which led to the loss of autonomy and a tsarist policy of Russification. The Polish language was replaced by Russian in schools as part of this policy, and the customs barrier between Poland and Russia was eliminated in 1851. That oppressive policy, however, helped the rise of Łódź as the "Polish Manchester," as it was called at that time. The huge and backward Russian market offered unlimited possibilities to Poland to produce and deliver industrial products for agricultural Russia, and to gradually emerge as the Empire's third largest industrial center. The coal, iron, and textile industries played the most important roles in Polish industrialization, and Łódź became the textile center. New textile factories mushroomed: in 1853, Karl Wilhelm Scheibler arrived from Monschau to build several factories with Julius Schwarz, and he became the textile king of the country. Jakub Petters, Szaja Rosenblatt, Israel Posnański, and several other Jewish entrepreneurs followed.

By 1864, the first telegraph station started operating. The next year, the city got its first railroad connection—a branch of the Vienna–Warsaw line, in 1869 the streets were illuminated by gas-lights, and in 1898 the electric tram transported people around the spectacularly growing city. The number of inhabitants totaled 40,000 in the mid-1860s, but by 1900 the population was 300,000, and by 1913, 500,000. At that time, 1.5 million cotton spindles and 12,000 looms were in operation. A great number of the new immigrants were Jews, who represented one-third of the city's population, while the share of Germans declined from 80% to 40%. The "Polish Manchester" was thus hardly Polish, because roughly three-quarters of its inhabitants were German and Jewish. The majority of the Polish elite, which still cultivated the noble-*szlachta* anti-business attitude, maintaining that business was for Jews but not for Poles, hated the city. Zygmunt Bartkiewicz, the popular Catholic journalist, named Łódź *złe miasto*, bad city, an alien social and cultural evil. Similar notions were expressed by the Nobel Laureate Polish writer, Władysław Reymont, who presented *Łodzermenschen* as ruthless, corrupt, exploitative aliens in his famous 1899 novel, *Promised Land*.

The growth of the "bad city," however, represented an American-type development in backward Poland. Łódź became the most densely populated industrial city of Europe: on each square kilometer of land in the town, more than 13,000 people were concentrated. Before the war, Congress Poland with its 15 million inhabitants produced 40% of the 124 million-strong Russian Empire's coal output, 23% of its steel, 15% of its iron, and 20% of its textile production. The Polish textile industry, beginning in Łódź, emerged as a par excellence export industry and sold 80% of its output on the Russian market. Textile employed 44% of the Polish industrial labor force and produced 45% of its total industrial output.

World War I ended the unparalleled boom of Łódź. The city was occupied by the Germans, who confiscated all the metal parts of the industrial machinery for armament production and halted the textile industry by 1918. After the war, a great part of the German population left the city, and their share dropped to 15%, but new immigrants increased the number of inhabitants to 600,000, and changed the ethnic composition of the city: 35% of the inhabitants were still Jewish, but half were Polish by the 1930s. One of the first victims of World War II was Łódź, which was occupied by Hitler on September 8, 1939. It was renamed Litzmannstadt, after a World War I German General, and attached—along with the entire area—to the Reich. After five months, a Jewish ghetto was established and 160,000 Jews were isolated there. Transports arrived from Germany, Austria, and Bohemia, and a forced labor camp was established. Jewish slave laborers worked in 100 factories for the German army, making uniforms among other things. In January 1942, about 70,000 Jews were removed from the ghetto and killed in mobile gas vans. Deportation stopped in September, however, and the ghetto continued working for Nazi Germany until May 1944, when 75,000 Jews were transported to Auschwitz. Only 5–8,000 Łódź Jews survived the Holocaust. Before the city was liberated by the Soviet Army in January 1945, 80,000 Germans escaped from the city to the West. In the end, postwar Łódź's inhabitants were more than halved to 300,000.

After World War II, when Poland was Sovietized and the communist regime followed a forced industrialization policy, Łódź emerged again as an entirely Polish city. Modern apartment blocks and shopping malls were built, and the population nicknamed the new districts of the city "Manhattan." During the anti-Semitic campaign of the late 1960s, journalists of this city were in its frontline. The best-known and celebrated Polish filmmaker Andrzej Wajda made a film in 1975 reflecting the same biases from Władysław Reymont's *Promised Land.* By the time the regime collapsed in 1989, Łódź had emerged as the second largest city in Poland, with 850,000 inhabitants. The post-communist transformation, the so-called "shock-therapy" of the early 1990s, which opened up the country and introduced a market economy from one day to the next, led to a dramatic decline of the economy and to rapid deindustrialization. The landmark Poltex Factory was closed. The traditional textile industry, the symbol of Łódź, disappeared. By mid-1992, industrial production in Poland hit bottom, at 40% below its 1989 level.

Nevertheless, the decline was halted in 1992 and a huge amount of foreign capital started to flow into the country. Foreign direct investments created new modern sectors. Infosys Limited, a multinational information technology giant with 2,000 firms throughout the world, opened business in Poland. The American Dell company and altogether nearly 1,000 foreign investors established modern industrial sectors by 2009, when the population of the city increased to 760,000, but the emerging agglomeration around it consisted of 1.4 million people. Around 2000, the city initiated an aggressive cultural reorientation and started celebrating the multicultural past of Łódź. A "Festival of Four Cultures" was held, and sculptures were erected on the main street of the city of famous former Jewish inhabitants such as the world-famous pianist Arthur Rubinstein, the poet Julian Tuwim, and the leading industrialists, Izrael Poznański and Karl Wilhelm Scheibler. The tourist industry marked and recommended walking tours in the "Jewish Łódź," and the "German Łódź." The cultural monthly *Tygiel Kultury* (Melting Pot) was published to cultivate a long disappeared culture and non-existent character of the "good city," as Łódź was re-nicknamed in search for a new culture, identity, and tourist business.

Rebuilding of Paris and Prague in the second half of the nineteenth century[15]

The old European cities, which inherited their structure and building stock from medieval times, became strait-jacketed in the age of industrialization and rapid urbanization by surrounding walls and fortifications. Their streets were narrow, dark, and overcrowded. The lack of sanitation, running water, and sewage systems made those cities a hotbed of diseases. When millions of people left the countryside and migrated to industrializing urban settlements, especially during the second half of the nineteenth century, most of those old cities had to be rebuilt, based on urban planning.

Paris is definitely one, if not the best, example of that. This was a gargantuan enterprise. Demolishing a great part of the old city, opening a geometrically planned, spider-web-like network of wide boulevards connected several ringroads, creating huge parks and squares, a gigantic water supply and sewage system, and—last but not least—doubling the size of the city, incorporating suburbs and neighboring settlements, and connecting them to the old city center. Most of this work was done with spectacular rapidity and success between 1853 and 1870. Although dozens of engineers and planners, and hundreds of thousands of workers, created modern Paris, its history is most closely connected to two people. The first is Louis-Napoleon Bonaparte, or Napoleon III, who sought to copy his uncle's 18th Brumaire (in the revolutionary calendar). Copying Napoleon's takeover by coup in 1799, the nephew made his *coup d'état* in December 1851, and declared himself Emperor of France. The other person, whose name is virtually synonymous with the renewal—or Haussmannization—of Paris, is Georges-Eugène Haussmann. The two men were only a year apart in age.

The *grand idée* was Louis-Napoleon Bonaparte's, the realization was accomplished by Haussmann. Napoleon III was not a great historical figure. He could owe his path to the presidency and then to becoming emperor to his name and legendary uncle. The contemporary Karl Marx in the first sentence of his brilliant historical study, *The 18th Brumaire of Louis Bonaparte*, stated: "Hegel remarks somewhere that all great world-historic facts and personages appear, so to speak, twice. He forgot to add: the first time as tragedy, the second time as farce." His example in his work was "the uncle and the nephew," and the "second edition" was only a "caricature" of the first. Historically speaking it is true.

However, regarding the rebuilding of Paris, Louis-Napoleon Bonaparte occupies the central historic role. During his 30 years living in exile in England, he nurtured this plan. He made a map of Paris with colored lines of the planned broad avenues and large parks. After having returned to France, successfully re-entered politics, been elected to the presidency, and then declared himself emperor, one of his very first actions was to initiate the realization of his plan. Several contemporaries and historians condemned him, maintaining that his real motivation was to rule the rebellious city by making possible easy military movements on the large, straight avenues in case of revolts. Indeed, in 1871, the Paris Commune was much easier to defeat in the renewed city. Even if it was among his motivations, his main goal was to build a sparkling imperial capital city, a kind of a monument to himself, a symbolic empire-building.

The emperor needed somebody to realize his ambitious plan, and he hand-picked Haussmann. The rebuilder of Paris was not an architect. He studied philosophy and law, and he trained as a musician who played several instruments. But he was a loyal Bonapartist, and an extremely efficient organizer. The Haussmann family was closely connected with Napoleon I. Haussmann's grandfather was an elected member of the revolutionary National Assembly in 1791, and he was commissar of the army during the 1790s. His father was war commissar and quartermaster in the Napoleonic wars. His father-in-law was General Dentzel, an adjutant of Napoleon's general staff. Georges-Eugène became an ardent Bonapartist.

He started his career as a civil servant in the state administration, first as a general secretary and sub-prefect of various prefectures, among others in Gironde. He gradually emerged in the hierarchy because his excellence and success in state administration and organization were recognized by his superiors. Louis-Napoleon Bonaparte, when already President of the Republic, was looking for capable and efficient local leaders, and he appointed him prefect of Var, Bordeaux, and then of the Gironde department. As Haussmann later noted, "[I] completely fulfilled the special mission I had received." His successful performances became a springboard for him. In June 1853, he was hand-picked by the new emperor and was appointed the Prefect of Seine, i.e., the entire Paris region. After the official inauguration "the Emperor took the new prefect into his office for a tête-à-tête and showed him the famous color-striped map."[16] That was his plan for the rebuilding of Paris. Haussmann got his life's work.

Rebuilding Paris was not a new idea. Some monumental classical buildings such as the École Militaire, the Théatre Français at the Odeon, the Pantheon, and the Saint Sulpice already started forming a new face for the old city in the eighteenth century. The revolutionary Convention appointed the "Artists' Commission" to prepare plans for the rebuilding, and in 1794 they recom-mended the opening of an east–west and a north–south road across the city. Napoleon I, although preoccupied by wars, was a passionate urban planner who dreamed of rebuilding Paris in a grandiose way. Under his rule, new streets were opened, and the most important project was the building of Rue Rivoli and four new bridges. The city, the second largest in Europe, outgrew its old structure and required major transformation. New laws on the expropriation of houses if public interest required cleared the legal way. From the 1830s to the 1840s, railroads started to be built to connect Paris with other cities, and banks were founded to offer financing. Nevertheless, the reconstruction hardly surpassed the stage of dreaming. Haussmann prepared the first complex and detailed plan and realized it with an excellently organized feverish effort in two decades. He formed a superb group of engineers and planners. The team was directed by Eugène Deschamps (the head of the Plan de Paris office), Jean-Charles Alphand (the designer of the parks), Eugène Belgrand (who realized the water supply plan), and several others. Haussmann collaborated with Fiolin de Persigny, minister of the interior, who assured the financial resources.

Great parts of the central city, about 20,000 buildings, were demolished, and 40,000 new buildings were erected around the new geometrically and harmoniously planned avenues and boulevard circles that were up to 30 meters wide. The average width of the streets was doubled in the new 160-kilometer-long road network, which was illuminated by 30,000 gas lamps. A network of more than 1,000 kilometers of service roads were added. Strict regulations prescribed the maximum heights of the buildings: 17.5 to 20 meters high on streets wider than 20 meters. Each building's façade had to be in line. At the fifth floor, a continuous balcony had to decorate the buildings and contribute to creating uniformity. This goal was mostly achieved by the compulsory use of the same yellowish lime stone facades along the newly built avenues. Haussmann, half a century before the Viennese Otto Wagner, pioneered the central idea of modern, twentieth-century architecture, and he became virtually the first modern city planner. He realized in Paris what Wagner conceptualized theoretically in the early twentieth century: namely that individual buildings have no separate aesthetic-ornamental purpose, and that aesthetic pleasure has to reemerge in the "monumentality of standardization" and the "heroic scale of the streets."[17]

The reconstruction was combined with the enlargement of the city by incorporating suburbs and neighboring settlements. By 1860, instead of the old 12 *arrondissements*, the new Paris comprised 20 districts. Paris was enlarged from 33 to 71.2 square kilometers, and its population increased from 1.2 million to 1.6 million. The newly incorporated areas were connected to the old city. Besides the new street network and the transformation of 60% of the city's buildings, significant new public buildings were also added to the new face of the city, such as the Opera House, several new town halls for the districts, new bridges and squares, and huge green parks. Among the largest parks were the Bois de Vincennes and Bois de Boulogne.

Besides the spectacularly visible changes, probably the most important modernization achievement of Haussmann—one that was not part of the dream of Napoleon III—was not even visible at all. He created the "blood circulation" of the city by building the water supply and the sewage system of Paris. Before 1852, only one-fifth of the buildings had running water. Six huge new reservoirs and a several-hundred-kilometer-long aqueduct solved the water supply of the large capital city. A new, roughly 800-kilometer-long sewage line was built to create a healthier environment. Walter Benjamin, the German philosopher, coined the phrase "Paris the capital of the nineteenth century" in the title of one of his articles. His fascination was strongly mixed with disgust. He condemned Haussmann for the destruction, and securing the city against civil war and erections of barricades. Benjamin maintained that every document of civilization is in the meantime a document of barbarism as well.[18] This bitter critique is certainly not fair. Indeed, Paris became the capital of the nineteenth century, the first big, integrated model city, a new paradigm of nineteenth-century urbanization. In the age of industrialization, the chaotic, uncontrolled, and rapid increase of the cities that undermined the social welfare of its inhabitants was put under strict control, and the new urban world became humanized.

The second half of the nineteenth century was a period of urban renewal in various countries. In the same decades that Haussmann transformed Paris, Prague, the Czech "capital" within the Habsburg Empire, went through important changes as well. Prague had a long history, and in the fourteenth century it was the capital city of the Holy Roman Empire under Charles IV. From that time, Gothic architecture predominated in the city, and several characteristic buildings, such as the Powder Tower, the Vladislav Hall at the Prague Castle, the old Royal Palace, the unfinished St. Vitus Cathedral, and the famous Charles Bridge, reflected the old greatness in modern times. Some remnants of the Renaissance also survived, but mid-nineteenth century Prague was mostly the result of the seventeenth- and eighteenth-century Habsburg period, with its prevailing Baroque style.

Until the 1850s, Prague was a small city within medieval walls with 150,000 inhabitants. More than 40% of them were German-speaking. As a hereditary province of the Habsburg Empire, and after 1867, part of Austria-Hungary, the Czech lands—unlike Hungary and the eastern parts of the Empire— represented the most developed and industrialized region together with Upper and Lower Austria. Prague, however, did not become a kind of "second capital city" like Budapest, and not even an industrialized city such as Brünn. Modernizing Prague, nevertheless, became an important national program.

As in Central Europe in general, a strong Czech movement of national revival also emerged. Newly born history writing discovered the glorious past before 1526 when the Czech kingdom was swallowed by Austria. Literature, poetry, language reform, and the national opera started mobilizing the population. Unlike in Paris, national awakening generated the attempt to modernize and "nationalize" the gradually increasing city. Its population increased to half a million by 1900. A new town emerged next to the old, and the old city walls were destroyed. The old Jewish ghetto, the so-called Josefov district, was demolished, and the medieval buildings and streets were replaced by modern roads with apartment houses.

The main motivation for the rebuilding of Prague was closely connected to the strong and rising national movement. The Habsburg period was simply characterized as "darkness." That period of more than 300 years was interpreted as "an interruption, during which the nation like some Sleeping Beauty awaited its awakening."[19] This attitude motivated the architectural renewal. The elimination of the Habsburg legacy stood at its center. The Baroque seemed to be the symbol of the Habsburg political rule and the counter-reformation in the country of Jan Hus. The new national movement turned to the glorious national past of the fourteenth century, and its symbol, Gothic architecture. What happened in Prague in the second half of the nineteenth century was motivated by the attempt to get rid of the Baroque. Between the 1880s and the turn of the century, almost all of the Baroque buildings were destroyed and replaced by neo-Gothic buildings as symbols of reconstituted Czechness. One of the most symbolic projects in this trend was the completion of the genuinely Gothic St. Vitus Cathedral in the royal palace area. The cathedral—with the castle—was built in 1344 by Charles IV. However, three generations of main architects died, and the building was never finished. The continuation was then halted by the Hussite Wars in the fifteenth century, and a great part of the cathedral was destroyed by a major fire in 1541.

In the mid-nineteenth century the completion of St. Vitus Cathedral became a national project. A Society for Completing Saint Vitus Cathedral was founded in 1859. The great bell tower, added in the sixteenth century and renovated in the eighteenth century, was Gothicized and completion in neo-Gothic style began, finished only in 1929. Charles IV's project was accomplished after half a millennium. As Derek Sayer interprets it, it triumphantly represented the idea that "we were here before Austria, and look, here we are after it!"[20] The demolished Baroque buildings were replaced partly by neo-Gothic, and partly by neo-Renaissance buildings. The latter style became predominant for important new public buildings such as the National Theater, National Museum, and Rudolfinum. The rebuilding of Prague turned back centuries to the Gothicization of the city, and it replaced the politically hated Habsburg-Baroque style with the glorious neo-style, resembling the past. Real modernization, including the enlargement of what was already the capital city by incorporating suburbs and nearby settlements, happened only after World War I.

Humanizing the cities: the garden city and pedestrianization[21]

Nineteenth-century urbanization was a major historic turning point, but also a punishing process. Millions left the countryside and migrated into emerging cities. Manchester, the first industrial city, increased its population from 10,000 to 500,000 inhabitants. The industrial agglomeration of the German *Ruhrgebiet* transformed a few walled medieval townships around World War I into one huge urban area with more than three million residents. Between 1840 and 1914, the population of London, including the surrounding settlements, tripled and totaled more than six million people at the turn of the century. By World War I, 100–120 million Europeans were living in some 70 major cities in Europe. Between 1850 and 1910, the urban population more than trebled and urbanization achieved a breakthrough: 75% of Britain's population was concentrated in cities, as were 57% of Belgium's, 53% of the Netherlands', and 49% of Germany's.

The change was dramatic, and the cities became dehumanized, as brilliantly described by writers such as William Blake and Charles Dickens. Housing and sanitary conditions could not improve at the same rate as urbanization progressed. Sometimes a dozen workers, who worked in shifts, were jammed in one room, often sharing the same bed in rotating shifts. Many lived in crowded attics and cellars. In the worst workers' slum in Manchester, 100 houses shared a single common "toilet," a large hole in the corner of the yard. A cholera outbreak decimated the population in 1832. Death rates were 25% higher among people who lived under roofs or in cellars, as 20% of Liverpool's population did and—even in 1880—10% of Berlin's population. Until the 1870s, the urban environment was a web of sicknesses, especially respiratory and digestive diseases, such as tuberculosis and diarrhea. In the 1870s, infant mortality was about 50% higher in the ten largest cities in Germany than it was in the countryside.

Small wonder that, at the turn of the twentieth century, the idea of humanizing urban settlements, the idea of the "garden city," emerged in England. Ebenezer Howard published his *Tomorrow: A Peaceful Path to Real Reform* in 1898, and he republished it with a new title, *Garden Cities of Tomorrow,* four years later. He had a simple idea: instead of the further growth of the big cities, a set of satellite garden cities should surround them. The garden city idea combined the urban environment with the countryside. Each of these settlements would concentrate only about 30,000 inhabitants. Independent single-family houses should be built in a low density settlement, and gardens should separate them from each other. Per hectare, 20 family homes were planned, with gardens in front and behind. The houses must not block the view of other homes. The streets, lined with trees, had to be wider than 13 meters and the façades of the houses on the two sides nearly 17 meters from each other. The gardens were not separated by walls but with hedges.

The exact plan of a garden city was prepared by Raymond Unwin and his partner, Barry Parker, and they built the first garden city of Letchworth, 34 kilometers from London, in 1904. Unwin published his *Town Planning in Practice* in 1909, which influenced city planning and the dozens of architects who followed it worldwide. In that year, he planned and built Hampstead, the first garden suburb, 8 kilometers from the center of London, around the huge Hampstead Heath. In 1919, 22 kilometers from London, a second garden city, Welwyn, was built, and 25 garden cities were gradually accomplished around London. In the first three garden cities and suburbs, the idea of semi-privatizing the streets was also realized by building closes, a blocking point formed by a group of houses to make a cul-de-sac. These streets serve the people who live there and exclude through-traffic. Sometimes, as in the case of Waterloo Court in Hampstead Garden Suburb, the houses formed a closed-square courtyard. The front gardens of the houses created a common garden, a kind of public space, while the backyards were isolated and entirely private. Special gateways connected the garden cities to the countryside. The architects used old existing pathways and preserved trees, and they combined them into the city plan. These small settlements were built in zones: a city center for commercial activities and the railway station, an industrial zone, and a separated residential zone.

The garden city idea spread. A special example was the Czech shoe king, Tomáš Bata, who built his factory in 1894 in the Moravian Zlin, a medieval township of 3,000 inhabitants. Bata, overwhelmed by the idea of the garden city, invited the best European architects and built a garden city around his factory for his employees, simple box-like red-brick family homes with gardens. Before World War II, the garden city of Zlin already had 45,000 inhabitants. Because the Bata Factory became a multinational enterprise with factories all over the world, the founder's brother, Jan Antonin, and son, Tomáš—who took over after the early accidental death of the founder—continued with the idea and built garden cities around the factories in Canada (Bataville), East Tilbury in Essex, and also in France, the Netherlands, and Brazil. The garden city idea conquered the world, especially the United States, and became predominant in the European suburbanization drive during the last third of the twentieth century.

The humanization of the old cities and city centers, however, remained unsolved. The big, old European cities declined into chaotic traffic traps during the second half of the twentieth century. Endless traffic jams, severe air pollution, the invasion of millions of tourists, and a deserting population rang the death knell of downtowns. As the London City Council's experts summed it up: "cities of half a million population and more begin to incur acute problems ... The conflict and congestion have caused environmental problems ... high accident rates, noise, air pollution, vibration, visual intrusion ... difficult to access. The consequences are well known: mounting levels of stress ... deterioration of the fabric of the city centres themselves, decay of the life quality ... all hampering the orderly functioning of the centre. As the situation gets worse, first shoppers and then shopkeepers tend to seek alternative locations ... This in turn leads to a commercial decline of the shopping core."[22] How to revitalize the overcrowded city centers and to give them back to the inhabitants? This question became the most burning urban problem during the unparalleled prosperity after World War II, when roughly half of urban inhabitants became car owners in Western Europe.

Urban planners turned to the idea of traffic-free zones, creating pedestrian streets and districts in historic city centers to give them back space for outdoor activities. In several cases, war destruction and postwar reconstruction helped realize this idea. Four major goals were served at once: solving traffic congestion, stopping environmental decay, improving the economy, and providing space for community activities in the historical central areas. In several cases, huge parking lots were built at the existing ring-roads and public transportation, while mini-bus service (in Leeds) and often newly built subways (in Vienna, Cologne, Copenhagen, and Munich), assured the connection to the center.

The first pedestrian street, the Vasterlanggatan, was opened in Stockholm in 1961. In the later 1960s, several other streets and six blocks followed. The pedestrian Strøget of three contiguous streets between two main squares was opened in Copenhagen in 1964. Munich's City Council ordered the plans for a traffic-free zone in 1964. The first pedestrian streets were opened between the medieval Karlstor and the Rathaus gate and the downtown area followed when the new subway system was opened in 1972. The first experiment, closing traffic on the Kärtner Strasse in Vienna, succeeded in 1971 and the pedestrian zone, together with a new subway system, was rapidly enlarged. The pioneering experiences encouraged other cities and countries to follow. In the fall of 1972, the Greater London Council sent a team to other countries to study the pedestrianization experience. The team presented and published a report about the similarity of the problems and the possibility of solutions.[23]

Pedestrian streets were repaved; trees and flower beds decorated the widened walking areas, buildings were renovated, fountains and statues were erected, and chairs, benches, cafés, and restaurants populated the areas and made them extremely popular. Traffic-free areas had a strongly positive impact on air pollution: in Gothenburg, Sweden, the carbon monoxide level of the downtown area dropped to one-sixth of the previous level. Noise decreased by three-quarters from previous levels in the Copenhagen pedestrian zone. The downtown areas experienced a vigorous business revival as well. "Pedestrian districts in operation for over 25 years, such as those in Essen, Germany, and Rotterdam, Holland, have reported an increase of 34% to 40% in their annual business volume."[24]

Since the old city centers were full of historical buildings, pedestrianization went hand-in-hand with the restoration of historic districts in Rouen, Vienna, and Bologna. The pedestrian areas became extremely popular for tourists: 3.7 million tourists visit the Munich pedestrian area per year, where movable chairs make it possible for visitors to sit where they like. Cultural activities reconquered city centers. Open air concerts and theater performances, and various kinds of happenings created new colors in city life. The old city centers of Europe became humanized, and an all-European Reconquista gave them back to its population.

Stalin's industrial fortresses: Stalingrad and Stálinváros[25]

Most of Europe's industrial cities emerged during the nineteenth and early twentieth centuries. Late industrializers, especially the Soviet Union and then the Soviet Bloc countries, created their own industrial cities around the mid-twentieth century and even later. Paradoxically enough, the Soviet industrialization policy that aimed to create in the isolated country an industrial basis for modern war, followed the nineteenth-century pattern of developing coal, iron, steel, and heavy engineering industries, moreover, mostly by building new industrial cities, new "black countries" of coal, iron, steel, and heavy engineering industries.

Stalin initiated his first Five-Year Plan in 1928–29 with very ambitious targets. Investments would be increased by nearly three times, industrial labor force by 40%, the output of so-called heavy industries, the main preference, aimed at a three-fold increase, and steel and machinery production was to grow by two-and-half times. History's most extreme industrialization drive to establish self-sufficiency, however, was soon modified, and the accepted "optimal version" of the plan was replaced by a "super optimal" version, and the five-year period was shortened to four years, moreover, in February 1931, Stalin announced that in the "basic, decisive branches" the goals would be achieved in three years. Instead of doubling machinery production, the new target was an increase of almost five times. In that year, Stalin clearly declared the central goal in a famous speech: "We are fifty or a hundred years behind the advanced countries. We must make good this distance in ten years. Either we do so, or we shall go under." One of the best economic historians of the Soviet Union, the British Alec Nove, added after this quotation: the Nazi German attack, "1941 was ten years away."[26] The Soviet Bloc countries after World War II followed the same pattern and also established industrial cities from scratch.

Gigantic industrial plants and cities were built. In the summer of 1927, 10,000 people started working to build the Dnieprostroi, a monstrous dam at the River Dnieper to produce 530,000 kilowatts of electrical energy. The new power source was connected to major industrial bases, including new industrial cities in Zaporozhye and Krivoy Rog. One of the pet-projects of Stalin's five-year plan was the Dzerzhinsky Tractor Factory in Stalingrad. The selected place was the sleepy, relatively small town, originally called Tsaritsyn, established as a fortress in the late sixteenth century on the western bank of the River Volga. In 1720, it had 400 inhabitants, but it was located on trade routes and had excellent water transportation possibilities, and so it became a trading settlement. In 1862, the city got a railroad connection, and before World War I, electric lighting was installed in the center and the first tram line was opened. By 1900, Tsaritsyn already had 84,000 inhabitants.

In 1925, the city was renamed and became Stalingrad, as an honorable sign of the city's role in the civil war after the Bolshevik Revolution. This city got one of the preferential investment projects of the first Five-Year Plan: the country's first mega-tractor factory. In 1930, the factory started production. Thousands of peasants, many of them illiterate, worked on the construction, and then as workers. As the first director of the factory later said, when he asked one of the workers how he measured the sockets he was grinding, he showed his fingers as his measuring tool. Nevertheless, in 1932, 51,600 tractors were produced (in 15-horsepower units), and 66,500 by 1937. The newly collectivized agriculture, and the State Tractor Stations established alongside them, started the mechanization of Soviet agriculture. Very soon, however, a more important product gained preference. The Stalingrad Tractor Factory began producing for the Red Army, and one of the most important parts of war preparation, the first famous T-34 Tanks with their 85-millimeter guns, began leaving the factory. These guns, as it was soon demonstrated, were able to penetrate the German Tigers, while the tanks' 45–50mm thick armor offered the best defense. As General Guderian, commander of the German tank corps, maintained in December 1941, Germany lost its superiority in tanks. Stalingrad and some other tank factories produced probably the best tanks during World War II. This weapon became the backbone of the Soviet army, and in 1944, 11,000 were produced in a year.[27]

Stalingrad's name, however, became world famous during World War II when one of the most decisive battles, and Hitler's first devastating defeat, changed the course of the war. In the summer of 1942, Nazi Germany concentrated its 4th and 6th Armies on Stalingrad, heavily bombing and attacking the city with 300,000 troops. In the winter, the Germans controlled 90% of the city, which resisted heroically and changed hands 13 times. In November, Marshall Zhukov's one million troops encircled the Nazi attackers. Field Marshall Friedrich von Paulus lost 400,000 soldiers, and 110,000 surrendered with him. Other Axis troops died, among them 130,000 Italians and 12,000 Romanians, and the entire 2nd Hungarian Army was destroyed, killed, or captured. Altogether 1.5 million people died in the Battle of Stalingrad. Hitler's offensive stopped and his retreat began, ending in Berlin in May 1945. Stalingrad was totally ruined. The giant factory, however, was evacuated to the Urals and Siberia, along with 1,200 others. After the war, the ruined Tractor Factory was preserved as a war monument, and a new tractor factory was built 15 kilometers away from the city. The former Dzerzhinsky factory was split into four independent factories. Stalingrad, renamed Volgograd by Nikita Khrushchev as part of his de-Stalinization campaign in 1961, became an even more important industrial city than before. Aluminum, steel, and chemical industries, oil refineries, and machine, vehicle, and shipbuilding industries operate in the entirely rebuilt city that grew to 80 kilometers along the Volga River with one million inhabitants in 2010.

After World War II and during the immediately emerging Cold War, Stalin followed the old (and old-fashioned) Russian military doctrine of building a buffer-zone between the West and the Soviet Union. Those regions that were liberated by the Red Army from Nazi and local fascist rule between August 1944 and May 1945—i.e., the whole of Central and Eastern Europe, including the eastern half of Germany—were Sovietized. The countries of the Soviet Bloc introduced a Soviet-type, non-market, centrally planned economic regime and copied Stalin's industrialization policy, preferring the same heavy industrial branches, from coal mining, to iron and steel, to heavy engineering. New industrial cities were created, among them the Polish Katowice and the Hungarian Stálinváros. Stalin sought to prepare for an anticipated and coming World War II during the 1930s. From 1947–48, the year of the "turning point" of Sovietization in Central and Eastern Europe, Stalin wanted his satellites to be prepared for an anticipated World War III. In 1948, Stalin actually sent a message to the Soviet Union's satellites that World War III was unavoidable in three years, and that they had to subordinate the entire economy to war preparation.

Communist Hungary started preparing its first Five-Year Plan in the late 1940s, and it was a copy of the first Soviet Five-Year Plan, to the extent that Hungarian circumstances allowed. The crown jewel of the plan was building a new city for the metallurgical industry. Although the realization of the plan started in January 1950, the government was in an extreme hurry, and it started the preparation of the iron and steel complex in the South-Hungarian Mohács already in the spring of 1949. After several months of construction preparation and earthwork, the government decided to change the location of the new iron and steel city to Dunapentele, a small settlement that got city status in 1833, a few dozen miles north of Mohács. The reason for changing the location was Stalin's split with Tito's Yugoslavia and the possibility of an offensive against Hungary's southern neighbor. The government was in such a hurry that construction work started in the new place without the usual three-month preparatory work, and with an investment plan only 50% ready. As the "economic Tsar" of the country, Ernő Gerő announced in the spring of 1949 that Hungary would be the "country of iron and steel." In the center of the Five-Year Plan was the development of the iron and steel industry "in a tempo unparalleled in the history of the Hungarian industry."[28]

The new iron and steel complex was built and started production in 1954. Since Hungary did not have iron ore, the giant factory was based on Soviet iron ore deliveries from Krivoy Rog, via the Black Sea and the Danube River. In imitation of Stalingrad, the small old agricultural township of Dunapentele was renamed Stálinváros, the City of Stalin, in 1952. Most of the investments during the Hungarian Five-Year Plan period were channeled into the iron, steel, and heavy engineering sectors. In accordance with the Soviet pattern, the five-year period was shortened to four years. Pig iron production was planned to increase from 0.3 million to 1.5 million tons, and steel output was to increase from 0.7 million to 2.7 million tons. As in the Soviet Union, a mania for huge scale meant giant companies were constructed on greenfields, and in the end, 40% of investments in the iron and steel industry were spent on construction and building works and an additional 30% was invested in additional projects such as stores, water and gas supply, etc. At the end of the day, Hungary built up an old-fashioned industrial sector, without real harmony with the possibilities and requirements of mid-twentieth century industry. Between 1950 and 1968, coal mining increased its production by more than two times, and the metallurgical industry by more than four times. By the mid-1960s, the metallurgical industry produced 13% of Hungary's industrial output, while in the advanced West, this share had already declined to less than seven percent. Near the Stálinváros iron and steel works, Hungary's first atomic power station—bought from the Soviet Union—was also constructed on the shores of the River Danube.

Again copying the Soviet Union, Stálinváros was renamed Dunaujváros (New City on the Danube) in 1961, exactly the same time as Stalingrad was renamed Volgograd. At that time, the city had 31,000 inhabitants. Although the heavy industrial complex virtually collapsed after the regime change in the 1990s, Dunaujváros was transformed by foreign investments. The new leading industrial company, the South Korean Hankook Company, built Europe's biggest tire factory in the city, which already has 55,000 inhabitants.

The emergence of post-industrial cities: suburbanization[29]

Two hundred years after the rise of the first industrial cities, the most advanced parts of Europe entered the age of globalization and de-industrialization. The leading European multinational companies employed as many, or even more, people in their subsidiaries abroad than they did at home. In the second half of the twentieth century, a service revolution transformed the structure of the economy and employment. The agricultural population dramatically dropped to 3–5% of the active population, and industrial employment also declined to one-quarter to one-third of the working population. The service sector became dominant, employing around 70% of the active population.

Because of a dramatic change in demographic trends, Europe's population started decreasing and aging from the 1980s. The retired layer of the society is often as large as one-third of the active population and in some places it approaches half of it. Meanwhile, Europe changed from a continent of emigration, to a target of immigration. In the first decade of the twenty-first century, 8–10% of the European population were already immigrants, mostly from Turkey, North Africa, and former Asian colonies. Some of these immigrants and their Europe-born children formed a new underclass, suffering from an enormous rate of unemployment.

All of these changes opened a new chapter in the urban development of Europe. The first change to mention is the all-round urbanization that occurred during the second half of the twentieth century. This trend was not new, but present for two to three centuries when urbanization gradually gained ground. However, in the European Union as a whole, 75% of today's population are already urban inhabitants. In some countries such as Belgium, Britain, Germany, Denmark, and Sweden, this share is between 83% and 97%. In the early twenty-first century, 36 European agglomerations concentrated more than one million people each. On the other hand, it is surprising to learn that only one-quarter of the population of the European Union lives in big cities with more than 250,000 inhabitants, while another one-quarter lives in middle-sized cities with 50,000 to 250,000 people. These seemingly contradictory figures, however, reflect a new development trend in urbanization in Europe. The traditional "compact" European city is disappearing and being replaced by a new trend of rural-urban, or "rurban," development since the 1970s and 1980s. The official jargon calls this new trend "losangelesization," the development of sprawling urban settlements and large-scale suburbanization.

Although the breakthrough of this trend is relatively new, the phenomenon itself has a history that is already more than a century old. Moreover, Lewis Mumford rightly noted that suburbanization was actually born together with urbanization. Monasteries often settled outside city walls, and then the cities gradually surrounded them. Universities looked for green park areas next to existing cities, as happened in Oxford, and then became incorporated into the cities. Rich people tried to escape from overcrowded, unhealthy cities and built homes and mansions outside the city. In modern times, however, suburbanization became a mass phenomenon. During the industrial revolution in Britain, around the turn of the nineteenth century, middle-class families escaped from London to Clapham and the Hampstead hills. In the nineteenth century, a ring of residential suburbs were settled in Barnes along the River Thames, St. Johns Wood in northwest London, Bedford Park (one of the first garden suburbs), and in the south and west of London in Putney and Hammersmith, respectively, and soon became part of the enlarging city.

Beside the well-to-do, middle-class residential suburbs, industrialization also created another type of suburbia: the industrial suburb with huge factories and workers' residential regions, sometimes as dormitory settlements for workers who could not afford accommodation in the city. Modern city zoning banned the establishment of polluting factories in inner cities, and pushed them outside. The previous essays on Brünn and Budapest clearly illustrate this phenomenon. The newly emerging suburban chain consists of independent administrative units of small townships or villages with a population of between 1,000 to 50,000 inhabitants. Not less than half of the population of the European Union lives in these kinds of settlements. Coastal urbanization in Portugal, Spain, and Ireland created long suburban strips at the country's seashore—in the case of Portugal, a 13-kilometer-long strip—that concentrates half of the country's urban settlements. Suburban settlements are loosely built up; houses have gardens and much more green area around them. While the built-up areas of European cities have increased by 20% in the last two to three decades, the population of those settlements has increased only by 9%. Huge shopping malls, mechanized households, better security, and cars for each adult person in gated communities eliminated the disadvantages of living outside a city, and offered several advantages and a better lifestyle for those who are living far from the noisy, crowded, and polluted city centers.

Surprisingly enough, this new trend rapidly reached the former communist countries as well, including the former Soviet Baltic republics. In Tallinn, Estonia's capital city, for example, the population decreased by 16% between 1989 and 2003, but in a 10–15-kilometer zone next to the city, new suburbs grew up, and one-third of their population lives in houses completed in 2005. The inner cities, previously elegant residential areas, lost most of their inhabitants and became the centers of banking and other service industries, packed with huge hotels serving the booming tourist industries. Former apartment buildings were redesigned and reconstructed as office buildings. In many other cases, parts of the inner cities sharply declined and become populated by immigrants, gypsies, and underclass layers. These developments became Europe-wide, including in the transforming post-communist countries. Prague's famous historic downtown lost one-third of its population in 15 years after the regime change and became a business, tourist, and administrative center. In the new suburban zone of the city, the number of completed apartments and houses per 1,000 inhabitants was three times higher than the national average. The seventh district of Budapest, a former Jewish ghetto, on the other hand, was mostly populated by Roma.

Settlements around big cities, instead of serving and feeding the urban population, and instead of offering cheaper homes for commuting workers and places for industrial firms, rapidly transformed into middle-class settlements. In the long Spanish coastal settlement strip, 50% of the area was sparsely built up with big houses. In one single decade, the 1990s, the population of the Madrid agglomeration increased by 50%. In European cities the built-up area in the last 20 years of the twentieth century increased by 20%, but the population of the urban-suburban inhabitants increased only by 9%. The small town development that dominated the postwar decades until the 1970s, stopped and reversed, since several of those small settlements became parts of huge urban agglomerations. Manchester, with its roughly 400,000 inhabitants, is actually the center of a 2.5-million-resident agglomeration. Because of the elimination of borders and the rapid development of transportation within the European Union, urban agglomerations started crossing former state borders and separating waters to create a London-Paris-Brussels and a Malmö-Copenhagen agglomeration. A similar trend started appearing between the nearby Austrian Vienna and the Slovak Bratislava, and between Vienna and Sopron and Győr in Hungary.

Some experts speak about "extreme urbanization" when urban and suburban settlements occupy more territory of a country than agricultural regions, and consider this trend decadent. Sometimes they call our attention to the lesson of history: urbanization represented the last stage of every civilization before their collapse. They also speak about the self-destructive character of the mega-polis.[30] The European Union's efforts to stop the process of city sprawling and to re-establish the traditional compact city structure, as the European Environmental Agency expressed this attempt in its 2006 report, is certainly too late and hopeless.

The two major types of urban sprawl[31]

Europe at the turn of the twenty-first century exhibits different types of suburbanization. One of them is as old as the cities themselves: the city starts sprawling in all possible directions and incorporating neighboring settlements. Formerly green, partly agricultural areas among the settlements also became part of the enlarging cities and were built up in a loose way by free-standing or semi-attached family houses. The other type of suburbanization, however, is new and different. It is, in reality, not the gradual enlargement of existing cities, but the creation of loosely connected suburban strips along seashores, lakes, or rivers. Both types of settlements have a relatively low population density where less than 80% of the landed areas is covered by buildings.

The first type is well illustrated, among others, by the examples of Madrid and Istanbul. In Madrid, during the high prosperity of the 1960s, new middle-class settlements were built in the northwest, and blue-collar ones were built southeast of the city. In the 1990s, urbanized land around the old city increased by 50 percent. While more than half a million new houses were built in the agglomeration, the population grew by only 240,000. In the early twenty-first century, beside the 3.3 million inhabitants in Madrid proper, more than six million people lived in the enlarged agglomeration that incorporated several small settlements such as Laganes, Getafe, Móstoles, Parla, Pozuelo de Alarcón, Las Rozas, San Sebastian, Alcobendas, Tres Cantos and Maja-dolousa. The latter, 10 kilometers from the center of Madrid, although it has existed since the thirteenth century, had only 560 inhabitants in 1850, which increased to 1,500 by 1960, but it became the home of 42,000 people half a century later. Most people go home to such "bedroom-cities" after work in Madrid. Madrid gradually spread and incorporated cities as far away as Guadalajara and Alcala de Henares. King Philip II moved his capital from Toledo to Madrid, but four-and-half centuries later, Madrid "went" to Toledo and incorporated it into its agglomeration. Several outer and inner beltways, an excellent 339-kilometer-long Cercanias–Madrid commuter railway system, the Metrosur rail-ring, and millions of cars connect the suburbs to the center of the enlarged city that occupies nearly 700 square kilometers.

Istanbul offers an even more dramatic example. The ancient city began growing extremely fast during the second half of the twentieth century and attracted 15% of the country's population. The number of Istanbul's inhabitants increased from one million to ten million. The built-up area enlarged by 600%. In a largely unregulated way, the city spread in all possible directions, and 300 gated communities were constructed in the immediate vicinity. On the European side of the city, a large agglomeration emerged with a 40–50-kilometer radius, with several administratively independent units such as Kemerburgaz, Zekeriyaköy, and Beyliklüzü, the latter with 186,000 inhabitants by itself. The city spread to the Marmara Sea, an inner sea connected with the Aegean and Black Seas via the Dardanelles and Bosporus, respectively. The coastline of the Marmara Sea at Florya and other settlements became popular places for the middle classes. Istanbul is also getting near the Black Sea. According to forecasts, another 2.5 million people will move to the vicinity of Istanbul by 2015. These sprawling, enlarged cities became so huge and the communication sometimes so chaotic, that instead of one city center, a polycentric relation was established, and the population basically lives around one of the smaller centers. This is also the situation in Dublin, where 40% of the country's population concentrates, and the 1.5 million inhabitants in the early twenty-first century are gradually increasing towards two million. Dublin's downtown is only one of the centers, and Newry, Droghda, and Dundalk also offer parallel city centers within the agglomeration.

The second type of new suburbia is not the sprawl of existing cities, but the creation of suburban style strips along sea-coasts. This development is closely connected to the rapid middle-classization of Western societies, and the explosion of tourism during the second half of the twentieth century, a major element in the rise of Western consumer societies. The sunny Mediterranean became the target of the middle classes from the colder northern countries. British and Dutch citizens bought summer houses to spend holidays in, before retiring to Spain, Portugal, and southern France. One of the best examples might be the urban coastal strip that grew up between Valencia and Murcia. On the Mediterranean seashore, the wonderful beaches of the provinces of Valencia, Castellon, and Alicante, especially the Costa Blanca, Costa Brava, and Costa Azahar, attracted part of the well-to-do Spanish population, but hotels and tourist institutions also built houses and high-rises in the coastal townships of Denia, Calpe, Benidorm, Peniscola, Oropesa, Morella, and several others, each of them generally with no more than 10,000 to 30,000 inhabitants. In the end, a consistent seashore settlement agglomeration emerged without any real center, or better put, with several small centers in the often independent medieval settlements. Similar developments characterized the Atlantic seashore of Portugal where, on a 13-kilometer-long strip amounting to 13% of the country's land, half of the country's urban area is concentrated. In this case, nearly half of the coastal land became a suburban-type agglomeration from Lisbon to Porto, and along the Algarve coast.

These new suburban-type settlements spread throughout Europe and became most characteristic in Belgium, the Netherlands, southern and western Germany, northern Italy, around the big capital cities of London and Paris, but sometimes also between major cities such as Paris and Brussels, along the Rhône valley. The urban face of Europe transformed and continues transforming.

Notes

1 This essay is based on: Stuart Hylton, *A History of Manchester*, Chichester: Phillimore & Co, 2003; Alan Kidd, *Manchester: A History*, 3rd edition, Edinburgh: Edinburgh University Press, 2002; W.H. Shercliff, *Manchester: A Short History of its Development*, Manchester: Municipal Publicity & Information Office, 1977.
2 This essay is based on: André Latraille and Richard Gascon, *Histoire de Lyon et du Lyonnais*, Paris: Privat, 1975.
3 W. Gregory Monahan, *Years of Sorrows: The Great Famine of 1709 in Lyon*, Columbus: Ohio State University Press, 1993, 125–26.
4 W.D. Edmonds, *Jacobinism and the Revolt of Lyon, 1789–1793*, Oxford: Clarendon Press, 1990.
5 Mary Lynn Stewart-McDougall, *The Artisan Republic: Revolution, Reaction, and Resistance in Lyon 1848–1851*, Kingston: McGill-Queen's University Press, 1984, 55.
6 This essay is based on: Anthony L. Cardoza and Geoffrey Symcox, *A History of Turin*, Torino: Giulio Einaudi, 2006; Alan Friedman, *Agnelli: Fiat and the Network of Italian Power*, New York: New American Library, 1989.
7 Cardoza and Symcox, 2006, 162.
8 Ibid, 200.

9 This essay is based on: Guy Greer, *The Ruhr-Lorraine Industrial Problem*, New York: Macmillan, 1925; Klaus Tenfelde and Thomas Urban, *Das Ruhrgebiet: Ein historisches Lesebuch*, Essen: Klartex Verlag, 2010.

10 This essay is based on: György Enyedi and Viktória Szirmai, *Budapest: A Central European Capital*, London: Belhaven Press, 1992; Ivan T. Berend and György Ránki, "A Budapest környéki ipari övezet kialakulásának és fejlődésének kérdéséhez," in Pesta László and Gerevich László (eds) *Tanulmányok Budapest múltjából*, Vol. XIV, Budapest: Akedémiai Kiadó, 1961.

11 This essay is based on: Herman Freudenberger and Gerhard Mensch, *Von der Provinzstadt zur Industrieregion (Brünn-Studie). Ein Beitr. zur Politökonomie d. Sozialinnovation, dargestellt am Innovationsschub der industriellen Revolution im Raume Brünn*, Göttingen: Vandenhoeck und Ruprecht, 1975; Herman Freudenberger, *The Industrialization of a Central European City: Brno and the Fine Woolen Industry in the 18th Century*, Edington: Pasold Research Fund, 1977; www.brno.cz/index.php?nav01=2222&nav02=5&lan=en.

12 Freudenberger and Mensch, 1975, 11.

13 Freudenberger, 1977, 183.

14 This essay is based on: Lucjan Dobroszycki (ed.), *The Chronicle of the Lódz Ghetto, 1941–1944*, New Haven: Yale University Press, 1984; Gordon J. Horwitz, *Ghettostadt: Lódz and the Making of a Nazi City*, Cambridge, MA: Harvard University Press, 2008; Joanna B. Michlic, "Lodz in the Post-Communist Era: In Search of a New Identity," Working Paper #65, Center for European Studies, Pomona, NJ; www.ces.fas. harvard.edu/publications/docs/pdfs/Michlic.pdf.

15 This essay is based on: Michel Carmona, *Haussmann: His Life and Times and the Making of Modern Paris*, Chicago: Ivan R. Dee, 2002; J.M. and Brian Chapman, *The Life and Times of Baron Haussmann: Paris in the Second Empire*, London: Weidenfeld & Nicolson, 1957; Nicolas Papayanis, *Planning Paris Before Haussmann*, Baltimore: Johns Hopkins University Press, 2004; Derek Sayer, *The Coasts of Bohemia: A Czech History*, Princeton: Princeton University Press, 1998.

16 Carmona, 2002, 190.

17 Ivan T. Berend, *Decades of Crisis: Central and Eastern Europe Before World War II*, Berkeley: University of California Press, 1998, 91.

18 Walter Benjamin, "Paris the Capital of the Nineteenth Century," in *Illuminationen*, Frankfurt am Main: Suhrkamp Verlag, 1969.

19 Sayer, 1988, 137.

20 Ibid, 180.

21 This essay is based on: Philippe Panerai, Jean Castex, Jean Charles Depaule, and Ivor Samuels, *Urban Forms: The Death and Life of the Urban Block*, Oxford: Architectural Press, 2004; Roberto Brambilla and Gianni Longo, *The Rediscovery of the Pedestrian: 12 European Cities*, Washington, DC: US Government Printing Office, 1977.

22 *GLC Study Tour of Europe and America: Pedestrianised Streets*, London: Greater London Council, 1974, v, vi.

23 Ibid.

24 Brambilla and Longo, 1977, 11.

25 This essay is based on: Alec Nove, *An Economic History of the USSR 1917–1991*, London: Penguin Books, 1992; György Ránki, *The Economics of the Second World War*, Wien: Böhlau Verlag, 1993; Ivan T. Berend, *Gazdaságpolitika az első ötéves terv megindításakor, 1948–1950*, Budapest: Közgazdasági Kiadó, 1964.

26 Nove, 1992, 190.

27 Ránki, 1993, 187–88.

28 Ernő Gerő's speech at the Political Academy of the Hungarian Communist Party, April 13, 1949, in Berend, 1964, 89.

29 This essay is based on: European Commission, *Urban Sprawl in Europe: The Ignored Challenge*, European Environmental Agency Report, No.10, Luxemburg: Office of the Official Publications of the European Community, 2006; Lewis Mumford, *The City in History*, New York: Harcourt Brace Jovanovich, 1961; Ivan T. Berend, *Europe Since 1980*, Cambridge: Cambridge University Press, 2010.
30 See Mumford, 1961, Chapter 17: "The Myth of Mega-polis."
31 This essay is based on: European Commission, 2006; Berend, 2010.

6 Bubbles, great depressions

Economic cycles

Introduction

Economic development is not linear. There is a pulsation, or cycles, with periods of rapid growth, followed by periods of near stagnation, even years of recessions and decline. This is inherent in the market system itself, which generates the cycles because millions of economic units, entrepreneurs, and managers make independent decisions about investment and output. In a period of prosperity, they easily overestimate the potential of the market. When they can effortlessly sell their products, they are ready to invest to increase production.

If millions of companies make this kind of overestimation, the outcome is too much new productive capacity, and overinvestment leads to overproduction. The products, consequently, cannot be absorbed by the market. Goods are piled high in storage, and companies lower their prices in order to sell. They also stop or decrease production, lay off a part of their labor force, and sometimes they lose liquidity, cannot pay back loans, and become bankrupt. Increasing unemployment further decreases the market. The manufacturing disease spreads to banks, which cannot get back their credit, and some of the banks also become bankrupt. Sometimes the banks are those that overstretch and provide more investments and credit than is reasonable. In this case, financial crises lead to restricted lending and the entire economy slows down or even declines.

Another natural characteristic of the market economy is speculation. Gambling practices sometimes create bubbles that push prices into the sky and at a certain point there are no buyers any longer, prices start declining, and financial collapse follows. This phenomenon is as old as capitalism itself. The famous Dutch "tulip bubble" of the late seventeenth century, and the English "South Sea bubble" in 1720, as well as the 2008 European crisis, especially the Irish and Spanish real estate bubbles, clearly signal this long history. Recessions spread internationally since markets for both goods and money are international. Export possibilities decrease, as well as the availability of capital imports from abroad. Bank failures, like contagious diseases, extend to other banks and countries. The 2008–12 Greek financial crises, even though Greece's economy represents only 2.5% of the Eurozone economy, endangered all the other countries and the common currency of the system. The interconnected market economies, although to different extents and depths, all experienced the recession.

These kinds of fluctuations were already recognized in the mid-nineteenth century by a French economist, Clément Juglar, who was originally a physician. He described and explained the cycle phenomenon, now called the Juglar cycle. He also maintained that market mechanisms actually automatically solve the crises. The decrease in prices and output gradually led to the marketing of the accumulated stocks of unsalable goods and the reinstallation of the balance between supply and demand. The 7–11-year pulsation, as Juglar described it, gradually leads to the return of a new prosperity. If the stocks are depleted, companies start replacing them, increase investments and output, re-employ workers, and a new prosperity starts again.

From the late nineteenth century, analysts recognized another type of cycle, but this time consisting of long economic waves that had a 20–25-year-long upward swing, and a similar length of downward or stagnating movement. The British William Stanley Jevons, based on the British experience, and the Dutch Jacob van Gelderen, described the existence of long waves before World War I. The first thorough statistical analysis, however, was made by the Russian Nikolai Kondratiev in 1922, and then in a more detailed way in 1926. He described in full what are now known as Kondratiev cycles from the turn of the nineteenth century up to his time. The last long cycle, he recognized, started its upward part in the 1890s, and, as Kondratiev stated, it reached its zenith during the war, and then it started its downward half immediately at the end of the war. He was unable to continue his research because he was arrested in 1930 and then executed on Stalin's order in 1938, but, indeed, the entire interwar two decades were a near stagnation, or a Kondratiev downward period, with a devastating Great Depression. After World War II, the cycle continued. Its upward half lasted from 1945 until 1973. Those years became the most prosperous period in European history. The boom reached its zenith and was followed by decline after the oil crisis of 1973.

The long waves are caused, according to the Austrian-born Harvard economist Joseph Schumpeter, by a "whole set of technological changes." Schumpeter was inspired by Kondratiev's hypothesis that the renewal of productive forces is the generator of the long waves. He sacrificed several years to accomplish a roughly 1,000-page-long book on the cycles. Schumpeter introduced the concept of the structural crisis, caused by "industrial revolutions." The mechanism works as follows: a major technological change makes the old leading and export sectors obsolete, and it inspires the rise of new sectors, based on the new technology. For example, the invention of hydroelectric power generation and transportation, and various kinds of applied use for electricity, led to the emergence of brand new electric industrial branches with huge potential markets. Coal lost out to electricity as the main energy source. Steam technology and the old engineering sectors lost ground in connection with this change. Coal output started declining, and dam construction and electric power generation increased. Electrical industries emerged. Over a period of one to two decades, this parallel decline and rise resulted in stagnation because it has a roughly zero increase outcome. The adjustment to the new technologies and to a series of new innovations takes time, but gradually the old leading sectors lost their importance. After one to two decades, however, the new technology offers the basis of a new prosperity, a new rapid growth period, and the new phase of the cycle begins.

During the high prosperity periods, speculation and manipulation to exploit possibilities for maximizing profit often create "bubbles," or artificially high market prices for certain goods or for real estate. When banks offered cheap credit and stopped monitoring the creditworthiness of their clients because they securitized their loans and sold them to other investors, a huge housing bubble emerged with skyrocketing home prices. The manipulated housing market bubble, of course, burst and resulted in a devastating crisis. During the long periods of stagnation and decline, great depressions endanger the functioning of the economy. In the interwar period, history's deepest and most international crisis paralyzed the world's economy. Leading industrial-economic powers such as the United States and Germany suffered a roughly 40% decline in industrial output. Agricultural prices dropped by 50–60%, and millions of Europeans lost their jobs.

While the 7–11-year Juglar cycles automatically re-establish prosperity and do not require outside interventions, the major structural crises, such as the great depressions in the long cycle-waves, do not lead to a timely automatic solution. Mass unemployment and bankruptcies, and the danger of major social-economic disruption, cry out for state intervention, crisis management, job creation by public works, and buying out companies. Most of all, governments have started assisting research and development to speed up adjustment to technological changes. They are assisting "sun-rise branches" of the economy, those new sectors that are based on the new technology. In backward countries, structural crises are often extremely deep and long because the peripheral, technology-importing countries are unable to adjust to the challenge of the technological revolution, or it takes a much longer time to do so. In those areas, outside intervention is especially important.

Cyclical economic development is one of the most exciting and troubling phenomena of modern economic history. Economic cycles are influenced by non-economic factors, such as wars and political upheavals among other things, but psychological reactions themselves can cause financial-economic panics and collapses. Although the cyclical pulsation of the economy is well-proven, neo-liberal economics rejected the possibility of cycles and crisis, maintaining that macro-economics invented all the required weaponry to eliminate volatility and recessions. They spoke about the "Great Moderation" of a recession-free economy. Although this argument met its Waterloo in 2008, recent analyses are much more stable and solid by rejecting the existence of a predictable, regular cycle, as previous cycle theories suggested.

This chapter offers case studies from the biblical "seven fat and seven lean years" phenomenon, the famous bubbles of the seventeenth and eighteenth centuries in Holland and England, the Great Depression of the 1930s, and its characteristic symptom of the suicide of Ivar Kreuger, the Swedish gambler-investor "Match King." Case studies present the "anatomy" of bank crashes, and the dramatic examples of the 2008 Greek and Irish economic collapse. Among the various economic disasters, an essay illustrates the story of history's greatest inflation in post-World War II Hungary.

The pharaoh's dream and modern economic cycles

Economic development does not mean permanent growth, but exhibits a kind of pulsation. Prosperities and crises, some theories suggest, rotate in an almost regular fashion. The very first instance of this phenomenon is strikingly old; it appears in the Old Testament. In Genesis, Joseph gives the following interpretation of the pharaoh's dream of seven fat cows emerging from the River Nile, followed by seven skinny cows that eat up the fat ones: seven prosperous years of plenty will come, followed by seven miserable years of bad harvest and starvation.[1] Joseph advised the pharaoh to gather and store enough food during the seven fat years to be able to feed the population during the seven lean years.

This first report of the existence of a cycle was also a report of the first—as modern economics calls it—"counter-cyclical" economic policy measure. One fifth of the harvest was taxed, collected, and stored by the state for the lean years when it was distributed. Sweden, thousands of years later, taxed companies in prosperous years, put the money into a special fund and then used this money to assist companies to come out of trouble in the years of recession. The American Obama administration initiated the same type of plan with the "bank tax."

The regular fluctuation of agricultural production was well-known in later centuries. For example, William Petty mentioned the phenomenon in 1662. He was a Renaissance man, physician general of the army in Ireland, a statistician who contributed to the creation of the methods of the modern census, but most of all, he was one of the earliest economists. He spoke about "seven years [to] make up the cycle."[2] A long time passed, however, until scholarly research offered a proper explanation. The German-born British astronomer William Herschel discovered the climatic and economic consequences of sunspot activities in 1801. Sunspots had been known for some time, but Herschel found correlations between the number of sunspots and the price of wheat at the London markets. High sunspot activity had a strong climatic impact, increased the energy output of the sun and the temperature of the air, while low sunspot activity had the opposite consequence. That fluctuation caused a series of good and then bad harvests, and, consequently, high and low wheat prices. In 1843, Heinrich Schwabe demonstrated an 11-year-long cycle between the periods of the high and low sunspot activities.[3]

When the modern industrial economy emerged after the industrial revolution, it turned out that it, too, had a similar fluctuation. Although not as punctual as clockwork, but approximately every seven to 11 years, prosperous, "fat" years rotate with seven to 11 "lean" years. "Commercial crises" were very well known in the first half of the nineteenth century. After prosperous years, all of a sudden, recessions followed when prices declined, goods were not salable, and companies decreased output and lay off their workforce. The repeated crises, especially the so-called defaults of public debts and "financial panics" in the 1790s, as well as the British recession of 1825, and then the major European recession of 1847–48, were regularly discussed in different kinds of descriptions and analyses.

In his monumental *Wealth of Nations* in 1776, Adam Smith did not deal in a methodical way with economic crises. The phenomenon, which he just mentioned, was discussed by others. Among the first economists to talk about them was the Swiss Jean Charles Léonard Simonde de Sismondi in his *Political Economy* of 1815 and *Nouveaux principes d'économie politique* of 1819. He called attention to the combined impact of limitless competition and mass poverty. While the first generates "overproduction," the second causes "under-consumption." Recessions reappear in a regular fashion. In 1823, Thomas Tooke recognized waves in prices, and John Wade maintained in 1833 that commercial cycles fluctuate in five- to seven-year waves. Five years later, Hyde Clarke noted periods of commercial distress that had been recurring in ten- and 54-year-long waves. Analysts, however, found different explanations for each of these crises. Why did they appear? Had there been any common causes effecting them? And how have they been solved? These questions did not get any real answers.

Our knowledge of economic fluctuation is based on the first convincing description and analysis of the crisis phenomenon by Clément Juglar. He was born in France and became a medical doctor. His interest in statistics drew his attention to economic problems and his science education led him to search for hidden interrelationships, causes, and consequences. Instead of occasional causes, he looked for "causes déterminantes." He realized that economic recessions are not disconnected individual events, but have common features and return in a cyclical fashion. In 1857, Juglar published a study in the *Journal des Économistes* on "Des crisses commerciales et monétaires de 1800 à 1857." A few years later, the Académie des Sciences Morales et Politiques launched a competition to "inquire into the causes, and indicate the effects, of commercial crisis that took place in Europe and North America during the XIXth Century."[4]

Juglar responded to the challenge with a book, *Des crises commerciales et de leur retour périodique en France, en Angleterre et aux État-Unis* (1862). He returned to the topic and produced a second edition, nearly three times larger, more than a quarter of a century later in 1889. Just as the Bible was the first description of a crisis phenomenon, this work was the first scholarly analysis of the economic cycles. Juglar realized that the cycle has no exact timing but returns in seven to 11 years. He distinguished among three phases of the cycle: prosperity, crisis, and liquidation. During prosperity, people become extremely optimistic and cannot imagine the end of the boom. Consequently, they start overspeculating. Gambling and speculation are human characteristics and the competitive market economy inspires these habits. Juglar speaks often about "excès de la spéculation," "extravagante application du capital flottant." Price increases generate "exaggerated extension" and "abuse of credit" to excessive expenses. Credit gets out of hand, and the "speculation spiral" gradually destabilizes the system. Overinvestment and overproduction lead to commercial crisis when products become unsalable. The cycle then reaches its second stage, the crisis. As stock accumulates and remains in storage, prices start to decline and companies dismiss a part of the workforce. Banks become overcautious in issuing (or advancing) credit. A portion of the debtors become unable to repay the credit and become bankrupt, pulling the creditors with them.

The crisis phase of the cycle automatically generates the third, "liquidation" phase when investments stop, interest rates decrease and, consequently, overinvestment and overproduction are gradually absorbed by the rising market. "L'espirit d' entreprise" awakens again, and a new prosperity gradually arises. Economic cycles and crises are thus organic parts of the market economy.

In spite of hundreds of years of experience, and a library that could be filled with studies on the recessions and the cyclical character of economic growth, people, including economists, are always unprepared and shocked when the cycle changes. After World War II and during the heightened prosperity of the 1950s to early 1970s, theories were born about the end of crisis phenomena. Recession and depression belonged to the past and would not return. During the decline or stagnation, in the years of crisis, a great many people lose hope, and significant numbers became ready to make alliances with the devil, to turn to ruthless, extremist movements, or to xenophobic populist and fascist regimes, as saviors. It happened in Italy in the post-World War I crisis and in Germany during the Great Depression in 1929–33. Mussolini and Hitler rode that wave to power. It helped conservative, xenophobic populist parties to gain power in some of the desperate Central and Eastern European countries in the 2010s.

A shocking new recognition: Nikolai Kondratiev and the long economic cycles[5]

At the threshold of World War I, two Dutch economists, Jacob van Gelderen and Samuel de Wolff, analyzed the price movements of the nineteenth century and recognized long waves in price formation. Their findings, because they were published in Dutch, remained unknown in other countries. A decade later, in Bolshevik Russia, a 30-year-old genius economist published a small book that introduced a new concept of economic fluctuation. Using historical statistics of international price movements and output data for basic goods,

Nikolai Dimitrievich Kondratiev documented the existence of 50–60-year-long economic cycles.

The Kondratiev cycle—as the Austrian-born Harvard economist Joseph Schumpeter named the phenomenon in the 1930s—exhibits a 20–25-year-long upward phase, and a similar length downward phase, in the international economy. The upward, or "A" phase, is the period of growth and expansion, the introduction of new products, and of rising but essentially stable prices. When growth reaches the "plateau," the entrepreneurial mood is euphoric, and speculation with shares, bonds, and real estate flourishes. High prosperity, however, undermines itself. All of a sudden, prosperity stops. High growth creates a shortage of resources. The political stability that characterized the growth period ends. Wars may follow. Those changes open the downward phase that starts with a recession and is followed by a long period of stagnation. The depression period, however, is a time of readjustment and of new inventions that establish future growth. When Kondratiev described those cycles in his book, he confessed—in a quite rare, modest way—that he could not thoroughly explain the causes of the phenomenon. However, he had an "initial hypothesis": "the long cycle is associated with the replacement and expansion of basic capital goods, and with the radical regrouping of, and changes in society's productive forces."[6]

The excellent economist of the twentieth century Joseph Schumpeter was greatly impressed by Kondratiev's findings in the 1930s, since the cycle theory virtually forecast the Great Depression that occurred in that decade. Schumpeter started working on the problem, producing a 1,000-page book on the cycles, which offered a more convincing interpretation of the long waves, in 1938. "An industrial revolution … periodically reshapes the existing structure of industry by introducing new methods of production … new sources of supply … new trade routes and markets to sell in … While these things are being initiated we have brisk expenditure and 'prosperity' predominates … and while those things are being completed … we have the elimination of antiquated elements of the industrial structure and 'depression' predominates. Thus there are prolonged periods of rising and falling prices, interest rates, employment … which phenomena constitute parts of the mechanism of this process of recurrent rejuvenation of the productive apparatus."[7] Schumpeter thus introduced the concept of a "structural crisis" caused by "a whole set of technological changes."

The first, upward phase of the Kondratiev waves emerged in 1780–90 and ran until 1810–17, followed by the downward period of 1810–17 to 1844–51, with a major crisis in the 1840s. The second full Kondratiev cycle covered the second half of the nineteenth century with 1844–51 to 1870–75 as the upward phase, and 1870–75 to 1890–96 as the downward phase, including the first so-called (and broadly questioned) Great Depression of the 1870s. The upward half of the third cycle characterized the years from 1890–96 to 1914–20. When Kondratiev published his work in the early 1920s, he diagnosed the beginning of the downward phase of the cycle. This, indeed, happened with the Great

Depression of the middle of the downward half of the cycle, and ended in the second half of the 1930s, between 1936 and 1940.

The late 1930s were also fatal for Kondratiev: his life ended in 1938. Kondratiev was born into a peasant family in 1892 in the province of Kostroma, north of Moscow. Before the war, he was a student at the University of St. Petersburg and studied under the best economist in Russia, Mikhail Tugan-Baranovsky. The young student soon joined the Socialist Revolutionary (SR) Party, a radical political movement, founded in 1901 and led by peasant intellectuals against the autocratic tsarist regime. At the age of 25, after the February Revolution destroyed the tsarist regime in 1917, he was appointed Minister of Supply in the Alexander Kerensky Provisional Government. The transitory government, however, had a short life. In October of the same year, the Vladimir Lenin-led Bolshevik Revolution ousted Kerensky and introduced the dictatorship of the proletariat. The November election of a Constitutional Assembly led to an SR victory by 370 seats out of a total of 703, compared to the Bolsheviks' 175. After the split of the SR Party at the beginning of the Bolshevik regime, the Left SR Party became a junior partner of the revolutionary government, but soon an absolute Bolshevik dictatorship followed.

Kondratiev, however, remained an influential economist and, in 1921, he established and directed his famous Conjuncture Institute in Moscow. He was one of the advocates of the so-called New Economic Policy (NEP) in 1921, a return to a market economy after the disastrous years of the so-called War Communism and the harsh exploitation of the peasantry and the famine that followed. In 1924–25, he traveled to the West, including the United States. After the death of Lenin in January 1924, a major and passionate debate ensued about the future road for Russia. Three main concepts emerged. Kondratiev belonged to the group of economists who suggested a well-thought-out economic policy road. Russia, an agricultural country, he argued, has to exploit its comparative advantages (David Ricardo's famous theory) and modernize and develop its agricultural sector. From agricultural exports, the income has to be reinvested into agriculture that will increase capital accumulation and in the medium-term, finance industrialization. The idea was nothing short of drawing the lesson of the British and West European economic history. The British industrial revolution became possible because it was preceded by an agricultural revolution.

A second, politically more influential group, led by Leon Trotsky, the actual military leader of the Bolshevik Revolution and the potential successor to Lenin, called his policy recommendation the "dictatorship of industry." In his group, the talented Bolshevik economist, Yevgeni Preobrazhensky, worked out the concept of this policy. He also based his argumentation on British economic history and its analysis by Karl Marx in his *Das Kapital*. The industrialization of Britain emerged on the basis of what Marx called primitive capital accumulation, the enclosure system that exploited and expropriated the peasantry, and which ousted the greatest part of them from their land. Trotsky and Preobrazhensky urged doing the same and starting a dramatic, fast industrialization of the backward country. They planned to eliminate the market system by introducing central planning and artificial prices, a "price scissor" with low agricultural and high industrial prices to exploit the peasantry and to accumulate capital for industrialization.

The third group, led by the Austrian-trained Bolshevik economist Nikolai Bukharin, rejected both concepts. The young Soviet state, he argued, must not follow an agricultural path of development because the country was politically isolated, had already survived a civil war and foreign interventions, was militarily endangered and had to be prepared for other attacks. On the other hand, the destruction of the market system and the exploitation of the peasantry would be a counterproductive and dangerous path because it economically undermined the domestic market, and politically alienated the majority of the population, the peasantry, thus endangering the Soviet system. Stalin and the majority of the political leadership shared Bukharin's view in the mid-1920s. The so-called industrialization debate, which took place at a high intellectual level, was closed by political considerations and brutal administrative methods in 1928. Stalin, rejecting their policy recommendation, physically eliminated his rivals, first the most dangerous one, the "left-deviator" Trotsky, then the "right-deviator" Bukharin, and, finally, he cynically adopted Trotsky and Preobrazhensky's strategy while murdering them.

Kondratiev's fate was also sealed. The advocate of market-led industrialization and the NEP, which was quietly put to an end, had no place in Stalin's Russia. In 1928, Kondratiev lost his position as director of his Conjuncture Institute; in 1930, he was arrested and sentenced to eight years in prison. However, he was not sent to Siberia to one of the infamous camps, but he was instead jailed in the monastery of Suzdal where he had the possibility to work and where he planned to write five books. In 1938, at the height of the madness of Stalin's purges, he was retried and sentenced to ten years in prison, but on the same day that the sentence was announced, he was shot dead by a firing squad.

The theory of the Kondratiev cycle survived him and characterized the Western economy in the second half of the twentieth century. From 1936–40, a fourth cycle emerged and its upward half ran until 1966–71, followed by a downward phase between 1966–71 and 1980–85, with the major crisis occurring between 1973–85. From that latter time, the fifth cycle began and its upward half covered the years until 2000–2007. For this cycle, however, the downward half opened with the dramatic financial crisis of 2008–11, and, according to the history of the long waves, may characterize the period until 2015–20.

The existence of the Kondratiev cycles are accepted by some economists and rejected by others. During prosperous times it is totally forgotten; when recession comes, it is always rediscovered. That happened in the 1930s, the 1970s–1980s, and again when the 2008 crisis started emerging. The British *Money Week* published an article about it with one of the sections titled, "Where are we now?", or "Which phase of the long wave are we in?"[8] As Eric Hobsbawm noted in a footnote in his *The Age of Extremes*, since Kondratiev and his long cycle theory predicted the Great Depression, it "convinced many historians and even some economists that there is something in them, even if we don't know what."[9]

From the Dutch tulip bubble (1637) to the Irish housing-market bubble (2008)[10]

Economic fluctuations probably have certain regularities, but sudden crashes may happen outside any pattern and cycle. The market economy is genuinely related to speculation to maximize profit and to generate huge wealth. Like gambling, however, economic speculation is always a risky business. Speculation may push prices into unrealistic heights, creating "bubbles" that, after a while, burst and generate mass bankruptcies, loss of lifelong savings, and the crash of the economy.

Unlike the cyclical pulsations of the economy, bubbles are created when prices rise far above the real value of a commodity or stock. It happens when certain commodities become extremely fashionable, or when a radical structural change leads to the sudden appearance and shocking spread of new products, and their market seems to be unlimited. Another reason might be the high prosperity that comes with the extremely rapid increase of stock prices. If this takes a few years, millions of people run to invest in stocks. It might also result in production of high-demand commodities. A natural prerequisite, however, is the large amount of mobile capital looking for profitable investment. In modern times, cheap bank credit, huge inflows of foreign capital, and low interest rates may also fuel speculation, using and abusing credit for investment into promising sectors. In good times, people extrapolate the trend into the future; they believe in further, continuous price increases, and then invest in the future by speculatively buying assets or commodities, hoping to sell them later at higher prices. High demand pushes prices further.

At some point, however, people begin to experience doubt and believe that price increases cannot be continued and that it is probably better to sell. If too many reach that decision, panic may easily emerge as more people rush to sell. If too many sell, supply surpasses demand and prices decrease, pushing many more people to sell, and prices may collapse. The bubble bursts. Bubbles and their bursting have accompanied the market throughout its history. One of the very first bubbles that history records—although it was not called by this name yet—was the amazing Dutch "tulip mania" of 1633–37. That was the zenith of the Dutch Golden Age: the Netherlands was the richest and most powerful trading country and the most urbanized in the world. Meanwhile, the Netherlands was also the home country of the agricultural revolution, with flourishing horticulture. In this environment, an exotic flower, the tulip, arrived from the Tien Shan Mountains and the slopes of the Pamir, via Turkey, and became extremely popular. Illustrated tulip-books were published and sold. People started buying tulip bulbs and florists invested huge amounts of money to sell the bulbs later at a higher price. In 1633, a stone house was sold for three rare tulips, and a rare bulb's price was equal to 1,000 pounds of cheese. In 1636, the price of some bulbs doubled in one to two weeks. But transactions were reported in which the rare "Admiral de Man" tulip's price increased 12-fold. The tulip mania reached its climax between December 1636 and January 1637. During that period, a "Semper Augustus" bulb sold for 10,000 guilders, an amount sufficient for a family to live on for three to four decades. Well-to-do merchants, weavers, and artisans entered the promising and well-paying tulip business. At the height of the tulip mania, a good businessman could make 90,000 guilders in one to two weeks, when the richest person of the country had 400,000, accumulated over generations. In the first week of February 1637, at the tulip auction in Haarlem, the boom suddenly ended. There were no bidders and the prices started declining. A devastating crash followed. Bulbs valued at 5,000 guilders were sold for 50. At the end, tulip prices dropped to 1–5% of prices at the peak of the mania. A few years later, the most celebrated painter, Jan Brueghel the Younger, painted his "An allegory of the Tulip Mania" with dozens of florists wanting to sell, and monkeys fighting for bulbs. One of the monkeys urinates on a tulip flower-bed; one speculator was carried to his grave.

This phenomenon was first called a "bubble" nearly 100 years later, when the powerful British South Sea Company went bankrupt in 1720. In the eighteenth century, a few state-chartered companies gained monopolies for colonial trade. The Dutch, British, and French East India Companies, the very first joint stock companies, were small empires with their own merchant fleets, navies, and armies, and they paid huge amounts of interest to their stockholders. The South Sea Company, established in 1711, had gained a monopoly for Latin American and African trade from the British Parliament. In 1720, the company took over the entire British national debt and converted it into its own shares. In April, £2 million of stock were offered for £300 each and sold out within an hour. In June, stocks peaked at £1,050. However, the debt conversion business and fraudulent practices soon ended the rush. In August, several investors withdrew, and by September stock prices declined by 75%. Arrests and the confiscation of private assets followed. This was a major shock, and the British Parliament enacted the South Sea Bubble Act in that year, banning the establishment of joint stock companies. This measure remained unchanged for 150 years. Exactly the same happened with the French *Compagnie des Indes* (or Mississippi Company) that had a monopoly for trading with French Louisiana and other colonies. In 1719, when the company issued 50,000 shares, promising 120% interest, 300,000 potential buyers lined up. In May 1720, however, the company's shares were devalued by half, and by November, they became worthless. Another bubble had burst.

Although the British Parliament drew the most draconic conclusion from the South Sea bubble, and the schools in the Netherlands are still teaching the moral lessons of the tulip mania, bubbles and their dramatic bursts accompany the entire history of the market system. Too much risk-taking by the over-extended financial sectors, the belief that stock prices would rise indefinitely, and the accumulation of huge debt burdens created multiple bubbles in 1873, 1907, and, in the most dramatic way, in 1931. Hundreds of banks collapsed, and severe recession followed. The Great Depression and World War II led to the introduction of strict regulations to avoid economic disasters, but regulations were eliminated from the 1970s on, and new bubbles developed and burst. The 1994 Mexican financial crisis, and the Asian one in 1997, called attention to a new factor causing bubbles and collapses: global speculation, massive capital flow, and speculative attacks against currencies, which led to panic among currency holders and a severe devaluation. The Asian crisis began with the real estate bubble in Thailand, generated by a huge capital inflow that totaled more than half of the value of the country's GDP between 1988 and 1995. The developing country's economy was unable to absorb the amount productively, and the real estate business started to run amok. Here too, foreign speculators took domestic credits and then attacked the local currency forcing devaluation to repay the credits with many fewer dollars. The collapse had a dramatic domino effect in Asia and in parts of Eastern Europe, including Russia.

The 2008–10 international financial crisis started as a consequence of the real estate bubble in the United States and several other countries. One of the most extreme examples was Ireland, the most successful economic performer in the European Union. In Ireland, 50% tax cuts, huge capital inflow, low interest rates, and unlimited bank lending to property developers created a huge real estate bubble. From the mid-1990s, house prices increased by two and a half times, and housing represented 14% of the economy. Household indebtedness jumped from 60% to 160% of GDP. In one of the most extreme examples, the property tycoon, Seán Quinn, paid €379 million for seven acres of land in an exclusive part of Dublin to destroy hotels and build fashionable shopping malls, luxury shops, and apartments. That was the highest amount paid for land in Europe. Similar to the seventeenth-century tulip speculators, the Irish developers also believed in unending price increases. Banks held this belief too: for example, the Anglo-Irish Bank increased its market capitalization ten-fold after 2000, basing its success mostly on its property-loan portfolio.

The bubble burst when interest rates started rising and the financial crisis hit Europe hard. As much as 60% of bank lending was concentrated on property. All of a sudden, Irish housing prices dropped by half, and bank shares fell by 90%. From super prosperity, Ireland declined into severe crisis. In 2009, the national income declined by 7.1% and unemployment reached 13%. Similar bubbles burst in Estonia and the financial crisis undermined Greece and endangered Spain, Portugal, and Italy, as well as the common currency of the European Union. As a result of bubbles bursting, millions of people and hundreds of banks became bankrupt in an unending chain from the seventeenth to the twenty-first century.

The greatest economic crash ever: the Great Depression of the 1930s[11]

World War I shocked the European economy and it took several years until it recovered in the mid-1920s. The second half of the decade, however, became the scene of a speculative boom, based strongly on inflowing American credits. After the extreme German inflation, 40% of investments in Germany in the second half of the 1920s were financed by American capital. Germany borrowed nearly $8 billion. In the late 1920s, indebted European countries paid the interest and principle from new loans, and their out payments reached 40% to 70% of the net inflowing capital. Examining the situation of the Central European countries, Derek Aldcroft speaks about "the most flagrant cases of over-borrowing."[12] On top of that, half of the inflowing foreign capital in several countries was short-term credits. Since foreign capital seemed to be guaranteed, irresponsible debtors—such as the Hungarian Viktoria Flourmill Company—sometimes invested short-term credits into establishing factories that offered only long-term income to repay. They did not care because they believed in the unlimited inflow of fresh credits to use for repaying. This situation reached its climax in 1928 when European debtors paid back $677 million a year, which was more than the new credits that they received.

In 1928 and 1929, all of the sudden, foreign, and most of all American, capital exports started drying up. In 1927, The United States exported $1,336 million, but only $790 million in 1929, and $363 million in 1930. From one year to the next, debtor countries received 50% to 70% less foreign credits and investments than before. All of a sudden, there was no fuel for the economic engine in Europe. The situation became much more severe because, in the case of Germany, half of the foreign credits were short-term, and they had to repay it within a year or so without new foreign money. In six weeks, Germany lost 2 billion marks worth of gold and foreign exchange. The reserves of the National Bank dropped to one-tenth of their previous levels.

After a long speculative boom, on "Black Thursday," October 24, 1929, the American stock market collapsed. "By eleven o'clock the market had degenerated into a wild, mad scramble to sell … [and] surrendered to blind, relentless fear. This indeed was a panic … A suicide wave was in progress, and eleven well-known speculators had already killed themselves."[13] By mid-November, stock prices declined by 40%, which discouraged investors and consumers throughout the world: a major crisis had arrived. Indeed, at the deepest point of the depression, the world's industrial output dropped by 30%: coal and iron production fell by 40–60%; grain prices declined by 60%; and the value of the European trade dropped to one-third of pre-depression levels. In the United States, 25% of the workforce became unemployed and industrial output declined by 41%. In Germany, 60% of the workforce became unemployed and industrial production declined by 40%. Investments dropped to 3% of the pre-depression level in Germany in 1931. Unemployment worldwide increased three-fold and reached about 15 million in Europe. While millions starved, grain, milk, and meat were destroyed because huge stocks of agricultural products became unsalable. In Brazil, storehouses holding 3.8 billion pounds of coffee did not find markets, and a great part of it was burned. In the summer of 1931, a tragic financial crisis followed. In the United States, 3,600 banks collapsed in 1930 and 1931. In the summer, all German and Hungarian banks were closed. The Vienna Creditanstalt, the most important bank of the entire Central European region, went bankrupt in May 1931.

The intensity, scale, and then the duration of the depression were all unparalleled. It was a dramatic worldwide crisis during the entire 1930s, unprecedented before and up to now. Thirty years later, the American economist John Kenneth Galbraith frankly stated in his book on the Great Depression that "economics still do not allow final answers on these matters."[14] There was only one country in the world that was not touched by the depression, Bolshevik Russia, which started its forced industrialization drive in 1928 and doubled its industrial capacities during the years of the Great Depression. Stalin took credit for that and declared that the socialist system was crisis-proof. In reality, Russia remained untouched because of its total isolation from the world economy.

The indebted countries were unable to repay their debts, and in the summer of 1931 they began rejecting repayment, beginning with Germany, but soon followed by others. New credits were no longer available on the international capital market, which crippled all of the debtor countries, while creditors lost a huge part of the money they had invested before. Although the two leading industrial powers, the United States and Germany, suffered the most drastic declines of production and the most spectacular bank crises, the less developed agricultural countries on the European peripheries experienced an even deeper and more complex crisis. Their agricultural exports declined by more than half, but because of the sharp agricultural price decrease, export incomes fell more sharply. In the case of Hungary, exports decreased by 42% but export incomes fell by 73%. Poland increased its agricultural exports by 28%, but its export incomes declined by 56%.

Agricultural countries had to export one-third more, just to be able to import the same amount, because their import prices declined much less than their export prices. Their foreign trade was thus virtually paralyzed. All of these countries became insolvent and asked for rescheduling of their debts. Instead of the traditional capital inflow that played a central role in the modernization of these countries, capital outflow made their depression permanent. "The economic collapse in Central and Eastern Europe was total, and international economic ties were broken."[15]

The extended depression generated drastic political consequences. A few weeks apart, in early 1933, two charismatic leaders emerged in two key countries of the world, the United States and Germany: President Franklin D. Roosevelt and Chancellor Adolf Hitler. Although they were politically totally different, both were elected because they offered an exit from the crisis. They promised jobs for the roughly 15 million American and six million German unemployed, respectively, and they offered work for industry. A drastic state intervention followed to cope with lacking investments, stagnating production, and mass poverty. Both Roosevelt's New Deal and Hitler's economic program focused on job-creating public works, stimulus to industrial recovery, and aid for the unemployed. In America, Roosevelt's interventionist policy was strongly criticized from the conservative side as a dangerous socialist endeavor, especially because of its social legislation, i.e., Social Security and the Labor Relations Act. In Nazi Germany, Hitler destroyed the unions and created a Nazi *Deutsche Arbeitsfront*; his job creation *Motorisierung* program, the extensive autobahn construction, already served his war preparation. Hitler made a series of economic agreements with neighboring Central and Eastern European countries in 1934 to create a *Grossraumwirtschaft*, an autarchic economic zone where the German war economy would be able to buy food and strategic raw materials for German industrial products in barter trade. In 1936, a four-year plan started open military-industrial war preparations.

Europe became strongly polarized politically. Fascist Italy turned to widespread nationalizations and 42% of industrial shares were in the hands of state-owned holding companies. The managers of private companies were responsible to state authorities. Austria and Hungary made a close political alliance with Mussolini and then with Hitler. Every Central European country adopted major elements of the fascist-Nazi economic programs. Poland started a state-led industrialization plan to establish an industrial triangle in the mid- to late 1930s; Hungary introduced a five-year plan for war preparation in 1938. Most of the European countries turned to an extreme economic nationalism and self-sufficiency, and joined the Italian- or German-led autarchic economic blocs.

In France, on the other hand, the Popular Front, a center-left coalition government, was formed in the mid-1930s. Prime Minister Léon Blum, "never concealed the fact he was inspired by the American New Deal and Roosevelt."[16] He introduced a 20 billion franc, three-year public works program. Social legislation served to counterbalance the impact of the depression. The Matignon Accords revolutionized working conditions and increased wages, introducing paid vacations and the 40-hour work week. In Britain, Winston Churchill praised Roosevelt as "an explorer who has embarked on a voyage as uncertain as that of Columbus, and … might conceivably be as important as the discovery of the New World."[17] The British industrial stimulus project was very similar to the New Deal, the Unemployment Act of 1934 established an Unemployment Assistance Board, and agricultural laborers were also included in the insurance system. Wages were increased by 10%. An extended social program transferred 5–6% of GDP from the rich to the poor.

The different kind of state interventions in the democratic and the fascist-Nazi oriented countries gradually led to recovery from the depth of the Great Depression in the late 1930s, but the real ending of the "endless crisis" came only with World War II.

Ivar Kreuger's suicide in 1932: the sensation and symbol of the Great Depression[18]

The Great Depression between 1929 and 1933 provided unpleasant sensations every day. Newspaper headlines shocked the reading public with the news that the world's coal output had declined by 40% and wheat prices by 60%. Newspapers reported that the unemployment rate skyrocketed to 44% in Germany, and 20 million Europeans lost their jobs. People learned that the Yugoslav government banned the use of tractors in order to provide more possibilities for working in the fields. The news reported on the collapse of more than 3,000 American banks and 17,000 German companies. As a shocking paradox, while millions of people starved, the news reported that producers destroyed unsalable food, including one million truckloads of wheat and 28 million kilograms of meat.

On July 13, 1931, the sensational news was reported that the German government had ordered the banks to close and had banned withdrawal of money from personal accounts. Hungary followed suit the next day. There was bad news every day. Still, the leading newspapers of the world rushed to publish special editions with the most sensational headline on March 12, 1932: the Swedish multibillionaire, Ivar Kreuger, one of the world's richest men, had committed suicide by shooting himself in his Paris apartment. The same year Hollywood released a film, *The Match King*, which told his story. Kreuger was the owner of a huge economic empire, including match companies in 33 countries and monopolies for producing matches in several others. He controlled two-thirds of the world's match production, owned mines, pulp and paper factories, banks, and iron ore mines, altogether about 200 companies, and the world's third largest gold deposit. In 1930, 64% of the entire trade on the Stockholm stock exchange was related to Kreuger's empire. He was a creditor of several governments, and provided a total of $350 million in loans to a dozen European countries. After World War I—when he offered a $30 million loan to Germany to pay reparations—somebody called him the "savior of Europe."

Who was Ivar Kreuger? Why did his suicide exhibit the essential characteristics of the Great Depression? Kreuger was born into a middle-class family in Kalmar, Sweden, in 1880. His grandfather established a small match factory that was inherited and run by his father. The young Ivar soon showed his intellectual brilliance; he skipped grades and at the age of 20 he graduated from the Stockholm Royal Institute of Technology as a mechanic and civil engineer. The restless young engineer traveled throughout the world and worked in South Africa, Canada, Germany, and the United States for years. He returned to Sweden in 1908 at the age of 28, and with a partner he established the Kreuger & Toll real estate and construction company. This enterprise became very successful, introduced new American technology, and built, among others, the Stockholm Olympic Stadium and participated in the construction of the famous Stockholm City Hall. The talented young entrepreneur was extremely ambitious.

He returned to the family business and revolutionized the match industry. In 1910, one giant match company, AB Jonköping-Vulcan AB, dominated the Swedish market, controlling 75% of the output and market. The young Kreuger skillfully arranged the merger of about 20 smaller match factories, including his family business, to create the AB Förenade Tändsticksfabriker. Based on this new company, he arranged a merger with Jonköping-Vulcan, which formed Svenska Tändsticks AB in 1917. He became president of the new giant company. Sweden was a world power in safety match production, based on an 1884 invention by Gustaf Erik Pasch of the Royal Swedish Academy of Sciences.

Kreuger launched an aggressive campaign to become, as he was soon indeed called, the "Match King." He provided credit to economically weak countries in Central and Eastern Europe in exchange for an absolute monopoly on the countries' match market. In 1928, Kreuger made an agreement with the Hungarian government to provide a $36 million loan in exchange for a monopoly on the Hungarian market. He bought the majority share of the biggest Hungarian match factory, Szikra Magyar Gyujtógyárak, and of all other smaller match factories, to create one single monopoly company. When the transactions were completed, the price of the match was trebled and he paid 18% from the income to the Hungarian government. The same time, a similar business transaction was realized with Yugoslavia, based on a $22 million loan to the government. Kreuger also bought or established match companies throughout the world, from Japan to Italy.

The secret of his unique and rapid success was his unparalleled talent as a financier. He broadly used—and partly invented—methods such as off-balance sheet financing and offshore subsidiaries in tax havens. Kreuger was a gambler and made business agreements for future buying and selling. He was involved in risky but highly lucrative business activities that are nowadays called derivative business. Eighty years later in 2009, when Bernard Madoff's Ponzi scheme collapsed in New York, and the deregulated financial transactions, including the derivative business practice spectacularly collapsed, Daniel Gross published an interview with the author of a newly published book on Ivar Kreuger with the title, "Grandfather of the Scam?" His business activities often bordered on illegality, but most of those financial activities were not regulated, and thus remained legal.

During the great American boom of the 1920s, Kreuger tripled his funds from America. He attracted investors by granting 25–30% interest while some of his investments and government loans resulted in only 6%. He covered the difference with new investors' money. He managed to do it because "when investors learned about the dividends Krueger and Toll had been paying, they simply went mad."[19] This activity was rather close to a Ponzi scheme. To attract and raise money, his company issued *kapitalandeslån*, or participating debentures, which were formally bonds, but in real terms they were non-voting stocks that paid high yields, often two to three times more than investment-grade bonds, but were high-risk, speculative-grade bonds, commonly called junk bonds.

His ambition pushed him into politics as an advocate of European peace and he was an advisor to leading politicians. President Hoover received him in the White House, and he had connections to Aristide Briand, Prime Minister of France. His loans targeted the reconstruction and consolidation of Germany. He was decorated with the Legion of Honor. The charming, elegant, and tireless Krueger had an air of mysterious greatness. He prepared for hours to make an impression by talking to people, and by delivering speeches by heart. As John Kenneth Galbraith noted, "Kreuger was an extraordinarily competent actor who discovered that a quiet forceful manner plus the ability to remember … were sufficient to win him the respect of the very best men. It cost them millions."[20]

When Percy Rockefeller visited him in Stockholm, Kreuger, using a fake third telephone set on his desk, pretended to receive telephone calls from Mussolini and Stalin, and introduced hired "ambassadors" to Rockefeller at the dinner party. Rockefeller said "That man is the salt of the earth. He is on most intimate terms with heads of European governments. Gentlemen, we are fortunate indeed to be associated with Ivar Kreuger."[21] Small wonder that he had built up and exploited lucrative American connections, and personal friendships with important bankers.

His lifestyle exhibited his extraordinary personality. He was modest in eating; quiet and reserved, and business was his public and personal life and entertainment. He did not need anybody, remained a bachelor, and did not maintain permanent relationships, although he sent regular allowances to several women, and appeared a couple of times with Greta Garbo. On the other hand, he built his four-story, 125-room marble and granite Match Palace in the center of Stockholm with a "tone of simplicity of line and furnishing."[22] On the top floor was his "Silence Room," hardly furnished and isolated. Kreuger ordered a specially made Phantom II Rolls-Royce, owned fast boats, and collected Dutch masters and rare Persian carpets. All these activities made him a celebrity and built confidence in his business transactions. He arranged his first loans in 1922, and sent over the American money to one of his subsidiaries in Lichtenstein. Kreuger traveled a lot and maintained apartments in New York, Paris, and Berlin since his business was based on connections and credits. His aggressive acquisition campaign of match companies throughout the world was financed from credits that were not visible to the outside world because of his skillful transactions. He also cooked the business records of his companies, overvalued them, and did not accept legal or other barriers. As one of his biographers put it: "he believed that superior men were not restricted by ordinary laws, and the end justifies the means."[23]

Krueger gained a majority share of the multinational Swedish telecommunication giant, Ericsson, in 1930 and, by misleading representation of Ericsson's business standing, he sold them the following year to the company's main rival, International Telephone and Telegraph Co (ITT). The latter discovered the illegal trick and initiated the elimination of the transaction. During the troubled times of the Great Depression, when the cash flow from America stopped and he had severe debt burdens, Kreuger went so far to forge $142 million worth of Italian government bonds, even personally forging the signatures on them. The nervous Kreuger, however, spelled one of the signatories' names three different ways on the 47 documents. His personal liabilities towered, and after two years of tremendous effort to save his empire, because of a total halt to credits and cash flow, all of the manipulations collapsed.

The Great Depression in Europe was closely connected to Black Thursday, the collapse of Wall Street on October 24, 1929, and the drying up of the American credit flow that financed the relative prosperity of Europe from the mid-1920s on. Exported American capital suddenly halved in the second half of 1928, when the Federal Reserve increased interest rates and attracted investments in the domestic market. However, in 1928, nearly $2.3 billion was still flowing abroad, but by 1930, only $0.36 billion. Since the relative prosperity in the second half of the 1920s was based on American credits, and repayment of principle and interest was based on new credits, the consequences were tragic. Germany's capital imports dropped from $967 million to $129 million between 1928 and 1930, and capital inflow to four Central and Eastern European countries declined from $246 million to $8.1 million, combined, in the same years. The Austrian foreign exchange reserves melted from 930 million to 114 million schillings. Several countries became insolvent and unable to repay credits. The same happened to thousands of seemingly flourishing companies, some of which used short-term credits—half of the total credit amount in Europe in the late 1920s—for investments that offered only long-term repayment possibilities.

When credit stopped, spectacular bankruptcies followed. That became the destiny of Ivar Kreuger as well. For the hyper-ambitious Kreuger, success and expansion was more important than his life. He committed suicide at the age of 52. His death remained as mysterious as his life. Rumors and theories spread that he was murdered, or that he escaped and substituted a corpse for his body. All of his assets were confiscated and auctioned. His brother was jailed. Sweden, as a lesson, outlawed some of Kreuger's practices such as participating in the debenture business. The Swedish match industry was taken over by the Stockholm Enskilda Bank and the Wallenberg family.

The anatomy of bank crashes in the 1930s[24]

Belgium became the cradle of the nineteenth-century banking revolution by establishing the first Credit Mobilier type of investment bank in 1830. In the later part of the nineteenth century, several local banks and cooperative societies were also established. The Middenkredietkas (Central Credit Cooperative of the Farmers' League) was established in 1895 as an umbrella organization for the farmer association's (*Boerenbond*) local savings and loan guilds. In the first third of the twentieth century, this institution emerged, expanded, and became one of the most important banks in Belgium. By 1932, it had nearly 98,000 members in more than 1,000 savings and loan guilds. It absorbed several "folks-banks" and other financial institutions. From the mid-1920s, the Middenkredietkas made significant financial transactions, and from solid savings and crediting activities it became a risk-taking investment bank. Consequently, it gained shares in several companies, including mines in Yugoslavia, diamond-cutting firms in South Africa, a large forestry operation in the Chiapas region of Mexico, and positions in the textile business, including industrial firms in Poland and Latin America.

The investment strategy of the bank radically transformed during the second half of the 1920s. As a solid savings and loan institution, it invested in safe fixed-rate government securities. Now, it turned to industrial and banking shares, and entered into the short- and long-term loan business. While shares represented only 10% of its securities portfolio in 1925, and government papers represented the overwhelming majority, by 1928 the share of safe government securities declined to one-third. The second half of the 1920s became a period of an overheated economic boom in Belgium as in some other European countries. Share prices soared and speculation, as Leen Van Molle stated, "became virtually a 'national sport', in which all sections of the population participated, including the deposit banks and the savings and credit co-operatives."[25] Financial institutions were not regulated, savings and loan cooperatives were allowed to go into the investment banking business, and the ratio between the banks' investments and deposits were not prescribed. In the speculation madness, the solid cooperative became a hazardous financial institution.

All the investments, however, were financed from the savings deposits of the members and clients. Deposits, of course, could be withdrawn at any time, eliminating liquidity, and the ability to repay. Long-term investments, in this situation, were extremely risky, but the bank, like everyone else, believed in endless prosperity, wanted to increase profits, and pushed caution aside. However, problems and difficulties gradually emerged. Affiliated and incorporated financial institutions suffered losses beginning in the mid-1920s. The difficulties of the affiliated Banque de Crédits et de Dépôts and the Yugoslav mining companies led to a 90 million franc loss in 1928. The Mexican (Chiapas) project caused 16 million francs worth of losses in 1929. Stock market speculation caused 53 million francs in losses in 1930, and the South African diamond business led to another 26 million franc loss in 1932. Only 87 million remained from the 691 million franc investments of the Middenkredietkas in the *Algemeene Bankvereeniging*. From 1929, all the share values that dominated the bank's assets decreased sharply. Between 1929 and 1935 the share index of the Brussels stock exchange dropped by a dramatic 70%. The overextended and gambling Middenkredietkas was unable to recover a great part of its loans. By December 1934, the bank's total assets of 1,800 million francs were dwarfed compared to the 2,297 million francs liabilities. Total losses reached roughly half a billion francs. Various actions, such as a moratorium on the repayment of deposits and a nearly 1.5 million francs National Bank credit, did not help. At the end of 1934, the *Middenkredietkas* collapsed and was liquidated in 1935. Harsh regulations and the establishment of a controlling agency followed. A Royal Decree of March 1935 ordered the reorganization of the Middenkredietkas and its affiliated institutions, and regulated the rights of the depositors.

The collapse of the Middenkredietkas had only local importance. However, thousands of similar cases characterized the entire Western world, and banks fell like dominos, pulling others with them. When the Vienna Credit-Anstalt collapsed in 1931, it dragged not only Austria's finances with it, but also the Hungarian and neighboring countries' banking institutions. As Fritz Weber stated, "Credit-Anstalt at that time was not just a financial institution, but ... *the* bank of the Danube basin."[26] The Viennese bank owned 85 industrial concerns in 1913, but it enlarged its empire to 340 big companies by 1931. Like many financial institutions in Europe, Credit-Anstalt launched a hyper-optimistic, aggressively expansionist investment and loan policy during the 1920s. From Western loans, it granted long-term credits to and made investments in Central and Eastern Europe. In the end, it had to write off 1.1 billion schillings, and its entire foreign empire. "Credit-Anstalt ... gave up its foreign business: from a significant international bank, it became an Austrian big bank."[27] The Austrian National Bank that rushed to save the banking system virtually lost its hard currency reserves. The gold content of the schilling decreased from 83% to 27%. Overspeculation and overexpansion destroyed banking in several European countries during the Great Depression.

History's greatest inflation: Hungary 1938–46[28]

Inflation is mostly a sign of the loss of economic balance. Just as high body temperature signals sickness, inflation signals some kind of economic ill. Inflation means an ongoing rise in price levels and a corresponding decline in the purchasing power of the money. The most common causes of inflation are either a lack of balance between demand and supply on the market, or the lack of balance between state incomes and expenditures, a situation that occurs when too much money is in circulation. In the first case, unsatisfied demand pushes prices high. In the second, the state turns to printing paper money to finance its expenditures, which, in turn, leads to a decline or total loss of the value of money. If those circumstances are extreme, inflation may reach double digit figures per week and we can then speak about hyper-inflation. While nineteenth-century orthodox financial theory maintained that balanced budgets and stable currency are the normal state of the economy, since World War II, an annual 2–3% inflation belongs to general practice, realizing the controlled and low inflation that John Maynard Keynes advocated as a weapon to stimulate the economy.

History records some famous examples of inflation. In medieval times, the gold and silver content of the coins were deliberately decreased and served as a form of taxation, called "lucrum camerae," or the income for the treasury. In the so-called "long sixteenth century" up to the mid-seventeenth century, the huge inflow of gold and silver from Spanish Latin America caused a long, 150-year permanent price increase, the so-called price revolution. In those years, prices increased six-fold in Europe. The French Revolution that opened the modern age arrived with the first modern inflation, when printed paper *assignats* lost their value in 1792.

After World War I, history's greatest hyper-inflation to date hit Germany, the main loser of the war, and also Russia, where the ruble lost its value after the Bolshevik Revolution and led to the introduction of the moneyless economy of War Communism. Almost all European countries suffered some degree of inflation at that time. Hungary already had hyper-inflation. The Hungarian korona had already lost half of its value during the war between 1914 and 1918. But the lost war, dramatic territorial changes resulting in the loss of two-thirds of prewar territories, two revolutions, and a counter-revolution shocked the country. Inflation started to run amok and, after a failed stabilization attempt in 1921,[29] reached its zenith in the spring of 1924. While 100 gold koronas was equal to 104 Swiss francs before the war, in May 1924 its value dropped to 0.0065 Swiss francs. Stabilization, at last, was based on a significant loan from the League of Nations in the spring of 1924, when the new currency, the *pengő*, was introduced.

During and after World War II, inflation hit virtually all European countries; price levels increased five-fold in France, three-fold in Belgium, 26-fold in Italy, and 110-fold in Greece. But a new historical record was born: the Hungarian super-hyper-inflation. This inflation actually started in 1938 as a consequence of war preparations. The Horthy regime, a close ally of Hitler since 1933, introduced the five-year plan, the so-called Győr Program, to develop infrastructure and armaments by an investment of one billion pengős, which was doubled in 1939. To finance the plan, the government applied the German model of hidden inflationary financing, formally as taxation on banks and companies, but to be repaid in the end by the National Bank, and thus it was in reality financed by printing paper money. The quantity of currency in circulation doubled from 1937 to 1938.

During the war, the Hungarian economy was subordinated to the Nazi war machine and armament production for Germany, including a huge Messerschmitt war plane production program, food, oil, and aluminum deliveries. In the end Germany did not pay for the deliveries, but considered them a contribution to the joint war effort. The financial burden was covered, again, by printing more paper money; currency in circulation increased more than 20 times until November 1944. Tax income covered only 30% of these expenditures. Hungary, consequently, suffered the biggest decline of the value of its currency during the war years. While currency circulation increased by eight times in Germany, and on average five to eight times in the occupied and satellite countries, in Hungary it increased by 14 times.

Inflation, however, started skyrocketing after the war. It was clearly expressed by the quantity of money in circulation: from 10.67 billion pengős in November 1944, it jumped to 765.45 billion by December 1945. War destruction was very severe in the country, which had been a battlefield for six months and suffered very heavy bombing as well. Half of the railroads, all of the major bridges, and 27% of the housing stock of Budapest were destroyed. The GDP of the country halved, the industrial capacities declined by 60%, and agricultural output dropped by 57%, compared to the 1938–39 level. In addition, Hungary had to pay war reparations of $300 million to those countries that she attacked in alliance with Hitler. Reparations themselves consumed half of the shrunken GDP in the first postwar year and were still consuming 17% in 1947. State incomes, on the other hand, almost totally dried up and, in the second half of 1945, covered only 6–8% of the state's expenditures. The government suspended the legal barriers to National Bank lending (or loans) to the government, and inflation became out of control. The banknote press worked in three shifts and the currency in circulation jumped from 765.45 billion pengős to 47.35 quadrillion by July 1946. The paper money lost its value; one 1938 gold pengő became equal to 1.4 quintillion paper pengős. In 1938, the real value of the currency in circulation was 512 million gold pengős, but in the summer of 1946, the value dropped to 3.5 million gold pengős. Post-World War I German inflation was nothing compared to this inflationary run. In the early 1920s, $1 was equal to 4.2 million German paper marks. In 1946, $1 was equal with five quintillion paper pengős.

Prices, in the early summer of 1946, increased by 12% per hour (!) and doubled in less than a day. No one accepted paper money any longer. The urban population exchanged clothing, furniture, family jewelry, and other valuables for food. In early 1946, the government introduced the calorie-wage system and companies had to "pay" 17,500 calories per week for a worker— 80% of the League of Nations norm, 3,080 calories per day! Wages were paid mostly in kind, by exchanging the companies' products for food in the countryside. At the deepest point of the inflation, real wages reached 13% of the 1938 level. Incredible poverty, starvation, and suffering hit an unfortunate generation that had already survived the misery of the Great Depression and the war.

Through the blood and sweat of the population, the ruined country was reconstructed, however, and made an impressive dynamic increase in output. The GDP reached 1938 levels by 1948. On August 1, 1946, a successful stabilization ended the nightmare. It was a masterful financial action without any foreign assistance. The new currency, the forint, replaced the unheard-of denominated banknotes—the largest banknote was 100 quintillion pengő!—that covered the streets like leaves in the fall. One new forint was equal to 400,000,000,000,000,000,000,000,000,000 paper pengős. This is not a misprint, it was a 30-digit figure, an astronomical number: 400,000 quadrillion.

The Hungarian world record was challenged in the late twentieth and early twenty-first centuries. In Russia in 1992, the rate of inflation reached 2,520% per year. Civil war ridden Angola had a long inflation during 1975–91. When the currency was stabilized, one new kwanza was equal to 1,000,000,000 pre-inflation kwanzas. In Yugoslavia, inflation reached the hyper-inflation level in the late 1980s, and prices doubled every 16 hours towards the end of the bloody civil war in 1994. When the Yugoslav *dinar* was stabilized, 1 new dinar was equal to 1,300,000,000,000,000,000,000,000,000,000 pre-1990 dinar. Zimbabwe in 2008 almost hit the Hungarian record with its 13.2 billion-percent monthly inflation rate. Nevertheless, post-World War II Hungarian inflation remains a world record.

How to make a state bankrupt: Greece, 1981–2010[30]

Greece did not declare bankruptcy for a while, but in real terms it became bankrupt. The deficit of the state reached 12% of the GDP by 2009—although the EU's rule prescribed a 3% maximum level—and the mountain of debt stood at 115% of the entire GDP of the country. Moreover, it peaked in 2012–13 with 149% of the country's GDP, although the European Union (EU) requires a maximum of 60%. In 2010, Greece had to borrow €50 billion to pay its annual bills. The country was unable to do it.

To avoid bankruptcy, the EU and the International Monetary Fund (IMF) put together a bailout fund, creating a nearly $1 trillion fund to help out Greece and some other, mostly Mediterranean Eurozone states in financial trouble. Greece, with its 11 million inhabitants out of 500 million citizens in the EU, and representing only 2.6% of the aggregate GDP of the so-called Eurozone of 17 countries, shocked the Western economies. The euro, the common currency of the EU, an economic superpower, was devalued by the market from €1 = $1.5 to €1 = $1.2. How could that happen?

The story begins more than 30 years ago in 1981. Greece, a backward, non-industrialized Balkan country with deeply rooted Balkan traditions of corruption and cronyism, a country that reached only 64% of Western Europe's average income level, was accepted into what was then called the European Economic Community, later the European Union. The inhumane and aggressive military junta that ruled Greece collapsed in 1974, and the rapidly democratizing country applied for membership. Cold War politics and psychology convinced the EU to accept the country that formally met the basic requirements of the European principles. Incorporating Greece into the West was crucially important, since the country had survived two civil wars that potentially threatened a communist takeover during and after World War II. A couple of years after the introduction of the common currency, Greece, which did not qualify in 1998, made strong efforts to fulfill the requirements about the levels of deficits, debt, and rate of inflation, and was hurriedly accepted for membership in the Eurozone.

Both acceptances—like many others by the EU in later years—were premature. Greece did not go far enough towards the Western economic, social, and cultural-behavioral standards to be a solid and strong member of the community. The government lied about its financial situation and doctored the figures, reporting economic growth when in reality the economy had declined, and reporting only a 6–8% deficit to hide the crisis. This became known only after the October 2009 elections when the new George Papandreou PASOK government was formed and made it public that the deficit was twice as much as the previous government has reported. The President of the country, Karolos Papoulias, urged punishment for those "who robbed the state coffers,"[31] and the new Prime Minister openly recognized that "Greece was riddled with corruption, which he claimed was the main reason for its economic woes."[32] His Minister of Finance added: "tax collection ... collapsed almost totally" because of corruption.[33]

History matters. In 1913 and 1950, Greece, reached only 44% and 38% of the Western income level, respectively. Education was backward, and industry hardly existed. True, the country increased its GDP by 4.5-fold between 1950 and 1980, but modern, competitive industry did not emerge. Moreover, in the common European market without protective tariffs, a de-industrialization followed. Greece, for example, did not produce durable goods, so these needed to be imported. Characteristically enough, foreign direct investments (FDI) did not rush to Greece. While FDI in Ireland and Spain surpassed inflowing EU money by two to three times, in Greece the EU money was twice as much as foreign investments. By 2008, after three decades of EU membership, the manufacturing industry produced only somewhat more than 9% of the country's income, and 18% of its exports. Greece, based on old traditions, developed a one-sided service economy. Service branches, most of all tourism and shipping, produced nearly 80% of the country's income. The average 16 million tourists that visit Greece annually produced 15% of the Greek GDP and created jobs for nearly 700,000 people, 17% of the labor force. Shipping is the other main industry, with more than 3,000 vessels and 163.4 million deadweight tons of capacity that represent 18% of the world's shipping capacities. Greece is number one in tanker and bulk carrier fleets in the world. From the mid-1980s, when prosperity returned to the world economy, income increased from both sectors.

It is more than telling that, among the roughly 15 less-developed countries that have joined the European Union since 1973, Greece was virtually the only one that did not produce higher growth rates than the advanced member countries, and thus that did not achieve even a partial catching-up process. This was understandable as fixed capital formation, which reached 32% of the GDP in 1979, declined to 21% a few years after the country joined the EU. Between 1975 and 2000, economic growth was less than 1% per year; that was a prolonged stagnation.

Membership of the EU was very lucrative for less developed countries. The so-called cohesion policy of the EU gave significant aid to regions that were considered backward, if they did not reach 75% of the average income level of the EU. From the 1980s on, huge amounts of EU money arrived in Greece, equal to 3% of its national GDP every year in the 1980s. The country rushed to join "Social Europe" and built up the previously mostly lacking welfare institutions. Retirement age became 58 years for a great part of the labor force. Wages that reached 5% of the GDP in 1960, increased to 13% of it. About $414 billion in credit flooded the country (but this amount, counting the repayment burdens, will reach close to $500 billion by 2013–14). Living standards significantly increased, and the middle class enlarged. There was no shortage of those kinds of investments that John Kenneth Galbraith called "symbolic modernization." *The Economist* reported in May 2010 that, "There were sporting and cultural extravaganzas, starting with the 2004 Olympics. Archeological sites were priced up; spanking new buildings erected ... the unprecedented prosperity enjoyed by most Greeks during the past decade ...

reflected the windfall of cheap euro interest rates, which stoked an exuberant consumer market, complete with smart cars, foreign travel and personal trainers."[34]

By 2004, there were 368 cars for every 1,000 inhabitants, virtually the same level as countries with twice as high income level. Consumption increased, and in a country with half of the United States' per capita income, the cost of living reached 84% of the level of expensive New York by 2008.

Budget deficits and public debt rapidly increased. Before joining the EU, the budget deficit was only 2% of the GDP, but by 1990, it had reached 16%. Public debt increased from 22% of the GDP to more than 100% of it between 1979 and the 1990s. "Public debt in its main part was financed through increased government borrowing ... Increase in 'non-productive' Greek public consumption and personnel expenditure are not followed by increase in Greek GDP ... The major fiscal expansion undertaken by Greece between 1975 and 1990 ... was mainly directed to personnel and 'non-productive' public consumption purpose ... [thus] the expansion ... has contributed ... to the prolonged economic stagnation."[35]

When the international financial crisis hit the world economy in 2008, and new borrowing became extremely difficult and much more expensive, when tourist and shipping incomes significantly decreased, the boat of the overspending, overconsuming, debt-ridden Greece started sinking. The tragedy would have been unstoppable without outside intervention and sacrifice of other countries' taxpayers' money. Papandreou, who launched his election campaign by promising pension and wage increases, was forced to introduce drastic austerity measures, cutting public expenditures, wages, pensions, and steeply increasing the retirement age to 65 years. The social pain generated endless demonstrations and riots. The story did not end in 2010 and a second bailout and further painful cuts of expenditures followed in 2011 and 2012. The irresponsible Greek policy endangered the entire Eurozone including the common currency. The only possible positive outcome of the Greek crisis might be some major step forward to fiscal integration, or as the old-guard of the leading German politicians, Joschka Fischer, urges, the foundation of the United States of Europe.

The European peripheries and the 2008–12 economic crisis[36]

On September 15, 2008, the American company Lehman Brothers collapsed, overburdened by toxic subprime mortgages. An international liquidity crisis emerged. A bank panic generated a bank crisis. Financial institutions stopped lending and several countries declined into recession. It soon became clear that Europe was hit the hardest. The reasons for this situation included irresponsible banking, irresponsible government and household spending, and huge real estate bubbles in at least ten European countries. As an immediate consequence of the liquidity crisis, these irresponsible policies came to light. Four countries—Greece, Ireland, Portugal, and Cyprus—collapsed and had to be bailed out by the European Union and the International Monetary

Fund. Three other countries—Latvia, Hungary, and Romania—soon followed. Although not yet unable to repay their huge debts, two more countries—Spain and Italy—were brought to the brink of insolvency.

If one looks at the map of Europe, it becomes immediately clear that the most crisis-ridden countries are located either on the Mediterranean or in the Central and Eastern European peripheries. It is well known in economic history that a core–periphery divide separated Europe beginning in the early modern centuries. Northern Europe emerged as the core of the world economy from the seventeenth and eighteenth centuries, and then Western Europe and Scandinavia joined in the nineteenth century. On the other hand, the Mediterranean and Central and Eastern European peripheries remained far behind. Their income level reached only about half that of the advanced core, and they remained agricultural areas and producers and suppliers of raw materials, while the Western core became industrialized and exported processed products. The core became rich, the peripheries remained poor.

The core and peripheries also exhibited a kind of relationship in which the latter depended on the former: the core offered markets for the peripheries' food and raw material exports, while exporting processed industrial goods, capital and technology to the peripheral countries. After World War I, a new dividing line emerged between core and periphery in Europe. The greater part of the peripheral countries turned to modernizing dictatorships. The fascist regime in Italy, which was copied in other Mediterranean countries, and the Bolshevik Revolution in Russia, which was later "exported" to other Central and Eastern European countries, changed the political map of Europe as well. Economic nationalism and protectionism flooded the peripheries. Core–periphery relationships hardly changed over centuries, and the core–periphery divide remained predominant until the post-World War II period.

From the 1950s–1960s, however, the economic miracles in Italy and Spain heralded some major changes. Independent Ireland, which was formerly incorporated into the British Empire and served as its poor labor supplier and market, became a member of the European Union in 1973, and soon experienced one of history's greatest rises in prosperity, especially from the 1990s on. The Mediterranean countries—after the collapse of their dictatorial regimes— also joined the EU. Italy was a founding country, and Greece, Portugal, and Spain joined in the 1980s. These peripheries became the success stories of Europe and at last experienced a rapid process of catching up to the West European core. Ireland surpassed Britain and achieved 115% of the income level of Western Europe in the early twenty-first century. Greece, at the same time, rose to enjoy more than 94% of the Western per-capita GDP, Spain surpassed 80% of that level, and Portugal advanced, too. Ireland and the Mediterranean countries thus virtually joined the European core. Their former backwardness seemingly disappeared, and the living standard of the population neared the level of the richest Western countries.

The Central and Eastern European periphery, however, had a much less successful postwar history. The region became the communist bloc after the war, and it remained isolated from the world market and Europe until the collapse of the regime in 1989–91. Only around the turn of the century did the region become an integrated part of the European economy and profit again from capital and technology transfer. Ten of the former communist countries were accepted into the EU in 2004 and 2007, but the adjustment process had begun in the early 1990s, when most of those countries were already knocking on the door of the EU. Their transformation was painful and caused severe economic decline in the early 1990s, when some of these countries declined to hardly more than one-third or 40% of the West European per-capita GDP level, but then the region slowly recuperated. The more successful Central European countries reached their respective 1989-levels by 2000, and then a process of catching up with Western Europe began. Some of the countries of the region reached 65% of the Western income level before the 2008 crisis. Russia, Ukraine, several other successor states of the Soviet Union, and the Balkans needed 20 years to reach their pre-collapse economic levels, doing so just around the time of the European economic crisis.

It was seemingly more evident that the transforming countries of Central and Eastern Europe, with their weak market institutions and freshly changed economic structure, and without an independent banking system of their own, were more fragile and exposed to the crisis. They were extremely dependent on foreign investments and markets, and the crisis endangered both of them. It is small wonder, then, that Ukraine, Russia, the three Baltic countries, Hungary, and Romania were extremely hard hit by the crisis. The real miracle, however, was that one country of the region, Poland, was the only European country to avoid the crisis. It is also admirable that the three Baltic countries, after 17–18% declines in their respective GDPs in 2009, returned to impressive growth beginning in 2011–12. Altogether, the former communist countries were not more devastatingly exposed to the crisis than the Mediterranean countries. Why? Partly because most of them wanted to be organically integrated into Europe. One may not forget the central slogan of 1989 in the communist countries was: "Back to Europe." Consequently, the countries of the region assiduously kept to the Maastricht rules of budgetary deficit and indebtedness rates (3% and 60% of the country's GDP, respectively) so as to be able to join the Eurozone. Indeed, they did so to a far greater extent than those countries that were already inside the Eurozone. The economic households of most of the former communist countries were in better order than in several Western countries. Furthermore, because 87% of the banking systems of the Central and Eastern European countries were in the hands of Western banks, these countries did not have to bail out their banks with state funds and taxpayers' money and, as a consequence, to decline into an indebtedness crisis. Foreign capital, which stopped flowing in only transitorily, supplied the countries with fresh capital. The Baltic countries profited highly from the fact that their banking system was almost entirely in the hands of Finnish, Swedish, and other Scandinavian banks. Strong German and Austrian banks continued financing the Central European region as well. At the two "Vienna Consensus" agreements, the financial leaders of the European Union agreed to continue financing the new Eastern members of the EU. Existing backwardness turned out to be an advantage.

Just the opposite happened to the Mediterranean peripheries. Although they did catch up with the West, they proved to be extremely fragile and declined in unison into the deepest crisis. By 2008, almost everybody has forgotten that the Mediterranean countries and Ireland were in the backward periphery only two generations before. What explains the dramatic and surprising collapse of the European peripheries, including those countries that had already achieved the economic level of the core of Western Europe?

The answer might be found mostly in cultural-behavioral factors, outside the economy. Although their economies rapidly grew, and their income levels doubled and trebled, the cultural-behavioral patterns in these countries changed much more slowly. The population of the "nouveau riche" countries that were integrated into the EU preserved their old habits and spent far beyond their real possibilities. People and governments built on credit and created welfare institutions, high living standards, and a real estate boom based on credit. They accumulated high indebtedness. Their governments' debt burden surpassed twice their countries' income levels. Household debts often surpassed twice the available income of families. Deeply rooted and flourishing corruption made the state household bankrupt. Tax evasion was the norm, not the exception. One-quarter to one-third of the population does not pay tax in appropriate ways in Greece and Italy. The "American Dream" of living in privately owned houses was realized to a higher degree in Portugal, Ireland, and Spain, where about 80% of the population moved into their own homes, than in the United States where this share is 67%. The living standard is virtually the same, the work weeks are shorter, the retirement age is much lower, and the welfare systems are much more generous in those former peripheral countries than in the United States.

The 2008 economic crisis was a cold shower and a wake-up call. Europe has to return to a solid spending policy and to a living standard that is commensurate with the real income of the people and the countries. Austerity measures are the bitter pills to swallow and the educational process required to return to an affordable lifestyle.

Notes

1 The Bible describes a second dream of the Pharaoh, immediately after the first, about seven healthy heads of grain, followed by seven empty heads of grain.
2 William Petty, *A Treaties on Taxes and Contribution*, London: N. Brooke, 1662, 43.
3 A Russian scholar, A.L. Tchijevsky, went even further and spoke about a correlation between sunspot activities and human activities, especially increased mass movements.
4 Daniele Besomi, *Clément Juglar and the Transition from Crises Theory to Business Cycle Theories*, paper presented in Paris, December 2, 2005, www.unil.ch/webdav/site/cup/users/neyguesi/public/D._Besomi_, and "Clément Juglar and His Contemporaries on the Causes of Commercial Crises," in *Revue européenne des Sciences Sociales*, Tom. XLVII, No. 143, 2009, 17–48.

5 This essay is based on: Nikolai Kondratiev, *The Long Wave Cycle*, New York: Richardson and Snyder, [1922] 1984; Vincent Barnett, *Kondratiev and the Dynamics of Economic Development: Long Cycles and Industrial Growth in Historical Context*, London: Macmillan, 1998; Joseph Schumpeter, *Capitalism, Socialism, and Democracy*, London: Allen & Unwin, 1976; Alexander Ehrlich, *The Soviet Industrialization Debate, 1924–1928*, Cambridge, MA: Harvard University Press, 1967.

6 Kondratiev, 1984, 94–97.

7 Schumpeter, 1976, 67–68.

8 Simon Wilson, "Kondratieff Wave Theory: Is it Any Use?" *Money Week,* June 8, 2006.

9 Eric Hobsbawm, *The Age of Extremes: The Short Twentieth Century*, London: Michael Joseph, 1994, 87.

10 This essay is based on: Charles Mackay, *Extraordinary Popular Delusions and the Madness of Crowds*, New York: John Wiley & Sons, 1996; Mike Dash, *Tulipmania: The Story of the World's Most Coveted Flower and the Extraordinary Passion It Aroused*, London: Victor Gollancz, 1999; Jeffrey D. Sachs, Aaron Tornell, and André Velasco, "Financial Crisis in Emerging Markets: The Lessons from 1995," *Brookings Papers on Economic Activity*, Vol. 1996, No. 1, 147–215; Landon Thomas, Jr., "The Irish Economy's Rise Was Steep, and the Fall Was Fast," *The New York Times*, January 3, 2009.

11 This essay is based on: John Garraty, *The Great Depression*, San Diego: Harcourt Brace Jovanovich, 1986; Derek Aldcroft, *From Versailles to Wall Street, 1919–1929*, Berkeley: University of California Press, 1977.

12 Aldcroft, 1977, 257.

13 John Kenneth Galbraith, *The Great Crash 1929*, Boston: Houghton Mifflin Co., 1961, 104–5.

14 Ibid, 174.

15 Ivan T. Berend and Knut Borchardt, *The Impact of the Depression of the 1930s and Its Relevance for the Contemporary World: Comparative Studies*, Budapest: Academy Research Center of East Central Europe, 1986, 261.

16 Joel Colton, *Léon Blum: Humanist in Politics*, New York: Knopf, 1966.

17 Winston Churchill, "While the World Watches," *Colier's Weekly*, December 29, 1934, 24–25.

18 This essay is based on: Frank Partnoy, *The Match King: Ivar Kreuger, the Financial Genius Behind a Century of Wall Street Scandals*, New York: Public Affairs, 2009; Robert Shaplen, *Kreuger, Genius and Swindler*, New York: Knopf, 1960; Daniel Gross, "Grandfather of the Scam?" *Newsweek*, May 29, 2009; Ivan T. Berend and György Ránki, *Magyarország gazdasága az első világháború után, 1919–1929*, Budapest: Akadémiai Kiadó, 1966.

19 Partnoy, 2009, 10.

20 J.K. Galbraith, "Introduction," in Shaplen, 1960, ix.

21 Quoted by Partnoy, 2009, 116.

22 Shaplen, 1960, 88.

23 Ibid, 251.

24 This essay is based on: Leen Van Molle, "Savings and Loan Guilds Under the Aegis of the Middenkredietkas 1892–1934," in Herman Van der Wee (ed.), *CERA 1892–1998: The Power of Co-operative Solidarity*, Antwerp: Mercatorfonds, 2002, 13–174; Fritz Weber, "Grosse Hoffnungen und k(l)eine Erfolge: Zur Vorgeschichte der österreichischen Finanzkrise von 1931," in Oliver Rathkolb, Theodor Venus, and Ulrike Zimmerl (eds), *Bank Austria Creditanstalt: 150 Jahre österreichische Bankgeschichte im Zentrum Europas*, Wien: Paul Zsolnay Verlag, 2005, 180–95; Dieter Stiefel, "Die Sanierung und Konsolidierung der österreichischen Banken 1931 bis 1934," in Rathkolb et al., 2005, 196–211.

25 Van Molle, 2002, 138.

26 Weber, 2005, 181.
27 Stiefel, 2005, 205.
28 This essay is based on: Berend and Ránki, 1966; Sándor Ausch, *Az 1945–46 évi infláció és stabilizácio*, Budapest; Kossuth Kiadó, 1958.
29 In 1920, Lóránd Hegedűs, the head of one of the leading Budapest banks, was appointed Minister of Finance. An orthodox financier, he initiated stabilization by introducing heavy single taxation of banks, landed estates, companies, and private wealth. This met with strong resistance. It also caused shortage of money and stopped the inflationary financing of reconstruction. The attempt failed in 1921, Hegedűs resigned and was hospitalized with a severe nervous breakdown (Berend and Ránki, 1966, 68–80).
30 This essay is based on: Stergios Babanassis, "Long-term Economic Development Trends in South Eastern Europe (1850–2003)," in Vasilis Angelis and Leonidas Maroudas (eds), *Economic System, Development Policies and the Enterprise Strategies in the Age of Globalization*, Athens: Papazissis Publisher, 2006; Michael G. Arghyrou, "Public Expenditure and National Income: Time Series Evidence from Greece," dspace.brunel.ac.uk/bitstream/2438/879/1/00–05.pdf, undated; Angus Maddison, *The World Economy: A Millennial Perspective*, Paris: OECD, 2001; *The Economist: Pocket World in Figures, 2008 Edition*, London: Profile Books, 2007.
31 *The Economist*, May 8–14, 2010, 52.
32 *The Economist*, November 21–27, 2009, 89.
33 Ibid, 53.
34 *The Economist*, May 8–14, 2010, 51–52.
35 Arghyrou, undated, 13–14.
36 This essay is based on: Ivan T. Berend, *The European Economic Crisis of 2008–2012: Bolt from the Blue?* London: Routledge, 2013; *Transition Report 2009: Transition in Crisis?* European Bank for Reconstruction and Development, London, 2009.

Index